Sitting Up with the Dead

Sitting Up with the Dead

A Storied Journey through the American South

Pamela Petro

Arcade Publishing • New York

For Marguerite Itamar Harrison,
who introduced me to the American South
and the Southern Hemisphere

FIRST NORTH AMERICAN EDITION 2002

First published by Flamingo, an imprint of HarperCollins Publishers, U.K.

The author and the publishers express their gratitude to the following: Louisiana State University Press for permission to quote from *Black Shawl* by Kathryn Stripling Byer (copyright © 1998 by Kathryn Stripling Byer); Copper Canyon Press for permission to quote from *Deepstep Come Shining* by C. D. Wright; Vintage Press for permission to quote from *North Toward Home* by Willie Morris; J. M. Dent and Sons for permission to quote from "Eheu Fugaces" from *Collected Poems 1945–1990* by R. S. Thomas; and Universal Music Publishing Ltd. for kind permission to quote lyrics from "Sweet Home Alabama" (King/ Vanzant /Rossington). Although we have tried to trace and contact all copyright holders before publication, this has not been possible in every case. If notified, the publisher will be pleased to make any necessary emendations at the earliest opportunity.

Library of Congress Cataloging-in-Publication Data
  Petro, Pamela, 1960-
    Sitting up with the dead : a storied journey through the American South /
    Pamela Petro. — 1st North American ed.
      p. cm.
    ISBN 1-55970-612-0
        1. Tales—Southern States. 2. Storytellers—Southern States—
    Interviews. 3. Southern States—Social life and customs.
        4. Southern States—Description and travel. I. Title.
  GR108 .P47 2002
  398.2'0975—dc2   2002018310

Published in the United States by Arcade Publishing, Inc., New York
Distributed by AOL Time Warner Book Group
Visit our Web site at www.arcadepub.com
10 9 8 7 6 5 4 3 2 1
EB
PRINTED IN THE UNITED STATES OF AMERICA

Contents

Acknowledgments

Writing can be a lonely occupation, but no book is ever written alone. More people contribute to its formation than can possibly be named and thanked: the waitress who called me "sugar" and made me laugh after a grim and sleepless night; the gas station attendant who told me dumb jokes about Boston; librarians who found countless books for me at Brown University's Rockefeller Library that were reputedly shelved, but actually were not. I can, however, thank all of the storytellers who appear in the following pages for sharing their tales and their wisdom with me. I have rarely met people happier in their profession, and their good humor — not to mention their kindness and generosity — made this book a pleasure to research. I reserve a special thank you for Vickie Vedder, who thought through the South alongside me, via e-mail, and who is one of the most insightful and generous people I have ever encountered.

I am also indebted to my wonderful friends such as Richard Newman, for the depth of his knowledge about African-American history and the civil rights movement, and his willingness to share it; to Mary Diaz and Tom Ferguson, for hounding me to store my manuscript somewhere safe, for their enthusiasm and encouragement, and to Tom, especially, for the title; to Laura Pirott-Quintero, who thought of Chaucer when I said I was going to the South to collect stories; to Nancy Levitt-Vieira for sharing her aunt's inspiring storybooks with me; to Michael LaRosa, for his hospitality and Caladryl; and to Stella de Sa Rego for her knowledge of Louisiana. I am grateful as well to Tim Huebner, of the Department of History at Rhodes College in Memphis, for his insightful comments and bibliographical recommendations; to Debbie Dunn, for her intimate knowledge of the Bell Witch legend; and to the many state arts organizations that keep records of the storytellers in their midst (thanks especially to Cydney Berry of the South Carolina Arts Commission, John Benjamin of the Kentucky Arts Council, and Wayni Terrill of the Canton, Mississippi Welcome Center).

My deepest thanks also go out to my parents, Pat and Steve Petro, for their ceaseless encouragement, and for selflessly looking after Tenby, the canine terror, while I took a short break. I would also like to give thanks to the many Harrisons who helped me throughout the summer: to Randy and Heline, for their gracious hospitality and depth of biblical knowledge; to Nat and Tina, for the use of their beautiful house in Chattanooga; and especially to Marguerite, not only for staying home and caring for Tenby — *and* dealing with computer glitches *and* serving as a telephone clearing house between me and countless storytellers — but for joining me in the heat of August and making the final part of my journey so much more fun.

There are a few final thank yous to extend. The first goes to Adele Nelson and Sara Schaff, for inspiring this idea at a party in the summer of 1998. I would also like to mention Georgina Laycock, whose encouragement and hard work have meant so much to me, and my editor, Philip Gwyn Jones: without him this book would not exist. I thank him for his good humor, patience, keen judgment and diplomatic demeanor, and especially, for his friendship.

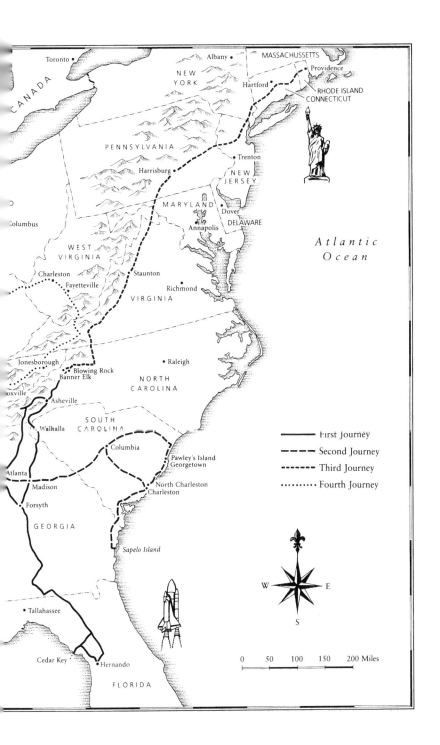

"In America, perhaps more than any other country, and in the South, perhaps more than any other region, we go back to our dreams and memories, hoping it remains what it was on a lazy, still summer's day twenty years ago — and yet our sense of it is forever violated by others who see it, not as home, but as the dark side of hell."

WILLIE MORRIS, *North Toward Home*

The Prologue

Chaucer said it was in April that people long to go on pilgrimages. I was two months late; the desire didn't come upon me until June. His Canterbury-bound pilgrims were moved "to seek the stranger strands/Of far-off saints, hallowed in sundry lands." A nice idea, but again, my journey differed in the details. No sundry lands for me. Like a contented lodger taken in by a big, unruly family, I lingered in just one place, or one household, you might say, within the United States: the American South. And I wasn't seeking saints.

What Chaucer's pilgrims and I have in common is that we chose stories as our waymarks. I traveled from the Atlantic seaboard across the high country of Appalachia to the Gulf Coast, listening to Southern storytellers tell me their tales. Like those of the Knight, the Nun and the Wife of Bath, stories served all of us — listeners and tellers alike — as compasses of understanding to high country and low, to the past and present, to ghosts and the living, to right, wrong, and finally, to the way home. Chaucer knew that stories are the surest guides on any journey. They are, in fact, journeys themselves, leading out of the graspable, sweaty present into the vanished or imaginary worlds that support it. They give depth and shading to the here and now, comment on it, contradict it, and crosshatch all that we think we know about a particular place with the shadows of lives long gone and schemes of characters who never actually breathed, but flourish in communal daydreams.

Visit the old coal-mining region of eastern Kentucky these days and you'll see the green hills roll by like a bright inland sea, buoying up Interstate 64 and the service industries moved down from the Northeast to take advantage of lower taxes. Then find someone with a minute or two to spare, and ask him to tell you a local tale. Maybe over a cup of coffee, or lunch of canned fruit and cottage cheese at a diner, he'll spin out *The Black Dog,* which is about a coal-mine collapse and the heroic pet who protected his master even in death. It's a tale about community and the fear of outsiders, even outsiders offering help; about trust and the habitual acceptance of death and the forgotten bond between men and animals. This is the heritage of the upland, coal-mining South, and it's invisible to the eye. But stories like "The Black Dog" are able to unearth an older Kentucky, one that still has relevance because it lives in the memories of service industry employees who drive to work on the Interstate, even though it may no longer be reflected in their daily landscapes. Travelers can't see it, but they can hear it if they listen.

Stories provide the connective tissues of a community, a region, or even a big, overgrown household like the South. They link the skin of the present to the unseen organs of the past, binding them into a continually shape-shifting body, by turns beautiful and terrible and occasionally — disturbingly — reminiscent of looking into a mirror. In my case, the glass reveals a surprise: a Northern woman, a Yankee who came of age in Britain, and now lives within the gravitational pull of Boston, Massachusetts — the geographic butt of nearly every dumb joke I heard in the South ("Hey," the Texaco cashier would say, as I paid for the gas I'd just pumped, "hear the one about the guy from Boston who bought his girlfriend a mink coat?" Or, "There was this guy from Boston with a chicken . . ." in which case I'd affect a Southern accent and say I was from Virginia). It's a fair question to ask what I was doing there. Tony Horowitz wrote in *Confederates in the Attic* that, "The South is a place. East, West, and North are nothing but directions." When I read that my kneejerk reaction was to agree; I couldn't explain why, but I wanted to find out. In my previous book, a journey around the world in search of Welsh expatriates — a group for the most part anchored by a concrete sense of identity — I had written of myself, by way of contrast, "To be an American, I sometimes feel, is to be blank, without a nationality or language." It was easy for me to write that sentence. I grew up in the suburban New York area, the heartland of the American communications industry that daily beams a facsimile of itself to the world. To be Northern, for me, is simply to be American. But Southerners, at least those in print, seemed to feel very differently, branded on the soul by the geography of their birth. Why? What place-bond did they have that I didn't? In *North Toward Home,* Willie Morris, a Southerner from Mississippi, wrote of himself, "The child . . . was born into certain traditions. The South was one, the old, impoverished, whipped-down South; the Lord Almighty was another; . . . the Negro doctor coming around back was another; the printed word; the spoken word; and all these more or less involved with doom and lost causes, and close to the Lord's earth." I had no such waymarks, and however fraught the Southern identity might be, I yearned for such a bond.

Growing up in the sixties, I had learned that the South was a scary place. Whenever I tried to conjure images of the things I knew to be there — tobacco fields, sharecroppers' shacks, flat-roofed stores on Main Streets and old-fashioned buses — I saw them in my mind's eye through an eerie blue light. These Gothic stage sets of mine had origin in a mundane reality: the fact that most of my childhood impressions were thrown into our safe, Northern living room by my parents' black and white television set. Unfortunately, they were usually disturbing: blurred scenes of race riots and fierce men with firehoses, dogs attacking crowds of protesters, and marchers in pointy hats and white sheets. It didn't help that the picture used to roll a lot (usually set right by a whack on the side), making the images even stranger. The South looked like the site of a haunting: a dream world, not a waking one.

I was a dramatic child, given to extravagant musings, usually involving hauntings closer to home, principally in my closet, and eventually outgrew most of my darker impressions. But scratch the surface of nearly all Yankees and there remains a prejudice against the South, an unvoiced, but understood, moral superiority. We won the Civil War because we were *right*. "Be careful down there." I heard that advice from more than a few Boston friends. "Will you be safe alone?" "You know, it's still pretty rural down there. All *kinds* of things go on."

Down There. The South has always been somewhere *below* my home. I have a semantic prejudice, probably endemic to the Northern Hemisphere, that North is "up" and South is "down." So to go *down there* was to descend geographically. And in many ways I discovered that it was also to descend metaphorically, Orpheus-style, not so much into the Under-world as a kind of national Otherworld, an ornery, land-wedded, once-and-future counterbalance to the here-and-now America of my experience, the latter made generic through self-promotion. In much of the world's oral literature — the old stories explaining the external world that lived through a spo-ken chain of memory — travelers went to the Otherworld be-cause theirs was missing something, usually some critical means of reproducing itself (hence the ceaseless abduction of magic women in Celtic lore). They were thieves, to put it bluntly, but their plunder usually saved the day.

In my case, I was missing two things: a sense of my country as a *place,* not simply a well-oiled machine ceaselessly turning out the future, and, on a personal level, a voice. I am a relentless daydreamer. I tell myself tales so intricate and involved that they blot out whole days of my life. Like storytelling, like travel, like madness and violence, daydreams lead out of the known world into exceptional places, some of which no one in his or her right mind wants to visit, others wondrous and wise. But unlike those other means of transportation, daydreaming is a solitary sport in which stories are hoarded rather than shared. The French philosopher Gaston Bachelard asked, "What is the source of our first suffering?" only to answer himself: "It lies in the fact that we hesitated to speak. It was born in the moment when we accumulated silent things within us."

Who better than *tellers* — people whose role it is to share stories — to help me make a personal voyage from silence to speech (or in my case to writing, which is little more than speech's shadow), and thereby ditch my accumulation of fictional silence? So I went down into the Otherworld of the American South and I came back with stories. With living, listened-to tales that would be my exemplars, and that also might help me understand the open-ended, unfinished place that Civil War historian Shelby Foote says gives us "a sense of tragedy which the rest of the nation lacks"— not to mention why my sense of America is incomplete without it.

I should note that I opted to plunder spoken stories, as opposed to written ones, because they are chosen *for* their listeners, not by them, as is the case with readers. It was better, I thought, to have my assumptions made for me by Southern storytellers than to make my own, loaded as my selections would be with outsider's baggage. I asked each teller for a story *or* a tale that revealed something of the nature of life in his or her corner of the American South. (These semantics mattered, as the word "story" often invokes the private realm and "tale" the public; this option left tellers free to choose the space in which they felt the most comfortable, or thought was the best cipher of the South.) The orality of the stories was important as well. Oral tales are a plural endeavor; they're the products of generations and geography and weather and all the other ligaments that bind a community together. Written stories, by contrast, are idiosyncratic and individual, and it was a public sense of the South I sought, not a private one. Besides, two covers, a spine, and a few hundred pages don't have nearly as much personality as living, cussing, dancing, spitting, smoking, eating, drinking humans. Storytellers are often their own stories. They certainly became mine.

First Journey

R.S. THOMAS, "Eheu Fugaces"

Between
One story and another
What difference but in the telling
Of it?

Akbar's Tale

I WAS WEDGED INTO THE AISLE OF THE PLANE, waiting impatiently to exit, when a fellow passenger whispered uncomfortably close to my ear, "They say that when you die, you have to change planes in Atlanta to get to heaven."

Atlanta's Hartsfield International Airport is the second-busiest in the United States. Although it looks like every other airport in the world, the talk there is exceptional. As soon as I arrived in the main terminal, a short, squarish security woman called me "baby," which I found unaccountably comforting (as in "You lost, baby," after I'd attempted to retrieve my luggage from the wrong baggage carousel; my suitcase was doing figure eights on another conveyor belt on the far side of the airport). A few minutes later a very tall African-American man questioned me about cigarettes in Japanese. When I looked confused he switched with great courtesy to chewy-voweled, Georgia English.

The South is a famously talky place. The quintessential Southerner, William Faulkner, wrote, "We have never got and probably will never get anywhere with music or the plastic forms. We need to talk, to tell, since oratory is our heritage . . ." Even bones talk sometimes. Even when they're in the ground. There is a story from the South Carolina coast called "The Three Pears," or "The Singing Bones," about a little girl who exasperates her mother by eating pears intended for a

3

pie. Understandably peeved, the mother chops the girl up with an axe and buries the pieces around the farmyard. The head is packed off to the onion patch, which next spring bears a "fine mess" of onions. Sent to pick them, the son hears the ground singing:

> Brother, Brother, Brother
> Don't pull me hair
> Know mama de kill me
> Bout the three li' pear

Eventually her bones testify to everyone in the family, and the mother gets so frightened she runs into a tree and dies.

When I first encountered this story I thought, imagine what a ruckus a Southern cemetery would kick up. So many bones prattling on about this and that, you wouldn't be able to hear yourself think. Strangely, this old rural tale is what surfaced in my mind as I was swept out of the Atlanta airport in my new rental car, into a twelve-lane funnel of life moving at top speed. "Such a metaphor," I scribbled on a note pad, risking annihilation as truckers passed me at 80 mph, and Highways 75 and 85 blurred together in a whirlpool of relentless motion. Atlanta is a city on the move, shamelessly advertising America's infatuation with roads and size and moneymaking right in its freeway-bound heart. No time for death here, much less quaint talking bones. If there were any, I felt sorry for them: no one would be able to hear their chants in the din.

Actually, that is not quite true. Atlanta discovered some of its own old bones a few decades ago, and they shout their message — "Make Money!" — loud and clear, which is probably why the story came to mind in the first place. In the center of the city is a four-block grotto of unearthed, nineteenth-century cobblestones called Underground Atlanta, excavated and rebuilt as a tourist mecca of glitzy shops and restaurants. These skeletal streets were the foundations of the original city, begun in 1837 and first called Terminus, appropriately enough, for the railroad speculation venture that it was. The district wasn't burned by General Sherman's Union troops in the Civil War; it was buried to make way for a railway aqueduct. What began as a commercial venture died as one, only to be resurrected over a century later on behalf of yet another kind of commerce. It is the Atlanta way.

Those who don't hear the call of money beneath the city chase it toward the sky. Office and shopping towers sprout in clusters throughout the metropolitan area like so many galvanized steel ladders to the future (getting from one to another means that Atlanta residents spend more time commuting in cars than almost all other Americans, each logging around thirty-five miles a day). It is no accident that Tom Wolfe's recent novel, *A Man in Full,* hinged on the fortunes of a reckless Atlanta speculator who built a skyscraper too high for his wallet. Not so much fiction as parable, Wolfe's story of success-run-rampant tells the tale of the city's recent history. In the 1990s, metropolitan Atlanta saw the greatest population increase in America. It currently consumes fifty acres of forest land *per day* to pave way for new construction. The city is, in fact, the epicenter of an economic boom so great that if the eleven states of the former Confederacy were lumped together as a separate nation, they could claim the fifth largest economy in the world (equivalent, so I'm told, to Brazil).

This is the "New South" that so many speak of: socially liberal and friendly to big business — an attractive combination paid for in road congestion, air pollution, and overdevelopment. Yet Atlanta was on the make long before CNN, Coca-Cola, and the 1996 Olympics arrived. It has always been what some are complaining it has now become: a work-ethic driven, live-and-die-by-the-dollar, *Northern* kind of city, noisy and fast and flush with money.

Atlanta was the first stop on my first trip to the South. Over the course of the summer I planned four separate journeys, with brief rest stops at home in New England in between. I knew that my travels would generously overlap themselves and one another: because I was using storytellers rather than states or cities as my coordinates, I expected to leave a messy trail on the map, but gather a rich earful en route. On this first trip I took Georgia for my base, with forays planned both north and south of the state. The other journeys would take in the eastern seaboard, Appalachia, and "the Deep South," which included Mississippi, Alabama, and Louisiana. More immediately, however, navigating Atlanta was my chief concern.

None of the people behind the desk at the Super 8 Motel in the heart of downtown had ever heard of Ralph David Abernathy Jr. Boulevard, which disturbed me. Abernathy was Martin Luther King, Jr.'s, right-hand man throughout the civil rights movement. While nearly every town in the South with more than one stop sign has a Martin Luther King Jr. Boulevard, or at least an Avenue, most of the major cities have named something after Abernathy too, and it's usually a pretty significant street. Atlanta is no exception, but it took two painters suspended on scaffolding in the motel lobby to shout directions down.

"No one's ever asked for Abernathy before," said one of the clerks.

I soon discovered why. Abernathy proved a conduit to Atlanta's West End, an old African-American neighborhood of bungalows with sagging porches, pawn shops, fast-food restaurants, and corner stores hidden behind antitheft grills. Conversational half-circles of chairs were set up here and there on the sidewalks but were all empty: already at 10 A.M. steamy, near-tropical heat had a stranglehold on the day. Here, at last, was a restful nook in the city — a little ramshackle, but pleasantly quiet. I was no longer surprised it had been so hard to find. This neighborhood was the Atlanta anomaly, more Old South than New, where time was to be had in greater quantities than money.

All the bigger buildings seemed boarded up, except one. Marooned on the shabby street was a well-kept monument to Victorian whimsy: a many-gabled Queen Anne–style cottage with yellow patterned shingles, tall chimneys, and a giddy wraparound porch that looked like a carnival train of painted wagons. This was the Wren's Nest, former home of Joel Chandler Harris, the nineteenth-century newspaper man who gave the world Uncle Remus, and wrote down the Brer Rabbit stories.

I made my way onto the tangled grounds and a teenager named Matthew ran up and shook my hand. He lived nearby and was a summer intern at the house, now a museum. We traded confessions of childhood fears. He'd been afraid of hockey masks because the killer in *Friday the Thirteenth* had worn one; I'd thought pink paint could only be achieved by mixing white paint with blood, and one day insisted (on pain of sleeping elsewhere) that my room be painted blue. After these confessions we were buddies, and he showed me around the musty Victoriana: a full set of Gibbon in the library, windows shuttered against summer heat, tasseled lamps lit in the gloom, and 31 five-year-olds racing up and down the long, "dog trot" hallway, the electric heels of their Nike sneakers flashing red. The five-year-olds and I had come to listen to Akbar Imhotep, a storyteller who had not yet arrived. While I waited for Akbar, I watched a slide show about Harris' life, slightly unnerved that the rest of the audience consisted of a stuffed bear and rabbit — both dressed for church — and a fox in need of a taxidermist's touch-up.

At thirteen, Joel Chandler Harris had been packed off to learn the newspaper trade at Turnwold, the only antebellum plantation in the South to publish its own newspaper. He had spent Saturday evenings there with the owner's children, listening to two elderly slaves tell stories about cunning animals who lived by their wits, sometimes comically, often violently, usually successfully. These were "trickster" tales that had come from Africa with the slaves, and had been adapted over generations into a grand, elastic body of oral literature. Later in life, working for the *Atlanta Constitution,* Harris hit on the conceit of having a fictional former slave named Uncle Remus recount these stories in a newspaper column, which Harris would write in "darky dialect." Remus became such a hit that Harris collected his stories in 1880 in *Uncle Remus: His Songs and Sayings,* making both their names — as well as that of the trickster hero Brer Rabbit — famous worldwide.

Harris died in 1908. In 1946 Walt Disney Pictures released *Song of the South* — the animated musical based on the Uncle Remus tales that brought the world the Oscar-winning song "Zip-a-dee-doo-dah, zip-a-dee-ay, my oh my, what a wonderful day" — which struck many as paternalistic, at best. For the first time Remus began to look like what he had been all along: a white man's projection of the grandfatherly, accommodating, unthreatening, forgiving jester he wanted all black men to be. Though he never fell out of print, Harris fell out of favor with a thud. In the late sixties Disney withdrew the film from circulation. Then slowly, a decade later, the tide started to turn. Harris's "darky" speech was pronounced authentic African-American dialect; had he not chosen the vessel of Uncle Remus, it was declared he would have been the father of American folklore. As it was, Harris saved a body of oral tales that otherwise might have been lost. Disney released the film again in 1980 and 1986, and has made an estimated $300 million from it to date.

Akbar had arrived, damp with the same summer sweat that had turned my cornflower blue shirt cobalt under the arms. Solid, strong, and rounded all at once: he was a comfortable man to look at, with close-cropped, graying hair and a goatee to match. He swept into Harris's "good" parlor (reserved for company) followed by an unruly wake of black and white children, who settled into a kind of bobbing pool at his feet. I joined them cross-legged on the floor. In his pink and black African-print shirt, flanked by a pair of drums, Akbar seized the Victorian room by its own good taste, setting off a chain-reaction tremble in the drapery tassels, lace curtains, dried-flower arrangements, even a marble-top table, with his seated gyrations. A tall carving of Brer Rabbit and Brer Fox, arm in arm, watched from a corner.

Listening to the slide show in the dark, empty room I had been aware of a white voice condensing and interpreting Harris's life. Now, here in his parlor, where Harris had been too pathologically shy to tell stories even to his own children, a black voice was conjuring new life from the briar patch for the children of strangers.

TAR BABY

One time, old Brer Fox and Brer Bear was out sittin' around in the woods, and they was talkin' about all of the things the rabbit had done to 'em, to make 'em look saaad. Old Fox, he looked at Brer Bear, he said, "You know what, bear? That rabbit, he always was a little bit too sassy for me. You hear me?"

Bear said, "Yay-yuh, I hears you Brer Fox. What we gonna do about it, huh?"

Fox says, "Bear, I don't know about you, but if I ever get my hands on that cotton-pickin' rabbit, I'm gonna take his little whiskers, and nick 'em out one by one."

The bear says, "When you get through with that, hee, hee, hee, you give him to me, so I can just nookie him — Bam! Boom! — clean out cold. Let's go get him now."

"No. You wait here till I get back. I gots myself an idea."

As Akbar spoke, my knees ached to stretch out, but I was penned in by cookie-scented children on all sides, effectively stuck in a kind of perceptual briar patch of my own making: a white man's house built with money wrung from the stories of slaves, now administered by a black foundation — which, word had it, faced an uphill financial battle because of the seesawing of Harris's reputation — principally visited by white tourists who made their way to an off-the-beaten-track black neighborhood, where, if they were lucky, they could hear a black storyteller spin ancestral tales preserved by the intercession of a white man.

Well, old Fox, he left Bear sittin' there. He went down the road to his house, and he got him a bucket. He got that old bucket and he went on down in the woods and he filled it up with some of that old sticky, yucky, mucky, ooey, gooey tar. And he come back out there to where the bear was waitin' on him. When he got back he showed it to old Bear. Then he went and got some turpentine and he poured that over it, kind of softened it up a little bit. Then he went ahead and stirred it. And when he got it good and stirred up, he started scoopin' it up and shapin' it up, and after a while he shaped up a little old head. He worked up some shoulders, and chest, some arms and some legs, and when he got through with it, it looked just like a little bitty person. Some folks say, a little bitty baby. Y'all got any idea what he might a called it?

Kids: "TAR BABY."

Well, after he got this tar baby thing all shaped up, he knew that he had to catch that old smart rabbit. And he didn't know if this old tar-shaped thing was gonna do it. See, one thing that fox knows about, he knew that little rabbit ain't nobody's fool. So he figured, he gotta dress this thing up to get that old rabbit to stop and be friendly with it.

So he looked around to see what in the world he could dress it up with, and he noticed the buttons on old Bear's jacket. He called old Bear a little closer. The old Bear got close to him and he just, Pluck! Pluck! He snatched off a couple of buttons and he stuck them on the tar baby for eyes. He got him a piece a coal and he stuck that on for a nose. Hee, hee, hee, hee! He went on and shaped up a little old mouth. And, aaah, he squeezed some ears on the side of the head. Hee hee, hee, hee, hee! Hooo-EY! He looked at all the hair on Brer Bear's neck, and he just . . . aaaah!!! . . . stuck that on top of the tar baby's head. Then he took his jacket off and he wrapped that around it. And to top it off, he got old Bear's straw hat, and he stuck it — eek! — right on top of the head.

Now. He knew that if that Rabbit saw this little dressed-up tar baby thing, he was gonna stop and try to be friendly. Then he and old Bear would see what would happen when the tar baby didn't say nothin'. Now, to set the trap, they got that old dressed-up tar baby thing, and they took him out to the big road. And when they got out there, they set it up right by the side of the road, then they went out into the bushes to hide. Now, what I want y'all to know, is that right over there (Akbar points; children all look) on the left corner of the imagination, was a thing called a briar patch . . .

Now, that tar baby thing was just sittin' up there just as quiet as could be. Old Fox and Bear, they out in the bushes tryin' to hide.

Harris's shyness prevented him from reading from his own collections in public (the public, in 1900, meant the middle-class, white public). The curious thing is that he lost his inhibitions in front of black people. There is a story about him hiding from crowds behind a railroad station while he waited for a train. There he met a group of black railway workers on their break, with whom he immediately fell into an easy-going, storytelling swap until his train came. Caution tells me this is a psychological quagmire I should leave well alone. But the fact is that Harris exclusively communicated with white audiences in print, as Uncle Remus, and with black audiences in his own voice, as himself. Did he simply take the Remus character to heart, and only feel comfortable with "kin," or did Harris have an inkling that Brer Rabbit — "Brer," by the way, means "Brother"— was really a guerilla?

"Brer Rabbit," wrote Robert Hemenway, introducing a recent Uncle Remus collection, "is black from the tip of his ears to the fuzz of his tail, and he defeats his enemies with a superior intelligence growing from a total understanding of his hostile environment." Brer Rabbit — the incorrigible trickster — was born prey rather than predator, yet he triumphs through his wits again and again. Passed on within the confines of slavery from one African-American to another, these stories held a kernel of revolution: they conveyed strategies, allowed for vicarious victories, and promised that organized systems could be overcome by cunning. Brer Rabbit doesn't always win — or when he does, it is often at great cost, through the sacrifice of allies or the unnecessarily cruel torture of enemies. Intelligence allows him to choose freedom by whatever means available, if he wants it badly enough: a message of hope, heartbreaking in its moral ambiguity.

Now look! Who's comin' down the road just as happy and sassy as can be? Was our friend Brer Rabbit. Old Rabbit, he skipped along there, and when he saw that tar baby thing he stopped. Screech! And he tried to be friendly. First thing old Rabbit said was, "HEY THERE!" But what did that tar baby say? Children: "Nothing." Old Brer Fox and Brer Bear, they just laaaay loooow.

Now, Rabbit say, "I see you!" What'd that old tar baby say that time? Children: "Nothing." Old Brer Fox and Brer Bear, they just laaay loooow.

Rabbit say, "Can you hear me? No, looks like you cain't!" Did he say anything then? No, didn't say nothin'. Old Brer Fox and Brer Bear, they just laaaay looow.

Rabbit say, "Wait. Now don't you know how to SPEAK? Round here we all speaks to one another." Did the tar baby say anythin'? No, didn't say NOTHIN! Old Brer Fox and Brer Bear, they just laaaaay loooow.

Rabbit says, "Wait. Now, if you don't take that hat off and tell me 'Hi!' by the time I count THREE, I'm gonna blip you on the nose!" Was the tar baby scared? Children: "Noooo." Did he say anything? No, he didn't say nothin'. Old Brer Fox and Brer Bear, they just laaaay loooow.

Brer Rabbit was serious. Rabbit say, "One. Two. Two and a half. Three! Eeeeeeh . . . Blip!" (Rabbit tries to free himself) "Unh! Unh! Unh!" Right there's where things got sticky, didn't it? 'Cause his fist stuck. He says, "Hey! Let go! Let go! Let go right now, before I hit you with this one, and . . . Blip! Unh! Unh! Unh!" That one stuck. He says, "Hey! Let go! Let go! Let go before I kick the natural stuffin' outta you! And, Unh! Unh! Unh!" Did any stuffin' come outta that tar baby? Children (sounding superior): "Nooo." "Let go! Let go! Let go! Let go right now, before I butt you with my head. And . . . Blip! Ah, ah, ah, ah, ah!" I think we know what happened to the head, now don't we?

Well, old Rabbit looked up and he was stuck completely to the tar baby. Old Fox and Bear, they peek out of the bushes and see that old Rabbit was stuck. They eased up behind him and old Brer Fox, he say, "Mornin', Brer Rabbit, don't you look kinda stuck up this mornin'?

Ha, ha, ha! We've been lyin' here for a mighty long time, but we got ya now. This is gonna be the last day that you see!"

Bear looked at him and said, "Huh, huh, huh, huh, huh, I'm gonna nuggie yo' head clean off."

Fox say, "Nah, nah, nah, nah, nah, nah. Quick! We gotta make him suffer. Let's start us up a FIRE. Let it get good and hot, drop old Rabbit in it and let him BAR-BEEE-CUE for a while."

Well now, Brer Rabbit, you know he was stuck. But two things about this Brer Rabbit I want us to never forget. Number one, even though he was stuck, he didn't lose his head. And number two, he never ever, never ever, never ever gave up. And out of the corner of his eye he saw that old thorny briar patch, and . . . Bing bing bing bing! BING! What'ja think happened? Children: "He had an idea!" He had an idea. He knew what to say to old Fox and Bear, didn't he? He say, "Brer Fox, I don't care what you do to me. Just don't fling me into that, ah, briar patch. Go ahead, BAR-beee-cue me, just don't fling me in that, uh, briar patch . . ."

Bear say, "Wait a minute, wait a minute. If we start a fire, we gotta make sure it don't get outta hand. Ain't that true? Won't you let me knock that here rabbit head off now?"

"Nah, nah, nah, nah, nah, nah. I want to hear him holler! I'm gonna haaaang you rabbit." Brer Rabbit say, "Oh hang me, Brer Fox, hang me, please hang me, ooh please, don't fling me in the, briar patch!"

"Hanging you a bit too nice a thing to do. Ought to just drag you down to the creek and drown you, Brer Rabbit." Old Rabbit say, "Drown me, Brer Fox. Won't you just drown me? Oh please, please, just don't fling me in the briar patch!"

"Think about it now. Think. What's the worst thing I could do to a rabbit? Uh! I know. I'm gonna get my knife, then I'm just gonna peeeeeel you hide off right here." Old Rabbit say, "Skin me, Brer Fox, pull mah eyes out, pull mah ears out by the roots, cut mah legs off! Boo hoo hoo hoo! Oh please, don't fling me in the BRIAR PATCH!!"

Well, after old Rabbit went on and on and on and on about not flinging him in the briar patch, old Fox looked over there to see what in the world he was talkin' about. Ah ha! He saw him some thorns stickin' up and twistin' round every which-a-way, and he figured the worst thing he could do to that rabbit would be to fling him where he didn't want to go. Do y'all think that was a good idea? Most of children: "Yes!" The rest of them, "No!"

OK, that's about seventy-five — twenty-five here. Let's see what we got.

Fox grabbed him, and he gave him a great big old swing, and he just fling him, Woooooooooooooooooeeeee! Ow!! Oooo! Ow! Well, when old Rabbit fell into the briars, he did so much screamin' and hollerin' and carryin' on, that old Fox and Bear thought he was just about dead. And they all commenced to celebrating. But they couldn't celebrate long. Um un, um un, um un.

After a while, way up on the hill, up popped old Rabbit. And when Rabbit come up out of the briars, he had a little piece of one of 'em, that he was using to comb the rest of the tar outta his hair. And he had to look back. He saw old Fox and Bear back there, shakin' their fists and stompin' and carryin' on. Old Rabbit hollered back like this, "Brer Fox! Hee, hee, hee, hee, hee! Didn't I tell you not to fling me in the briar patch? Hee, hee, hee hee, hee! I was bred and born in the BRIAR PATCH! Didn't you know I was born and bred in the BRIAR PATCH?" And that old Rabbit skipped off to live almost happily ever after.

Akbar, the heat and I sat together in an improvised little amphitheater behind the Wren's Nest. Beneath a canopy of mature trees, the late morning still smelled new as the vegetable scent of condensation evaporated slowly and sweetly. He told me that he'd got his start as a storyteller by working as a traveling puppeteer. He used to set up a special suitcase as a stage from which he would manipulate his puppets. One day in the middle of a performance the legs he had rigged on the case had fallen off, and he wound up having to tell the story he'd intended to perform. And that was that.

I asked him if Atlanta ever played a role in his tales. "Not really," said Akbar, "but it keeps me from telling some." He explained that he was in the process of learning a new story called *The Man Who Knew Too Much.* I thought he meant the Hitchcock movie, but he was referring to an African tale that had been adapted into a short story by Julius Lester. Akbar condensed it for me. A woman works daily in the field, stopping now and then to nurse her baby. One day as she's nursing, an eagle appears, watching her closely. The next day after she's finished nursing, she leaves the baby in the shade of a large tree; the eagle reappears and to her horror heads straight for the child. But instead of killing him, the eagle strokes the boy gently with his wing. The woman is amazed, and tells her husband. He refuses to believe in the kindness of eagles, claiming he knows their ways, but agrees to accompany the woman the following day. When the eagle comes and begins stroking the baby, the man shoots an arrow at the bird, who quickly moves away. The arrow kills his son instead, and the eagle tells the man, "You are responsible. Now all men on earth will mistrust each other and fight because of you. Because you knew too much."

How nice to know that in other cultures Eve was a man. I secretly felt sorry for the husband.

"I told that story to a men's group, and man, they hated it. Their reaction was, 'Well, the husband did probably know more about eagles than the wife.' Can you believe that? They refused to put any blame on the guy. It got to be real sexist." Akbar went on to explain that there had lately been a rash of baby killings in Atlanta, which was why he felt uncomfortable telling the tale right now. "A story's only half the equation," he said. "The context you tell it in makes all the difference, twists the meaning. Ignore the context and you're being irresponsible. Look, if I were to tell that story in this city right now, who knows what message people would hear. I don't even know what it means. The context," reiterated Akbar Imhotep, in Joel Chandler Harris's garden, "is everything."

When a billboard on the way to Cyclorama, just south of downtown Atlanta, told me, Jesus Was A Vegetarian, I immediately resolved to keep a record of interesting highway signage.

During the morning I had become infatuated with circuitousness: everything I had encountered at the Wren's Nest seemed to wind back up on itself. So I decided to conclude the day with a visit to Cyclorama. It seemed fitting to visit a narrative where the end literally merged with the beginning.

Cyclorama is billed as the world's largest painting. It is fifty feet wide by nine hundred feet long, stretched on a circular canvas in the middle of which is a small, rotating auditorium. All of this is housed in a rather grand building in Grant Park, a leafy spot in Southeast Atlanta where everyone else seemed intent on going to the zoo. In the eighteenth and nineteenth centuries, cycloramas were authentic marvels. When they came to town with a circus — which is how this one wound up in Atlanta — people would come out in droves and spin around while the painting stood still: motion pictures with the onus of motion on the viewer. Once there were three hundred cycloramas cluttering the earth, now there are only twenty. This one, which was inexplicably painted by a troupe of Polish and German immigrants in the 1880s, depicts a bloody day (July 22, 1864) in the Battle of Atlanta.

I crawled up into the rotating auditorium and immediately felt seasick. I fixed my eyes on a railing at the bottom and watched it move against the stationary backdrop of what looked like paint-by-numbers carnage. It was like being on board ship, except that Sherman's army was standing in for the sea, the men's blue jackets far outnumbering the Rebels' nobly tattered gray.

"Now, the blue is the Union, the gray is the Confederacy," explained a mother to her two little boys — my only cyclomates, but a welcome step up from stuffed animals. "Oh good," said one child, "we're the gray."

I guess I overextended my metaphor. Cyclorama was pretty corny. The foreground was strewn with bushes and mannequins to lull us into seeing three-dimensionality (it didn't work). When we stopped spinning, I jumped out of my seat to leave, only to find we had completed just one of *two* revolutions. A voice on the loudspeaker told me to sit down. This time around — only because a guide pointed it out — I noticed something. Among the mayhem of bayonets and dying soldiers (one of whom had been touched up to look like Clark Gable) and dead horses and smoking ruins — imagine sixteen thousand feet of this — was *one* woman and *one* African-American man.

Now I happen to know that amid the six hundred and twenty-five soldiers and five hundred and five animals in the Bayeux Tapestry there are only two women, one of whom has a name: an embroidered nun named Aelthgyva, who appears to have done something untoward with a monk. Aelthgyva is far more interesting than the red blur in a dress depicted in Cyclorama. But having just learned that two hundred thousand black soldiers fought for the Union in the Civil War in 1864 and '65, the inclusion of one token black man seemed grudging, to say the least.

The problem with Cyclorama, and with circular orbits in general, is that they confuse the eye, and the eye confuses the mind. Is the painting spinning around us, or are we turning while the painting stands still? This afternoon we were the ones in motion, but it didn't seem so; we — the two little blond boys, their mother, and I — were nestled securely in the center of our universe, just as the Polish and German artists had been. What we thought we saw revolving around us was just a reflection of *our s*tory, not history.

I left Cyclorama still awaiting its Copernicus.

Colonel Rod's Tale

I HAD ALL DAY TO GET FROM CENTRAL GEORGIA, where
I had stayed at a Budget Inn after breaking out of Atlanta's
endless spaghetti junctions, to Hernando, Florida: a more
or less straight journey of about four hundred miles. The air
conditioner at the motel had tirelessly pumped a bad smell into
the room (decaying rodent? dead body? sewage?), so after what
would become my standard breakfast of bad coffee with nondairy creamer and a Krispy Kreme donut, I thankfully took to
the road.

There wasn't much difference between the Interstate and
the secondary highways. The latter threaded through cultivated fields, watermelon patches, a few pecan orchards, pine
groves baked to the scent of turpentine, and towns so small
that only the change in speed limit — from 55 mph to 35 —
affirmed their existence. Car washes did a big business here in
this dusty, rural world. I noticed that most of the large, formerly
fine houses were in ruins; the smaller ones, without exception,
brokered with the street through either open or screened-in front
porches. (The architectural record in southern Georgia, and, as
I was later to discover, much of the South, tells a tale of uneven wealth. The older housing stock — pre-1930, at a guess —
consists on one hand of large, multistory homes and mansions,
and, on the other, of small, one-level shacks and bungalows.
Most midsize, middle-income homes are post–Second World
War.) When I stopped by the roadside to drink a Coke, the

metal on my sunglasses holder got so hot in the sun it actually burned my skin.

Interstate 75, by way of contrast, offered cultivated fields, watermelon patches, a few pecan orchards, pine groves — and lots of signs. Shelled Pecans! We Bare All! Couples Welcome! (that from an "adult" bar that seemed to have spent a fortune on advertising). Jesus Is Lord at the World Famous Catfish House. All You Can Eat! And, from a mysterious series of black billboards with white lettering, You Think It's Hot Here? — God.

I tried to fill in the blanks between signs — together they held the makings of a spanking tale of sin and redemption — but my attention was ultimately claimed by the road itself. The Southern sun nearly beat the blackness out of the blacktop. It shone so hard on the macadam that every fleck of quartz or mica in the road surface glinted white, tinting the Interstate the glittering, grainy silver-gray of an old-fashioned movie screen. My parents had a screen like that when I was a child, on which they had shown slides for family entertainment on Sunday evenings. Now, from my mind's eye, I projected the same images I'd once seen in our living room onto Route 75: my grandmother wearing a visor hat, cotton dress blowing in the wind, squinting against the sun; my brother looking uncomfortable in a pair of tight Hawaiian shorts; me posing like Marilyn Monroe with a tiny fish I'd caught. All of us silent and still on a distant northern beach.

Or maybe not so still. In *my* memory the family is gathered watching slides when — inevitably — one of the screen images waves to us. My mother nudges me and says, "There! Did you see? Wave back to yourself!" And we all laugh and wait for the next small miracle to occur. It's like a household secret, these ghosts of our living selves left behind to carry on being young and warm and on holiday, not just in memory but in the photographic record. My parents tell me this never happened. "You must have been dreaming," said my father. I don't know. If it were a dream, wouldn't the slides have spoken as well? In my memory bank of images, we are always silent.

I arrived in Ocala, Florida at the same time as a tornado warning. When I pulled off the Interstate the sky looked like bruised peaches, bluish-gray and yellow all at once.

Here, in the United States, the Road is supposed to be one of the big stories: the seduction of motion, of progress, of speeding away from the past. But today I felt the same as I did leaving the Atlanta airport — that the highway pulled me in and knocked the breath out of me, like an undertow with the force of a hundred oceans, sucking me into motion and away from all the stories nesting in the countryside. Maybe that's because the last time I encountered the world-at-rest it was sunny and dusty and utilitarian. Now, leaving the same road, I found myself inside an extravagant purple storm that tugged at the Spanish moss on Ocala's old trees. The pictures didn't connect, and I wondered at the glue that held them together.

Ocala looked like a Southern town in drag. Everything there was exaggerated: the steamy heat; the campy Victoriana of the wood-frame houses; the trees! The trees were downright Gothic. Magnolias, palms, and best of all, live oaks. The latter, characteristically shorn of fussy, incidental twigs, always look gnarled and old. Dripping with Spanish moss, they were biblical. It was as if rows of Old Testament prophets lined the side streets, waiting to convert paper boys and joggers.

As I headed southeast, Ocala gave out onto a commercial strip, as tawdry and generic as any in America. This soon petered out into aluminum-sided, pastel-colored retirement villages, then horse farms, then swamps, and finally, a down-at-heel holiday community on a lakeshore, planted with a sign that read, Hernando. I asked a woman in a beauty parlor which of the three motels I should stay in. "Go for the Mid-Florida Motel and Trailer Park," she concluded. I pictured the ranch-style units I'd just seen down the road behind a parking lot of slimy green puddles, shadowed by clumps of Spanish moss. "I might stay there if I had to. I wouldn't set foot in the others."

I had just time to take a cold shower — ringing Colonel Rod for directions from an outdoor pay phone had given me a prickly heat rash — before finding my way out of town through darkening, uninhabited stretches of piney outback to his Spanish-style ranch house. I had been eager to talk to a well-known Atlanta storyteller named Chuck Larkin: a real character, by all accounts. But Chuck was unavailable, so he gave me Colonel Rod's name, and told me he was "a good ol' swamp boy, and a helluva storyteller." I imagined a gruff military man with gruff military stories. One who would spurn white panama hats, Hawaiian shirts, and small poodles with jeweled collars. But these were the attributes of the person who answered to Colonel Rod.

"Colonel Rod Hendrick of the Cracker Brigade, at your service, ma'am," he said.

He led me into a spacious, open-plan home with the world's largest television screen in one corner. When we stood in front of it, the TV characters' heads were three times bigger than our own. In his study, Colonel Rod sat down beneath a stuffed raccoon and a model airplane, locked me with his turquoise eyes, and said in a dreamy voice, "Once upon a time, on the far side of the moon . . ." — he paused, looked around, and winked — "these two crackers went into a bar . . . Ha! Gotcha! I hate that kind of vomity storytelling, don't you?"

Colonel Rod explained that a local reporter had given him the nickname "Colonel." He was actually a retired salesman from Miami, who had also been a cop and happened to be a "pedigreed Florida cracker."

"I grew up dirt poor, south of Miami. You know what a cracker is, girl?"

I grimaced in half-knowledge. In Tom Wolfe's novel, crackers had been Georgia good old boys.

"You're eatin' grits for breakfast; you know a couple a guys named Skeeter or Gator; you're huntin' white tail deer with a six-beer handicap; then you're a cracker. Used to be a derogatory term, you know, like Redneck, or White Trash. But not anymore."

Colonel Rod gave me an essay he'd written on Florida Crackers, which put the derivation of the term down to the cracking sound pioneers made with bull whips as they rounded up cattle from the palmetto swamps. These pioneers, Colonel Rod added, had headed south "to get away from Yankee oppression" after the Civil War.

"Now I'm a storyteller. Say the American Tobacco Company has a conference. I'm the entertainment. I get $500 a gig, and a dollar a mile for transportation. I also teach these workshops in storytelling. There was a teacher who took one of them. Afterward, every Friday afternoon, she held a storytelling hour . . . the kids were taking to it like, I don't know, a fish to water or something like that. They loved it."

"That's really great," I said politely.

"Well, she called me later and told me about a little boy in her class called Leon, who is a fantastic storyteller. She said, 'He can tell tales, and he tells them with a gift like Mark Twain. He's fantastic. But what I think is, that he's lost touch with reality. Now Leon is just lying. And I've created a monster. What should I do?'"

When Colonel Rod got to the part about Leon his voice changed. He started tugging on his vowels as if they were made of spandex, stretching out "lying" to sound like "li-on." It occurred to me that a story might have started without my knowledge. I was a little confused until he said he'd advised the teacher to tell Leon the silliest, most outlandish, "most lyinist" story she could think of — "maybe that will break him out of it." Then I knew I was right.

Colonel Rod held my eyes to his, almost without blinking; my peripheral vision caught a ceiling fan spinning directly above his head, like a whirligig hat. He was saying that the teacher could see Leon was getting worse. So she told him a tall tale about being attacked by an Alaskan bear on the way to school, on the corner of Alligator Avenue and Center Street. A little black-and-white dog had killed the bear and saved her.

"Leon," Colonel Rod concluded, "just sat there goggle-eyed. Big-eyed as a bug. You got to believe me. And the teacher looked over and said, 'Now Leon, do you believe that story?'

"And Leon said, 'Yes ma'am. That's my dog.'"

Colonel Rod was on a storytelling jag. He'd told me he'd numbered his stories one through twenty one as a fail safe mnemonic for when he's performing. "Okay," I said, "quick: what's number seventeen?"

"A cracker in a bus station!" he roared, and he was off.

After dinner — a healthy, low-fat meal fixed by his wife, Brenda — Colonel Rod led me through a shouldersized gap in the electric cattle fence surrounding his house to a replica of an old Florida Keys fishing shack that he'd built out back. It looked like the retreat of a degenerate boy scout. Kerosene lamps for atmosphere, even though it was wired for electricity; pots and pans hanging from the ceiling; two sets of bunk beds; photographs of people who had caught big fish; a makeshift bar stocked with gin and bourbon; old Southern state flags emblazoned with the stars and bars of the Confederacy (all since replaced as politically incorrect, except that of South Carolina, which is the subject of a bitter debate).

A violent thunderstorm had trapped us in the shack and Brenda in the house with our cappuccinos. "This," Colonel Rod had said, beaming, "is where friends of mine come and turn the monkey loose. Y'know, guys getting together to get drunk and fart."

As the storm worked itself into a full gale so did Colonel Rod. I could feel him shrewdly calculating audience response — in this case, a captive audience of just one — judging if he had succeeded in his two favorite, occasionally incompatible, aims: to startle and to please. As I betrayed only pleasure (politeness is like a hormonal imbalance with me, I can't help it), he got a little reckless. Not only did he slip into what he called his "cussin' stories," but others that took tired, if belligerent, potshots at women, gays, and a variety of other minorities. On cops: "There are no policemen left. Only social workers." On blacks: why there should be highway signs for exiting white drivers in parts of Miami that read, "Beware: Ghetto ahead." But then he added, "I guess the same goes for them, too. Man, I wouldn't want to be a black guy made a wrong turn in South Boston."

Colonel Rod was a storyteller caught between personae — Florida cracker or worldly businessman? — in the presence of a fastidiously indulgent listener who refused to offer directional signals. He veered all over the place, from cracker jokes to a troubling tale inspired by a Flannery O'Connor short story, and I liked him for having humility enough to lay bare the lifeline between storyteller and audience. Or perhaps he just couldn't help himself. During a long tale about a pulpwood truck driver and a psychiatrist, I decided that I would trust Colonel Rod with my life, but not my sensibilities.

After an hour and a half the storm grew worse, and I got too tired to consider anything but the sounds coming out of his mouth.

THE MULE EGG

It was the Depression. Everybody was broke all over the whole country. And in Atlanta, Georgia, there were two city slickers up there, worked downtown, lived in an apartment downtown, had never been anywhere except downtown. All they knew was asphalt and concrete. Well, when the Depression slammed in here, both of them lost their jobs. So they decided — they wasn't too smart, but they was good old boys — they decided they was gonna pool their money, come to Florida and go farming. Now I wouldn't think that was too smart, but they was industrious. So they bought an old black Model A truck, and here they come south with this Model A truck, looking like the Beverly Hillbillies.

They was comin' down Highway 27, which was a gravel road in them days, and they got just south of Ocala, and they seen a sign nailed to a live oak tree, and the sign said, Plough Mule For Sale. Old Slem was driving the truck, and he said to his partner Clem, "Look at that, Clem! I forgot about that! We got to have us a plough mule." Said, "We can't farm without a mule. Pull in there, we'll see what that guy wants for it."

So they pulled in this farmyard, and the guy was sittin' there. He said, "Get on out, boys, get on down, come on in." And he said, "Sir, sir, we saw your sign back there says you got a plough mule for sale." Farmer said, "That's right, and he's a good 'un too, son." Clem said, "Well, we want to buy a mule for farming. We're from Atlanta." So the farmer heard opportunity knocking right away, see. He recognized these guys being city slickers. They said, "What do you want for that mule, sir?" Farmer said, "I want two hundred dollars for it."

TWO HUNDRED DOLLARS? They couldn't believe it. Their eyes was bulging. "We just come from Atlanta wantin' to be farmers. But two hundred dollars? We can't afford that." Now I'm going to give you a little history here. During the Depression, you could buy a ridin' horse for five or ten dollars, but a trained, young pack mule was running a hundred seventy-five, two hundred dollars. Worked just like a tractor. Anyway, Clem said, "No, we just quit our jobs, we can't afford that." Farmer said, "Well, how much money you boys got between you then?" They said, "We ain't got but twenty-five dollars."

Well, the farmer said, "Boys" — he had been peddling them old central Florida watermelons from his watermelon patch, and he had two of them left over, on a wagon over there where he'd been sellin' 'em, and he was just fixin' to bust 'em up because they was rotten, you know, and throw 'em over the fence and feed 'em to his cows — he said, "Boys, see them two green things over there on that wagon?" They said, "Yessir." He said, "Do you know what they are?" They said, "No sir, we don't." He said, "Boys, you just happen to be looking at two of the finest mule eggs in the state of Florida, right there." They said, "Mule eggs? Never heard of such a thing."

The storm was directly overhead at this point and the shack was shaking. Thunder followed lightning before I could start to count the seconds. About the time Colonel Rod pronounced the words "mule eggs," a lightning bolt lit up the window behind him, stinging my eyes with an instant image of cross-hatched tree branches across a background of seared white shards. I thought incongruously of the German Expressionists, and felt anxious.

The farmer said, "You're lookin' at two of the finest mule eggs in Florida. Look, I'll tell you what I'm going to do. I'll let you have one of them mule eggs for five dollars." He said, "I'll tell you what else I'm going to do. I'll get some straw out of the barn, and I'll make you a nest up the back of your truck. You put that mule egg in there, you throw a blanket or a jacket over it, keep it warm, and in about two weeks it'll hatch out, and you'll have yourselves your very own baby mule. It'll be gentle as a house cat, and you'll have a fine mule there."

"Boy, luck is on our side," said Clem and Slem. So he got the straw, and he made this big old nest, and they put that watermelon, I mean, ah, mule egg, up in there, and they put a blanket on it and paid the farmer, and they took off down Highway 27, comin' south. And now I live in that part of the country. A hilly part. And they come to Clairmont, Florida. Now Clairmont is in a valley. A great big hill goes down in there, and up out the other side. Well these old boys wasn't too smart. Here they come, they come down into Clairmont, and they did all right then, but when they started out the other side, the mule egg went, dumpty, dump, dump, dump, and it fell out in the middle of the road and — splat! — busted all to pieces. Big old pile of rotten red mess. And you know how them swamp rabbits get on the side of the road, late in the evenin'? Well, it was late in the evening, and there was a swamp rabbit standing there, and it spooked him when that watermelon hit the road, and he jumped out and got right in the middle of that red mess.

Well these two boys slammed on the brakes. Pulled over to the side of the road and jumped out, and looked back, and there sat that rabbit right in the middle of that mule egg. They said, "Look, he's alive! He survived it! He's OK! Get him! Catch him, catch him!" And boy, they took off after this baby mule. They had five dollars tied up in him. They yelled, "Catch him, catch him!"

Well that old rabbit took off. He went through a briar patch, under a barbed wire fence. They chased him about a half a mile or so and they got in this kind of shape — Colonel Rod gasps like he's dying — they just couldn't even breathe. They couldn't go another step. And as I said, old Clem was the smarter of the two, he was hanging on a tree, and Slem was sittin' on a log. And Clem said, "Let him go, son, let him go. Just let him go. I don't believe I want to plough that fast no-how."

*

I desperately had to go to the bathroom. The storm had stopped abruptly, and Colonel Rod offered to direct me through the dark, dripping thicket of the backyard to his reproduction outhouse (also wired for light). When I got up to leave the shack, I noticed that behind me all along had been a framed photo of John F. Kennedy and Martin Luther King, Jr., shaking hands. "One of my favorite possessions," said the Colonel, sounding like he meant it.

Back at the Mid-Florida Motel, around midnight, I sat cross-legged on my bed taking notes, thinking for some reason of Cyclorama. I had an uncanny sensation of motion. All of a sudden I realized that the floor *was* moving. I put my glasses on and a dozen immense, scuttling cockroaches resolved into focus. Having just read Redmond O'Hanlon's *No Mercy,* his saga of traipsing through Congo with God knows how many parasites attached, I tried not to panic. But then again, this wasn't Congo, and I had a choice. I grimly packed my things and slept — or rather lay awake all night listening to rain pelt the roof — in the back seat of the car.

The next morning, I remembered I was actually in Florida and decided to take a detour to the coast. Central Florida, or rather the northwestern part of peninsular Florida, has no big hotels, no crowds, no Disney characters. The accents are rural, the land more inclined to scrub forest than cultivation or pasture. This may have been the Sunshine State, but I wasn't in the playground part. It was still the South. And it actually looked like rain.

Colonel Rod's cracker shacks dotted the landscape: tiny clapboard houses, often raised on cinderblocks to avoid flooding, leaning heavily on makeshift front porches. They were almost always half-hidden by shade trees, rarely exposed to the sun. I imagined dark rooms inside and mildew, windows democratically open to both breezes and mosquitoes in equal measure. In this climate it is air-conditioning that draws a line between real poverty and the lower rungs of middle-class comfort. Without artificial coolants, people still have to stop what they're doing and sit in the shade, as they have for generations, and wait to cool off, and tell each other stories while the sweat dries (or maybe these days they just sit inside and watch TV). The majority of Southern stories aren't *about* poverty any more than they are about heat or shade. They're simply one by-product of a lifestyle that has either vanished — which is why tale-telling is so often associated with the elderly — or that we now call "poor."

The sky began chucking it down. An unrelenting series of fierce rain squalls, really like thimblesized monsoons, belted the car as I drove toward a small town on the West Coast called Cedar Key. Whenever one hit I was nearly blinded for about seven nerve-wracking minutes, and had to inch along Highway 19 at 25 mph; when it let up the windshield revealed an unbroken flatness grown over in stumpy, grayish-brown scrub.

Cedar Key is marooned three miles out in the Gulf of Mexico at the end of a series of low bridges. It is a small town, only around seven hundred residents in summer, given over to dissolute, late nineteenth-century buildings with peeling paint and sagging clapboards, columns staggering to support second-story porches. Palm trees and hand-lettered signs advertising bait and cold beer cheered the place up in a spirit of easygoing unconcern, rather than neglect. I drove the two blocks separating the last bridge from the Gulf and parked near the harbor. The sky over the water was the color of pigeons, smudged gray and white, and sheet lightning flashed offshore. The air was so heavy that the smell of beer from nearby bars hung in it like a net.

I wandered into one and sat next to an old man who was

simultaneously smoking, drinking a Bud, and eating a Fudge-sicle. He told me he was hiding out from the cancer that a doctor said was going to get him. I looked alarmed and he laughed. "Better wait for it in a bar than at home watching TV." In the next breath he said that a fishing ban had killed the commercial fishing industry in Cedar Key about five years ago, and now clamming was the big thing.

"What do you get?" I asked. "Cherrystones?"

His glance at me was the fastest I'd seen any part of him move. "Aw, you must be from Boston or somewheres up North, am I right? Nobody says cherrystones 'round here."

The bartender looked from me to the beer I had ordered (Newcastle Brown Ale), seemed to satisfy some internal inkling, then lost interest and returned to her phone call. "Storm's knocked the power out at my mom's, down by Rosewood," she yelled to someone in the kitchen. I'd seen the Rosewood highway sign on the road to Cedar Key, but it had seemed to apply only to empty acres of scrub forest. Beside it stood a hand-painted placard that read, Rosewood Memorial.

Cedar Key relies on its wonderfully degenerate buildings to set the disreputable, rum-running mood of the place (residents did actually run guns and booze during the Civil War). Because Rosewood had no buildings, however, I had to call Dick Newman, who works in African-American Studies at Harvard, to find out why the name stirred an uneasy association with violence deep in my memory. He told me that in 1922 a white woman had accused a black man from Rosewood — a predominantly black town — of raping her (her accusation was reputedly false, covering up an affair). White vigilantes from the surrounding area retaliated by burning every structure in Rosewood bar one, a farmhouse owned by a white man, and massacred every black resident they found. With the help of the spared white farmer, the mothers saved some of their children by hiding them in a well on the farm property. A grand jury subsequently looked into the matter, but never brought any charges, and the town ceased to exist in all but name.

It had occurred to me earlier that morning, as I was driving through the rain, that while stories ideally link us to the past and to other cultures and traditions, opening the world wider, storytelling itself can sometimes be a way of narrowing experience, of not hearing. To tell (and tell and tell and tell) is not to listen. The teller effectively becomes like a television set, capable of disseminating stories but not of taking them in. Colonel Rod's barrage of tales the night before had effectively kept me and my disruptive, feminist opinions at bay; I don't think that shutting me up was his intent, but it had that effect. Like violence, which strips stories from the landscape or buries them with its victims, storytelling can occasionally be a reactionary device, a reflex of the fearful that may be wielded like a defensive — and now and then a deadly — weapon.

I drove out of Cedar Key in a dispirited mood, back past the town that was only a story, and retraced my route north toward Georgia.

Vickie's Tale

E VERYBODY THINKS I'M A PENTECOSTAL, but I'm not, I've just got long hair."

This last word came out sounding like *hi-yar*. Vickie Vedder was a striking woman in her early forties, tall, softly athletic, with an easy smile and what could only be called tresses of long dark hair. With her good looks went an accent that you could grow fat listening to, sweet and sticky-worded ear toffee. My own voice sounded brutally utilitarian by comparison.

I had met Vickie on the Internet, and she'd invited me to her home in Forsyth, Georgia, before she had stopped to consider whether I might be an axe-murderess. Later she told me she had been worried.

Forsyth is in Georgia red clay country, where the earth swells and bucks under the farmland. When exposed, it is the color of raw beef; and on dry days, like this one, a haze hovers above the roadsides like rusty fog.

Vickie lived outside town in one of the quiet places I had been fretting about missing on the Interstate. To reach it I drove along a secondary road past woods and fields until I came to her signpost: an old barn half-consumed by trees. It would have had the look of a Dutch landscape etching but for the corrugated iron roof, which was painted with enormous letters that read, See Beautiful Rock City. Or, as Vickie had warned, See Beautif Rock Cit, because some of the iron slats had recently fallen off. Rock City is a kind of giant-scale rock garden in Chattanooga, Tennessee. Barns all over the South once advertised it, though Vickie's is now one of the few that remain, making it a legitimate Southern icon.

Her farmhouse and outbuildings artfully married wrought and found, decay and care, in a way that suggested a relaxed appreciation of the visual world. Vickie kicked at the red dirt and said that the difference between "home" — Wilkinson County, not far to the south — and "here" — Monroe County, where her husband was from — was that the earth in Wilkinson County was white and chalky. "This," she said, scuffling it again with her foot, "is just red dirt."

Vickie's house was nicely cluttered, but her "office," which was really a nook just wide enough to stand sideways in, looked more like an experiment in sedimentary rock formation than any part of an ordinary household. Her desk and bookshelves were barely visible, overlain by strata of photographs, trinkets and souvenirs, scattered overtop with scribbled notes and sheets of paper. The effect was of a secular altar, which it may very well have been. I peered into one photograph and met the eyes of an old lady who seemed as aware of me as I was of her. She had a neat nest of white hair, severe black-framed glasses, blue eyes, and a crumpled mouth set in a straight line. "Granny Griffin," said Vickie. "All cleaned up."

I had been eager to meet Vickie, ever since I had learned she told stories in the character of her grandmother, but especially keen after phoning her the previous evening from my motel room. Rarely in the course of chatty conversations do people bother to dredge their hearts and intellects for their deepest opinions, especially on difficult subjects like race or religion. It's too hard, and most people are out of practice in the discipline of thinking, much less translating thought to speech. Yet the latter skill had been Vickie's inheritance, and in between giving me directions to her barn and laughing over the urban legends of the Internet, she had spoken like a true child of Faulkner's talk-besotted South. "The North-South thing isn't real anymore. It's dangerous to perpetuate that stuff. But there are differences. The South carries a deep kind of pain, and the North a sense of moral duty. Both can cripple a person, or a family. Or a country, I guess." On race she was upbeat: "Look, we're still a young country, we'll work it out. We have to find a big porch to sit on and tell each other stories, and not try to solve everything immediately . . . You know, I grew up with black kids and we loved each other. We still do. Why don't people ever talk about that?"

The following morning, in her living room, over the course of an hour and a half, Vickie did something I didn't expect. Instead of distilling her conclusions for me, she verbally re-created the world in which she had formed them. It was like taking a crash course in someone else's life.

This strange new universe began with its people. Granny Griffin was tall, had big feet, and wore support hose held in place with rubber bands just above the knee. Daddy Runt, her husband, was extremely short. Jesse H., Vickie's father, was famous in the family for pointing at you with his middle finger. (Vickie squinted, scowled, and jabbed at the air: "Now you listen to *me* . . .") There was Ladonia Griffin, Daddy Runt's mother, whom Granny loathed, calling her "Old Lady Doughknee Griffin." And *Aint* Hattie, Daddy Runt's sister, whom Granny also disliked. Granny had been born a Kitchen — pronounced *Keet'chun* — "I weren't born no Griffin," she'd remind Vickie. The Kitchens were mean as snakes, but it was another branch of the family that, according to Granny, "had let the meanness in the door." Everyone on Granny's side of the family was "peculiar." As Granny said about one of her sons, "one more inch and he'd be over."

All these people ("I hate that you can't meet them!" cried Vickie several times), lived on the same street: Harberson Walker Road, known in the family for unexplained reasons as Habersham Walker Road (Granny and Daddy Runt could "kinda sorta read," said Vickie). Across the way was the Mixon's cotton field, which "Old Man Mag" plowed with a mule. Granny feuded with Eva Mixon as well. "She didn't *hate* the Mixons," said Vickie. "It's more that she saw through the outer crust of them — what they were trying to be versus who she KNEW them to be." Granny's insights didn't stop her from retaliating, however, when Eva took drastic measures to protect her chicken coop. "They killed each other's dogs and chickens under cover of night and poison," Vickie explained.

Granny ate hog brains with a cut-up onion for breakfast, and put soda in her tea to make it black. She "had a hard opinion on religion." She liked country churches, which taught you to be more scared of God than the Devil, but "she had no inhibitions with God. She could talk to him anywhere, it didn't have to be in church." Granny believed that the first thing that happened when you died was that you went blind. The incentive in becoming a ghost was to come back and "take a peek at something familiar," but since ghosts couldn't see they bumped into things and scared you. Turpentine and kerosene made into a poultice kept them away.

Jesse H. (the H stood for Hamm) had come from a family of tenant farmers — Granny had a hard opinion on them, too, "cause they wuz high-falutin" — but her own family worked in the Kaolin mines (Kaolin is a wet, white, sticky clay used to make chalk). Daddy Runt, who had made moonshine whisky during the Depression but never drank a drop, had a talent for charming honeybees. He began each morning by pulling up peanuts (they grow underground in the pods of peanut plants), then put in a full day at the chalk mine, went fishing in the chalk pond, cleaned and ate the fish, and spent summer evenings shelling peas.

"Now, none of us was gonna starve in 1960," said Vickie, "but we still had to put up food for winter as if our lives depended on it." Granny, Daddy Runt, and Jesse H. — who was the oldest of ten children and near to his in-laws in age — carried the stresses of the Depression, "when eatin' was a privilege," into Vickie's childhood. Every night in summer the whole family sat on the front porch and shucked peas, butter beans, and corn. Besides being useful, shucking accomplished two other goals: it ensured Granny's admonition that, "There ain't no good young 'un unless it's a tired young 'un," and it provided an opportunity for storytelling.

"It was ungodly hot, shelling all those peas," recalled Vickie. "Southern heat: it's a cross between you and the weather. It has an attitude about it. Ignorance, immaturity, and devastation are all mixed in there, because you had to *function* in it. It was never just a hot night, but what you brought to that hot night. Like resentment. What made it bearable were the stories and songs. Otherwise it was just like a black drape over you."

Often as she spoke, tilting her head back, closing her eyes, and reaching out with both hands, as if she were conducting an invisible family choir, Vickie would say, "Now hold it a minute, let me get this just right." I imagined her childhood as a great jigsaw puzzle in her head, stored in pieces, and that she would rather be tortured than not give me a perfect verbal model of each one, so I could grasp the big picture (a critical challenge, as that big picture is fast fading from the Southern landscape).

Vickie spoke sadly of the people she'd known as a child not realizing that they sat on top of the largest chalk deposit in the world. Now she had a precious resource of her own — memories of her childhood among these people — but the difference was that she fully grasped its value. I had an uncanny feeling that she had intuited the worth of her growing-up even as a little girl, and had been hyperaware of every incident, every relative, every syllable uttered, and collected these as treasures she would draw upon in adulthood. (Vickie explained, slowly and carefully, that her family's high spirits had sometimes crossed the line into violence; her powers of perception were honed young, reading signs in people's behavior so as to be on the lookout for trouble, the better to avoid it.)

Now it had become her God-given responsibility to bring this vanished world and its prickly inhabitants into the present, without letting them fall into caricature. "I'll die before I let Granny Griffin get plucked out of context by someone," she warned, "and turned into Granny Clampit [from *The Beverly Hillbillies*]."

By this time my hand, from taking notes, and my head were both aching, but Vickie's obsession was infectious. I felt as if I were attending the birth of a storyteller as she painfully translated the particular, the personal, the people whose breath she had felt, into characters whose lives were no longer composed of strings of disconnected incidents but were in the process of taking on larger meanings. "Until 1997, when I started performing, I saw 'em as real people, y'know, who they really were. Now they're dramatized. If it's not actually her [Granny] on stage, the audience at least has to recognize the *idea* of her."

That idea conveys Vickie's feelings about age, among other things. "Granny was *old*. And being old was a privilege." Not just for the elderly, who had survived, but for the youngsters who lived with them. Age connected worlds, tethered vanished relatives and their strange ways to everyday life. Old people took up the domestic overflow, could be counted on to be at home even when parents weren't. They were a safe harbor in a tough world: something she considered most kids to be without these days, which is one reason she decided to give the children of central Georgia a communal grandmother.

Vickie had originally tried to write about Granny and her clan for a local newspaper, but repeatedly felt tugged back to the verbal. She found she'd had to make tapes and then painstakingly transcribe them to get at the spelling of Granny's dialect. "Sand bed" wasn't what Granny had said, when she was yelling at the kids to sweep up the chalky dust in her front yard; it was *say'nd beyd*. Without hearing Granny, even when her voice is filtered through the eyes, her stories leak into the modern "anywhere" world of Standard English. Dialect, according to Vickie, is a place marker, and maybe a marker in time as well; without it, the gulf between Granny's world and ours narrows, and the truth, she said, is that they are not at all contiguous.

Once she decided that sound was more important than words, Vickie started telling stories at the local library in the character of Daddy Runt. "It was at Christmas. I decided to show the children the way Daddy Runt did his Christmas tree. He'd a cut a pine saplin', then pull every needle off that poor thing. Then he'd dig a hole in the corner of the yard, set it in there, and wrap light bulbs — though he'd call 'em *leyt boolbs* — around every limb. Granny and I would sit on the porch and watch him. She had an eye for humor, struck through with a big vein of cynicism. Since she couldn't control Daddy Runt, she'd give him a hard time. 'Jus look at that poor-ass pine tree,' she'd say, 'that thang's as bald as Old Man Brown.'"

After a few incarnations as Daddy Runt, Vickie decided the costume was too hot, and switched to Granny. Instead of simultaneously portraying and narrating every move her grandfather made — self-narration had been a longstanding habit of his — she became Granny, and in character would describe what Daddy Runt had done to that poor tree, and then take on the shortcomings of almost everyone in Wilkinson County, and in neighboring Twiggs, Bib, and Baldwin Counties as well. "My daddy's family was strong-willed and aggressive, but Granny was *obstinate*. As you probably already know from just knowing people, period"— she looked at me and I nodded hesitantly — "the outgoing fellers in life who talk big just slam into a stone wall when they come face to face with a passive-aggressive — emphasis on passive. Granny called it 'bide'n her time.' She'd ugh-huh and ugh-huh (that means fake it), grimace and gesture when the 'greats' from Daddy's family were around. But, later, she'd say, 'Ooooh-wee, listen heah. Them Roberts ain't nothin' but trash. Heah they all come up the highway from Ocilla like a band'a gypsies, thankin' Macon, Georgia was *Somewhere*. Back then Macon wut'n nothin' — a one-trawf waterin' hole maybe fer a tired mule, but'je Granny, heah, she ain't got nothin' in her heart fer Macon or nobody out'a Macon, includin' them Collins'ses and that bunch'a Hamms. They ain't nothin' but talk. Granny could whup 'er one of 'em if she took the notion.'"

When I said Vickie became Granny, I meant it. Even without the costume — she'd shown me a picture of herself in a long dress, apron, and bonnet, the bottom edges and corners of her mouth smudged with brown eye shadow to imitate snuff stains — sitting in her air-conditioned living room on a sunny June morning, in her fashionable summer dress, fingernails and toenails painted bright red, Vickie Vedder *became* Granny Griffin. She scrunched her face, fixed her eyes wide, never once taking her pupils off mine. Her voice came out high and scratchy, like the ragged end of a rook's cry, sustained and riding on a fast, cocky trot of vowels and consonants — utterly different from any other sound I'd heard her make. When she finished a particularly pithy phrase, she'd make a kind of "put-that-in-your-pipe-and-smoke-it" S curve with her head and shoulders, dropping the left one, raising the right, following it up with her left jaw, and ending with a cock of the right eyebrow. Now and then she'd splice in a mannerism of her father's — the middle finger in the "know-it-all" position — for extra emphasis. The effect was mesmerizing. The old lady was smart and funny, but because she had been so quickly conjured to life in a pretty, young body, I was too amazed (and a little alarmed) to laugh.

I stumbled into downtown Forsyth at an extreme ebb tide. I wasn't depressed. On the contrary, I found Vickie elating, just utterly depleting. The town looked settled in its well-to-do ways, and baked pale in the midday heat. I parked in the shadow of the Monroe County Courthouse, a ponderous Victorian comment on law and order in red brick, topped by an Islamic-looking dome, which sat smack in the middle of town and effectively quartered Main Street into a square. Then I wandered into Russell's Pharmacy to buy a pen (Vickie's talk had used up my ink) and found that the Russells also ran a sandwich shop next door, with an old-fashioned ice cream counter and wrought-iron tables and chairs. The funny thing was that each chair and table foot was covered in a slit-open, neon-yellow tennis ball. The effect against the otherwise black and white floor was surreal, as though it had been decorated by Magritte. I hoped the floor had recently been waxed, but I never found out.

A friendly woman at the counter offered me a pimento and cheese sandwich with extra mayonnaise, a combination I'd never heard of but Southern friends consider a kind of holy food, and coaxed me into a Coke float to go with it. I could barely understand her accent; in fact, she had to repeat "pimento" several times before I got it. All of her words seemed glued together.

As carbohydrates and sugar rekindled my brain cells, I remembered what had been nagging at me all morning: Bertram Wyatt-Brown's classic study, *Honor and Violence in the Old South*. One of the cornerstones of Wyatt-Brown's argument stressed the honor code of the antebellum South: the idea that Southern morality was based on honor, a public virtue conferred by the community, as opposed to the self-regulating morality of private conscience, and that, consequently, slavery could function without contradiction in such a world, because honor required its opposite — abasement — in order to have value. The public element of this system intrigued me. When virtue is an external construct, an individual must base his self-worth on the opinions of others; no space is sanctioned for the consolation of private dignity. As Wyatt-Brown wrote, "public factors establishing personal worth conferred particular prominence on the spoken word and physical gesture as opposed to interior thinking or writing." He went on to add that, at heart, the "archaic concept that thought itself was a form of speaking" had not died out in the prewar South.

Thinking as a form of speaking remains a self-perpetuating legacy in parts of the South, or at least it did during Vickie's childhood in Gordon, Georgia. If I had learned anything from her that was alien to my experience in America, it was precisely this. I wrote and Vickie talked. "My family is predisposed to talk," she had said, laughing, "and *maybe* think." Speech not only brought Granny Griffin back to life, it triggered something very like a dialogue in Vickie's head between her childhood memories and her adult analysis. Following an in-character lecture on how ignorant folks *rhernt* (ruined) perfectly good peas and beans, Vickie paused to consider her grandmother. "From what I could tell about Granny," she explained, "is that as she aged, she began creating a private world of thought. She actually didn't like her in-laws, her husband, the neighbors; a lot of the community style also didn't jive with her natural inclinations to be a loner. Family life crowded in on her thoughts, and I feel like Daddy Runt was a 'too' busy person to talk through things with her. This was observable from anyone watching them live out their lives."

Vickie's observation was made for my sake: it was the result of public display, of having an audience. It was, literally, thought as a form of speech. In *North Toward Home,* Willie Morris said there was something "spooked-up and romantic" about a small town childhood in the South, which he attributes in part to growing up in a place where reading books was unacceptable. The imagination had to work itself out somehow, he said, and that was usually through talk, the endless telling of tales. In a rural world without access to other means of preservation — today Vickie mourns the fact that she never had a camera as a child — talk was both a family legacy and the means to a kind of private immortality. On countless summer evenings, shelling peas on the porch, Vickie's living relatives made the dead as familiar as Old Man Mag, Eva Mixon, and the mule, but as they spoke, they were in turn laying down their own investment in Vickie's memory, for now she tells stories about the way they told stories.

"I think my Granny Griffin, Daddy Runt, Daddy, Mama, and all their relatives have actually become characters and stories unto themselves," Vickie had said. "That's because their storytelling styles, their lifestyles, and their mannerisms . . . are what's worth knowing about them. It's not what they said; it's how they were affected by what they were saying, the people they thought of to remember . . . And it became a joy to the living members of our huge family to sit and listen to stories about the dead members and how they had acted when they were alive . . . To hear my daddy talk about the Collins family was funnier than actually knowing a Collins . . . All by himself, he could take you back to the spot where it all happened, so we were taken into his mind, and we loved him and his voice and how he raised his big old hands, his grin . . . He would say, 'I can't tell ye another word, I'm s'tickled by that crazy Ethel Collins. If her mama had know'd what that gal was doing . . .' And on he'd go. And it was as if the whole clan, the whole farm, the whole scene was *still* important."

My grandmother had only waved to me in silence in my dream-memory of the slides. Vickie's grandmother had done one better: she had come alive again and spoken to me that very morning. In Vickie's experience the past lived through speech. Granny Griffin was inside her and could come out at her bidding, because when she had really been alive they had *talked*. Granny had lived next door and talked to Vickie and through a constant funnel of stories had lent her not only her own life, but the lives of hundreds of other relatives stretching back down the ages. My family, by contrast, had shared landscapes — the beach at Cape Cod, Nantucket Sound, and the big jetty where we'd fished into countless blue twilights — and it was into these places that we had spilled our love. They and the images we took of them silently testified that we had been happy together. They were our stories. But when we were pictured within them, waving or not, it was almost as icons of age or gender or some other universal attribute, like pleasure: Smiling Young Girl in Seascape; Heroic Man Fishing on Jetty. We individuals kept our narratives battened inside as silent memories, held close but not mythologized into family stories. Places glued us together but they were not wells into which we poured our spoken history, as Vickie's family poured their words into Georgia.

Vickie and I are almost the same age; we both grew up in the 1960s. But whereas my memory is infiltrated with public television and private photographs — images concurrent with my childhood — Vickie, who grew up without a television set, remembers stories with roots trailing back into the deep, deeper, deepest past. What does it mean that I had lived in the suburban North, and Vickie in the rural South? Does it mean anything at all? I didn't have answers yet, so I scribbled these questions on a napkin smeared with pimento cheese, and very much hoped I'd figure them out before the end of my pilgrimage, two months later, in the bayous of Louisiana.

"Where ya from?" asked the woman at the counter.

"Rhode Island," I guessed, hoping I'd understood the question. For good measure I complimented her on the Coke float.

"You didn't get that accent in Rhode Island," said a voice behind me. "There's London in that voice."

I was floored. LaMar Russell, owner of Russell's Pharmacy, had read the invisible pedigree of my speech and found Wales in it (he thought it was London, but from the perspective of central Georgia, they're close enough). It was uncanny. The thing is, I don't think I have a discernible British accent; in fact most people think I'm from Virginia. I explained that I had gone to the University of Wales for graduate school, and had come to love the country so much that I often woke up astonished that I continued to live and breathe without the Welsh landscape and language. LaMar looked triumphant. The only other people to have spotted rogue signposts in my American diction were a gas-meter reader in Rhode Island and an elderly couple at Gatwick Airport. In the midst of discussing the outrage of delayed flights, the woman had grasped my hand and with feeling told me how good it was to meet someone from home. "We've been traveling for five months," she enthused, "and you're the very first fellow Tasmanian we've met!"

As I told this story to LaMar and the woman I couldn't understand, it occurred to me that Vickie had never told *me* a story. I laughed out loud. I hadn't noticed until then.

Rosehill's Tale

I CONTINUED ON A MORE OR LESS northerly route out of Forsyth. I had called a storyteller with the engaging name of Nancy Basket from a pay phone in Cedar Key, and made an appointment to see her in Walhalla, South Carolina, the following afternoon. Walhalla is in the westernmost corner of the state, a region that has more in common with its hilly northern neighbors — North Carolina and Tennessee — than with the low country of coastal South Carolina. In fact, it is officially part of Appalachia, and not a long drive from central Georgia. I had time to get there slowly.

What I really wanted was to get a pedicure. Vickie Vedder's glamorous toenails had put the idea in my head. Besides, I thought, beauty parlors were probably breeding grounds for all kinds of local stories: what else can you do while your perm sets or nails dry but talk? Unfortunately, piney woods — I now understood why this phrase comes so easily to Southern songwriters — had the countryside in a vicelike grip, leaving towns few and far between. The first substantial one I came to was Monticello, where I stopped a noticeably well-coiffured blond woman at another courthouse square, beneath another Islamic-domed edifice, and asked her about pedicures. She gave me convoluted directions to a little house outside town, with a hand-painted Beauty Parlor sign out at the front.

"No, sweetie," said the girl in the front room, between careful strokes of nail varnish, "we don't do no ped-i-cures on Fridays. You're outta luck."

I went back to the courthouse square to get my bearings, and just behind the spot where I'd questioned the woman earlier was another beauty parlor; I figured it must have been obscured by her minivan.

"Don't do nails. No toenails neither," responded the receptionist, who was wearing an old-fashioned, wraparound blue robe, hair glistening with gel. All the customers and hairdressers were black, and all were staring at me. "You not from here, girl, are you?"

Undaunted, I decided to try Madison, just up the road, where I parked on yet another sober, red-brick courthouse square, dominated by yet another cupola straight out of the Arabian Nights. I asked about beauty parlors in the chamber of commerce, and was told they'd all be closing about now.

While waiting my turn to talk to the woman behind the counter, I'd been fingering a book of Madison, Georgia, matches emblazoned with two messages: "The Town Sherman Refused to Burn" and "For Safety Strike on Back." Some promotional material nearby asserted that Madison's claim to fame was its thirty-five antebellum houses that had miraculously survived the Union Army's torch-and-pillage march across Georgia (apparently a Madison resident and former U.S. senator named Joshua Hill had not only opposed secession, but was a friend of General Sherman's brother; a plea from him was enough to prevent Sherman from toasting the town). I learned this from a brochure with a cover photo of a handsome young couple got up to look like a Southern belle and a Confederate officer. Another version lay beside it, printed in Japanese.

"How about storytellers?" I asked on a whim. "Anyone in town with a reputation as a good talker?"

*

"Am I talking too much?" Colonel Dan McHenry Hicky ("Laddie" for short) asked his wife, Hattie. We both assured him he wasn't. "Well, then," he continued, taking my arm in a courtly way, "let me show you this mantlepiece in the dining room. See? It doesn't quite fit. That's because this is the mantle from the old slaves' quarters. We had to sell the original during the Depression."

Both Hickys were far too polite and attentive to be bores, but they lived in a house that prattled on with a vengeance. "Rosehill," as it had once been called, was the only home in Madison to have remained in the same family since before the Civil War (Dan was the sixth-generation owner). Every room, every rug, every piece of furniture told a story, and like the parents of an accomplished but mute child, they spoke enthusiastically on its behalf, translating the sign language of beams and boards into three continuous hours of patrician-toned English. I had been referred to Hattie by the chamber of commerce — "She does costume tours of town; she's a great one for stories!" — and given directions to their house. Typically, I missed the street and pulled into a driveway to turn around.

"Are you the lady who wants to hear stories?" an elderly man asked, emerging from the garage. He generated kindness and mild curiosity. I said Yes, but that I was at the wrong house.

"Oh, this is one of our houses," he replied. "Come on in."

The Hickys were both in their eighties. He was nearly blind from glaucoma, with thick glasses and an endearingly unhip notepad and pen in his shirt pocket. She was small and slender, self-conscious in her not-for-visitors trousers, with hair the color of champagne touched by a drop of cassis. Both had inherited homes in Madison, bringing their total in this historic town of white-columned gems to three. Of these, Rosehill was the showplace. The easy graciousness of those whose lives had been devoted to the appreciation of beauty, rather than the necessity of work, still clung to it — like an invitation to a ball.

Iris Murdoch said that beauty "unselfs" us. "The sight of a bird, or a bank of sweet peas, or a lovely cloud formation," she wrote, "breaks us out of our narrow egos." She believed that anything that promotes "unselfing" is conducive to goodness, and that the best example is beauty. I bring this up because while some people are swept away by sweet peas and others by ankles and calves or particular shades of table linen, I am seduced by architecture. Beautiful houses encourage imitation. The harmony of design that makes them calm makes me want to be calm; their lack of rough edges makes me want to shed whatever ill emotion is pricking my skin like a stubble of thorns. Their sure lines guide my eye on a seamless journey up pilasters and over eaves, into corners, down staircases, through spaces dark and secret, light and open. Murdoch said this is the accomplishment of beauty, to lure the eye off the self. Stories do the same thing, and equally well; they, too, draw me out of the easychair of the ego and into motion along a route of words — calisthenics for the soul. Storytelling houses are the ultimate exercise.

"We have a ghost livin' next door," said Hattie, giving "door" a well-bred Southern "ah" at the end, rather than the West Country "r" most Americans chew on at the ends of their words. "McCooter is her name. She was murdered on the property. And she likes to drink. If you have a party and don't leave a drink out for McCooter, she'll knock the slats out of your bed . . . Sure enough, a new family moved in and didn't know the story, had a housewarming party. That night, didn't the slats fall right out of their bed!"

We left the front porch and its Egyptian Revival doorway — the Valley of Kings transposed into white clapboard — and entered a world decorated by the dead. "As a little boy I couldn't wait to get new furniture," said Dan. I had no sympathy. The front parlor was cavernous, swallowing up a crystal chandelier, several pieces of immense Empire furniture, a gilded floor-to-ceiling mirror, and a rare nineteenth-century piano. The carpet dated to the 1840s, purchased by an ancestor of Dan's from a traveling peddler with a sewing machine.

"That's my grandfather, John McHenry," said Dan, pointing at a pastel portrait of three children from 1859.

"It was made while the family was taking the Grand Tour," interrupted Hattie. She got up to show me John McHenry's ancient passport. "See, it goes into great detail. Forehead: Full. Eyes: Light. Nose: Aquiline. Chin: Oval. Complexion: Dark. And then it says here, 'Accompanied by Wife.'" She made a face.

"See, in the picture," Dan pointed but didn't look, "he's wearing the uniform of the Georgia Military Institute. His whole class enlisted in the Confederate Army on March 20, 1864, when John was fifteen years old. He was put on sentry duty: his first post. It was dark, and he heard a rustling in the bushes. He hollered 'Halt!' but there was no answer. So he hollered again, but the noise just got louder. So he fired his musket at the noise, and he heard something drop. It was a pig. His only casualty in the Big War."

"Now, see this picture," Hattie showed me a hand-tinted photograph. "This is Laddie at seven, with his head on that little boy's lap. Only the little boy was an old man by then. It was taken in the nursery upstairs."

We moved into the entrance hall. It had been added in 1848 to what was once the outside of the house, in effect becoming the central hallway when another wing was built on the other side. One half of the house has closets, the other doesn't.

"During the Big War," began Hattie, "the town was occupied by Northern troops. One elderly man from Madison, Mistah Smith, was escorting two ladies downtown when they were accosted by a drunken Yankee. While trying to protect the ladies' honor, Mr. Smith was shot and mortally wounded. He was brought here to die. See, he passed away right there, on the third step." She patted a stair-tread and I instinctively spun the melodrama in my mind's eye, giving it lots of blood and weeping.

"Another Yankee rode his horse up and down the hallway," tisked Dan. "Ruined the black and white checkerboard floor."

The depth and continuity of their knowledge stunned me. Generation upon generation, harboring the same memories in the same house, of a war fought on their doorstep, carried, even, into their front hallway: it was completely alien to my experience of the United States. Half my ancestors were peasants who would have been smarting under the thumb of the Austro-Hungarian Empire while the American Civil War was in full swing, and the other half, though probably in the States, are shadowy figures who lived out their lives in unknown locations. The intimacy of the Hickys' relationship with the past — both the personal and the national past, intertwined into a breathtakingly accessible history — fascinated but gave me goose bumps at the same time. My reaction to their stories reminded me of staring dispassionately into a gaping hole in my leg after an accident, and thinking, how interesting, it looks like the pith of a carrot, even while alarmed that it was my own bone and flesh I was seeing. No wonder so many pilgrims to the South return with reports that the War Between the States, as Southerners call it, or better yet, The War for Southern Independence, lingers so vividly in the contemporary mind. In *Confederates in the Attic,* Tony Horowitz quoted an Oklahoma man working in North Carolina, as saying, "In school I remember learning that the Civil War ended a long time ago. Folks here don't see it that way. They think it's still halftime."

We moved into another parlor where there was framed Confederate money on the wall, a tiny set of scales used to measure ore during the California Gold Rush, a silhouette of someone who had danced at General Lafayette's ball, and a photograph of another ancestor who went down with the *Titanic*. Showing me an elegant little powder keg, Hattie, eyes glinting with wicked pleasure, said, "If our little mother-in-law [Zoe] were here, she'd say, 'Dahlin', I do apologize, but this is what we kept the gunpowder in when we were shootin' at *you*.'"

The wonders continued. I saw Hattie's grandmother's wedding dress, with a waist just about the circumference of my upper thigh. I learned that glass used to be shipped rolled into cylinders to prevent it from breaking, then reheated to be stretched flat and cut (which is why there are so often bubbles in old glass); that Zoe's mother's name was Philoquia; that Hattie had a Yankee grandmother from Nashua, New Hampshire. I saw chests stuffed with muffs and boas and velvet hats from winters long past, and a desk of Georgia pine that had survived a fire in Arizona, the heat from which had resurrected long-dormant insects which woke, gnawed, and gave a fabulously ornate burling to the wood.

Hattie showed me the pink satin "Southern belle" dress she wears for summer tours. I asked if it had been specially made. She burst out laughing, glanced conspiratorially around, and whispered loudly, "Forty dollars, off the rack. It's a prom dress, from the Juniors department!"

Dan wanted me to look at his poetry. One poem was about a dog, another a sensitive meditation on the sky from his perspective as a fighter pilot in World War II. As we pored over his work, Dan knowing by heart what he could no longer see, Hattie turned on the radio and began a kind of private, swaying dance, singing along to "Summertime" in a breathy alto. Then they wanted to take me out for fast food, but I was exhausted, and badly needed to make sense of my notes. Suddenly sad at the idea of leaving them alone in their beautiful temple, I ran to the car and fetched a crumpled bag of what Granny Griffin would have called sorry-lookin' peaches that I'd bought earlier to give to Nancy Basket, and presented it instead to Dan and Hattie by way of thanks.

"He didn't bore me. That's why I married Laddie," Hattie said as she saw me out. "It doesn't do to be bored in life."

The next day in the breakfast room of Madison's Days Inn (set on a commercial strip a respectable distance from the historic downtown), I ate my Cheerios under an amateur watercolor of Rosehill. The contemporary painting imagined the house in pre–Civil War days, with several Uncle Remus–looking figures toiling — they were too picturesque to be merely working — in front. Yesterday, Dan Hicky had said that an old man, a former slave, had knocked on the door around the turn of the century and told his grandmother that the house used to have a balcony in the shape of a heart leading to a second story porch. The painting, however, portrayed mid-nineteenth-century Rosehill in its current incarnation, with a traditional porch stretched vertically across the façade. I felt smug for hours.

I also read a booklet Hattie had given me that she'd written about Madison — I was trying to avoid several elderly members of a bus tour who were holding bagels over their eyes like Lone Ranger masks — and learned two things: how to make "Georgia's Coke-Cola [sic] Salad" (red Jell-O, crushed pineapple, Bing cherries, cream cheese, and "two cans Coke-a-Cola"), and that the former owner of Cyclorama had lived in Madison. This was big news.

A house near the Hickys' called Luhurst — another monument of white-clapboard respectability, with a wraparound porch — had once been home, appropriately, to Lula Hurst, who had an amazing talent. She could levitate people and objects. Her most famous feat was to stand on cotton scales and, unaided, hoist two grown men in a chair over her head while the scales showed only her own weight. Her father contacted Paul Atkinson, who chaperoned the Battle of Atlanta cyclorama around the country along with other marvels, and arranged for Lula to join the act. Before long, however, Paul and Lula were married, and moved back to Luhurst to levitate no more.

The Kudzu's Tale

I STOPPED AMID THE BROAD-BACKED HILLS of Northeastern Georgia, not far from Walhalla, to get more peaches and a barbecued pork roll at a roadside shack that looked like it had been abandoned by a mobile flea market. The owner, squinting from beneath a battered Atlanta Braves cap, barked, "Girl, you got people in Georgia?"

I told him that close friends lived right over the Tennessee line, and he let it pass. "These here're South Carolina peaches. Just so's you know. Georgia peaches be runty right now." So much for the plump peach on Georgia license plates. I also bought some scuppernong preserves because I liked the name. Vickie said that Daddy Runt had made wine from "scuplins'," and I thought these might be the same thing (they were, but it took borrowing a dictionary to learn that scuppernongs are wild grapes, and scuplins' one of Vickie's family's innumerable verbal shortcuts).

As the greenery rolled by I had the same curious feeling I'd had for days: that the South badly needed to comb its hair, metaphorically speaking. Mile after mile, the tree and shrubscape along the roadsides was hopelessly tangled in kudzu, the plant *Time* magazine had voted one of the worst ideas of the twentieth century. It was easy to see why. Kudzu is a leafy vine that was first introduced to the South from Japan in 1876, then promoted with gusto in the thirties, with the idea that it would prevent soil erosion and provide shade. The problem is, in optimum conditions — for instance, the climate of the American Southeast — kudzu grows up to a foot a day, and eventually smothers every object in its path. In seventy years it has crept everywhere, turning stands of mature trees into wild, giant topiary gardens. Imagine if Christo, the artist who wrapped the Reichstag in cloth, decided to cover the entire state of Georgia in very high pile green carpeting: it would look exactly like the work of kudzu.

I made up a sport called kudzu-spotting, which is similar to cloud-gazing, though earthbound. The dense green masses take on all kinds of shapes: bears, swooping eagles, several species of dinosaur, all leashed together like shaggy green circus animals. The idea is to spot them while driving at 70 mph without having an accident (I narrowly avoided two crashes that I can recall). Kudzu is so universally despised that it has become a sub-genre of Southern chitchat to bash it. Everybody hates kudzu . . . everybody except Nancy Basket. Nancy makes paper out of it. She told me on the phone that she's also built a kudzu barn in her backyard.

"The leaves talk to me; they told me to use them," Nancy said, sounding like she meant it.

Oh great, I thought, even the kudzu talks.

We were sitting in what I'd call Nancy's Native American room, though her whole house may have been similarly decorated. I had arrived late, having been stuck on a two-lane highway behind a behemoth thresher, or some other ungodly large piece of farm equipment, and in my rush, hadn't glanced at the rest of her house. An animal skin was thrown over the sofa on which we both sat, curled up on our respective feet, and her daughter's Cherokee dancing outfit hung on the back of a door near an American flag, the latter superimposed with the image of a Native American man in full headdress. Antlers, feathers, animal skulls, and beaded necklaces were scattered along the mantlepiece of a large fieldstone fireplace. It was a comfortable room, earthy, with soft, overstuffed furniture — the very antithesis of Rosehill — and Nancy suited it. She wore her hair in a long black braid; bare feet poked out from under the hem of her denim skirt.

There were baskets everywhere.

"I'll explain later why I went to the kudzu for help," Nancy said. "But the baskets come first."

Nancy had been born in Washington State, but moved to South Carolina ten years ago after learning how to weave and braid baskets in the early eighties. Shortly after her apprenticeship, a great-uncle had contacted her out of the blue, sending hitherto unknown information about her third–great grandmother, Margaret Basket, a Cherokee basket weaver who had been born in Virginia. Margaret had been one of thousands of Cherokee forced westward along the Trail of Tears, after white settlers drove them from their homes. (I thought uneasily of Rosehill. Hattie Hicky had told me the day before that one of the branches of the Trail of Tears had passed just in front of the house; it later became the Charleston-to-New Orleans stagecoach route. "We ran the Indians out of heah," she'd stated, characteristically telescoping past and present with her free use of pronouns.)

"When a young Native American woman shows promise as a basket maker," Nancy continued, "out of respect she takes the name of the ancestor who's helped her in her art." Which is why, encouraged by her uncle's intervention and a timely divorce, she became Nancy Basket.

The stories grew out of her basketry. After she got to Walhalla, Nancy continued her apprenticeship with Native American artists in Cherokee, North Carolina, just across the state line. "They told me stories as we worked. Native people

59

believe that there are stories in the landscape. Stories in mute things, in objects, like baskets." Nancy had a rhythmic way of speaking, soothing but with muscular emphasis, as if she were kneading her words the way bakers knead dough. "They also believe that stories have medicine. That stories find you when you need them. And if you become a storyteller, it's a sacred responsibility. You have to give your audience the medicine you think they need."

I wondered what medicine I would get, as I sipped a Diet Dr. Pepper. Now, she continued, she worked as an artist-in-residence in the South Carolina school system, traveling and teaching Native American culture, basketry, and papermaking, and telling stories. "I tell the children about the drowning of Cherokee towns for reservoirs. There are some of us," she was almost whispering now, "who can still hear the drums sounding underwater."

Half-hypnotized by her delivery, I was jerked wide awake by this last bit of information. In Wales, my touchstone for oppressed nations, Welsh-speaking villages had also been submerged — recently, in the 1960s — by reservoirs created so that towns in England could access water more cheaply. Instead of drums, Welsh nationalists claimed to hear chapel bells tolling underwater. I told Nancy this and she nodded solemnly. "Yes," she said, "I see you understand." Then she excused herself and ran out to drive her reluctant teenage daughter to work at McDonald's.

These missing places, drowned, or decimated like Rosewood, take revenge in ghost stories of phantom drums, and long-dead children crying in the bottoms of wells. Landscapes do hold stories, only sometimes they are so old, or the victims of violence were so powerless, that the tales become dislodged, and the "hauntings" that began as collective conscience, a community remembering, get swept up into the dominant, collective conscious as folktales of ghosts. I heard eerie stories, usually in pubs in North Wales, about church bells ringing under the sea long before I ever learned about the Tryweryn Reservoir. I wondered how many spooky tales contained an ember of subversion at their core — a protest of the vanished, pushed from the margins all the way off the page — that smolders there either to be ignored or bellowed into flames according to the teller. Everything depends not so much on the tale, but on who tells it.

One of the original feminist manifestos, aptly titled *Diving Deep and Surfacing,* by Carol P. Christ, makes the succinct point that those who tell the stories wield the power. "Women," she wrote, "live in a world where women's stories rarely have been told from their own perspectives." Carol Christ wasn't the first, of course, to point out the power of storytelling in shaping knowledge, especially in relation to women trapped in men's narratives:

> "On women . . . the clergy will not paint,
> Except when writing of a woman-saint,
> But never good of other women, though.
> Who called the lion savage? Do you know?
> By God, if women had but written stories
> Like those the clergy keep in oratories,
> More had been written of man's wickedness
> Than all the sons of Adam could redress."

This wonderful diatribe was delivered by the Wife of Bath in Chaucer's *Canterbury Tales.* Her admonition, and Christ's — for the characters to seize control of the narrative — applies to all marginal-dominant relationships, as Nancy well understood. It was her particular goal to wrest control of the storyscape from the settlers, so to speak, and return it to the Cherokee.

Audiences hear different drums, no matter how deep the water, depending on who is speaking them to life.

She pursues this task with zeal, but with delicacy. "Because I work in the school system, I have to be so careful. Remember, this is the South. I can't say the word 'imagination'" — I must have looked aghast, because she stopped, nodding her head — "really, I'm serious, I can't say 'imagination' to the children because some parents complain it leads to devil worship."

I was trying not to choke on my Dr. Pepper. Nancy raised her eyebrows and rolled in her lips, as if to silently reiterate, It's true. "The South is so controlled. You have to break the rules without making people bleed. Stories do that."

This was my cue: I asked her if she would tell me a tale that she felt grew out of her environment, her Appalachian corner of South Carolina. Nancy nodded and said that this was her version of a tale she heard years ago from an Abenaki storyteller named Tsnaqua. She cleared her throat, and began.

GRANDFATHER CREATES SNAKE

A long, long time ago, the Creator, the one who made us all, red-yellow-black-white-and-brown, had a huge stone bowl. He reached deep down into it and he picked up the last little bit of clay that he had in there, and he said, "There's not much here, I guess I can throw it away. Hmmmm. But if I do, then the two-leggeds that I made will all know I threw something away. I told them not to do that, and I want them to listen, so I'm going to show them how to take a little bit of something and make it better."

So the Creator took this little bit of clay and he molded it and he shaped it and he gave the new thin thing eyes and Snake could see. He said, "Snake, wait here in the bowl. I need to go down to the river . . . to get more clay."

Snake waited and waited. And he waited and waited. And the Creator didn't come back. So he started looking around, and the snake looked in the sky and there were stars there, and he was warm, and when he looked down he saw color for the first time. He saw red-yellow-black-white-brown-blue-pink-purple-and-green, and he said, "Oooo, what's this? I want to go into the world and find out about color." So he slithered out of the bowl and he went down into the world. When he did that the Creator came back with a big armful of clay, put it in his stone bowl, and said, "Snake, where are you? I have enough clay and I can give you arms and legs. Snake! Where are you? I have enough clay and I can make your skin."

But Snake was not to be found. "Oh no!" cried the Creator. "You crawled off into the world and you weren't ready yet. You'll never have arms and legs now. You'll have to slide on your belly forever. How are you going to keep yourself warm? It's going to be winter and nighttime when you get down there and you don't have any skin! I wish you well, but I wish you would have waited." So the Creator just had to wait to see how Snake took care of himself.

Snake crawled off into the world and it was winter and nighttime and he had to crawl underneath a rock to keep warm. He was shivering and he was shaking, and he knew he had to get warm or he was going to die. So he looked around and he saw this Cherokee round-house, and there was a fire coming up out of the floor, and he said, "Maybe the fire is like the stars, and I can crawl over there and get warm." So Snake crawled over, got warm, and he was happy and grinning like this [Nancy grins extravagantly]. And there was a girl in this roundhouse, and she took one look at that new and different thing, something she'd never seen before, and she screamed. "ACH!" And it hurt Snake's ears. Then, in Cherokee, she said, "Get out of my house, ugly nasty person!" And the snake said, "Ugly? Nasty? I'm new and different and you're hurting my ears!" And the snake crawled out of the roundhouse crying, back underneath the rock.

The snake cried so hard — it was so cold outside — it froze his eyes open, and today snakes cannot close their eyes. It was so cold underneath the rock, all by himself, that the tail of the snake froze and cracked into little pieces, and today rattlesnakes, as you know, have the same kind of tail. And the snake said, "I'm cracking up. I'm going to die. And then the Creator will have made me for no reason. I can't let that happen. I have to take care of myself."

And so the snake found another roundhouse — because Cherokees never lived in teepees, you know — and he went into that roundhouse, and he was by their fire, and he was getting warm and he was real quiet, but there was a boy in the roundhouse. And the boy took one look at that new and different thing, something he'd never seen before, and he didn't scream or anything — because guys don't scream — they just pick up big sticks AND START HITTING. He WHACKED that snake. And then the snake had a horrible limp. Did you ever see a snake limp? It's real hard to do without legs.

The snake limped on out of the boy's roundhouse, and he said, "I've been frozen, my tail's all cracked up, I've got this horrible limp, my ears hurt because the girl screamed at me, I guess I'm going to die in the backyard of that boy and girl. And then after I'm dead I'm going to STINK. They're going to kill me for no reason."

So he went to the backyard of the boy and girl and he found that they'd left some beads lying on the ground. Maybe they didn't want them anymore. And he saw the beautiful colors. So he said, "At least I'll be able to die in the colors that I love so much." So Snake went over to the pile of beads, and he wriggled and he rolled, and he wriggled and he rolled, and the beads — because his body was still clay — began to stick. And he said, "I know what I'm going to do," after he looked down and saw he wasn't dead yet. "I'm going to bead myself my own belt. And I'm going to tell all my other snake relatives when they come down how to bead belts out of different beautiful colors and patterns and designs."

And that's why snakes today have their different colors and designs, but they still have to seek out places to keep warm.

Haboo? . . .

. . . Pam, that means, Are you listening?

She'd startled me. "Haboo!" I shouted back.

Nancy finished the story by adding, "We need to remember that different isn't ugly or bad or right or wrong. Different is just different." I wished she hadn't beaten the tale with a didactic stick at the end. It was obvious enough already, I thought, preferring to think of it as a creation myth rather than a we-must-learn-to-live-together sermon. I wanted to see the kudzu barn.

The afternoon was warm but the humidity had lifted a little here in the higher elevation. It was actually pleasant to be outside. Nancy told me that when she began storytelling, children would occasionally ask to see pictures. She decided she needed a visual aid that would draw in Cherokee culture in another form. That's when she turned to the kudzu.

"I went to it and asked for help," said Nancy. "It taught me to make paper from its leaves." Kudzu should get a teaching certificate: Nancy makes a lovely, deeply textured paper from the stuff, which she stains with natural Cherokee dyes. She presented me with a kudzu collage depicting a bunch of carrots. On the back it told me that in Asia kudzu roots are ground into a powder that's used as a thickener in cooking, the vines exported as grass-cloth wallpaper, and the purple flowers — which incidentally smell like grape bubble gum — used in jelly-making.

My little gift in no way prepared me for the glory of Nancy's kudzu barn. Raised up on short stilts and cinder blocks and sagging slightly at the sides so that it arched in the middle, with exterior walls of bundled straw, like a castaway's palm hut, it was homely and exotic at the same time: a cross between homes I'd seen along the Chaophraya River in Thailand and the covered bridges of New England.

"See," said Nancy, poking the roughage on the exterior walls, "it's made of bales of kudzu. Each wall is one bale wide.

It's great insulation. When I'm finished, I plan to stucco over both the outside and inside walls, but I'm going to leave a square inside exposed, that I'll cover with Plexiglass, so you can see how it's constructed."

The interior looked like the nest of a big, tidy bird — the dried bales were still exposed behind the wall studs — divided into neat rooms by walls made of antique windows that Nancy had scavenged. "It had been a livery stable," she said, "belonging to the house next door, when it was an old coaching inn. But I'm going to use it as a paper studio."

We stood in admiring silence. When the wind blew, the dried kudzu rustled in the walls, whispering, I guess, about fecund youth and topiary animals, and the romance of purple bubble-gum flowers.

Walhalla was a thriving little place, with more than its fair share of antique shops, and brochures advertising upcoming events like the annual Oktoberfest. A gas station attendant told me the area had been heavily settled by Germans.

The most surprising thing in town was a Mexican-Salvadorean restaurant, a bit of a dive decorated with big, old-fashioned Christmas lights, where I stopped to pick up some takeout. It was an off-hour, around four in the afternoon, and as I pulled open the door a premonition flashed across my mind of a bunch of beery guys hanging out around a pool table. I steeled myself, but as it turned out I couldn't have been more wrong. It was empty but for three Puerto Rican women — mother, daughter, granddaughter — who were eating at the bar, each pursuing her own version of a seated salsa to the piped backbeat. They told me to order the vegetable quesadilla and join them while I waited, so I climbed into one of the high, twisty swivel chairs at the bar and began to spin it with my foot. We looked like a quartet of exhausted Motown backup singers.

In 1986, they said, the local quilting and textile factory began hiring Hispanic workers; now there is a fledgling community of about five hundred or so Spanish speakers around Walhalla. They were thinking of organizing a Fifteenth of September Party to compete with the Oktoberfest. "Not compete, really," said the grandmother, "just, you know, add to it."

"What happened on September 15th?" I asked.

"That's the real Mexican Independence Day. *Cinco de Mayo* was just independence from the French, you see."

I commented on her lack of accent in English.

"Oh, I grew up on Long Island," she said. "We moved here because the cost of living is so much better for retired people. You can buy a nice house for $30,000."

I asked if the Hispanic community ever felt vulnerable here, being such a small minority. No, she said, they didn't really have any problems. A few seconds later she added, as an afterthought, "People just see us as different, and that's okay. As long as different is just different, not bad or threatening in any way."

At that moment, if Grandfather had tapped me on the shoulder and passed me Snake's long-overdue feet, I wouldn't have been surprised. Those were the woman's words. I asked her if she had ever heard of Nancy Basket, the storyteller. She shook her head "No." Nancy hadn't recommended any restaurants in town either, but I no longer doubted her ability to hear the drums sound from the depths. Occasionally a takeout quesadilla helps the medicine go down.

I was fast exchanging the culture of heat for the culture of hills. My route now was due north, destination Asheville, North Carolina, just about an hour and a half's drive from Walhalla. I was supposed to meet a storyteller named David Holt at his home near Asheville in two days' time, and had a daring plan for the intervening day.

As I approached North Carolina, I felt as if I were leaving one version of the South behind, a process already begun in northern Georgia and Appalachian South Carolina. There were fewer farmsteads, fewer smallholdings, fewer modest, fifties-style ranch houses and sagging shacks. Instead, forests claimed the land almost without exception. I missed what had become my favorite icons of rural living: unpainted barns that sat expectant but stoic in flat fields, like aging beasts of burden, their vertical gray boards softened and mottled by weather into velvety, strokeable hides.

The omnipresent greens of the Southern landscape were clustered vertically now rather than spread across the earth in plantings, and were less sun-faded; the rising land grew darker, rearing up before me into the Great Smoky Mountains and the blues of highland distances. The conifers and kelly-green deciduous trees had a Northern look, as if I were on the cusp of a world better known to me (a heart-sinking disappointment), where autumn and its candle-flame leaves make an impact undreamt-of in southern Georgia. My ears crackled in the clean air. Even the sunlight in the hills was different, more matter-of-fact, sharper; gone was the easy-going, late afternoon haze the color of whipped sweet butter, spangled with free-floating dust mites.

But the signs of the South continued. I stopped at a gas station cunningly disguised as a log cabin, and found that I could still buy beer at highway-side convenience stores, even on *Sundays* (handy, but scandalous to the New England Puritan that occasionally wags her finger in my conscience). Mammoth lumber trucks still ruled the highways, barreling along laden with freshly cut timber in a convincing display that the country was being felled around me. Hot boiled peanuts remained the snack of choice. And everything from live bait to chicken livers to ice cream to twenty-four-ounce soft drinks for 50 cents were hawked on portable electric signs that looked like debased offspring of old movie theater marquees (the above quartet was all advertised on the same sign). These simple things are unknown to me at home in Rhode Island, but for the electric marquees, which only appear in the rural corners of the state, and rarely at that.

Things took an ill turn in Asheville. My devil-may-care approach to lodging — basically, drive until I came to a sign advertising a cheap chain motel — was thwarted by a nest of converging highways. Every time I glimpsed a likely sign, it was on a route that I was either passing over, under, or paralleling, never the route I was actually on. Nearly an hour of this put me in a fierce and rather desperate mood, and I resolved to simply exit and take whatever I found. Unfortunately, I exited on the city's south side and wound up in the shadow of the Biltmore Estate: the largest private mansion in America, built by one of the Vanderbilt clan in imitation of a chateau from the Loire Valley. For a $30 entrance ticket I could ogle a handful of the two hundred and fifty rooms — names like Ming, Wedgewood, and several Roman-numeraled Louis jumped from the furnishings brochure — and all seventy-five acres of formal gardens, if I so chose. I didn't really want to do either, but lots of other people did, which meant rich tourists, smart hotels, and high prices. I picked one, blanching at the cost, but was so eager to eat my vegetable quesadilla and drink my convenience-store beer in comfort that I stayed.

That night I sent an e-mail to Vickie Vedder, reminding her that we'd talked so much the other day that neither of us noticed she hadn't told me a story. I proposed that perhaps she could send me one on tape, or even over the Internet: I would check my ethereal mailbox for a reply.

Orville's Tale

THERE ARE ALL KINDS OF ORAL STORYTELLERS, who tell stories for all kinds of reasons. Preliterate cultures told stories not only for entertainment, but, like Vickie's family, as a way of codifying the communal past and passing it from generation to generation. The Druids — the priest class of the early European Celts — instructed initiates by requiring them to memorize Druidic lore in the form of linked three-part narratives, called triads. Anglesey, a large flat island off the coast of North Wales, functioned as a kind of university for would-be priests, where students spent eighteen years committing the *mythos* of an entire culture to heart. Even when Celtic tribes picked up writing from the Romans, still the Druids clung to mouth-to-ear learning, not trusting knowledge not internalized in the human memory.

While memory is tenacious, what the Druids didn't count on were the Roman legions that stormed Anglesey in A.D. 61. The legionnaires lined up with their swords and shields on the mainland side of the Menai Straits, a narrow inlet that separates Anglesey, or Ynys Môn in Welsh, from the rest of Wales. When the tide was high, the Druids and their followers — faces painted blue, hair streaked with lime, waving torches and hurling curses — struck such fear into the troops that they almost ran from their posts; but then the tide turned and the Romans got hold of themselves, waded across and slaughtered everyone on the island, effectively wiping out a civilization in an afternoon. When the stories a culture tells about itself disappear, when there is no one left to listen and no one to tell, then not even ghost stories are left. There is, simply, no more culture.

I learned the story about the Romans and Druids from Tacitus, who helpfully wrote it down. Many people who practice storytelling today get their information the same way, from books or recordings, which may actually broaden their art rather than diminish it, untying the parochial knots of family and geography and bringing new experiences to bear on old situations. These people value the spoken word, whatever its source. They enjoy performance and the verbal acrobatics it entails, and are seduced by the intimate bond between listener and teller. A few years ago, I went to a Ghost Story Concert in Tennessee, and sat in a park with hundreds of other people, listening to storytellers populate the darkness with haints and blood-sucking ghosts and dancing corpses that wouldn't die. Their words came over an invention of this century — a microphone — but I've never before felt such kinship with the tens of thousands of generations that preceded mine on earth We were obeying a human impulse as old as fear, just as they had done: make the dark hours better by filling them with voices.

These "book-learned" tellers often perform in untraditional venues, such as schools, museums, or organized festivals. But what interests me about the South, more than any other region of the country, is that it provided "natural" contexts for tale-telling long before the modern storytelling revival ever got underway. In *Storytellers: Folktales and Legends from the South,* John Burrison identified three traits that have historically made the South a hotbed of the storyteller's art: a socially-instilled reverence for the spoken word; a population base with roots in West Africa, Ulster (the wellspring of the Southern Scotch-

Irish), and southern England, all of which are rich in story-telling traditions; and finally, physical isolation in a rural land-scape. To these I would add the lingering poverty of the Great Depression, which ensured that much of the Southern population remained rural and remote throughout most of the technologically plugged-in twentieth century.

These are the very conditions that create the parochial knots of family and geography that, for good or ill, are the wells from which traditional tellers haul up their tales, still dripping with the rich, distinctive murk of the Southern soul. Shucking corn, keeping the kids quiet, entertaining neighbors: whatever the incentives that brought stories to their lives, these Southern Druids — minus the face paint, though not beyond the occasional hurled curses — learned their art the old way, mouth-to-ear. They first *heard* most of the tales they now tell themselves, or like Vickie, learned telling techniques and then applied them to stories of their own. Some tell family tales, or personal anecdotes. Others tell legends, or trickster tales, like Akbar's story of Brer Rabbit, or even "jokelore," which is Colonel Rod's stock-in-trade. Many tell folktales; a few, the most isolated tellers, furthest from outside influences, tell very old folktales. And then there is Ray Hicks. Ray tells Jack Tales.

When I woke up in Asheville, I knew I was within an hour or two of Ray Hicks's home. This was so exciting that I splurged on biscuits and sausage gravy for breakfast (one of the perks of lodging well), nodding between bites as an old man told me how he'd worked in the dairy up at the Vanderbilt Estate when he was a boy. His job was to jump off the milk wagon and run bottles to customers' houses, racing to catch up with the horse if he'd had a big delivery. Now the dairy is a winery: most people prefer Chardonnay to milkshakes these days, though I doubt Ray Hicks would endorse the change.

In 1983 the National Endowment for the Arts made Ray a National Heritage Fellow — a very grandiose title for a man who probably couldn't care less. I had book-learned a few things about ol' Ray, as people called him, although I had never met him. He is nearly eighty; he stands seven feet tall; he rarely leaves his Appalachian home on Beech Mountain, in a remote corner of the Blue Ridge; he speaks with a vestigial accent that, according to a *New Yorker* profile "preserves Chaucerian and Elizabethan locutions"; and the stories he tells are his birthright, the current expression of an oral family tradition that in this country, at least, goes back to around 1760, when a certain David Hicks, Sr., arrived in America from an unknown village in Somerset, England.

I had read that Ray is "the patriarch, the classic American storyteller." I'd read, too, that once when his truck broke down and he'd been unable to pay for repairs, he'd prayed to Jesus for help, and that night an illuminated map of an internal combustion engine had appeared on his bedroom wall. He fixed the truck easily the next day. Isolated up on his four-thousand-foot-high mountain, Ray was to Anglo-American storytelling what Picasso was to visual art: a master, a genius to whom narrative digression came as naturally as shopping lists do to people with empty cupboards. I'd further read that Ray was on record as claiming that he learned everything he knew from his alter ego, Jack.

You know Jack too, and so do I: "Jack and the Beanstalk" and "Jack the Giant-Killer" are two of his better-known exploits. Jack is the hero of a cycle of English wondertales so ancient that they were already part of the folk-culture when first set into rhyme in the 1400s. Several centuries later, Jack emigrated to the New World with David Hicks, Sr., and became a Southern mountain lad. Meanwhile, back in Britain, even though the giant never got the best of him, nineteenth-century editors did, and trapped Jack in bowdlerized children's stories, which is how most Americans now know him as well. Most, that is, but for the descendants of David Hicks, Sr., of Beech Mountain, North Carolina. On their summer porches and beside their winter fires, they kept alive a Jack meant for the adult world; a young man who through cleverness, a little magic, and sheer good luck outwits throughout all eternity his dastardly brothers Will and Tom, various supernatural adversaries, and most of the hurdles life throws in his way.

The partnership of an elderly American mountain man and a figment of the imagination of medieval English peasants ("my best friend," as Ray calls Jack), is based on a good-hearted nose-thumbing at five centuries and the Atlantic Ocean. I can open a book and read the words of Jack's contemporary, Geoffrey Chaucer, but we are not intimates; Chaucer is dead, so he can't be my friend. Jack, on the other hand, has been an immortal lodger with the Hicks clan, living alongside each generation. Ray has said, "I'm Jack. Everybody can be Jack. Jack ain't dead. He's a-livin' . . . Like I tell 'em sometimes . . . I ain't everything Jack has done in the tales, but still I've been Jack in a lot of ways. It takes Jack to live. Now I wouldn't have been livin', probably, if I'd not been Jack's friend."

My compatriots may enjoy freefalling into an unseen future, but the invisible world I perversely cherish is the one that has passed. I want to fall backward, not forward. That vanished world — still invisible to the eyes, but accessible to the ears — lives on in Ray's stories, by grace of a marriage of New World and Old that is far more genuine than the uneasy union of European plunder and American folly at the Biltmore Estate.

I wanted very badly to find Ray Hicks.

In the words of someone else who must also have been searching for ol' Ray, "Easier said than done." I looked up "Hicks" in the phonebook and found two listings under "Hicks, Orville" in the Banner Elk area, which is the town closest to Beech Mountain. I had heard Ray had a younger cousin named Orville, who was also a storyteller, so that was promising. I rang both numbers: no answer. There was nothing else to do but try my luck in the Blue Ridge Mountains.

I followed the highway as far as I could, then started sidewinding up into the foothills. The temperature dropped twenty-five degrees in half an hour. Sham "Trading Posts" by the roadside sold souvenirs and apple butter for cash; the only trading they were doing these days was on a two-hundred-year-old memory of the area — a stone's throw from the Tennessee line — as the Wild Frontier. However hokey, their presence conjured vague thoughts of Daniel Boone, the eighteenth-century pioneer, woodsman, sometime Indian captive, and habitual poor speller (carving on a tree in these parts "D. Boone cilled a bar"), for whom a nearby town was named. Boone's homespun swashbuckling — the story of his rescuing his young daughter from the Shawnee Indians made its way into James Fenimore Cooper's *The Last of the Mohicans* — coupled with Ray's legendary inaccessibility (folklorist Joseph Daniel Sobol described fans "making the pilgrimage up the rocky road to Ray's house, their ears popping and their cars' suspensions rattling"), kindled a belief that I really was entering something very like wilderness.

Thick fog settled as I drove higher, and when it lifted I found myself in Blowing Rock, North Carolina. Volvos and BMWs jockeyed for position on streets lined in cafes and galleries. I saw a restaurant called Cheeseburgers in Paradise. There were antiques and estate jewelry shops and potters' studios, and the mild smiles of well-dressed tourists resigned to "having a nice time." This wasn't Ray's world, it was a twee tourist town. Winter population: 1200. Summer population: 6000. I felt like a cartoon character whose thought balloon had just been exploded. Matters didn't improve in Boone, but merely slipped down the commercial scale from The Wine and Cheese Shop to the Hillbilly Trading Post. The mountains weren't distant, now, as they had been yesterday; I was among them, like an insect buried in thick carpet, with knobby green mounds on all sides. Whenever there was a straightaway, it was cluttered either with kitsch — old motels, miniature golf courses, and places where families with children young enough to be stupendously gullible could "pan for mountain gemstones" — or slick purveyors of outdoor recreation.

Banner Elk was given over to the latter. In fact, it looked like an Olympic village set on a small plateau, ringed by mountains and scattered with hiking shops, ski shops, fishing gear stores, and white-water rafting centers. On top of Beech Mountain, Ray's fabled Olympian home, reached only by turning my car wheels inside out on a road so steeply interlaced that its design would have made an Irish monk proud, I did not find Ray whittling on his porch, but a resort village of prefab condominium units.

This was heartbreaking. Maybe Ray had moved into a condo. I berated myself for turning him into a kind of holy hick; he was as entitled to wall-to-wall carpeting and air-conditioned clubhouses as the rest of us. Still, it was with no mean measure of desperation that I corraled a cop in the parking lot of a trendy toy store and asked about Ray.

"Oh, you're looking for Ray-the-Storyteller." I was as relieved as I have ever been: at least she'd heard of him. "He gives out Beech Mountain as his address, but that's really not it." She then gave me excruciating directions to the Mast General Store in Valle Crucis, about twenty minutes away. "They'll know how to find Ray there."

*

"Ray who?"

My heart sank. Pretty college students on summer vacation were weighing bags of day-glo penny candy — sassafras drops, Gummi strawberries, candy buttons, clove puffs, and Charleston Chews — for tourists' children. No one knew Ray.

"You might want to try up at the Mast Store," one finally suggested.

"I thought this was the Mast Store."

"No, this is the Mast Annex. Store's half a mile up the road."

I sighed loudly enough for people to stare. My guidebook called Valle Crucis (which means Vale of the Cross and is pronounced Valley Cruise by the locals), "an offbeat settlement" on a "pretty back road." This was true enough. Despite the penny candy, the detritus of tourism had remained on the highway, leaving handkerchief-size fields and pastures nestled between the switchbacks. One, indeed, cupped the Mast Store, a rambling, sagging thing of many rooflines that looked like a brontosaurus constructed out of white clapboard. An ancient Esso gasoline sign hung out front, and an American flag flew from the roof. The Mast family had been selling everything from bowler hats to chicken feed and live chickens there since 1883.

Now it was stocked with useful stuff for modern life, though ancient advertising posters still hawked turn-of-the-last-century goods. There was a hardy smell of dust, canvas, fertilizer, and coffee. In the center of the main room sat a wood-burning stove surrounded by rockers: a central focus even in the middle of summer. An old man with a gourd-shaped head, huge eyes and no teeth rocked by himself next to a checkerboard; the red squares were set with Coca-Cola caps, the black ones with silver-and-black, twist-off beer tops. I took the facing chair and asked if he knew Ray Hicks.

"Yeah, I know ol' Ray. He been down here a timer two. Sittin jus' whar ye are now. Wha ye lookin' fer 'im? Ye kin t'ol Ray?"

I explained that I was an admirer, and he gave me a loose collection of directions to Ray's house. At first, I was relieved to hear that Ray did indeed live "way back deep in th'mount'n" — so no condo for the Hicks clan, I thought triumphantly — then, an instant later, decided that this was more bad news than good. I would never find him now. I was silently weighing my chances when the old man said, "Ole Ray's as tall's that big ole stove."

"No."

"Yes, ma'am, he is." He added that he'd personally been coming to the Mast Store since he was six years old, and it hadn't changed at all but for the stock. The Masts used to sell pig feed and grain, but now the farmers were all gone. Then he leaned over and whispered conspiratorially, "Upstars wus the funeral parlor. That's a-whar they kept th'caskets, up thar. They feed ye all ye'r life, then they dress ye up and pack ye off." After that, he stretched himself and got up to take his leave, bowing and saying his mother was waiting for him at home. I must have looked incredulous, because he added, "She's eighty-four, but I look older. Ye'r not too big, but she's half ye'r size, and still a whip'snapper. She makes th'ony canned green beans I kin eat."

Another two hours of searching turned up wave after green wave of mountain ridges, each skirted by precipitous valleys fast now falling into shadow, but no Ray Hicks. Another young cop told me, "Yeah, I seen him on TV tellin' his old-timey mountain stories, but I don't know where he lives." I finally gave up, returned to Boone, and checked into the Franklin Court Motel. One whole side of my room was covered in a wallpaper mural of birch trees in autumn, which struggled to a bitter draw with the floral-print bedspreads and knotty pine paneling. When I went out to dinner, I discovered that members of a beefy motorcycle gang had occupied the rooms on either side of mine. I would have despaired then, except that my final, halfhearted effort to reach Orville was successful: he would be happy to meet me the next day at the Blowing Rock Recycling Plant, where he works. I could barely understand his accent, but I thought we had made a date to meet at noon.

It was ten past twelve: twenty minutes at the recycling plant, and no sign of Orville. That morning, someone had told me he plays Santa Claus in the Blowing Rock schools each Christmas, and that I couldn't miss him. But I was; each minute that passed I was missing Orville. Just as I'd christened the phrase "The Hicks Hex" in my notebook, a truck pulled up. The driver worked at the plant, but had never heard of Orville Hicks. "Why don't you try the Dumpsters just up the road," he suggested kindly. "Maybe that's where he's at."

I sped up the highway then literally ran, backpack filled with tape recorder, notebooks, pens, and corn muffins bouncing wildly on my back, into a bivouac of big metal Dumpsters. I kept on running until the sight of Orville stopped me cold. From pictures I knew Ray was tall, gaunt, and clean-shaven; Orville wasn't exactly short, but he was bearded and stout. I thought he looked like a great, ambling composite of all the earth's creatures, plants and animals alike. The bib of his denim overalls, incongruously graced by a gold watch chain, bulged with a belly big and round enough to take on a life of its own, like he had a young piglet hidden in there. His head supported two landmarks: a Carolina Tractor baseball cap and a curly, graying shrub of a full beard grown right up to his laugh lines. Between the beard and cap smiled the face of a brawny elf, nostrils arched with mischief, very blue eyes glimmering beneath bushy brows. The easy good humor that spilled from this man salved my immediate fear that he was consciously parodying himself.

"I reckon you want t'hear a sto-ry," he said cheerfully. I assured him I did.

"Well come 'round here to ma lyin' bench." Gesturing with the antenna of his mobile phone, Orville indicated a salvaged plank pushed up against a chain-link fence, next to one of the Dumpsters. Peeling paint and decomposing plastic littered the ground like eternal snowflakes. Maybe because it was a recycling dump, there was no smell. We settled in and Orville said, "Oright, I'm a-gonna tell you 'bout this boy named Jack, okay?"

The good luck of this made my palms ache with pleasure. "Did you learn this one from your cousin Ray?" I asked.

"No ma'am, from ma' mama. I had six brothers and four sisters. I'm th' youngest. See, in th' evenin'-time, sto-rytellin' was part of our growin' up. Mama, she would holler at us, 'You young 'uns wanta hear a tale? Then come on in th' house,' and we'd go in th' house and sit down thar and do chores while mama'd tell the tales." Orville stopped and expertly spat tobacco juice at the dumpster. "We'd break beans, er shell peas, er bunch galax. And we'd set thar and do th' work, and mama'd tell us these Jack tales. And that's how I learned 'em, by listenin' to mama up thar on Beech Mountain. This here one's called 'Jack and the Varmints.'"

Orville made a noise in his throat like children do when they're imitating a machine gun, except that he was smiling. It was an extraordinary chuckle, half pure joy, half rhythmic device.

JACK AND THE VARMINTS

Now Jack, he lived waaaay back up in th' mountains thar with his mama, and they got up one morning, and went to get something to eat, and looked, but didn't have a bite to eat in the house. Didn't have nuthin'. And Jack's mama said, "Son, you gonna have to go out and find some work. If'n you don't, we gonna starve to death."

Well, Jack, he didn't like to work too good, if he could get by with it. But he finally headed down th' road lookin' for work. Well, Jack got down th' road a little piece, and found an old board layin' beside th' road that come off an old wagon. Well Jack got his old pocketknife out of his pocket, and got to whittlin' on that board. Walking down th' road, he wasn't carin' where he's going, er if he found work er not. Got down th' road a little piece and Jack looked and he'd chewed down a big old round paddle outta that board. Well, Jack put his knife in his pocket and got that old paddle, walking down th' road with it, swing-ing it this way and that way. Wasn't long before he come by a mud hole [pronounced hough]. Jack got to lookin', and there was a big bunch a flies flyin' around that mud hough. After a while the flies lit on th' mud hough, and Jack snuck up on th' mud hough with that paddle, and he come down in that mud hough, ka-wham! Right in th' mud hough with th' paddle he went. And he picked up th' paddle and looked under it, and he'd killed seven flies! [Orville chuckled.]

Well, Jack thought he'd done something big.

"Excuse me, can I put this in here?" A man held pieces of an old kitchen chair for Orville to inspect before he tossed them in the Dumpster. Orville looked them over and thought he could do something with them, and stockpiled them at our feet.

"I'm a salvager," he said, a little sheepishly.

So Jack went on down the road and he come to the blacksmith shop. He went in 'ar and he got that blacksmith to make him a belt [pronounced bey-alt]. And Jack put that belt on, and that belt, it read, "Big Man Jack Killed Seven at a Whack." Gosh, Jack went down the road with that belt on feelin' big [pronounced be-eg].

Well, it wasn't long before Jack come by the king's house. The old king was settin' on the porch thar smokin' his old corncob pipe, leanin' back in a rockin' chair, and he seen Jack a-comin', and he said, "Howdy son."

Jack looked up thar on the porch and seen the king, and said, "Howdy-do, daddy."

The old king said, "Can I hep you?"

Jack said, "Yeah, I'm a-lookin' fer work."

"Well, Jack," he said, "I need a man. But you ain't bigger enough fer what I need you for. But come on up here and set down and talk to me awhile anyway."

Well Jack went up on the porch, set down in the old chair, and him and the king got to talkin'. D'rectly the king looked over and he seen Jack's belt. And he read it and said, "Big Man Jack Killed Seven at a Whack." He said, "Gosh, Jack, that belt mean what it says it does?" [Orville chuckled.]

Jack said, "It sure does." The king thought he killed seven men at a whack, din't know he was talkin' about flies. He said, "Gosh, you just the man I'm a-lookin' for."

Jack said, "Whaddaya mean?"

He said, "'Cross the mountain here, there's a big old wild boar on the loose. That thing'll weigh ya up to two thousand pounds, it got tusks stickin' waaaay up outta its mouth, and that thang's knockin' down fences and killin' horses and sheep. Nah I need to get that thang killed. If you can kill that thang and bring it back ta me, I'll give you a thousand dollars."

Jack said, "Gawsh, a thousand dollars. Well, king, I'll see if I can go back thar and kill it fer you."

Well, the king went out and got his horse, and put the saddle on it, and put Jack up behind him, and rode 'cross the mountain to where he last seen that wild boar at. And the king was sa scared of it, he knocked Jack off the horse and he beat that horse to death gettin' outta thar, very nearly. Jack got up, dusted hisself off, and said, "If that king's that scared o' that wild boar," he said, "I'd better not mess with it. I believe I'll just go on home [pronounced haum] and forget about it."

Well Jack started 'cross the mountain haum. He got 'cross the mountain, got down in the holler and got lost [pronounced lawes-t]. He got to beatin', thrashin' around in the laurel bushes, tryin' to find his way out [pronounced a-yout]. The wild boar's on the other side of the mountain, and it hear Jack down in them bushes, boy here it come. Whipty-cut, whipty-cut, here come that wild boar 'cross that mountain. And Jack seen that thang comin' down the mountain, them big tusks is hangin' out, knockin' rocks down this way, knockin' trees down that way, gosh it scared Jack ta death.

Jack took off a-runnin' as hard as he could run. Wild boar right behind him, whipty-cut, whipty-cut, whipty-cut, hear it come [chuckles]. Well Jack tucked through the bushes, dodgin' this way and that way a-runnin', and Jack run and run 'til he's just about gived out. And the wild boar's about to ketch 'im. Jack said, "I gotta do somethin' quick. That thang's gonna ketch me and kill me." Well, Jack looked, and he seen a little old log cabin up thar in the woods. The top of the cabin had fell in, but the rest of it was still standing. Jack went ta that log cabin as hard as he could run, that wild boar right behind him, whipty-cut, whipty-cut. And Jack got to the door of that log cabin, the wild boar grabbed him by the coattail and ripped a big chunk outta it.

"I'll just pull up this old chair, will that be all right?" An elderly man had been circling our lying bench for the past five minutes, dispersing his glass and plastics with enormous deliberation, the better to keep listening to Orville. He had his hands hopefully on the back of a folding beach chair that had seen better days.

"That's what it's a-thar fer," said Orville, and sent a missile of tobacco spit back at the Dumpster.

I gave the newcomer a firm smile that said, Fine, but sit down and be quiet.

Gosh it scared Jack, and Jack run inta that log cabin, and the wild boar come in behind 'im. Well Jack clumb up the log cabin and jumped outta the top of it, and run around thar, and pushed the door shut, and put a big rock up against it. The wild boar couldn't get outta the log cabin.

Well old Jack went on back down to the king's house. The king was settin' on the porch, he seen Jack, "Hey, Jack, ya kill that wild boar?"

"Well no, king, I didn't see no wild boar."

The king said, "That's funny. Last ten men I sent up 'ar, that boar's tried to kill 'em and scared 'em to death. And you didn't see no wild boar?"

Jack said, "No, only thang I seen was a little old pig up on the side a the mountain. That thang got ta followin' me around, I made a pet outta it. I was gonna bring it back here and give it to you, but that thang bit me on my coattail and jerked a chunk outta it and made me mad, so I picked it up by the tail and the ear and throwed it in a log cabin up thar. You can go up thar and see if that's what you want."

Well, the king jumped up on his horse, rode up on the mountain, looked down in that log cabin, seen that wild boar, and gosh it like to scared him to death [pronounced day-yuth; chuckles]. He went back to town [pronounced ta-youn], and got sixty of his men 'n Winchester rifles. They all went back up thar. That wild boar's sa big, a-rootin' down thar in that log cabin, and beatin' around with them long tusks, it scared the king's men — they wouldn't get close enough to shoot it. Jack said, "Give me the gun, I'll shoot it." And Jack went around the old log cabin, and finally found a crack. He stuck the gun in thar, and bang! Shot it between the eyes and killed it deader'n a hammer [Orville chuckled]. That wild boar fell over. It'us so big, that when they skinned it out, it took twenty-four wagonloads of meat to haul it back to the king's house.

Two other men joined us, acknowledged by a nod of Orville's Carolina Tractor cap.

"You Ray Hicks?" asked one.

Orville explained that he was Ray's younger cousin, and related to Ray's wife, Rosie (Ray and Rosa Hicks are also distant cousins). "It was Ray that got me a-tellin', though," said Orville, spitting again. "I was a-shy, but Ray wouldn't have it. He made me go up on stage once't, and I told a story, and I haven't stopped since. Sometimes I do twenty-two shows a month. And people bring thar children and grandchildren out here to th' dump."

"Does anyone mind?" I asked.

"Th' county hasn't complained yet," said Orville, chuckling mightily. "Now ma own daddy, he was a Missionary Baptist preacher, and he didn't care too much about th' sto-rytellin'. When Mama told us tales, she'd have ta look out th' do-or to see if Daddy was a-comin' home; if she seen him comin', she'd quit tellin'.

"Ma daddy didn't have no car or driver's license, so we just stayed up on th' mountain. We didn't have no 'lectric'ty 'till 1964, and then we didn't have no TV. Daddy thought that was a sin. I'll tell you about the hardest whippin' I ever got. We'd worked all day in th' fields, worked real hard. My brother come up to th' house — he had an old '42 Chev-e-rolet, I think this happened about 1959 — and he took us young 'uns up to th' store to buy us a sody pop. Well, we got in th' car and got up to th' store there, about three miles, and I looked at th' store and saw a sign. And th' sign said, 'Drink good ole' Mountain Dew.' Well, Daddy started in th' store and he said, 'What kinda drink do you want, Orville?' and I said, 'Daddy, get me one o' them good ole' Mountain Dews.' Well, Daddy turned right around and broke a switch off a tree, and he gave me th' hardest whippin' I ever got. Daddy thought it was a moonshine I was askin' fer. But it was just sody pop. He didn't find out 'til years later."

Orville chuckled his rapid-fire chuckle again, as if he'd been recalling pain inflicted on someone else's backside.

"Ma daddy was real strict," he continued. "Fer him Christmas was just 'nother day. Mama'd get ta feelin' sorry fer us kids, though, and fill a white rag with sugar and dip it in water er milk and tie it off, give it t'us ta suck on. She called it a sugar tit. Now ev'ry night come 7:30 we had to go to bed, even if we weren't a-tired. Daddy'd blow th' lights out, and if we talked we'd get a whippin'. But now, fellers, I was a-tellin' a story to this lady, and I'll go back to it, if that's okay."

Everyone shook his head very earnestly, and Orville picked up the flow as easily as if he'd been holding it in his hand all along.

Well, tha'll went back and Jack got his thousand dollars. He put it down in his pocket. Boy, Jack was tickled t'death. A thousand dollars! He said, "I'll go home, won't have to work." Well Jack started down the road. He hadn't even gotten outta the king's sight, and the king hollered and said, "Heeey, Jack, hold up a minute." Jack looked back and said, "What is it, king?"

He said, "Jack, I just got word in that a big old lion's got loose. It's done eat one little boy, and girl, and Jack, me being the king, I gotta have that thang killed. People's scared of it. If you kin kill it, I'll give you another thousand dollars."

Jack said, "Get somebody else to do it, king, I'm a-goin' *haum*."

The king said, "Aw, c'on Jack, you killed seven at a whack. You killed a big old wild boar fer me. You ain't scared of an old lion, are you?"

Jack said, "Well, I reckon I can see if I can kill it for you, king."

The king went on out and got his horse, put his saddle on it, and him and Jack got on his horse and they rode across the mountain. Well, they see that big old lion thar. The king was s'scared of it he knocked Jack off that horse, boy he took off, whippin' that horse, gettin' outta thar.

Jack got up and dusted hisself off, and said, "I'm a-goin' haum. I'm not gettin' messed up with no lion, and I'm stayin' on this little bitty road here'll take me haum, and I'm not gettin' lost [pronounced law–ust]."

Well Jack started on that little old road towards haum. He got down the road a little piece and he come around a bend in the road, and right smack dab in the middle of the road set that big old lion all rared up. It seen Jack. It lioned, "Rarrrrrrrr." It roared s'loud, the king heard it from in town. He said, "Oh no, Jack's a goner this time."

And it scared Jack s'bad, that instead of runnin', Jack clumb up a big old tree. Clean to the top of it. But that old lion came and got under that tree, and looked up and seen Jack up that tree, and got its big old teeth and got to gnawin' on that tree. Had the tree nearly cut in two. Jack was up thar scared t'death. But d'rectly the old lion dropped off [pronounced ough] to sleep. And Jack said, "While that lion's asleep I'm a-gettin' outta here."

Jack put his foot down, put it on an old brickly limb and it broke, and Jack fell outta the top of that tree smack dab on the lion's back. The lion jumped up and felt Jack on its back. It tried to bite him and tried t'claw him. And tried to run through the bushes ta knock him out. But Jack was scared t'death. He was hangin' on that lion's back fer dear life.

The lion took ough a-runnin'. Right into town that lion went. And the king was settin' on the porch. He looked, and seen that lion a-comin' with Jack on its back, and he run in the house and grabbed his rifle. They come 'round the king's house, the king shot and missed and shot Jack's hat ough. Boy, Jack was getting scared on that lion's back, and the king shootin' his hat ough.

The lion come around the king's house again, the king took better aim, and Bang! Shot the lion right between the eyes and killed it. The lion fell over in the street and Jack did too. Well, the king walked over thar where Jack was gettin' up, dusting hisself off, and the king got up to Jack, and Jack said, "Looky here, king, I'm mad, I'm good and mad."

The king said, "What you mad about? I shot that lion."

Jack said, "That's what I'm mad about." Said, "I caught that lion up on the mountain, and I was trainin' it for your ridy horse. I've been a-trainin' that thang for nearly two hours, and you up and shoot it like that. King, that makes me mad."

The king felt sorry for Jack, give him an extra thousand dollars, and old Jack went on haum with three thousand dollars in his pocket. The last time I's down by thar to see Jack, that lazy rascal still ain't done n'work.

Orville chuckled so hard he almost drowned out the clapping. I was freezing — fog had settled again, bringing with it a chill better suited to a November afternoon — but I was too absorbed to care. Orville's voice fascinated me. Akbar, Colonel Rod, and Vickie all had Southern accents, but when they began their stories they slipped out of standard grammar into dialect, as well as thicker, curlier versions of their own voices, which they either borrowed from their own past selves — as, I think, was the case with Colonel Rod — or from friends or relatives. The change was a marker that conversation had stopped and storytelling had begun. But with Orville it was different. His voice never altered. As an educated, African-American professional, Akbar would never say, "Ah hears what you're saying," the way Brer Bear does. But to Orville sody pop was always sody pop.

"I like to tell ma kids now, 'cause they live like lit'le rich kids, with a TV set'n all, what it was like when I growed up," continued Orville, after he spat some more jet streams of tobacco juice. "I didn't like school much. I was always a-lookin' out the winder, day-dreamin' and such. So I used ta hide in th' woods and not go ta school. I'd swing on grapevines and set rabbit traps. Maybe I'd go two, three times a munth. My parents never found out 'till we got the 'lectric'ty, 'cause then a phone come in, around 1965. Th' princ'pal called and said I hadn't been in school. You know I got a whippin'.

"Before I went ta school, *if* I went" — Orville chuckled and his beard shook up and down — "I had to get up at five in the mornin' and run th' milk cow down from the mount'n, cause whar we lived at was in th' holler.* That'us just one a ma chores. Another was raisin' pumpkins. In the fall o'th' year, people would drive up thar t'get these pumpkins, specially round Haloween time er Thanks-givin'. We raised some great big pumpkins. One Saturd'y, Daddy left me down at the barn sellin' them pumpkins. It was long 'bout one or two o'clock, I hear'd a car come up, a great big old Cadillac. A feller got out with a big old coat on and a necktie. And he looked like a rich city feller."

The *déjà vu* switch tripped in my brain. I waited expectantly, then sure enough, Orville sold the rich city feller a mule egg. My mind raced: if I'd had trouble disentangling the under-growth of Colonel Rod's conversation from his tales, it was impossible to tramp through the audible kudzu thicket of Orville's monologues and separate memories from perfor-mance. And perhaps that was the point: his memories were his performance. The storyteller *was* the story. In real life Colonel Rod is a composite figure, half mule-egg seller, half city slicker; perhaps because of this dichotomy he's more comfort-able presenting the tale in the third person. He doesn't quite have the credentials to sell mule eggs himself. But Orville does. If I hadn't heard the story previously, I might have believed him. The parts about the sugar tit, the whippings, and playing

---

*Holler is a backwoods term for hollow, a valley or the downslope of a mountain; it is often used in the proprietorial sense, as in "our holler," meaning a family's ancestral patch of land. Despite being a regional varia-tion, it is recognized, though not used, throughout the country. The *Ox-ford English Dictionary*'s first written citation dates from 1845.

hooky were all true, so why not passing off pumpkins as mule eggs?

Despite his isolated upbringing, Orville's storytelling betrays a very modern self-awareness. He is conscious of his own exoticism, of how the "mountain man" image is perceived and valued — and ridiculed — in the world at large, just as Vickie is conscious of Granny's uniqueness. Because it is presented in the first person, however, Orville's double-vision is even more unsettling. As I discovered later, listening to his storytelling tape and thumbing through a written profile of him (when the group broke up, Orville offered to sell me his latest tape and CD, which he kept in the passenger seat of his truck), Orville codifies his childhood experiences, remembering them as stories, almost as if they had happened to Jack and not to him personally. His telling of the Mountain Dew incident on tape, and in print, was word-for-word the way he'd told it to me.

It is clear that Orville is on the cusp, one foot in the contemporary world, one foot in the otherworld of his parents, Gold and Sarah Hicks. But what made my drive to David Holt's house, outside of Asheville, shot through with twined veins of relief and regret, was that the old world of his daddy's day is past. If it weren't, Orville's stories would not have petrified into legend in his middle age (he's forty-eight); the flotsam of daily life would polish their edges, as silt burnishes gemstones in a tumbler machine, and his tales would change shape and luster day by day. But daily experience is so different now in these Southern mountains, with the arrival of condos and tourists and wider roads and better jobs and cheeseburgers from paradise, that it doesn't bear any more on Orville's childhood memories than it does on Jack's fifteenth-century escapades. And in some private place beneath his chuckles, that makes Orville sad. In the book he sold me, he is quoted as saying:

With my children and the new generation coming along, I can't live the old ways. Can't even buy a wash pot. We've got a car and a VCR and television, and our children are growing up fine. But if it was up to me I'd take all the electricity out of the house and have oil lamps. Live the old way.

Before I left the Blowing Rock Recycling Center, I asked Orville two crucial questions. One was how to get to his cousin Ray's house, to which he replied with a tangled web of directions. I'd have liked nothing better than to turn around and march back up into the mountains, but I was due back at the Atlanta airport the following day, and so set them aside for a future trip. The other was what on earth I had been perching my feet on as he had talked.

Orville laughed, chest heaving, spat hard, and said, "That thar's a gut bucket. It's a subst'ute fer a bass. See." And Orville began strumming a cat-gut string that was threaded through a tiny hole in the bottom of an overturned metal washtub, attached at the other end to a makeshift handle held aloft by a four-foot stick. Dum dum dum it went, recycling the sound of Orville's childhood from the percussive thrum of his memory, up through his fingers, and out into the chill mountain air.

David's Tale

A DIFFERENT MAN, a different mountain.

Like Orville, David Holt is a "mountain man," but only in the sense that he lives on a mountaintop. In Butler Mountain Estates. To reach his house I more or less pointed the car straight up, jammed it into second gear, and ground past increasingly big homes until I reached the crest, where David's was perched. The first floor clung to a ridge that looked across a scalloped valleyscape so far-flung and full of beauty it made me gasp; the lower level sprawled down the mountainside. Wet suits and scuba gear hung drying in one of the garages.

After two hours of contemplating Orville's beard, David himself appeared almost obscenely clean-shaven. He was handsome, with smooth, regular features; I imagined he would be extremely photogenic. He greeted me in a black baseball cap, Hawaiian-style shirt with carp swimming on it, a pair of hip, high-tech sweatpants, and with a laidback ease and thoughtfulness that spoke of professionalism, success, and intelligence. He gave me a glass of water and we went out to talk on his deck.

"We just got home from an overnight bus trip to Key Largo," he said. "It was great. You sleep all night, wake up and you're there, then you dive all day and come home. I'd do it again anytime."

"I was just in Florida too," I said lamely, then came to an abrupt stop because I had completely forgotten the names of everyone I'd seen there and the places I'd been. Instead, I told him about my hunt for Ray Hicks, and my meeting with Orville. He knew them both well, and later gave me a photocopy of a map drawn by Ray's wife, Rosa, that showed the way out to their holler.

"It's best to write ahead of time and ask for an audience," he said. "Ray and Rosa are the nicest people in the world, but they don't have a lot of money. I like to bring them groceries — you know, canned goods, maybe a ham or a chicken, rice, that kind of thing. Ask what they need. Then you'll have to fight Rosa to get her to stop cooking it all up to serve you. They'd both give you the shirts off their backs, even if that was all they had. And they don't have much more."

David explained the convoluted trajectory that had led him to storytelling. He'd grown up in Texas and California, but his grandmother's legacy — a '62 Chevy with 62,000 miles on it and two thousand dollars — had led him to the Appalachian mountains to learn "old-timey banjo." He'd picked it up so well, adding other mountain instruments along the way, like the paper bag ("Really," he said, when I looked as if I hadn't heard right, "I learned it from a mountain fiddler; I've played the bag at the Grand Ole Opry"), that he's become an expert on traditional mountain music. The stories came from his mentors, the mountain musicians who had taught him in the sixties and seventies, and now he weaves their tales into his music just as they had done, the better to hold an audience's attention.

"You know what I like about storytelling, are the unlimited possibilities," he asked-and-answered. "There aren't any rules. With folk music there are rules, unspoken ones. You can bend them pretty far, but once you break them you're in another genre. The Kingston Trio broke 'Tom Dooley.' But storytelling is different. You don't want to lie, if it's historical, you want to keep it true at the core, if you know what I mean, but you can be any first-person character from the past that you like. I find that really liberating."

Very like travel, I thought, which also allows you to try out different personae from that of your homebound self, to the extent that every time you cast a shadow on a new spot of ground, you can fill it in with whatever details you choose. No one knows the difference. That, too, is liberating.

"A lot of the stories I tell start out as anecdotes that I hear from local people, and I add characterization, and try to make them as visual as I can. Like 'The Great Dana Baby Swap.' That's a story I tell now, but it started as an anecdote I heard at a church homecoming around here. There was a guy there talking about the Methodist Revival meetings of the 1830s, when people would come from all around to hear visiting preachers. Well, at one of these, in Dana, North Carolina, all the adults were at the meeting — they'd come down from the mountains with their families in covered wagons — and they'd left their babies asleep in the wagons. The teenagers thought it would be funny to switch the babies as a joke. Well, the next morning everyone took off for home, and only later discovered that they had the wrong children. He said that pretty much nobody came back to trade: it was too much trouble back then. This was still the wilderness. So they just kept each other's kids."

David got up and ran into the house and came back with an armful of his storytelling tapes, to explain the provenance of some of them to me. "Groundhog and the Hogaphone" was a true story about a mountain man named Uncle Ike from Rosman, North Carolina, who had invented a hogaphone. I gave David the same look I'd used on the paper bag.

"No, really," he insisted. "He caught himself a groundhog, killed it, tanned the hide and stretched it taut over a windowpane where the glass had gone. Then he stuck a wire through the middle of it, tied it in a knot, and ran the other end down the mountain to a friend's house, where there was another groundhog hide tacked across a broken window. And they could speak to each other. Supposed to be true." David shrugged his shoulders and smiled, while his cat vigorously clawed away at one of the deck supports as if it were a scratching post.

In David's story, Uncle Ike runs the wire to Granny Beecher's house, a mile away. He plays the banjo for her — "Cripple Creek" is her favorite tune — and she plays the radio for him. One day a bear gets into Uncle Ike's cabin and Granny hears the commotion over the hogaphone and thinks he's a goner, but when she gets there with her shotgun the bear is dancing as Uncle Ike feverishly strums the banjo.

"You see, the bear comes from another anecdote," David explained. "I heard this true story about a guy who shot a female bear, not knowing she had a cub with her. The cub was real little, so he brought it home and reared it. His wife suckled a baby on one breast, the cub on the other."

My eyebrows were in springboard position again.

"Really! I swear. They kept it for a long time and it was completely tame. But then a circus came through town and they sold it. It all happened during the Depression."

"Oh, that's terrible," I said, instantly regretting my kneejerk softness.

"Mountain people aren't real sentimental. They can't afford to be."

David went through the evolution of several other tales, including one he was working on at the moment, which he hadn't yet performed as a full-blown story. It was another true anecdote, going back only four or five years or so, about a snake-handler. "Snake handling is illegal in North Carolina," said David, "but not in Tennessee. So this preacher crossed the line one Sunday with a bunch of rattlesnakes, and got a crowd together. He shook 'em and sang and stuff, and the police came and broke it up, saying they'd arrest him next time they found him with snakes. So the following week he shows up again, shaking his snakes, and the police arrive. One cop got so mad he grabbed the snakes out of the guy's hand, and they bit him. He dropped the snakes in the crowd and everybody screamed and shouted, running every which way — the cop almost died, but in the end he lived — and they arrested the guy, fined him, and let him go. Well, the next week he came back again without the snakes, drank strychnine in front of everybody, and died. Now how do you tell that one?"

How indeed. It occurred to me that most of David's mountain stories had a hard kernel of pain inside them, but only if you listened from a certain angle. The bear sold to the circus, the preacher and his followers, some of the parents from around Dana, North Carolina — probably the younger, more sentimental ones — didn't fare so well in these tales. But it takes a cosseted modern mind like mine, freed from subsistence living by education and economics, to indulge in maudlin scenarios. The great promise these stories hold, the reason they were remembered and valued and passed on to David, is the pledge they make on behalf of the extraordinary: for good or even ill, the mundane, workaday life of the mountains, a hard life full of sacrifice and tough labor, can sometimes be overthrown by humor or invention or miracles and become memorable. It's crucial that the people who told David these anecdotes stressed that they were all *true*. These tales are simply testimony that *things happen,* that jokes of enormous proportion can be pulled off, that preachers don't always know best, and this delight in the prospect of everyday dullness suspended overcomes the tiny, acute angle of grief that broods inside them. For centuries stories like these have offered hope to dreamers who haven't had time to dream.

On two recent occasions my father and I had been walking my dog in my parents' neighborhood in New Jersey when we came to a thin, rocky river in a shallow ravine. My father told me how he'd gone for a walk late one winter evening on a very cold, clear night, and had come to the river. It was completely iced-over, smooth and solid gray. So he walked right down the middle of that lane of frozen water for miles, winding through the heart of suburban housing developments, completely hidden by the wooded riverbanks from all but Orion and his fellow winter constellations. I thought this was a distant boyhood memory he'd dredged up from the 1930s, but no, he said, he had done it fairly recently, when I'd been in college. I was enchanted by the idea of my father gliding along on a frozen river. It was so uncommon, it was unearthly, beautiful, wild.

The next time we came to the river I mentioned his story. "That was when I found the raccoon," my father said. I thought he was going to add to the enchantment, but he told me that it was dead; it had been someone's pet, and was still wearing a little red collar and leash. The leash had gotten tangled in a bush and the raccoon had been unable to free itself, and had starved to death there.

I was devastated by his coda. I am not a mountain woman; I'm of the suburbs, where there is money and time enough to lavish love on the animals we turn into pets. The story changed for me then, and turned into a metaphor about the dark side of domestication, the dangers of leashing creatures and rivers and men. Now I only tell it in a rogue mood, half-predatory, half-melancholy. But here in the hills, where people eat raccoon (in fact I was given a recipe later in the summer), my father's story would be remembered for its magic: The Man who Glided down the River. The raccoon might play a clownish, walk-on role, like the bear in the Hogaphone tale, but nothing more. I was surprised to hear Akbar's words, clogged with Atlanta heat, coming back to me in the thin mountain air: audience and context are everything. Not only in the way a story is heard, but, I understood now, in how it is created as well.

The late afternoon had grown itself a blue chill, so we moved inside. David showed me his instrument collection — "I'm instrument poor," he had joked, and I'd believed him — which ran the gamut from handmade banjos to glamorous steel guitars. The latter looked like Art Deco toasters from the thirties, but were far sexier. David pulled out a mountain bow — "the oldest stringed instrument in the world," he said — which is played with the mouth and resembles either the bow of a bow-and-arrow set or the Brazilian instrument called a berimbau. I wasn't sure which.

We settled in his living room, where another collection, an extensive grouping of African masks, was suspended on the wall behind me. I wondered how much this man paid in insurance.

"Speaking of snakes," said David, smiling like a little boy with something slimy in his pocket, squeaking back and forth in his stylish sandals, "I've got a real story for you now."

ROSS AND ANNA

This is a true story, they say. People say that it happened up around Burnsville, North Carolina. I don't have the names of the real people, but I'm going to call them Ross and Anna. Now Ross and Anna — this happened about a hundred years ago — Ross and Anna were married. And in those days young people got married when they were about fifteen or sixteen. And Ross's father gave them about sixty acres of mountain land. Now it's very steep up there in Nancy County, North Carolina. The only flat place Ross could find on the land was a big granite outcropping of rock that stuck out over the valley. It was just a big flat granite rock, and he decided he would build his home right on the center of that rock, because it was the only flat place there. Now, right in the center of that rock was a hole that went straight down. It was about the size of your fist, and went as far down as he could see. So it seemed like a perfect place to build a cabin. They'd build the cabin right over that hole, so if there was any rain, or water, it would just drain down through the center of the cabin.

Everybody in the community got together for the wedding of Ross and Anna, and after the wedding they had a pounding. Now a pounding is an old mountain custom where you give them a pound of whatever they need to get started: a pound of flour, a pound of wheat, a pound of lard, a pound of coffee. And they took it up to their new-made cabin. And they put it above the fire on the mantle. It was kind of a cold, early spring night, and Ross built up a huge roaring fire in that fireplace. And he could see it was going to be beautiful to have the bottom of the fireplace be the same granite rock that was the floor of the cabin, because the whole rock began to heat up. And they went to bed, and it didn't even begin to get cold in that cabin until about four in the morning. That was when Ross got up out of bed. He leapt out of bed onto the floor, and when he did the entire cabin was filled with a loud rattling sound. He hollered out to his wife, "Don't get up!" and he fell to the ground.

Well, the next morning some of Ross and Anna's friends came to see how they were doing. And they knocked on the cabin door, and nobody came to the door. And so they knocked again. It was only a one-room cabin; somebody had to be in there because it was locked from the inside. They knocked harder, and they could hear this rattling sound on the inside. They hollered out "Ross! Anna!" They put their ears up to the door and they could hear somebody crying. And then they realized that the only way to open the locked door was to smash it open. So they got a log that was left over from the building and they reared back and hit the door. And it flew open.

The sight that met their eyes was unbelievable. There was Ross in the center of the floor, stone-cold dead, with rattlesnakes writhing all over his body. They could see what had happened. They saw that the fire had heated up that rock, and that those snakes had been hibernating down inside the center of the rock, and had come up through that hole. There were still snakes coming out of the hole and crawling all around the cabin. There was no way they could walk across the floor and get Anna, who was still on the bed with her head in her hands, crying. So they walked around the cabin and they climbed up the side, and they ripped off some of the shingles, and they lowered a man down in the cabin with a rope around him. He grabbed onto Anna and pulled her up through the roof and down the side.

The only way they could get Ross's body out was to stand at the door and take a lasso and just throw it until at last they got it onto his foot, and pulled his body out. Well, they had a big meeting of everybody in the community, thinking about what should be done. And after the burying of Ross they decided the proper thing to do would be to wait a week or so, and then go back up there and tear down that cabin. Then they would build it again for Anna down in the valley below, for it was a new cabin and she would need a place to live. And so they waited a week and went back up there. But there were still snakes coming out of the hole. They waited two weeks and they went back up there, and now there were snakes on the bed, all inside the cabin . . . the snakes hadn't moved at all. They waited three weeks, and this time when they went up to the cabin it was completely surrounded by snakes, they couldn't even get close to it. Well, it disturbed the people of that community so deeply they decided something had to be done. And so they lit that cabin on fire and they burned it to the ground. And that ended the true story of Ross and Anna and their House of Snakes.

As David talked I was right there with him, high up in the mountains on Ross and Anna's granite ledge; but a couple of times my eyes wandered to his mantlepiece. The light was fading and I'm nearsighted, so I couldn't quite make out what I was seeing. After I finished clapping I asked him.

"David, are those what I think they are?"

He blushed a little. "Yeah, they're Grammy Awards. I've got two of them. They're for the category 'The Spoken Word.'"

Like me, David Holt is a seeker. He may not be from "The North," but he is as much a product of generic America as I am (and it is "Generic America" or "Corporate America" or the U.S. Government or "Management" — they all mean more or less the same thing, having supplanted "The North" as the great infiltrator, or oppositional pole — that the "exceptionalists" of the South rail against: more on this later). In David I recognized a fellow pilgrim, someone seeking to feel anchored to a tradition, the way Orville and Vickie are anchored, rather than to the mere shifting pleasures of scuba diving or photography or creating collections of things. And David has anchored his sensibilities in the Blue Ridge Mountains. The stories he creates don't break faith with the impulses that created them. They celebrate the exceptional, the weird, the exciting; they carry no traces of suburban sentimentality.

Yet he knows his limitations as well. Like so much in the South, it comes down to voice. When we had discussed the open-ended thrill of storytelling, David added a qualification: the Jack Tales. Like folk music, they could be broken by the wrong sound. "Ray is Jack," David had said. "I can't separate Jack from Ray. I can't imagine my voice telling those stories. Orville's, yes, mine, no. At least not right now. I see it as a challenge: how to find the voice for Jack. You know, can a guy who grew up in Texas and went to school in California tell a Jack tale and make it work for me? Come back in a few years and see if I've found a way."

After I left David's, a wrong turn onto Interstate 40 sent me into a purgatory of beauty. Instead of heading south toward Atlanta, I wound up barreling west into the heart of the Great Smokey Mountains. Mile after mile went by without an exit, or even the promise of one. As afternoon gave way to evening, each component of the view through my windshield grew too dramatic to bear: the hills rose to staggering heights, then abruptly fell, then rose again. The trees turned back their leaves in submissive acceptance to the growing wind. The distant mountains went purple, then ultramarine blue after the sun set behind them. The sky paled, then like a broken yoke, yellowed, then reddened. Nothing around me was tame, nothing stayed still; it was a beauty out of control, excessive, beyond what I'd ever ask for. The trucks drove too fast, and I couldn't get off the road.

I went almost an hour out of my way, and when I finally righted myself and found a Days Inn, it was full. I felt betrayed by the great American promise of lodging for all. Thankfully, the manager put me onto an independent motel just up the road. "Run by Indians," he said, "they're taking over the motel business, and more power to 'em. Do a good job."

An overwhelming smell of simmering potato and cauliflower curry filled the office of the Sapphire Inn. The Indian proprietors glanced at my fast-food dinner, a sandwich from Blimpie's, and gave me a look usually reserved for underprivileged pets. Once in my room, I immediately put on the basketball game (the Knicks, my team, were losing in the playoffs) and checked my e-mail, to see if Vickie had responded. She had.

Pam — Hello!

I was happy to hear from you . . . As soon as I finish editing the stories about the Dead Man, Sister Collins and the Bald-headed Bohannon Boys, I will send you a tape. Along with it,

I'll send the Bedbug, which is really about Granny and a rattlesnake gittin' reeleejun . . .

After I saw you, it dawned on me that I skipped a part about eccentricity, particularly Granny Griffin's, that would better fill in your imagination with specifics rather than the general overview that I gave.

I think Granny may have started off her life with a few physical attributes and personality traits that probably got her on the path that eventually led to becoming eccentric. It took years, though, for her to fully develop into the gnarled old lady that I came to adore. Granny was tall, about 5'7" or 8". She had big feet; her shoe size was what she called a number Nine — she actually said, "These number nines down here at the end of my leg." She married Daddy Runt who was about 5'1". So all through this marriage Granny's impression of herself was that she was big. Her mother was high-tempered, and Granny inherited that, as well as a very, very stubborn nature. That, in my opinion, is the real root of her road to eccentric behavior . . . She was a self-made oddity among her own clan, as well as the rural area where she lived out her time . . . So, yes, she was unusual among the unusual (the whole family was full of peculiarities — and that would take time to explain because there were so many, and each of the many had deeply imbedded roots in ignorance and some deliberate deviance, unaccountable fears of outsiders, superstitions, and self reliance). In other words, these people aren't easy to describe, especially when trying to explain their beliefs and actions to an overly-educated and politically correct culture. The more I think about Granny and Daddy Runt and their kin before them, the more I come to realize how much Southern culture has changed — and most of the changes were GOOD ones . . .

Telling stories was a pastime for everybody when I was

growing up, and over the years as the stories were told, they were embellished and humorized. We laughed at the old folks and their unnerving ways. But I'm afraid that, if we backed up to those days, we would come to find that they were harsh and coarse. Which is why my parents and grandparents developed a psychological shell that sort of bounced the wounds off with laughter. And which also accounts for why painful comedy is still funny today . . . That's how I interpret Mama and Daddy when they're talking about somebody getting a "whuppin" with a hickory stick, and how the mule almost killed Hansel but how hilarious it was to see him sliding up through the corn rows with the mule in charge — considering how Hansel loved to try to boss everything and everybody. My daddy would say: "That learned 'im. That shore did show Ol'Hansel a thang or two about who he really is, and WHO that mule was, for that matter!" And he'd laugh. Daddy always let you ask the realistic question about stories like that, and so did Granny Griffin. "Did you help him get loose from the mule?" Daddy would say: "I had to. That mule would'a killed ye Uncle Hansel. Hansel was a fool, gal. It took all we could do to keep that young'un alive; it's a wonder he ain't done killed hisself five times over. Some folks don't know what they doing. Remember that!"

. . . Bye for now. Vickie Vedder

I sat on the bed vaguely watching big men jump on the television screen, feeling a little of that same rush of overabundance in my head that had twisted my viscera on the ravishing highway. Vickie's message was like her conversation: exhilarating and wonderful and a little scary in the relentlessness of her perception. I wrote back and asked why she wears a costume when she tells stories. I figured that was limited enough to avoid sparking an overflow of eloquence. Then I did something I almost never do in motels: I opened the drawer of the night-stand and took out the Bible.

A phone call to my friend Marguerite's father, Randy, a Presbyterian minister, sent me straight to the Book of Mark. The last chapter ends on a rising heartbeat: Mary, the mother of James, Mary Magdalene, and Salome race to tell the apostles that Jesus has risen from the tomb. But, said Randy, some people must have been unhappy with the abruptness of Jesus' return, so a longer ending was added around the second century A.D.

Sure enough, following the last verse of Mark in my Bible, in small print, was a note that some versions add eleven more verses, which were quoted at the bottom of the page. In them Jesus upbraids the apostles for not believing in his resurrection. In no uncertain terms he orders them to get a move on, to go out and preach the gospel throughout creation. Those who believe, he says, will be saved. "And these signs will accompany those who believe: in my name they will cast out demons; they will speak in new tongues; they will pick up serpents, and if they drink any deadly thing, it will not hurt them . . ."

No, but believing in stories will. I wondered if it had been arrogance or gullibility that killed the snake handler. Not for the first time, I felt that in stories I had chosen powerful but dangerous guides to the American South — and, I suppose, to myself and my silent inner voice: curative, intoxicating, entertaining, necessary, and, occasionally, deadly.

Second Journey

C.D. WRIGHT, "Deepstep Come Shining"

First the light sinks to shadows. The shadows become
Flooded with broad washes of dark. Watch. As the
dark comes
Entirely into its own. Watch. The light being eaten.
Devoured . . . The light murdered that the truth
become apparent.

Veronica's Tale

Excuse me, but do you follow the news?"

"Yes," I said warily, unable to imagine what was coming next.

"Then look, there, that short black man who's going through the gate. That's Desmond Tutu."

It was Desmond Tutu. On my plane to Atlanta. The woman who had alerted me to my good fortune of flying out of Boston with the Archbishop was called Dixie Lemons. I wondered if she could ever be unhappy with a name like that. Even occasional low spirits would seem ungrateful. Dixie said she was going to Blowing Rock, North Carolina — I told her to have a cheeseburger in paradise for me — but that she also had friends on the South Carolina coast, where I was headed. She wrote down their names and telephone number, and made me promise to call them.

This bit of good fortune cheered me on my way back *down there.* I had been home for ten days, during which time New England had broiled under the biggest, hottest sun ever to wander into the northern latitudes. And the South would be hotter still. But meeting Dixie was a good omen. "Dixie Lemons, Dixie Lemons, Dixie Lemons," I chanted to myself, putting my faith, like a medieval pilgrim, in fortuitous names and happenstance.

After we were airborne, I opened an envelope from Akbar that had arrived just as I was leaving home. It was a story he had promised to transcribe for me about his Uncle Line, known to the grown-ups in Akbar's childhood as Catman. Both names, including his Christian one, were chiseled on Catman's tombstone in central Georgia. The story was called "A Polar Bear's Bar-Be-Cue"; this is how it began:

A POLAR BEAR'S BAR-BE-CUE

Just when I thought I'd seen and heard everything, my cousin told me about the day a polar bear came to Uncle Catman's bar-be-cue. Uncle Catman was famous for his finger-licking, lip-smacking, melt-in-your-mouth bar-be-cue. Some people from New York wanted to buy his recipe but he wouldn't sell it. He said it was secret; he learned it from his father, who had learned it from his father, who had learned it from his father, who learned it from an ancient African in Middle Georgia. But that's another story for another day. This is a story about a polar bear who came to Uncle Catman's bar-be-cue and made it totally un-forgettable.

Uncle Catman had let the meat soak in his special sauce all night. He got up and started a fire in a pit he made himself. He was about to put on the first batch of meat, when he looked up and saw a thousand-pound polar bear staring at him. He stepped back and started to run, but knew that with animals, you are not supposed to show fear. So instead of running, he said, "How you doing, Mr. Polar Bear?" and reached out to shake his paw.

The polar bear said, "I'm fine. This Georgia heat is a little warm, but I'm okay."

"You have a seat and I'll be right back."

Uncle Catman went to get some ice-cold lemonade for his new friend. The polar bear drank the lemonade and said, "Thanks, that was good. Can I help you with the bar-be-cue?"

And so it progresses. Catman gets the polar bear an apron and they start cooking. Naturally, the guests are scared out of their wits; Aunt Louise wants to call animal control. But Catman vouches for his new friend, and soon everyone's playing music and cards, and Catman and the other men are swapping stories with the bear. He tells them about how cold it gets in Alaska, "where your breath turns into ice crystals before your eyes." The men tell him Georgia heat stories; about days "when it was so hot the shade was afraid to come out"; or the time they put vegetables in an ice cooler in the back of a pickup, and wound up with vegetable soup. As the stories get wilder and louder, an announcement comes over the radio that a dangerous polar bear has escaped from the zoo. Sounds of sirens and helicopters are heard. Uncle Catman, thinking fast, hides the bear in his garage.

Uncle Catman asked the polar bear what did he want to do?

The polar bear said, "I want to go home. I miss the snow and my friends and family. Can you help me get home?"

Everyone knew that the ice plains and snow mountains of Alaska were a long way from the cornfields of Middle Georgia, but what could they do? Surely they weren't going to send him back to the zoo.

That night Catman summons his cousin, Willie C., a long-distance trucker, over to his house. Willie C. is about to make a run to Seattle, Washington. Catman explains that the polar bear escaped from the zoo and helped him that afternoon with the bar-be-cue, and that they have to save him. After a bit of convincing, Willie C. agrees to give the bear a lift. The story ends with the polar bear "real happy," but Willie C. even happier: he finally has someone to help him with the driving.

As I read — or rather, eyed words that Akbar's voice was speaking in my head — the plane thrashed around in the unsettled air like a bucking bull. The pilot came on and told us there were heat thunderstorms below, and made the flight attendants sit down. "Dixie Lemons, Dixie Lemons, Dixie Lemons," I repeated like a mantra, trying to concentrate on Akbar. I hate to fly.

For the past few days I had been irritated with myself for overthinking my experience in the Wren's Nest: my hyper-awareness of the racial strata overlying Akbar's performance seemed so artificial — so *Northern,* I'd thought. Stories can effectively overcome their origins and be made fresh for a fresh audience. No one else, least of all the delighted children nor, seemingly, Akbar, had given a hoot about the racial overtones. But now, here was this gem of his own creation, a reverse Underground Railroad story. Instead of good white folk hiding runaway slaves in their basements and attics, covertly chauffeuring them to the next safe house, and so on, until they reached freedom, here were good black folk helping the whitest, most northerly creature of all, a polar bear from the snow mountains, escape to Alaska. I smiled at my memory: Akbar and I must have been equally alive to the shudderings of history — I imagined a flock of ironies like hummingbirds, furiously beating invisible wings — that day at the Wren's Nest. Even as the plane lurched, I applauded him. He had achieved what the Wife of Bath and Carol P. Christ had advocated: seize the narrative. Become the hero yourself.

Dipak Patel welcomed me to the Super 8 Motel in Decatur, Georgia, wearing a shiny maroon tie embossed with the Super 8 insignia. He pointed to a sign on the desk that read, Life is Great at Super 8! "It's true!" he said. His English was superb, though his wife, fussing behind the desk with a baby ingeniously wrapped into her sari, barely spoke a word. A modem screeched hoarsely in a back room. He's Indian, I thought, he has Caucasian features and dark coloring. That's why Indians have come to the South! They represent the races meeting in the middle . . .

"Stop it!" I warned myself, furiously chewing the inside of my cheek to replace inane thought with pain. "Stop thinking tripe. Stop it!" To avoid interpreting myself off the deep end, I wrote down everything I could about Room 100, my room for the night:

Supposed to be nonsmoking, but last month's cigarette smoke lurks beneath aggressive air freshener; latter smells like aftershave, is remorselessly sprayed into room every ten minutes from electrical wall-mounted pump. Standard features include: waxy wall-to-wall carpeting, damp to bare feet like most motel carpets in the South — probably from having been laid over concrete, now sweating in humidity. Old-fashioned desk phone; bucking toilet uncertainly riveted to floor; plastic cups sealed in plastic wrap; blankets pocked with old cigarette burns (proof!); wafers of soap embossed with Super 8 logo — smell like my Hungarian grandmother; big expensive TV with remote; dark furniture; floral bedspread; generic framed prints fixed to walls at all four corners; ancient heating/AC unit underneath inoperable windows; thin white towels; gleaming fiberglass shower; "maid's ribbon" over toilet seat.

I pulled out road maps and studied the triangular route I'd proposed for my second journey. I would head eastward from Atlanta through South Carolina to the coast, down the seaboard past Charleston to the Georgia sea islands, then back to Atlanta where I had to interview jailed asylum seekers for an article I was writing about the Immigration and Naturalization

Service. Tonight I had an appointment at a recording studio, but first I was going to see Stone Mountain.

As its name suggests, Stone Mountain is a great, bald brute of a stone hill. It rises above the treetops of suburban Atlanta like a breaching granite whale, so immense it has a circumference of five miles at its base. Its appeal, besides just unaccountably being there, is that in 1924 sculptor Gutzon Borglum, apparently wanting something to practice on before he hacked the presidents out of Mount Rushmore, began a 90 foot by 190 foot relief carving of Confederate heroes Jefferson Davis, Robert E. Lee, and Stonewall Jackson on the mountain's flank. Stone Confederates seemed more of a genuine marvel than even Cyclorama, so I turned off the highway — Stone Mountain has its very own exit — paid my five dollar entrance fee, and approached the hulk.

Despite my anticipating incinerating heat, it had become a damp, chilly evening. No one was around. I assumed it was a dinner-hour lull before the big sound and lights show began, which promised a recording of Elvis singing "Dixie." I walked as close to the base of the great mound as I could; it was so big I had to tilt my head back forty-five degrees to squeeze the top into my frame of vision. The granite itself was surprisingly smooth, a slightly darker maroon than Dipak Patel's tie and striated with vertical green bands. On the side, not unlike an insignia on brand-name jeans, was indeed the world's largest relief carving. A guidebook informed me that Lee is as tall as a nine-story building, but the image seemed puny compared to the mountain itself. Perhaps victimized by the too-lavish attention of the chisel, the three rebel horseman sat stiff and stilted, but their horses' half-finished bodies flowed into the hewn granite like waves.

A large grassy knoll knelt below the mountain, outfitted

with giant loudspeakers. In the center sat a middle-aged African-American couple in folding chairs, eating a picnic dinner. They were three hours early for the sound and light show that promised to heap gaudy shades of praise on men who had fought to preserve the institution of slavery, but, curiously, they seemed determined to get good seats. I bowed out of their view and studied my brochure: I could visit an "authentic" antebellum plantation, an antique car museum, a petting zoo, a fake general store, or ride on a scenic railroad or the riverboat *Scarlett O'Hara*. There were also "Southern replica" antiques to buy, or dinner at The Depot Chicken Restaurant, which looked enough like McDonald's to put people at ease. Instead, like the German couple in line before me, I opted for a corndog — a hotdog on a stick, coated in fried cornbread batter — and counted all the shiny black trashcans I could see without moving my head (sixteen).

Two weeks earlier David Holt had told me about the Civil War's effect on the banjo — how an African instrument had been disseminated throughout the South by the great coming-together of soldiers, eventually to become associated with white, Scotch-Irish mountain musicians. A similar scattering was currently underway on the Internet. Web sites like The Moonlit Road were casting Southern stories upon the ether, to change or mutate depending on what their listeners heard.

The Moonlit Road was the brainchild of Craig Dominey, a young man from Atlanta who loved Southern stories, especially spooky ones, and wanted to share them with the world. He wrote on his Web page that visitors were welcome to enjoy these "ghost stories and folktales from the dark backroads of the American South, told by the region's best storytellers. By selecting a story, you embark on a journey to a storyteller's home in the land where the story was born." Internet visitors could select to hear the tale if their computers were equipped to download sound, or read textual versions complete with historical background notes.

I loved the creaking gate that opened to invite viewers to the site — it led onto a dark road overshone by a full moon — and called Craig to compliment him. He invited me to a Moonlit Road recording session. A teller named Veronica Byrd was going to tape her version of a story called "Taily Po" in a garage in Decatur: why didn't I come along? I agreed on the spot, and Craig directed me to the house of his audio engineer, Henry Howard: just off Interstate 20, past Wal-Mart and the Stone Mountain Festival Mall, right at a little sandbox of a cemetery (most of the graves decorated with plastic geraniums), and into the modern housing development down the street.

Henry Howard lived in a large white house half-heartedly glamorized by a pair of rectangular columns at the front entrance. As per instructions, I knocked at the side door, and Craig ushered me into the tidy studio that had once been Henry's garage. Henry, a quiet man with pens clipped to his shirt pocket, like Dan Hicky, was deservedly proud of his sound-effects library. He had hundreds upon hundreds of CDs that reproduced any sound imaginable.

"Listen," he said, grabbing one, "that's a sliding glass patio door." I nodded in agreement. He took it out and put in another. "What's that?" he asked.

"Um, a car drag racing?"

"Car tires on gravel," he corrected, adding "Ah, but consider this: what *kind* of car, what model, what make?" He showed me a catalogue that listed tires-on-gravel sounds for literally hundreds of different cars, broken down into model and year. I imagined armies of technicians systematically taking apart the heard universe sound by sound. Windshield

Wipers; Hand Brake Applied; Door Opening with Person Outside; Door Opening with Person Inside. And this was only the automotive section.

"Show her how many hits we had on the Web site today," said Craig, who was slight with sandy-colored hair and seemed mild-mannered, but for mischievous eyes. Henry's computer monitored the number of Internet users who visit The Moonlit Road each day. On July 12, 1999, the most "hits" had come from the U.S. No big surprise. But the runner-up was the United Arab Emirates, followed by Canada, Singapore, Australia, Malaysia, and the U.K.

"Hi everybody, sorry I'm late!" Veronica Byrd swept into the room like a benign tornado. Cornrowed hair bound on top of her head, tied with a purple scarf; Hawaiian print shirt; large, gold hoop earrings. Veronica's trappings were flamboyant but her beautiful, friendly face added grace and dignity — she had an impressively high forehead and cheekbones — and humor. She saw me taking it all in.

"I like to grab 'em with color!" she laughed, indicating her shirt. "I'm not one of those African-American storytellers who's into dressing in African garb and all that stuff, blah, blah, blah." She rolled her eyes. "Martin Luther King, Jr., gets shoved down the kids' throats in Atlanta. So my African-American heritage stories are about other black explorers and inventors — women, especially — who aren't so well known but equally important, if not more so." She took a wheezy breath, explaining that she had asthma. "I went to *Spelman,* you know, oooh-la-la!" She made this last pronouncement in a fake English accent, rolling her eyes again. Spelman is arguably the most prestigious African-American university in the country. "And I can't win there either. I wore my hair in cornrows at my tenth reunion, and my classmates were *horrified.*"

Coming to storytelling through acting, Veronica and her husband call themselves storyperformers, and do most of their work in the Georgia school system. "You have to be really careful what you say in the schools . . . ," she said, trailing off into an echo of Nancy Basket's sentiments.

"That's why she comes here," said Craig, "to do *demons.*"

"Yeah, for Craig I do the scary-bloody-gory things that make you jump. Remember, Craig, when you broke up with your girlfriend?" Turning to me she continued, "I was recording a story called 'The Boo Hag.' He'd say, 'C'mon, make it gorier. Make her *suffer.*' Remember?" asked Veronica, giggling and digging Craig in the ribs.

Craig looked embarrassed. "I guess the stories kind of record my personal life. At the core they're all probably deadly serious anyway."

"Let's get this show on the road," said Henry, looking at his watch.

Veronica took her place in the sound booth. Henry sat down at a controlboard and asked Veronica to speak. When she did, horizontal bands of green lights jumped under his fingers. Craig was busy turning a row of stuffed animals around to face Veronica's glass booth. "Every storyteller needs an audience," he explained.

"This is an old African-American folktale, Pamela." Veronica's voice was magically clarified and magnified, made holy, almost, through Henry's equipment. It sounded as if I were being addressed by a goddess. "It's about a man who chops off this creature's tail and eats it, then the creature wants it back."

"I know this story!" I said excitedly. "The creature comes into his cabin and asks, 'Can I have my tail back?'"

An explosion of digital-quality laughter shook the room; Henry's soundboard shone like a radar panel.

"Ooooh, please sir, might I please sir, have my tail back, sir? I won't trouble you again for my tail. Please?" Veronica roared asthmatically, helpless with laughter, between English-accented takes on my pitiful attempt to impersonate the creature. "Jeez, girl, no one's giving their tail back after some polite little wimpy white-girl question like that. GIVE ME MA TAIL!" she bellowed so loudly she fell into a prolonged sneezing fit.

"Are you getting this?" Craig asked Henry. "The sound effects are great. That was a really ripe one."

While we were waiting for her to recover, Henry swiveled around and said, "You asked about my favorite sound effect." He'd evidently been thinking about this. "The BBC does the best stuff, like 'Nails Pounded Through Flesh.' That might be my favorite."

Veronica very audibly snorted, sniffed, laughed, and cleared her throat. Then she began:

TAILY PO

The trials and tribulations of living in today's modern society can tend to wear on your nerves. One can grow very weary of dealing with paying bills, taxes, insurance, morning and evening traffic — and the pollution! Not to mention anything about keeping food in the refrigerator. Oftentimes the whole thing can make you want to holler! Throw up both yer hands! And that's exactly what old Bill Smith did.

He gave up the luxuries and, if you ask me, some of the necessities, of modern life. He loaded up just the barest of essentials and his three hunting dogs into his truck. And he moved way up into the north Georgia mountains . . .

Veronica's words stirred a stereo effect in my memory. They were replaying words already there, almost matching up but not quite, like a mental double exposure. I knew what was coming: Smitty, as the townfolks knew him, would become the isolated old codger in the mountain cabin, hunting to feed himself and his dogs . . .

Once, a long time ago, down in the big woods of Tennessee, there lived an old man in a log cabin all by himself. Now that cabin was just one room, and at one end was a big old stone fireplace. And every evening, the old man would come in and cook whatever he caught on that big old open fire . . .

This was the opening to David Holt's story "Taily Bone," which I had listened to just days earlier on one of his cassette tapes. It gave me goose bumps. David's version had also touched off another echo in my memory, which I pursued to the Internet. Months earlier, I had read "Tail Een Po" on Chuck Larkin's Web site (Chuck was the Georgia teller who had introduced me to Colonel Rod). He said he'd first heard the story as a child, then again in the 1970s, before it was disseminated in print, in the Cookville area of Tennessee. A folklorist had told him that *taileenpo* is Irish Gaelic for "the tip of my dear tail," and that the story has ancient roots in Ireland. Chuck's version is set in his own Depression-era childhood in the tidelands of Maryland. Instead of the old man, the hero is a boy named Aggie (short for Augustine) who rode the schoolbus with Chuck.

Aggie lived in a log cabin. When people built a log cabin they started with one room about sixteen feet by sixteen feet. After they started living in the one room they would later build on additional rooms. Aggie's mom and dad slept on a homemade mattress back against the wall. Above their heads was a platform halfway up the wall just big enough for Aggie's mattress, with two poles holding the platform and a ladder to climb up and down. To the left of the bed

*was a fireplace and to the right was one window. Across from the beds was the
front door.*

Veronica's voice reverberated through Henry's garage:

"Now Smitty built himself a nice little cabin way back in the woods.
It wasn't very big, but it was just enough for him. The cabin only had
two rooms. One he used for a bedroom, and the other for every other
room: living room, dining room, den, and even kitchen. He built
himself a nice big fireplace, where he could cook his food and warm
his body on chilly nights . . ."

*This day Aggie was out in the garden chopping weeds . . . As Aggie was
swinging [his] hoe . . . he suddenly saw a whole head of cabbage disappear
straight down into the ground. That surprised him because there were no
varmints big enough to pull a whole head of cabbage underground. In those
days all your food . . . was grown in the garden, and Aggie knew he had a
problem. When he saw another great big watermelon disappear underground,
he raced over and started swinging that huge hoe at the spot. Whatever was
in the dirt turned and was digging down faster than Aggie could dig.*

". . . during the warm months," continued Veronica, "Smitty had
no problem catch . . . oops. Let me try it again, Henry. Had no
problem catching small game, but the colder months pro . . . Oh
bother! Blather, blather blather!" said Veronica, choking on
her words.

"It's okay, it's a raw tell," said Craig to me. "Henry'll just
splice it together."

Veronica went on, ". . . but the colder months proved a little
more difficult to keep his stomach full. Well, it was on one of those
cold wintry nights that Smitty went to his storage shed to see what he

could find for dinner. All he found was a small piece of fatback meat and a handful of rice . . . He ate the fatback and a little bit of rice, but he gave most of it to his dogs. 'Iknow, Youknow, Comptiko Callico, come on, dogs, and git some of this here dinner!'"

He made one more swing as hard as he could and hit something, and he could hear a squeal going deeper into the ground. When he cleared the dirt away . . . he pulled out a bloody, muddy tip of a tail with no hair, about five inches long, pointed on the end and real thick and meaty where it was cut . . .

Aggie carried the tail in the house. His mom and dad had gone to town. His mom had a big pot of greens cooking in the fireplace. Aggie put the tail into the iron pot to cook . . . His parents had not returned and Aggie had not eaten any meat for about nine days. The only meat the family ate was game they caught in traps, and they had not caught any lately. Aggie fished the tail out of the simmering water . . . and carried it out behind the barn. He ate the whole tail and did not save any for his parents. He buried the bones in the ground.

"The sound of the wind blowing around, and in some places through, the tiny cabin had almost lulled Smitty to sleep. When he heard something. He opened his eyes and saw a shadow on the wall. He eased out of bed and tiptoed into the other room. There, he saw the oddest-looking creature he'd ever seen. It was short and stubby, with pointed ears and short, fat feet with long nails, and it had a long, bushy tail . . . Smitty quietly picked up his axe, crept over to the odd critter, who was devouring an insect of some sort, raised his axe, and came down squarely on the creature's tail. Whack! Smitty turned to catch the varmint, but he was too quick. It hurriedly escaped, er, through the wall? It went right through the wall."

It was late that night when Aggie woke up. Some noise had woke him, his parents, and their three hound dogs. The dogs were growling and barking at the door. Aggie's daddy Orville got up and let the dogs out. They took off after something that had been in the yard. Orville closed the door and placed the locking bar down. Next he put a log on in the fireplace and stirred up the fire. Last he closed and locked the big shutter over the window and went back to bed.

The next time Aggie woke up, the fire in the fireplace had burned out. The inside of the cabin was dark, dark, dark . . . Aggie wondered what woke him up and then way off in the distance he faintly heard what sounded like a voice. Slowly Aggie heard the voice coming a little closer and getting a little louder . . . Then he realized there was something outside in the dark whimpering, "Tail een po, tail een po, where is my tail een po?"

. . . When Aggie tried to get up he found he was unable to move or speak. All he could do was wiggle his fingers and toes and roll his eyes.

The voice came closer and louder, "Tail een po, tail een po, where is my tail een po?" By this time Aggie's mom and dad were awake and they told us later that they could hear this eerie voice moaning, "Tail een po, tail een po, where is my tail een po?" but they could not move or speak! . . . Wham! Something hit the front door. "Tail een po, tail een po, where is my tail een po?" Aggie thought, "I ain't scared. My daddy bolted the door, ain't nothing gone to get in."

"Smitty thought the wind was playing tricks on his ears, but then he heard it again. 'Taily po, taily po, I want my taily po . . .'" Veronica's voice quivered and shook in its highest register when she spoke for the creature. It sounded like the wind wailing up a bad storm. "Smitty jumped out of bed and called his dogs. 'Iknow, Youknow, Comptiko Callico, come in heah and see what's makin' that noise!'"

"Tail een po, tail een po, where is my tail een po?" Then Aggie heard something big slowly dragging itself around the cabin toward the window, now quietly whimpering, "Tail een po, tail een po, where is my tail een po?" . . . Wham, bam bam bam, it hit the window hard several times and still whispered with quiet fury, "Tail een po, tail een po, where is my tail een po?" Now the thing was crawling slowly around the cabin . . . Aggie could hear what sounded like claws sinking into the wood as the creature slowly crawled up

over his head, furiously whispering, "Tail een po, tail een po, where's my tail een po?"

"Well, I ain't scared, my daddy put thick strong overlapped shingles of oak wood on the roof, ain't nothing can get through that roof." . . . Now Aggie could catch a small whiff of some ghastly smell coming through tiny spaces between the logs. "Tail een po, tail een po, where is my tail een po?" . . .

"Oh oh, that sounds like something is sliding and sliming down inside the chimney. It's in the fireplace!"

"Tail een po, tail een po, where's my tail een po?"

"Well, it can't get up here on this platform. It can't climb a ladder. I ain't scared." But then he could hear what sounded like claws on the bottom rungs of the ladder and he could feel the platform shake a little bit as something slowly climbed the ladder. "Tail een po, tail een po, where is my tail een po?" Aggie could feel a presence coming over the mattress at his feet . . . Now it was right over his face. Aggie held his breath, the stench was horrible. Then two little red beady eyes opened up right above his face and quietly whispered, "Tail een po, tail een po," then screamed, "HAVE YOU GOT MY TAIL EEN PO?"

"Smitty ran to his bed and jumped in. The scratching and the voice grew louder and louder, and Smitty yelled louder, 'I ain't got no taily po! Why don't you leave me alone and go on about your business. I ain't never hurt nobody or nothin', just leave me alone!' The scratching seemed to be inside the house now. The voice was so loud it was deafening. 'TAILY PO, TAILY PO, YOU'VE GOT MY TAILY PO. AND NOW I'M BACK TO GET IT. GIVE IT TO ME NOW!'

The next morning all Aggie's parents found were his fingers and toes. After the thing ate the rest of Aggie, it went over and unlocked the cabin door and left. A week later the three hounds were found several miles away in the next county and brought home. A few months later some hunters found a pile of bones that some say were Aggie's bones, out in the swamp. AND THAT'S A TRUE STORY.

Craig and Veronica wanted to retape parts of the story to make it sound fiercer. That was fine with me: I sat in Henry's studio, my feet tangled in a nest of interlaced wires, and tried to sort out the rich, schizophrenic harmony of "Taily Po." I was dazzled and exhausted by its elasticity: that the same premise could be stretched in endless directions, not so much by altered details, but by *voice* alone, had resounding implications. Storytellers working with the same material literally use their voices to sow different realities in the mind's eye of their hearers. I hadn't realized until Veronica's performance how vision-saturated voices really are. Images of race, gender, social status, even geography float along on the spoken word, invisible to the eye but unavoidable to the mind. Veronica's voice conjured up an old black man, a loner who chose to retreat to the hills, decent but gruff, touched by the supernatural that turns up in so many African-American tales (Smitty's creature walks through walls; Aggie's has to come down the chimney). Chuck Larkin's voice summoned a different picture, a more moralistic one: a no-nonsense, poor white family — I painted them white because Chuck has a white voice — living on the edge of a swamp, and a son who pays the price for not sharing his food. The creature that eats Smitty warns us against the otherworldly foes of the night; the one that wolfs down Aggie, also responsible for first devastating the garden, is more the incarnation of a natural disaster.

Even more amazing than the story's potential for difference, however, is its constancy: "Taily Po" is told throughout the South by groups who have historically defined themselves in reaction to, indeed against, one another. Not only is the story told by these disparate groups — highlanders and lowlanders, blacks and whites — it has become so expressive of their cultures that its origins are claimed by them as well. One says it's an old Irish tale, another that it grew out of the African-American tradition. Whatever its real birthplace, in becoming Southern "Taily

Po" became accessible to all who live in the South; by becoming enamored of it, the sometimes warring factions of Southern society, despite their enduring distinctions, betray that they, too, have become Southern. And that through centuries of living in the rural oven of the American South, fending off varmints and cutting back kudzu, they have come to share enough similarities to express their lives, fears, and fantasies through the same simple tale. One room or two, Smitty's or Aggie's, "Taily Po" will always take place in a cabin. A poor man's house. The owner must always hunt for his dinner. Animals are held close and depended upon. Fear is a constancy. Death is a consequence of poor planning, or poor judgment. Stories like "Taily Po," and there are hundreds of multiversion stories haunting the South, are spoken palimpsests: roadmaps of overlaid identities, all on their way to meeting at a middle ground, all on their way to becoming Southern.

Suzannah Lessard once wrote of a tidal estuary on Long Island, much like the northern beaches that silt up my memory, "The landscape was a map of my spiritual reality. It represented feeling that I could not feel and as art it expressed what I could not express. It was a substitute for an interior to which I had no other means of approach: it was a map of me." Perhaps in a similar way, for a region imaginatively dependent on narrative rather than scenery, stories are the spiritual maps of the South. Into them are poured the elemental experiences dealing with weather and topography, disease, hunger, darkness, light — the ahistorical, very human responses to *place* — that pride and conscious selection tend to overlook in forging the collective self-image of a social, racial, or economic group. In stories there is room enough for everyone.

Considering "Taily Po" — or rather "Tail Een Po" — on its own terms, if the tale truly hails from Ireland, as Chuck Larkin's "Folk Lorest" claimed, it is chilling to realize that a story conceived centuries ago in the rural Irish countryside still fits an existing profile in contemporary America (it is hard to imagine the tale taking root anywhere else in the country but the South). "Taily Po's" popularity is a glimpse not only into the knitted threads of Southern culture, but of how very old the ways of the New World can sometimes be.

"You know, Smitty's my dad," said Veronica, coming out of the recording booth, letting the door soundlessly close behind her. "That's his name: William Smith. He lives in California and loves to hunt and fish. So I borrowed him."

I gave her a tired laugh. I had wrenched my back at home in Rhode Island — starting the lawnmower, of all the unglamorous things — and ached to lie flat. Just as I was leaving, however, the four of us got into a compulsive storytelling jag about pet near-death experiences. I don't know, perhaps it was human revenge on the "Taily Po" creature. We couldn't stop: Veronica led off with a miraculous hamster revival; I told a squashed hamster story; Henry added an account of a fish re-animation. We were all yawning desperately as the others talked, but we couldn't help ourselves. It was like a game of pickup football, but played with stories, mostly for fun, a little competitive. I rounded off the night with the tale of Wilma, the Mean Siamese Fighting Fish, who had once jumped out of her bowl attempting to attack my finger, slid down a burner on our gas stove, and landed in the bowels of the oven. She had been out of water ten minutes when we finally recovered her body, shrouded in bits of ancient charcoal. The coda is that after floating on the surface for a while, she survived to swim another six years, ornery as ever, with a net over her bowl.

Kwame's Tale

I DROVE THROUGH ROLLING FARMLAND to Columbia, the capital of South Carolina, in agony. Every twenty minutes or so, the sensation of being scored by a hot knife from my lower back to my left thigh would become so overwhelming I would have to stop the car and do stretching exercises. These greatly amused passing truckers, who would unfailingly hoot, honk, or whistle. One waved his undershirt out of the window. Adding to my increasingly bad mood was the fact that I was driving on Strom Thurmond Parkway (Thurmond, the notoriously conservative senator from South Carolina, will be one hundred when his term is up in 2002; he has used the filibuster so often, setting a record in 1957 by speaking for over twenty-four hours against civil rights legislation, that the Capitol could have been heated with his hot air alone).

As I rolled into Columbia, a church marquee asked me, Who Was the Last Man to Actually See Jesus? I was too hungry to give this question serious thought, and drove instead along an avenue of towering palm trees — seemingly out of place in the center of the state, far from the subtropical coast — along a strip well-stocked with used car lots and fast-food concessions, straight to Maurice's Gourmet Barbecue. Maurice's (also known as "The Piggy Park") had been recommended to me on account of its unusual barbecue sauce. Instead of the typical sweet-and-tangy, brown, sometimes bourbon-laced sauce that holds sway throughout the South, Maurice had invented a mustard-based sauce that looks exactly like the reflective, neon-yellow paint used on no-parking lines. A label told me it included apple cider vinegar, mustard seeds, water, tomato paste, sugar, soya oil, peppers, salt, powdered onion, molasses, turmeric, paprika, spices and herbs. I ordered the "Little Joe Basket" which came with two hush puppies, french fries, coleslaw, and two ounces of pulled pork with Maurice's barbecue sauce, served on a bun.

In local hangouts like Maurice's, I confess to drawling my vowels and dropping my g's. It is an almost unconscious gut instinct: the urge to blend. Unfortunately, anybody sounding like a South Carolina native would not have had to ask what hush puppies were. The waitress had both suspicion and pity in her eyes — maybe she thought I was an amnesiac — when she answered, "Fried corn batter, girl. Everybody knows that." Later I read that hush puppies were reputedly invented by hunters or fishermen, and are ideally fried in the same fat used to cook fresh fish. The name comes from tossing leftovers to howling hunting dogs, ravenous at the smell of anything frying, to hush them up.

Later, sitting in a booth and tucking into my pulled pork, I wrote on my napkin, "Good taste — sweet yet piquant, complex — enough pork to prevent sauce building up too high a crescendo on tongue." While I reviewed my meal, country and western music throbbed through nearby loudspeakers. All the tunes were curiously upbeat. Country notoriously indulges in the "tears in ma cigarettes and whisky" school of songwriting, but no one misbehaved in these songs; instead, they were about things like "staying up all night to watch my lover breathe." For the first time since my meal arrived, I stopped eating long enough to take in my surroundings. The parking lot was actually a working, 1950s-style drive-in, outfitted with menus and speakers under a chain of individual carports. I had never seen one in person before. Above the carports rose an immense neon sign topped by a pig in a "Little Joe" tee-shirt, who wore a curiously world-weary expression, something like the tragic tough guy in an old movie. On the far side of the drive-in was the Piggie Park Employment Office, draped in an American flag and a banner that read, Christ Is the Answer. A sign in front of the building added, For All Have Sinned and Fallen Short of the Glory of God. I recalled the Jesus Was a Vegetarian notice from Georgia, and assumed there was some self-laceration involved.

There wasn't much to see in Columbia that dated before 1865, the year the city was burned to the ground by Sherman's men on their destructive trek from Atlanta to the sea (Sherman's systematic destruction of the Georgia and South Carolina countryside was probably the first example of "total war" in modern history, and it effectively ended Southern resistance; Nazi strategists reputedly studied the Union Army's methods in developing the blitzkrieg). One of the few complexes Sherman left standing was the University of South Carolina, a genteel-looking compound of bisque-colored buildings draped with bougainvillea, where my next story lay in wait.

Kwame Dawes had been recommended to me by the South Carolina Arts Commission as a storyteller "not to miss." When I called him from Rhode Island, he sounded frantically busy, but agreed to tell me a tale. When I demurred, he said, "No, no. I've resigned myself to a crazy summer. You're just fitting into a picture that's already misdrawn."

I liked his thinking, and agreed to meet him at the Welsh building — another good sign, I thought — on campus, where he teaches in the English Department (I later discovered he is also an award-winning poet, having received Britain's Forward Prize for Poetry in 1994). I found Kwame in a white, utilitarian box of an office, lit by unforgiving fluorescent light. As twilight turned into darkness, the beautiful campus disappeared from his window, at first commingling with, then replaced by images of us, our mirrored selves growing ever more substantial, like two ghosts gaining confidence, in the blackening glass. Kwame's reflection was contradictory, his casual polo shirt at odds with his close-cropped hair and full beard, clipped tight in a way that flattered his square jaw. The effect gave him a benign, Shakespearean dignity: Othello in his thirties, as Associate Professor of English.

"Fundamentally, at heart, I am a storyteller. I tell stories any chance I get, in whatever mode available to me." Kwame targeted his essential self in the rhythmic clip-clop of a Jamaican accent. He had been born in Ghana, moved to England, lived in Jamaica through his schooling years, including university, put in a stint in Iowa, and received his Ph.D. in the cold and unlikely setting of Fredrickton, New Brunswick, in Canada. "Storytelling — not just me telling stories, but exchanging them, learning other people's stories — is a way for me to get inside a culture. How people listen to my stories, too, is as important as the stories I collect from others; the questions they ask are clues to their thoughts, their culture . . . Storytelling, more than anything else, is a dialogue, and through dialogue you can discover what needs to be told. Minorities, especially, need to tell their stories, because if they're not heard, they're not part of the national consciousness. They don't exist."

A phrase from a novel I had been reading — *Night Letters,* by Robert Dessaix — bobbed up, begging consideration. "One of the advantages of being Australian," he wrote, "is that you are a kind of blank to other people . . . and so of little interest to them until they have written on you." So far this summer I'd had scant experience with dialogue. Narrative had flowed only in one direction: I listened, but I rarely told. The storytellers I met were nothing if not likeable, but on the whole they were an incurious lot. Like Dessaix, I was a blank to them, especially coming from Rhode Island (the name had a magical property in that it caused people's mouths to drop open in looks of clueless incomprehension; the phrase "near Boston" snapped them shut again). I wondered what unspoken stories had been written on me, or whether the old, self-protective, isolationist instinct of the South manifested itself in the present as an indifference to lives lived elsewhere. Maybe I had simply been left blank.

I remarked to Kwame that he'd had rather a lot of experience with new cultures. "That's why I have so many stories," he laughed, explaining that in order to tell them all he'd become a playwright, poet, novelist, teacher, author of short fiction, teller of oral tales, and singer in a reggae band. But fundamentally, through all these incarnations, he was, simply, a storyteller.

THE STORY OF THE GIRL AND THE FISH

This is the story of the girl and the fish. Now a lot of people don't know how we got water lilies. You see water lilies all over the place, and you think, How lovely! But the question is, where did these water lilies come from? Well, this is a simple story, and I'll tell you, but you have to pay attention because it's very sad. A very sad story.

Once upon a time there lived a man and his daughter and two sons. The two sons were very, very untruthful. They were terrible. They used to compete to see who could burp the loudest and who could fart the loudest, and that kind of thing. Now the daughter was a wonderful daughter. She was the oldest. Well, it turned out that after a while the father began to think he had to marry off this girl, as you know fathers tend to do. And so he went around the town asking all the men what kind of sons they had, so he could marry off his daughter.

Now she didn't want to get married. She had other things in mind. So as soon as her father started that she became very sad. She'd go down to the river and she'd sing a sad song, and she'd say, "Hello trees, hello water, hello spirits. I'm sad today, I'm sad today." The women who were washing the clothes down by the river would hear this sad song blowing through and they'd start to cry. Because they knew what was going on.

Well, the father tried and tried, and he finally found someone. A fellow who spent money. Knew money very well. Rich boy. The father came over and said, "You're going to marry him." And she said, "No, No! Not him! That is a terrible boy. That boy have no sense. That boy don't know how to talk to people. That boy is a fool." The father says, "You are, and that's the end of that. In four months the wedding should happen."

But it is almost as if all the elements conspired against this marriage. Because as soon as the father said that, it stopped raining. The first month, no rain. And this was the rainy season. The second month the ground was hard, tough, nothing could grow. And you know, the girl felt funny, because on one hand she was thinking, if it goes on like this there's no way there can be a wedding, but on at the same time she could see people suffering . . . The third month, no rain. And father was getting very upset. There was no water in the house . . . The girl was the one who would go to the river and try to dredge up whatever water she could. One day she went to the river and everything was dry, bone dry. Just a little mud. And she started to cry. And she was crying, crying, crying, crying, and all of a sudden she heard somebody say, "Hey, you, what you doing up there?"

And she looked around and she saw nobody. She said, "I must be losing my mind!" So she started crying again. She said, "Now I'm losing my mind too!" And she heard, "Hey, stop that noise up there!" Then she looked, and she said, "Who is that? Who is that?"

Said, "Me, look down here." And when she looked down on the ground in the bed of the river there was a fish. A fish sticking his head out of the mud. And she said, "You're a fish." And he said, "Yes, go to the top of the class." So she said, "But you're talking." And he said, "Oh, you're a really bright one." She said, "But you're a fish, you're not supposed to be talking." He said, "Well you are the idiot because you're talking to me." And she started to cry again.

The fish said, "Oh my goodness, why don't you take your crying and go somewhere else with your crying. You know it's hot out here, and I'm trying to get a little rest, and, and . . ."

She was crying, she wouldn't stop crying. And she said, "You're so mean and you're so wicked and you don't care . . ."

"Okay, okay, what's the problem?"

So she told him the whole story, and the fish felt really bad. A nice fish. That's the beautiful part. A nice fish.

"Give me the bucket."

"My bucket?"

"Yeah, give me the bucket."

So she gave the fish the bucket and Poof! So she waited. No fish, no bucket. And she said, "Oh my goodness, now I've lost my bucket to a fish. How am I going to tell everybody I lost my bucket to a fish?" So she started to cry again, and she heard, "Hey YOU!"

And up came the fish with a bucketful of the coolest, clearest water you ever saw in your life. And she said, "Where did you get it?" He said, "That's for me to know, and you to find out. Take the water." So she said, "Thank you." And he said, "Hey, any time you need water, come down here."

So she took the water home and gave it to her father, and her father said, "Thank you! Nice. Where you got it?" She said, "Oh, down by the river." And her father said, "Okay, good, give me the bucket."

And what the father did was he poured half the water for home use, and poured the other half in a huge vat. Everyday she'd come with three or four buckets of water and the father would pour half for home use, and half in the huge vat. And the vat was getting fuller.

Now you're probably wondering what all this has to do with water lilies.

I nodded my head vigorously.

Time will tell.

So anyway, the vat began to get higher and higher, and ah, the girl and the fish became closer and closer. Ah yes, they'd sit down for hours and talk. Oh, it was beautiful, they were just loving it. Because you know, fish, they actually have some fantastic stories to tell, because they're stories you wouldn't know about, because they're under the ground, in those deep waters. And she would sit, oh it was beautiful. And she would sing, "La, la, la, la, la," and the women who were down by the river would hear this voice and say, "What a beautiful voice, what is going on?" And their hearts would be lifted up, they'd be so happy.

Well, after about four months, the father said to her, "You're getting married next week." And she said, "But Daddy, Daddy, we can't get married! There's no water, no water to bathe . . ."

"No, no, no, no," he laughed. "Look over there in the vat." And she saw all that water that her father had been saving. And the father started to make plans. Well, she was so upset, she ran down to the river and she was crying and bawling, and the fish came up, and the fish said, "What? What?"

"My daddy said I have to get married and I don't want to marry this man and it is you that I really love," and so on. And she kept going on. And she kept going on. And she ran back home. And her father said, "What is the problem?" And she said, "I hate you, I hate you, I don't want to marry anybody," and said the father, "Get out of my house, get out of my house, I'm sick of you, go and get some more water."

Now one of the things you have to remember is all this time, the brothers are hanging around, watching. And they'd been keeping out of it, but when this crisis happened, the brothers started to get very suspicious. They said, "You know, she's too upset about this thing. Because after all, most women in the village get married that way." So they followed her down to the river, and I'm telling you, they saw her with the fish. She went down to the river and said, "Hey fishy fishy fishy fish," and he came up. And she said, "Daddy won't listen!" And the fish said, "Hey, come here." And the fish held her, and the fish kissed her. Well. That was it. The brothers said, "Ooooh, disgusting. A fish and my sister!" They ran back to the father and said, "Oh Daddy, you wouldn't believe what we saw." The father said, "What is it?"

"Oh Daddy, you won't believe what we saw!" The father said, "What is it?"

"You wouldn't BELIEVE what we saw." The father said, "Look, don't play with me." And the boys said, "Daddy, Daddy, Daddy, your daughter is kissing a fish." Well, this just completely destroyed the father. He said, "You must be lying." The sons said, "Come with us." And they went down to the river, and it was true.

And the boys said, "Let's beat him." And the father said, "No, no, let's go back. It's better." So that night, the girl walks in, and the father says, "Where have you been?" And she says, "Down by the river."

"Who were you with?" And she said, "Well, no body, no person." And he says, "Are you lying to me?"

"No, no, no, no, no, I was with no person down there." So the father says, "Go to your bed." Then at midnight the father got his sons and they went down to the river. And one of the sons said, "Here, fishy fishy fishy fish." And the fish said, "Hey, who is that?" The boy said, "It's the girl." And the fish came up. And as soon as the fish poked out his head, Whack! They started to beat that fish. They beat the fish, they stomped on the fish, they mashed up the fish. Finally the father picked up the fish by the tail and dragged it up to the house. It was dawn by then. The fish was barely alive. He called her downstairs, and said, "Look, this is your fish." And she just lost it. She screamed at them, she said, "How could you do that to me? How could you? This is the only creature I've ever loved and cared for! And look what you've done." But the father said, "This is a fish! How can you love a fish? It's just a fish. I brought you up to love a fish?"

And she said, "But, but, but it's a dear fish. I love the fish." And the father said, "You must be mad." And she said, "No, no!" And she grabbed the fish in her hands and she started to go to the door. And the father said, "You stop this minute. Put the fish down, because we're going to eat that fish tonight." And she said "NO!" and she started to walk off with the fish. The brothers came after her, and dragged her, but she kept walking away, and the brothers said, "Oh, she's crazy," and the father started to follow her and said, "Come, come girl, you can't do that." But the girl just kept walking, walking, further and further, till the father started to get worried. He said, "Oh my goodness, she's serious." And he said, "Look, look, I'll get you another fish. I'll get you another fish." And she said, "This is not any fish. This is my dearest friend." It became clear to the father that he was losing his daughter. And he sat down on a tree and started to cry.

And this girl was walking, and she climbed up the hill, she was singing this sad song, so sad, you know, so sad. And women in the village could hear this song from their rooms and they knew something was happening and they started to cry. And they started to sing. And she went up the hill with the fish, over the valleys and across the forests, and came to a high mountain. And just at the bottom of the mountain was a large, wide lake. And the moonlight hit that lake, silver and smooth. And she walked down to the lake with the fish in her hands, and as she stepped into the water, the water began to cover her legs, and the fish began to move slowly. And then the fish began to swim around her. And move in and around her, and soon she started to feel her fingers stretching and opening up. And the more she moved in the water, her fingers were stretching and turning green, and out of this flowers, white flowers, all over the place. The flowers came from all over, from her hair, from her lips, from her mouth, from all over her body, and they began to cover this lake. And the place was covered in water lilies. And the fish danced through the water lilies. And you could hear wafting out of the water this beautiful sound, this sweet sound, "We are happy, We are happy." And the women could hear it in the village. And the father could hear it as he sat there crying. And that's how you got water lilies.

My notebook had fallen to the floor; the tape recorder spun its spools, unattended. I'd even stopped quizzing myself on how to drive back to Motel 6, lest I forgot. Kwame had made the night extraordinary. His story hollowed out a space in the pressing mountain of worries and chores and ideas and plans that surrounded both of us: a hole in which he'd left room for nothing but sheer, simple entertainment. My viscera — I'm not sure which organ, it was a communal feeling — chimed like bells with something very akin to joy. I felt immensely lucky, and understood a little of Vickie's and Orville's remembered delight in their pea-shucking story-telling summer childhood nights.

Kwame said that he likes to tell "The Girl and the Fish," which is essentially a West African folktale, possibly with some Asian elements thrown in, to children, as a lesson in tolerance. "Black children, especially," he said, smiling, knowing I'd be surprised.

"What's their response?" I asked.

"They always want to know how she gave birth to water lilies if they just kissed," said Kwame, laughing.

Alice's Tale

Pam — Hello!

I received your message a few days ago. My typical procrastinating self took its time to get motivated, in the mood, and energetic enough to return you a note . . .

About the clothes: the gray sweater I wear was actually Granny's. She gave it to me years ago, and her precious safety pins are still pinned where she left them. She always carried "extrees" in case sump'n come undone. There are the tiny gold safety pins on the pockets where she "stitched up" the holes . . . The long dress, shimmy (petticoat), and bonnet are how Granny used to dress. She considered herself modernized because she wore shorter dresses in her later years — but she honestly thought it was disgraceful — that's why she kept her thick support hose on all the time. She didn't want her legs to show. One of the other reasons I used the longer dress and bonnet was due to my recollection of Ms. Eva Mixon (I told you about her already) . . . Ms. Eva DID NOT modernize, never. You could see her bent body out there in the cotton field with Ol' Man Mag, that oversized bonnet completely covering her face . . . I suppose any dress she put on after she turned about fifty years old would have touched the floor. She wasn't a large woman in the first place, and hard times and hard work had withered and grizzled her terribly (which was her appeal to me). Mr. Mag and Ms. Eva were absolutely perfect visual aids (aides) for a peek back into the Depression Era . . .

My regret regarding my childhood? That I wasn't a camera buff. So much varied country life could be appreciated now if I had filmed it — pictures are often worth a thousand words. But since we don't have those, my visual representation of life on Harberson-Walker Road in Gordon, Georgia, is the best I can give. Granny's "flavor" is caught and held in that representation. Ms. Eva and Granny were both very, very much typical of ALL country women in Wilkinson and Twiggs Counties, Bibb and Baldwin Counties, too . . . I mention Bibb and Baldwin because they offered a "go to town" spot, and on top of that, there were many rivalries between the small towns and small counties — still are. (Family feuds, you know, fist fights, car races, the haves and the have-nots.) Granny used to say, "Cross that line, and they ain't no tellin' what'll hap'n to ye." She meant the county line between Twiggs and Bibb. She didn't like the Bibb County people, and that basically was based on the fact she didn't like my Daddy's family because . . . his daddy . . . was a no account (according to Granny), who wore [his wife] out and didn't feed what he bred . . .

Granny convinced me over the years that she had a low opinion of procreation and men folks, sorry dogs. "Men's a sorry lot to bear. Jes wait, you'll find out sooner'n ye want to know. Ol' Granny has been put thoo it, chile, by that very thang a'standin' yonda." And she'd point to Daddy Runt and keep eating her ice cream, not batting an eye or worrying that I was only nine or ten years old . . .

One more thing: I don't want Granny to come off sounding like a hard old witch with a bad attitude. I focused on her gnarled ways because they stood out to me as strong. Granny had the courage to tackle the truth about herself and other people as well. Wrong was wrong with her, and she didn't hold back her view of what she saw and sensed. It's not that she opined day and night about other people's faults; it's just that as you lived out your life with her, you came to notice this security within her to see through life into its core motives . . .

I hope you are enjoying your wonderful job — I am jealous and pea-green with envy (borrowed from Scarlett O'Hara) . . .

Sincerely, Vickie Vedder

IF I HAD COME TO THE SOUTH in search of a national Otherworld — and it was becoming clear to me that what I was looking for in America was Europe, and Africa and Asia as well — I had found my spiritual medium in Vickie Vedder. What I really craved, I think, was a place in my own country to replace Wales. There, I had found the horizontal paths of lives-in-progress, the temporal trajectories we all tread from birth to death, made infinitely richer than my own for being crosshatched with depth-sounding vertical shafts, driven deep into the well-remembered past by the touchstones of landscape and folk memory. This kind of crosshatched living — inherently place-oriented — contradicts the very core of the American ethos, so seductive to so many, which promises a sleek, synchronous journey unhindered by baggage of any kind, from clingy national memories to economic shortfalls. The American promise is of a forgettable past, not a well-remembered one. Yet I have always longed to reach down rather than out; when, at ten, I learned my house had been built on a nineteenth-century landfill, I immediately got a shovel and went out to dig. I desperately wanted to live in an Old World rather than a New one.

Similarly, and just as contrarily, crosshatching is what the South is all about, and stories are its vertical shafts, putting many Southerners in daily touch with the dead and done-with (a predilection, it must be said, that simultaneously grounds people morally and socially and cripples them with outdated ideas about everything from women to race). Vickie, with her open line to Granny Griffin, was undoubtedly my medium, my guide to the American Otherworld. She introduced me to her own circle of Southern ghosts, and provided me with clues to understanding those of the others I would encounter as my journey led me deeper and deeper into the American South.

"Georgetown County, South Carolina, is the ghost capital of the South." I copied that off the Moonlit Road Web site at 4:30 in the morning, having been awakened by a car screeching up and down the off-ramp of the highway that led to my motel. It raced up the ramp, jammed on its brakes, then raced down again in reverse, repeating this at least twenty times or so before the police finally arrived (I wondered what make and model had made those particular sounds). Even hermetically sealed in my motel room I could smell the burning rubber.

Much later that morning I tried to decipher my middle-of-the-night e-notes while having breakfast at a nearby I-HOP (International House of Pancakes). I ordered Cream of Wheat pancakes, bacon, and tea.

"Swee' tea, darlin?"

"No, I . . ."

"That's okay, we got a batch without sugah."

"No, no, not iced tea. I'd like hot tea, please."

"Hot tea?" She took a step away from me as if I carried an exotic disease. "Really? Sure?"

When my tea came, it was surrounded by its own little entourage: sugar, honey, pitcher of milk, pitcher of cream, the ubiquitous nondairy creamer, wedges of lemon and lime: every conceivable additive for the betterment of so strange a beverage. I used the milk, and pocketed the limes to suck on later.

I had read that there have been more ghost sightings per square mile in Georgetown County — the tidewater lowlands of the upper South Carolina coast, including a narrow, fifty-five-mile-long slice of land between the Waccamaw River and the Atlantic Ocean, called the Grand Strand — than anywhere else in the South. My only notation at the time had been, "Why?" I hoped the next days would offer some insight.

As I approached the coast, stopping every twenty minutes to unwind the corkscrew of agony into which my vertebrae were still twisted, I felt the farthest from home I had ever been in my own country (the Southwestern desertscape excepted). The kudzu had given way to palm trees and the greens had lightened, lost their temperate, hardy darkness and taken on the chartreuse vulnerability of perpetual new growth. These were the colors of India and Thailand, of the subtropics. Heat weighted the air and brought the sky oppressively low, curdling its clouds into blue-gray thunderheads. The earth was unremittingly flat, bedded with acres of corn and tobacco planted in neat, exuberant rows. One field of very tall green plants with large heads caught my eye; after I'd driven past I glanced in my rearview mirror and gasped at the golden blur of five hundred sunflowers all staring east.

The dwellings on these tidewater flats got not an ounce of respect from the earth. There were no rises or swells, hillsides or valleys to suggest location sites that would make sense in terms of shelter or even picturesque views. Just flatness, which bred a kind of haphazard, helter-skelter quality in the situations of communities and individual homes. The latter managed a little fierce dignity, but towns, especially new ones, looked absurd. Why here and not there? Commercial strips — Shoney's, Waffle House, Dairy Queen, Burger King, Red Lobster — surfaced now and again in a blight of plastic colors, then petered out into bedraggled woods and fields. The poverty was of a level so unexpected, so deep, that it wrenched modernity right out of the air. The radio claimed that this was

America, 1999, but my eyes told me otherwise, sought comparisons in the Depression, and in past centuries. Women and children, mostly black, sat on the sagging porches of unpainted shacks; fieldworkers clustered together under shade trees at the noon hour, the way cows do. A church marquee read, If Jesus Is in Your Heart, Notify Your Head.

Closer to the coast, near the congested resort of Myrtle Beach, developments began to spring up: communities of identical condos with inane geographical names that had nothing whatsoever to do with the topography, like "Cedar Ridge" and "Blackmoor," that elevated comfort and convenience above individuality, and were gated, to keep the locals out. I had recently seen similar, fortress-style resorts in the Dominican Republic. It was telling that the attitudes of corporate developers toward both local populations were identical; the gates said that they were alien, "other," frightening, threatening — and black — not, like the warm winters and white beaches, part of marketed America.

More appealing than the developments were men selling "Today's Shrimp" from the backs of pickups along the roadside, and the signs that I had begun to see advertising psychics. I sped past a neon announcement in a bungalow window that read, Sister Laura — Psychic Readings, then two miles later spun around in a U-turn and came back. But I obviously wasn't psychic myself: Sister Laura was out. More than half of me was relieved.

The act of traveling is essentially the act of creating narrative. When you travel you leave a trail on a map, much like a plot line; and where stories are shot through with metaphor and resonate with subterranean meanings, so travel is laced with memories of home and previous adventures that harmonize with the here and now. Storytelling and travel differ only as dreams differ from waking stories. Bert States, writing in *Dreaming and Storytelling,* said, "Dream is . . . unlike a fiction, structurally and effectively, in that it is a lived experience as well as a narrative; it belongs to both art and reality." Travel, done well, with none of the serendipity weeded out (that makes it tourism) is the art of lived storymaking. Did I really want to look at the last page of my trip in advance? Ironically, I was too superstitious. I could wait for the calendar to end my tale, not Sister Laura, and so continued down Highway 17, which small roadside markers labeled Evacuation Route, to the town of Pawley's Island. (I confess to an ugly encounter with my own prejudice; to my surprise, the Evacuation arrows point south. I had just assumed that in times of storm and flooding the way toward safety would be north . . . .)

In Pawley's Island, on the Grand Strand, two ladies at the Chamber of Commerce gave me directions — "like ladies," they said, "in time, not miles" — to All Saints Waccamaw Episcopal Church. In the middle of the night I had read a story on The Moonlit Road about a young woman named Alice Flagg, who lived on the Grand Strand in the 1840s, when Waccamaw Episcopal was new. She was a member of the plantation class that had grown rich on rice paddies, tended by slaves along the swampy freshwater rivers on the Strand's leeward side. She and her crowd lived inland during the winter, then traveled ten miles or so to their healthier, sea breeze–cooled beach houses in summer, to avoid "Country Fever," as they called malaria (the Spanish had tried to settle this area in 1526, but disease got the better of them). Alice had the misfortune to fall in love with an unsuitable lumberman, who was banished by her evil brother, Dr. Allard Flagg. She pined away, and was buried in the All Saints Churchyard under a headstone that bore "no other inscription than her first name," because she had so disgraced the family. Her ghost was said to haunt the cemetery, looking for the lumberman's ring that her brother snatched from her dying finger.

I followed the ladies' directions to a long, colonnaded building, which looked too slick to be very old. I was enormously disappointed, until I turned around: right behind me, on the other side of the street — observation is not always my strong suit — sat the old church and cemetery. The colonnaded structure was simply a new administration building. I crossed the street and found that the church itself appeared to be a perfect little Greek Revival temple, full of architectural optimism about democracy for all the white men of the planter class, painted a warm, late-daylight ochre, with an Egyptian door lintel just like the Hickys'. Big sash windows with moveable black shutters flanked the entrance.

A weathered notice by the door informed me that "during the turbulence of the mid-nineteenth century, members of the church were active in governing the state of South Carolina." Very circumspect, that. It also alluded to the fact that, "in spite of the romantic legend," the only Alice Flagg buried in the cemetery had been a very young child when she died (her headstone, however, did simply read "Alice"). But even without a set of bones, the churchyard had the ability to conjure the lovelorn Alice's legend from thin — or rather hot, heavy, damp — air. The gravestones, for the most part simple, upright slabs, were weather-worn and mottled with lichen; some were veiled by wisps of gray-green Spanish moss that dripped from tree limbs above. It was a quiet, well-cared-for spot, languid, solitary, and perfectly still. The sky was overcast and the sweet pine-and-floral scented air so oppressive it squeezed out the light from beneath the thicker trees, casting the day into premature shadow. As I hunted unsuccessfully for Alice's grave, the thunder of an approaching storm began to rumble toward me. It was odd, even troubling, so strongly to sense anticipation in a garden of irreversible conclusions. Perhaps this is the gap in which the haunting instinct is born.

In full rain now, I crossed the Strand to Pawley's Island beach, not ten ladies' minutes away, and the site of another Moonlit Road story. On the seaward side of the modern coastal highway, clinging to a fragile finger of land between a green thicket of tidal marsh and the ocean, Pawley's Island is one of the oldest beach communities in the United States. Its sturdy summer cottages date to the mid-nineteenth century, most darkened with age and weather to a deep pitch, or sodden-bark brown. They were all wrapped with porches, and often raised on stilts to avoid flooding, even though they faced the relative safety of the tidal marsh (newer, bigger homes unwisely thumbed their noses at the weather gods, their front picture windows staring brazenly at the roaring Atlantic). This is where Alice and her family would have "summered." A brochure called the look of the place "arrogantly shabby," which seemed about right.

The wide, surf-slicked beach was zebra-striped with short black jetties and pounded by the hazel-colored ocean. The rain had become a tumbling mist and thunder echoed off the face of the water. It was a perfect setting for "The Gray Man," a clever tale-within-a-tale about a man who brings his family to his ancestral home on Pawley's Island for the summer. One morning, walking along the beach, a mist rolls in and he is shadowed by a gray figure who mysteriously disappears when he turns to confront him. Later that night a storm comes up and knocks out the power throughout Pawley's Island. His daughters demand a story by candlelight, and he tells them "The Gray Man," about another pair of doomed lovers in the old rice plantation days. This time the woman's fiancé drowns in quicksand on his way to her. She mourns excessively, then one day, walking the beach, sees a shadowy gray shape approaching her which looks more than a little like her dead lover, Beauregard. Her family fears for her sanity and takes her to a doctor in Charleston. That very day a hurricane rips into Pawley's Island: houses are destroyed and many die. The woman realizes that the Gray Man's appearance saved her life, and she revives from her depression.

In the present-day part of the story, the storm increases in intensity and the man becomes superstitious, spontaneously deciding to take his family back to Atlanta. History repeats itself: that afternoon, Hurricane Hazel — which devastated much of the eastern seaboard, including my home city of Providence, Rhode Island, in 1954 — hits Pawley's Island dead on. When the family returns, all is shambles and destruction; nearly every structure built since World War II has been demolished. But their home is intact. Even the laundry is still pinned to the clothesline. The moral: those who heed the Gray Man will be protected. Never mess with wind nor water.

I woke the following morning in a Georgetown motel with a hangover on just one side of my head. I had been so chilled the previous evening by wind, rain, and other people's afterlives, that I drank a bottle of red Zinfandel for dinner, offset only by a bag of cheese doodles and a peach. To add bad luck to foolishness, the storyteller I was supposed to visit was now suddenly unable to meet me. I called a man about taking a kayak tour of salt marshes and old plantation canals, but he wasn't in. Then I tried to visit an historic home, an old rice plantation that boasted "an original slave street, with wooden shacks and a church," but it was closed due to water damage. Feeling travel-cursed, I settled for wandering the streets of Georgetown with half my head weighed down by a dull brain ache.

Georgetown was nicely historic but not precious. The flat-roofed, painted brick façades of the Front Street shops summoned the 1950s rather than the 1750s (though the city was founded in 1729); the new harborwalk was a fine idea, but instead of pristine marshland it faced the towering steel works — where rods for radial tires are made — that dominated the western harborfront opening onto Winyah Bay. But I liked the place for its self-reliant shrug of the shoulders at tourism. It had a steel mill and a paper mill: if tourists could put up with that, fine, if not, let them go elsewhere. The historic district was equally egalitarian. Brick mansions and white clapboard houses with regal front porches sat next to tiny, wooden A-frame cottages one notch above shacks, many of the latter painted with a cobalt-blue trim, said to ward off ghosts. All were fighting a dignified battle against the weather, which buckled paint and warped wood and felt leaden and malarial in the lungs.

I asked a young man at the rice museum if he knew any good stories about Georgetown. He immediately directed me to Renee (pronounced "Renny") Cathou. "Old Renee's got a fish house down the end of St. James Street," he said. "He has a circle there, you know, kinda like King Arthur's round table, 'cept Renee's only got chairs, no table." I was confused but he was too busy laughing at his own wit to explain further. So I checked my map and found St. James; I imagined an open-air seafood restaurant on the water, overseen by the venerable chef Renee and his cronies.

At first St. James boded well, but the fine old houses with manicured lawns at the upper end of the street soon petered out into shacks, then sheds, then, at the water's pungent edge, a parking lot of crushed shells with a boatyard on one side and an enormous plank-board barn of a building on the other, weathered to the color of a very dark horse. I was about to leave when I saw a tiny sign over the doorless entrance: "Fish

House." My heart sank. I didn't like the look of the place, but I forced myself to go inside.

After the searing glare of sunlight on white shells, it took my eyes ten seconds or so to adjust to the dark interior of the old fish-gutting warehouse. My skin instantly began to perspire in the coolness. Pupils widened, I took in what was obviously a working fisherman's lair: parts of ships' motors lay about in states of half-repair; tools, ropes, nets, lures littered work benches and walls. Like a structural mermaid, half the fish house was built on land, the other on pilings above jasper-green water. The whole building was soaked in a deep marine smell, so familiar to me from New England: a crossbred scent almost sexual in its lowest register, like salty, sweaty flesh, and sharp in its uppermost, with the gassy aroma of vegetable matter rotting slowly under water, all cut through with diesel.

Near the harbor end of the building was a circle of mismatched chairs around an ancient heater. In one sat an old man in a khaki shirt and trousers. His face wasn't wrinkled, but looked rather to have been peeled and polished by the elements. His skin was fair and stretched taut over his features; his pale blue eyes were wide and as deeply lidded below as they were above. He didn't smile.

I explained my quest and Renee politely declined to help. "Ah don't have anah stories for yah, ma'am," he said, in a genteel accent that pried open the consonants at the ends of his words. I thanked him anyway, but stalled, noticing a set of antlers hung with lures and bobbers on the wall behind me. I stared down an open boat ramp to the water beyond.

"Well now," he said slowly, seeing I wasn't moving, "I s'pose yah might just call Dickie Crayton, up they'ah in Pawley's Island. Tell 'im I could still beat him and his brothah both." At what, he didn't say.

I used Renee's phone to call Dickie, who agreed to see me

later that day, "between naps." A young man had arrived while I was on the phone. I should have taken his presence as a sign to leave, but, inexplicably, didn't. Instead I hung around, making awkward small talk, waiting . . . waiting for what, I wasn't sure. I just thought it would be wise to wait. Two more men arrived, one elderly, one young and robust, in his early forties, with a stout, friendly face. With him came pots and pans gripped securely with potholders, cups, thermoses, a roll of paper towels, paper plates, and plastic utensils. It seemed I had been waiting for lunch.

"Well," said Renee, smiling at last, "yah heah now, yah might as well stay and eat."

The pots and pans brimmed with red beans cooked with onions and ham bones, and simmered duckling. The young man who had produced the feast had been up since five that morning, cooking. He had shot the ducks himself over the past winter; he guessed he bagged about a hundred in a season, and had cooked up eighteen that morning.

"Teal, eh?" said a newcomer with his mouth full.

"Yeah, teal," said the chef. "Little ducks about yea big," he explained to me, indicating the size of his hand. "They'ah the best tastin'."

"Man, the whole breast's heah," said another man in admiration.

"That's cause I shoot 'em in the tail or the head. You don't get a mouthful'a lead that way."

The ducks had been cooked whole. Even so, they were tiny — I tried to ignore my once-vegetarian conscience — and musty-tasting, with the wild flavor of creatures that never intended to be eaten. The meat was the color of dark brown earth. I tried to balance my paper plate on my knees, acutely aware of my Northern accent, my short black-and-white dress, sunglasses, and sex. More men had arrived while we were eating, swelling the party to about ten. There were both young and old; all seemed to have plenty of time for a leisurely, gracious meal and low-key conversation in an old fish house. One had brought his lumbering blond labrador, who kept trying to sneak into "the circle" on his belly to beg for tidbits.

"How often does the circle meet?" I asked. "Once a week?"

"More like once a day," laughed Renee, winking and offering me another duck. The conversation shifted to the shops along Front Street. "It's a damn shame so many of 'em are run by Yankees these days," said a man sitting next to me, smacking his knee. He suddenly remembered my presence and bowed low from the waist. "Spent some time up theyah in Newport, Rhode Island," he added by way of apology. "Think she'll ever win back the America's Cup?"

I shook my head no.

"I slept in the seaman's bethel in New Bedford, once," added another. "Nice place."

"You get some pretty bad storms too, don't yah?" said Renee. "That big old hurricane of '38 really did some damage."

"People have been telling me you're still recovering from Hugo," I replied, referring to the massive hurricane that trampled the Carolina coast in 1989.

As we spoke of storms, I detected a shift in the atmosphere of the fish house: the community of weather and water was banding together to transgress bonds of geography and history. These men sailed the same Atlantic that washed my beaches; like New Englanders, they too read the tide charts, watched the phases of the moon, and became anxious in September and October when tropical storms begin to brew in the Caribbean. I'm no sailor, but I know the history of Rhode Island, and it hasn't seen a worse disaster than the unpredicted 1938 hurricane, which sent a tidal wave into downtown Providence, washed away hundreds of families, and blew whole houses fifteen miles from one side of Narragansett Bay to the other. For the first time since I had arrived in the South, in, of all places, a dank, fishy warehouse full of duck hunters, I felt accepted as kindred — a sentiment I never once detected in the polite, but remote, interior.

The South is awash in whimsically named supermarkets: Food Lion, Harris Teeter, Winn-Dixie, Kroger's, and my personal favorite, Piggly Wiggly. I stopped at Food Lion to buy a lemon cake for Dickie Crayton before calling on him at The Blue Anchor, his stilt-hoisted house in a modern district of Pawley's Island. Dick, as he identified himself, was frail and painfully thin, dressed in white and attended by two little lap dogs. As a navy man and a sailor he had been all over the world, but reserved his deepest pride for his birthplace, Georgetown.

"There's no place in all America that goes so well with the blacks and the whites," he said proudly. "Now I've never had a black man in my house, unless he was carrying a mattress or something, but they're the nicest people. They always say hello."

He went on to tell me that in 1900 Georgetown had boasted the largest lumber mill in the world. "Longleaf pine," he said reverently, "that's what we've got here in our forests. The termites can't get into it. Take a look at your door frames and windowsills back up North: bet they're longleaf pine."

And rice! Ah, rice. Georgetown County had produced half the world's rice supply in the early and mid-nineteenth century. "We were the richest rice capital in the world," remembered Dick, about a time before he was born. "They cut the cypress trees to make rice fields." But then, he said, rice had been planted in Texas, where there was a subterranean water supply. In South Carolina, dikes and canals had to be dug to keep the rice paddies moist — a fine solution in the days of slave labor, but too painstaking and expensive after emancipation. "Finally, around 1900," he said sadly, "the great hurricane came and broke through the dikes, and salt water came in and poisoned the fields. That was the end of Carolina rice. There's not a field left."

To my astonishment and relief, Dick refused to lament the demise of a grain that had literally ridden on the backs of eighty-five percent of the local people (because rice plantations were so labor-intensive, killingly intensive, slaves represented the vast majority of the Georgetown population until the Civil War). "You want to know what my great thing in life was?" he suddenly asked, leaning forward, full of eagerness. "Dancing. Ballroom dancing."

Dick did a little seated shuffle. "When I was a young man I had leather dancing slippers. Oh, they made me feel like I was floating." His eyes shone with decades-old happiness. "How did you learn?" I asked.

"In the summertime, when we were kids, nobody had a shoe on on all Pawley's Island. Only the Yankee tourists wore shoes. We took gramophones to the beach every evening and played records. And just danced. We danced and danced, barefoot in the sand. By the end of summer I could throw a cigarette down and crush it with my bare toe. That meant I'd been dancing for months — I had the calluses to prove it. And you could buy corn whisky in Coke bottles for twenty-five cents. Sometimes you had to drink three or four bottles to get drunk. Then you'd lie in the dunes and look at the stars. And you knew everybody. There weren't so many people back then. You'd never find men on the beach during the day — they'd all be out dragging for shrimp."

An image came back to me then, from the previous day, a caught glimpse from the car window of a man tossing a shrimp net into the water. It had hung in the air like a smoke ring for just a second before disappearing from view.

I asked Dick if he had lived through any of this century's big hurricanes. He chuckled. "Well, I was born on White House Plantation, outside of Georgetown," he began. "In 1916 I was just a baby, and my father was up at White House. My mother, my twin brother, our black maid, and my five-year-old sister and I were here at Pawley's Island for the summer, staying on the beach. Back then there was no warning system, no way to tell people a big blow was on the way. Only one old man walking door to door . . .

"Well, my mother didn't get word before the storm hit. So she put all our lamps in the windows on one side of the house to let people know we were still there, if anyone came. Well, an old man did show up in a horse and buggy.

"'What you doing here?' he asked. 'There's a bad hurricane coming!'

"So he put us in the buggy and we tried to cross the two-hundred-yard causeway [the bridge over the swampy leeward side of Pawley's Island] to the mainland. They tied my sister and the little black girl in the back, and Mother sat with the old man up front, holding us twins in her lap. The causeway was well under water. Every time a wave came it would lift the horse clean up off the ground, then set him down again. My mother thought we were goners, but we made it, and put up in the attic of a friend's house. And that was the 1916 hurricane."

Weather. Actually, weather and topography, they were the story-makers in this part of the world. These tidal lowlands had a fragility, emotional as well as environmental, that only someone who had been on the roller coaster at Myrtle Beach one too many times could possibly miss. Georgetown County was the topographical equivalent of a consumptive, nineteenth-century heroine, superlatively beautiful but doomed to die. The beaches were wide and white, the soil rich, the crepe myrtle in glorious, pink bloom, the fens thick with animal life and luxuriously green; but this was loveliness born of a geographic deal with the Devil. Storms came here. The coast lay down at sea level and the sea had its way with the land. Come late summer, early autumn, hurricanes flooded and destroyed man's diversions even as they enriched the biosphere — and this happened year after year after year after year. And all this heat and water bred mosquitoes, and for generations that had meant early death from malaria and yellow fever. A morbid glamour clung to this place, and out of it grew ghost stories.

Dickie Crayton had survived to dance his summers away, but I discovered that the real Alice Flagg, the little girl, had drowned with her father during the great storm of October 15, 1893. A very real tragedy — of seawater, not tears — lurked behind the fiction. The thing to remember is that there have always been ghost-makers aplenty in the Waccamaw Episcopal parish: it simply took storytellers to embroider them from tropical depressions and disease into the equally capricious killer, forbidden love. And the Gray Man: what was he but the embodiment of storm clouds on the eastern horizon? Heed him and he brings hope, ignore him and he wreaks destruction.

How different these tales are from those of the high, dry ground, the Appalachian Mountains and the dusty fields of central Georgia. Neither Jack nor Brer Rabbit nor even the mule-egg seller, with their shared brutal optimism, opportunism, and luck, could begin to outwit the Gray Man. The terms of conflict in highland and lowland stories are utterly different. The seaboard climate is too elemental, too unpredictable for the kind of mortal cleverness that wins the day — or loses it, in the case of Taily Po — against the prosaic antagonists of the interior. Antagonists that include living opponents, near-comical creatures with funny tails, or even temporary conditions like drought or depression. By contrast, these coastal stories, even when cast in terms of human conflict (Alice versus her evil brother Allard), have an inner core of fatalism wrung from the innate knowledge that there can be no protection against wind, rain, high seas, and disease. Strip away their fictional bark, and at heart stories such as *Alice* are ringed like the pith of a tree: in them, careful listeners can hear a record of floods and hot summers, malaria outbreaks, storms and early freezes. They are the real almanacs of the lowlands.

This eyewitness account of the 1893 hurricane, from a plantation worker named Reverend Cato, is what the real Alice would have experienced before she and her parents and her four siblings were washed from their beach house by a forty-foot tidal wave:

> The tide ain't run out that day. Not even for to show the oysters on the rock, nor the sand bar. Water rushing in. Over on the beach, the sea been light up. Been light up like lantern lights up the house. Looked same like fire. That sea make us think of judgment and hell. Sea looked like it on fire. And the creek been light up. And the tide. She rolled in fast. The moss was flying from trees same like bird. Every which-er-way, the trees snap. Rotten limbs fall all round. The sound of prayers reached us. They was all praying. Good and bad was united. We go down in prayer. Speak to the Good God. Ask him to calm the elements. Beg him to say, "Peace. Be still."

Cornelia's Tale

ORNELIA BAILEY OF SAPELO ISLAND, Georgia, was a busy woman, but after several telephone calls finally consented to see me. There was, however, one hitch: the State of Georgia owned much of Sapelo as an estuarine reserve. This meant that to take the ferry from the mainland and not return the same day, visitors had to be sponsored by someone from the island. Cornelia owned one Bed and Breakfast, but it was full. She suggested the other one, but it was also full. On a whim, the man at the second B&B told me to try Mr. Gardner, who sometimes rents out his house. I called and spoke with Mrs. Gardner, who agreed to a deal: for $100 cash I could have the whole, three-bedroom house and a bike.

I was in Georgetown, and to catch the 3:30 P.M. Sapelo ferry the following afternoon, I had to drive a distance of about two hundred and twenty-five miles through the heart of the South Carolina Low Country — an experience as close to traveling underwater as dry land can offer. Rain came first. A heavy, blanketing deluge battered the earth and turned my windshield into a watery prism, making the chlorophyll-drenched landscape swim before my eyes. It looked like the rolling image on my parents' old television set, but monochromatically green instead of blue. The rain stopped just before I reached the Charleston bypass, allowing old black women to emerge from tarpaulin-covered shelters by the highway side, where they sold woven sweet-grass baskets. I stopped once in a pine clearing to read my map, and opened the windows to let in the scented air: instantly the car filled with swarming mosquitoes. I slapped two and smeared my thigh with my own blood.

Between Charleston and Beaufort (pronounced Bewfort) I turned off the air conditioning and let the rain-cooled wind tangle my hair. The land here was plaited with rivers and inlets and marshes: like Renee's fish house, a kind of mer-place, half of the earth, half of the sea. The sky was too heavy for the heavens and fell around me, damp and milky-white, settling atop the Ashepoo River, which in open places was the color of pearls and in shaded ones deep black. The marshlands looked corrupt, their bright Easter-colored grasses — lime green and pink-tipped — underlaid by coils of inky water that shimmered with a noisome, oily iridescence. Pine forests; boiled peanuts for sale; long, straight avenues leading to picture-book plantations: these things filled the dry land between swamps. Spanish moss, called "ghost hair" by an old man I'd met at a gas station, wrapped everything. The whole world seemed to be fermenting.

Because of the sheer numbers of slaves required to work this part of the country, first in indigo, then rice, it stands to reason they would have left an African imprint on the land. And they did, in speech, especially the creole language called Gullah, or Geechee; in religion, which often betrays a creolized mix of Christianity and ancestral spirit worship, like Brazil's Candomble; and in their folk stories. According to local belief, the swamps and woods of coastal South Carolina and Georgia are awash in evil spirits. Boo-hags, boo-daddies, haints, and plateyes: they'll all get you if you don't watch out.

I popped one of Henry Howard's studio tapes in the car's cassette player, and Veronica Byrd's voice rang out into the swamps.

THE PLAT-EYE

Nellie Bale and Jean Le Rue were sisters. Besides being sisters, they were the best of friends . . . Now, one of their favorite things to do during the hot South Georgia summer months was to go swimming at the old swimming hole and pick scuppernongs along the way. Well, it happened on one of those hot and humid days that the girls could not cool off for anything. They tried going down to the well and splashing their faces with cool water. Eating little chips of ice. They even tried standing in front of the small, oscillating fan that their mama kept in the living room window. But nothing worked. That was when they both decided to go down to the swimming hole. That's when their adventure began.

Nellie, who was the oldest, put on her pink swimsuit with purple polka dots. And Jean, the more practical of the two, her basic blue with red trim. The girls quietly closed the door to their bedroom, tip-toed to the kitchen, got their pails from the shelf under the sink, and oh so quietly made their way to the back door. You see, they were trying to stay as quiet as possible so as not to waken Gran'ma Mathilda, who had a room in the back of the house. But just as Jean put her hand on the doorknob and turned it,

"Jean! Nellie! Y'all trying to sneak past me? Come here! I got something to tell you before you go."

The girls looked at each other, and with a sigh of disgust they shuffled towards Gran'ma Mathilda's room. They knew what they were in store for. Their usual lecture. "Y'all stick together. Don't wander too far off the road or you might get lost," she'd say. Or, "Don't let darkness catch ya on a dirt road. Make sure you're home afore nightfall!" Or her all-time favorite, "Stay out of the Gongetcha Woods, at all cost! Strange things been known to happen in those woods." But on this particular day, Ma-tilda, that's what the girls called her, seemed even more anxious to give the girls their usual lecture. She sat them both down on her bed and looked them straight in the eyes, and said the strangest thing.

"If ya hear a chain rattlin' on a tree nearby, be careful. 'Cause it might just be a Plat-Eye." Then she reached into her pocket and pulled out two smelly little pieces of burlap, each tied into a tight knot. She then handed each girl a bundle and told them, "Keep this witcha at all times today, make sure it's always in your pocket no matter what happens."

The girls took the bags out of respect for their gran'ma, gave her a kiss, and bounded out of the room. But before they could clear the doorway she belted out, "Make sure you stay out of those Gongetcha Woods. Strange things been known to happen there!"

I stopped the car and the tape and hunted for my notes. Veronica had been born in Atlanta but raised in California. Every year, as soon as school was out, she flew back East to spend the summer with her Grandmother Nellie, who told her old-time, African-American stories. "My surface life was in California," she had said, "but my imagination, my ancestral imagination, lived in Georgia."

Her grandmother had been born with a caul over her face; she had been able to see spirits as a child. At bedtime she would creep into Veronica's room on her hands and knees, acting out the story she would tell that night. Veronica would squeal with equal parts of delight and fright, yelling "Grandma!" and her grandmother would bellow in a deep, slow voice, "I am not your grandmother . . ." It was in these sessions that Veronica first learned about plat-eyes. Much later she discovered the dark legend behind their penchant for chain-rattling. It was the folk belief that a plantation master would bury his gold beneath a large tree, and to protect it, he would find the biggest, meanest slave on his estate and chain the slave to the tree and let him die there — the idea being that his restless, bad-tempered spirit would keep thieves away and protect the treasure.

As I traveled, I collected books, so that by this time the back seat of my rental car had metamorphosed into a mobile library shelf. I reached back and pulled out *A Treasury of Southern Folklore,* and continued my plat-eye research. Plat-eyes are angry spirits that were not given proper burial. If a body is buried with prayers and respect and still can't stay put, it rises to become nothing more than a "harmless haint"; ignore the funeral rites, however, and you'll have a plat-eye on your hands. Animals have second sight and can see them all the time, but only humans born with cauls over their faces, like Nellie, are capable of spirit-vision. "As a rule," the entry continued, "spirits resemble the bodies they occupied. The most unfortunate ones become plat-eyes and take on many shapes, changing quickly from one to another. Now a dog, then a horse, a man without a head, a warm cloud or a hot smoke that suffocates all living creatures. Plat-eyes fear nothing and stop at nothing. Wise people and beasts flee from them . . ."

Once the girls were out of Ma-tilda's earshot they laughed and giggled about the silly things their gran'ma had told them. They thought it was awful strange her telling them to carry those smelly little bags in their pockets. And rambling on and on about chains and trees, and the Gongetcha Woods, and Plat-Eyes, whatever they were. But they dismissed it as the babbling of a half-senile old woman, and they grabbed their towels, dropped the burlap bags on the table, and headed for the ever-beckoning coolness of the swimming hole . . .

Well, the twenty-minute walk seemed to take no time at all, and before they knew it, there they were. The swimming hole! The girls dropped their pails and jumped straight into the water — what they had been waiting for all day long. Pshew! They were finally cool. The girls splashed around and played in the water for hours. They played so much that they were completely exhausted. So they got out of the water, ate a few scuppernongs, talked a bit, and before they knew it — Yawn! — they had both drifted off to sleep.

Well, Jean was the first to awaken. When she realized where she was she looked around and saw that the sun was setting and that the warm summer day was giving way to the coolness of evening. She quickly awakened her sister. They grabbed their towels and pails and started back down the ever-darkening dirt road. They had walked about five minutes when Nellie remembered what Ma-tilda had said. "Don't let darkness catch ya on that road. Make sure you're home before nightfall!"

There was no way they would make it back before nightfall if they kept on the dirt road. But Nellie had an idea.

"Jean! Jean! Let's cut through these woods. That way we'll get home waaay before dark. So we won't have to listen to one of Ma-tilda's silly old lectures."

Like I told you, Jean was the more practical of the two. "We can't go through those woods, Nellie, we might get lost. Besides, those are the Gongetcha Woods. Ma-tilda warned us not to go in there."

"Don't be silly!" Nellie protested. "Ma-tilda just made that up just to scare us. There ain't no such thing as the Gongetcha Woods. Come on, girl!"

Well, with very little effort at all, Nellie had talked Jean into going through the woods. With nothing more than getting home before dark on their minds, they started through the woods.

At first, the path through the trees was quite visible, but the deeper they got into the woods the denser the leaves on the trees became, making it much harder to see where they were going . . . The girls made their way as best they could, through the barrage of tangled weeds and vines, towards what they thought was home.

Well, they were doing just fine until they heard an unusual noise. Coming from behind them. Or was it in front of them? They really couldn't tell. They stopped. And so did the sound. So they continued on. But there it was again.

"What is that? I've never heard anything like that before," Nellie whispered. And as if to answer their question, a large black cat jumped in front of them. Hisss! Well this put both of their minds at ease, for there was nothing at all scary about a cat. Nellie walked up to the cat to pet him, when she let out a loud scream. For you see, the closer they got to the cat they saw that he had two front legs, but four back legs. And his eyes glowed in the dark. What in the world? There was that strange noise again. What was that? And where's it coming from? The girls gave each other that look, and there was no need for words. They both knew they had to get back to the dirt road and take the long way home. They turned around and tried to figure out which way was out. Everything looked the same . . . Jean grabbed her sister's hand, and they started as fast as they could to what they thought was the way out of the woods.

The occasional eerie beams of what was now moonlight, streaming through the leaves of the trees, confused the girls even more. They were moving as fast as they could when they heard that sound again.

"What's that? Let's get out of here!"

They continued a short distance when they saw a large, shadowy figure in front of them. They turned on their heels and started away from the ominous thing. But there seemed to be shadowy things everywhere they looked. As if out of nowhere a large dog with wiry hair and big, bloodshot eyes walked directly in front of them. He had a hole in his side, exposing all of his innards, which dragged along the ground as he walked. The girls let out a blood-curdling scream, and the dog screamed back, mimicking their voices. The girls were completely beside themselves with fear. They knew if they could make it back to the dirt road, they could at least see where they were going. They were blindly running in who-knows-what direction, when the sound seemed to be coming from everywhere.

"It sounds like, it sounds like, a chain or something. Like a chain. A chain rattling against a tree." At that moment they remembered that Ma-tilda had told them, "If you hear a chain rattling on a tree nearby, be careful, it might just be a Plat-Eye."

They didn't know what a Plat-Eye was. And after seeing the dog and cat, they weren't sticking around to find out. The sound kept growing louder and louder with each step. It seemed to be all around them. They thought they were almost out of the woods, when there was an awful stench that permeated the entire area. And floating down through the trees was what appeared to be a large hunchback hog, both eyeballs hanging from their sockets, dripping blood on the girls, and it made the most horrifying noise. "Eggghhh, egggggghh."

I pulled over and made a quick note: Veronica's story played like the blockbuster remake of an original black and white plat-eye movie, in its preference for gore over unseen menace. In fact, there is a much older version of the tale in which the plat-eye simply appears as a suffocating, sulfurous cloud. I was both disappointed and relieved: in the growing, swampy darkness, gory eyeballs were less frightening than disembodied threats. I was grateful for Veronica's high-spirited, Technicolor vision.

Nellie and Jean screamed as loud as they could, and . . . ran as fast as they could until they made it back to the dirt road. Once they were back on the dirt road they could see exactly where they were going, but this was no reason for them to slow down. Nellie and Jean ran all the way home. They didn't stop until they collapsed exhausted on their front porch. When they caught their breath they looked up, and standing in front of them with arms folded was . . . Ma-tilda.

Best they could they tried to tell her about all the spooky things they'd seen while they were in the woods.

"Ma-tilda, Ma-tilda, we saw a hog, and he had blood dripping out of his eyes, and there was a dog, and there was a cat, and it was so scary, it was so scary, boo hoo hoo hoo!"

Ma-tilda let the girls finish telling of their adventure. Then she calmly pulled out the small burlap bags from her pockets, and told them that they could have avoided seeing all of this, if they had obeyed her and carried those bags with them. For you see, the bags contained sulfur and gunpowder. A sure-fire way to ward off Plat-Eyes.

Ma-tilda has long gone on to meet her maker, but from that day to this, my sister and I make sure we always carry a small burlap bag filled with sulfur and gunpowder in our pocketbooks. Just in case there are any Plat-Eyes hanging out in these modern-day woods. Oh, I forgot to tell you, my name is Nellie Bale. It was my sister Jean and I that learned this lesson firsthand. And oh, what a lesson it was. So next time you dismiss those things your elders tell you as mumblings of senile folks, you'd better think again. Sometimes old folks know what they're talking about. And don't forget. Stay out of those Gon-getcha Woods. Strange things have been known to happen there.

That night, in a motel in Beaufort, I hardly slept at all, and got up looking a little gothic around the eyes. Soon a plague of chambermaids came upon me: I could hear their housekeep-ing carts rolling like thunder on the pavement outside my room. I stumbled to the door and hung a Do Not Disturb sign on my knob, he modern equivalent of blue-painted trim to keep unfriendly spirits at bay. I'd read on a notice posted in the lobby that the average time it took to clean a room was twenty-two minutes.

By three that afternoon I was swaying along with the wave-ridden dock in Meridian, Georgia, where the Sapelo Queen was moored. Although the crossing only costs a dollar each way, one does not approach Sapelo Island casually. A visitor's center on the mainland underscores its environmental unique-ness as the token of a passing glacier: a delicate barrier island of pristine marshlands, beaches, and forested uplands, roamed by white-tailed deer and overseen by over two hundred and fifty species of birds. Seeing as I was taking the second-to-last ferry of the day, the national park officials politely but firmly asked where I would be staying. "At the Gardners," I said proudly, pretending I was an insider. Since there are only about sixty-five residents on Sapelo, I expected instant recognition, but the park people looked stumped. They chatted among themselves: Gardner. Gardner? You know a Gardner?

"Oh," said one of them, finally, "you mean *Dan* Gardner. Sure. All right, have a good trip."

All the portents suggested that Sapelo was special, a little prickly, different. I cautiously took my place on the small ferry alongside a dignified, middle-aged lady in a straw hat who was reading the Bible — she later proved to be a minister — and two house painters who looked like they'd been caught in a paint squall. All around us was water: heat-stilled flatwater, strewn with puddles of golden-green spartina grass in a very convincing reversal of the land-sea equation. I was the only white person in sight.

The crossing was brief and smooth. As everyone else chatted about weekend plans or hummed to themselves with Friday afternoon contentment, I scribbled furiously, making lists of questions, trying to remember the color of Renee Cathou's eyes (blue).

"What you doin', girl? Calm down. Look at the view." I glanced up with my pencil in my mouth and found the painters laughing at me. "Be calm, be calm, it's the weekend." I took a deep breath. It was going to take a conscious notching-down of gears to get along with Sapelo. For the first time all day I let my shoulders quit bookending my neck and drop into their natural slouch.

As we docked I asked the painters to point out Dan Gardner. "The one with the hat and glasses," they said. I marched up to a gentleman of that description and announced brightly, "I'm staying with you tonight!"

"You ARE?" he replied, startled.

One of the painters silently took me by the shoulders and steered me around forty-five degrees. "There's Dan," he wheezed, helpless with laughter.

Mr. and Mrs. Gardner and I sat leg-to-leg in the front seat of their shockless pickup truck, and lurched to the interior of the island. She had on a big straw hat with a flower in the front; he wore a pressed, short-sleeved shirt with a pocket clip for pens and pencils. They talked in unsynchronized stereo the way so many older couples do.

"Now, we've left the air conditioners on for you. Just turn them off when you leave," said Mrs. Gardner.

"Did you tell her about the air conditioners?" he asked a second later.

In less than three minutes we pulled up in front of a tidy, mint-green ranch house with a squat palm tree in front. The Gardners gave me a key and fussed like parents for a few instruction-filled moments, then roared off in their truck to catch the returning ferry to their full-time home on the mainland.

Cornelia Bailey's house was a short bike ride away, but not an easy ride. The dirt roads, booby-trapped with drifts of soft, tan sand, had directional opinions of their own, and sent me weaving in an uncertain course past a few modest homes and a sign that read, Hog Hammock — An Historical Community, Established 1857. Pop. 70, to Cornelia's shocking-blue bungalow. I rapped on the door a couple of times, but got no answer. Soon a little girl appeared with a bag of sunflower seeds, and let me in. "Gran'ma's got the TV on," she said, leaving a trail of husks behind her.

Cornelia greeted me casually but kindly. There was so much ebb and flow through her dark lime-colored kitchen — sons building bathrooms in need of cold drinks, granddaughters and their friends demanding to be paid for chambermaid work, friends wanting to borrow hairstyle magazines, a family of microbiologists, also old friends, come for the weekend — that to function at all she had to prioritize her attentions. I came in somewhere below the televised soap opera, and above her teenage chambermaids.

Cornelia calmly took her position in the center of this maelstrom like the matriarch she was, in purple pedal pushers, a "Gullah Connection" T-shirt, cowrie-shell earrings, big, gold-framed glasses, an orange-beaded head band, and bare feet. We talked about mosquitoes. My shins looked like bug-eyed tropical fish from the bites I'd gotten while unlocking the Gardners' bicycle. Cornelia pointed out that most people in the Low Country wear at least one piece of dark clothing, so that when you swat a mosquito you'll have a place to wipe your hand where the blood won't show. She asked where I was staying.

The Gardners, I said, and she looked dazed for a minute. "Oh, you mean *Dan* Gardner's place. Oh, that's good."

Cornelia wanted to know if I'd done my homework. Had I seen her Web site? Had I read *Sapelo's People,* by William McFeely? I answered no to the first, yes to the second, and she immediately discounted McFeely. "He don't know nothing about us. He lived here two weeks and he calls his book *Sapelo's People.* Like he knows Sapelo's people."

McFeely knew more than I did, at least. From him I had learned that Sapelo had been the site of one of the largest pre-war rice plantations in Georgia, under the ownership of an inventive entrepreneur named Thomas Spalding. It was Spalding who brought six hundred or so slaves to the island from markets in Charleston and the West Indies. When Union troops blockaded the sea islands during the Civil War, Spalding's son marched his slaves inland, to central Georgia, where he thought he could avoid their liberation. Unfortunately for him, he settled them smack in the path of General William Tecumseh Sherman, who freed them as his troops burned their way to the sea.

For practical reasons — to rid himself of hangers-on, rather than from any soft-hearted sentiment — Sherman issued Special Field Order 15 in January 1865, which literally gave the sea islands south of Charleston to former slaves, allotting forty acres for each head of household. The majority of Sapelo's liberated slave families eventually walked back to the island to take the U.S. Government up on its offer. It was they who founded Hog Hammock, named for Samson Hogg (a pig raiser whose family later changed the name to Hall). Their descendents exclusively comprise the current population of the island.

The former slaves stayed, but did not prevail. Under pressure from wealthy Southern planters, it didn't take President Andrew Johnson long to overturn Sherman's order, by then an act of Congress, and return the land to the men who had owned it before the War. This arrangement effectively turned freedmen, who for a short time had been land-owning farmers, into sharecroppers, working the land for the same families that had once owned them. Over the years, Sapelo's residents avoided the worst of the sharecropping system, and the Spaldings' attempts to revive their plantation never took hold. Wealthy outsiders eventually bought up huge tracts of the island, though today those parcels have been sold to the state of Georgia as scientific and wildlife reserves, with the ever-dwindling population of Hog Hammock — the number has fallen below three-digit figures in Cornelia's lifetime — sandwiched in between.

The soap opera had ended, and the TV blared the news, now, from its place of honor between Cornelia and me on the kitchen table. In between visitors she talked about the generous pace of island life. How there is always time for get-togethers, which tend to be phone-planned, and stop-bys, which are spontaneous happenings of the sort I was witnessing in her kitchen.

"You feel part of you is working so hard to retain this part of Georgia . . . My ancestors walked here, and we're walking on the same soil. I'll fight to stay here. But then, sometimes, I start to wonder how long we'll be able to hold on." Cornelia stopped for a moment, then made a fist and gave the table a little pound. "Then I say, No, I won't think that way. There's a saying, 'The positive works you the hardest.'"

". . . And in another item, today the authorities seized more than five hundred barrels of marijuana. And listen to this, folks, it's worth over one million dollars! They arrested forty-year-old Jose Mendez of El Paso, Texas . . ."

I lost the thread for a moment, seduced from Cornelia and Sapelo by canned footage of healthy marijuana fields gleaming on the television screen. Cornelia was saying that she likes to tell "human interest" stories, as she called them, in which she tries to convey the island's history and culture — stories she learned sitting with the elders as a child, stories that "don't need no copyright, that represent my papa and mama and all the people of the island" — as well as Brer Rabbit stories, and "Why" stories. When I looked quizzical, she explained, "You know, kids bug you to death with 'why' questions. I like to make stories out of the answers."

She expounded on her storytelling philosophy. "I can take a story and change it around for any audience. For example, if parents came to me and asked me to tell their child a story, I'd tell a black child a human-interest story about the island, so he'd get to know his roots. If it was a white child, I'd just tell a made-up story. See, the black child's parents would be able to fill in the details, but the white child's wouldn't."

"What would you tell a black child whose parents weren't from around here?"

Cornelia conceded she'd have to tell him the same story she'd tell the white child. Did she have a human-interest story for me, I wanted to know, to help me learn about Sapelo?

She looked at me for a moment as if sizing up my worthiness, or perhaps the potential for this Northern white girl to listen with an empathetic ear. I must have passed some test, because Cornelia cleared a space around her with her hands, as if she were setting up an invisible podium, then began to speak.

People ask me, What religion are you? Umm. Born Muslim and became a false Christian, I say. My great-great-grandparents were of the Islamic faith, but they weren't allowed to practice it as slaves. When their children were freed they formed the First African Baptist Church here in 1866. Well, it was formed by people who still had the ways of their parents and their grandparents in them. Christianity and Islamic faith rolled into one.

Now one of the stories about that church goes like this. It's about my grandmother Winnie. Her mother Harriet and her father John was very strict. According to the church rules . . . well, everybody was strict. They were strict with their children like everybody else. And you couldn't get pregnant out of wedlock. That was a no-no. And if you did by chance, the church stepped in, and you were made to marry that young man.

So, my grandmother broke all rules. She decided she wasn't going to marry nobody she didn't want to marry. No matter how many kids she had. So she had one child, two childs, three childs, four childs, five childs, without benefit of getting married. Now that was unheard of. Grandma was a free spirit from the get-go. So finally the church told her that we cannot take this no more . . .

". . . and the police are searching for a woman wanted for shoplifting [photo shown], and a man accused of terroristic threats and trespassing . . ."

"Winnie," they said, "you have to come before the board of elders and tell us who is the father of your children." So Grandma got all dressed up that day and she went to a church conference. And she went there and she looked around, and all she saw was a church full of women who were her friends, and cousins, and others. And I can imagine them all sitting on the edge of their seats, saying to theirselves, Lord, I hope she don't call my man's name.

So she looked at the elders up there who were waiting for her to speak and say who is the father of her children. She looked at them sitting up there — they were all men — and she said, "Now, if I tell you all who is the father of my children — I wonder which one of you all up there might be the father of my babies? — there wouldn't be nobody in this church but me now, would there?"

All heads went down and the women let out a sigh of relief, and nobody questioned Grandma no more. That was the end of that. She later got married to my grandfather and had three more daughters, and they lived happily ever after . . .

All this happened before I was born, but Grandma and others told that story and retold that story and retold that story . . . I knew grandma well. She was stubborn until the day she died.

The weather forecast, full of rain and humidity, came onto the television, and I asked Cornelia if she knew any good weather stories. She said that they didn't have weather stories on Sapelo, just weather predictions. But then she remembered the tale of Mr. Hamp Wilson and the Hurricane of 1898.

There is one about the Great Hurricane of 1898, when water went over most of the island. They didn't lose anybody. They lost some cattle and some chickens and some stuff like that, but nobody was lost on Sapelo during that time. But after the storm they did have to round up everybody to see who was there. Well, they took a head count and they couldn't find Mr. Hamp Wilson. And they looked far and wide, and they looked all over for Hamp Wilson, but they couldn't find him nowhere. So they went to Hanging Bull, and they called out for Hamp. And they heard this music playing. And they were going, "Now why would there be music playing with all this water all over and everything?"

But you see, the church is located in a part of the island called Hanging Bull, and Hamp was afraid the water would come up over there. So he gone and got the little organ that the church had, and he drug it all the way to the steeple up there, and he was sitting there playing music. So they found Hamp Wilson by the music of the organ. They found him safe and sound in the steeple, playing that organ. His wife — Miss Sylvia — was quite happy. They found her husband.

"Did you know him?" I asked.

"No, I didn't know him, but I knew his wife well."

"Was that her story?"

"No, that was everybody's story. She told it, but other people did too. My father was born a few years after that, and it was told to him as a child. Everybody knew the story."

With the exterior stairs missing, the crumbling threshold of the door to Sapelo's *second* First African Baptist Church, in Raccoon Bluff, came up to my waist. (According to McFeely, the *first* First Church, in Hanging Bull, was destroyed in the hurricane of 1898. Now this rendition of events stranded me in a war zone between McFeely's facts and Cornelia's stories — academic and islander also differed on loss of life in the 1898 hurricane — and I instinctively sought refuge in Cornelia's tale. McFeely's version leaves the past empty; Cornelia's replaces

destruction with the miraculous image of Hamp Wilson playing as the rains came, and lends us a glimpse into a value system which placed music and the Lord over life itself.
Understanding is often a more useful resource than truth.)

I peered inside the church into a monumental space that had
once been holy. It was dark and gray with dust, but I could
make out the wainscoted ceiling and walls, an uneven floor
that listed like a sinking ship, chandeliers knitted with cob-
webs. What little light there was filtered into the church through
colored-glass windows, filling the sanctuary with a filmy, ame-
thyst haze. Earlier, in Hog Hammock, I had asked a local resident what he thought was the most striking thing about the
island. "People's religious customs," he'd said without missing
a beat. "There's nothing extraordinary about their relationship
with God, but here people have a reverence for life after death,
the existence of a Supreme Being. It's not showy, not passed
down mouth-to-ear, but by precept, by example." The con-
fidant, matter-of-factness of the building confirmed his perception.

I couldn't linger long at the abandoned church· I had
worked up such a sweat biking the five miles there from Hog
Hammock that whenever I stood still I became a big slab of
mosquito bait (Racoon Bluff village had been deserted at the
urging of an off-island landowner who bought up the property for himself, and consolidated residents in Hog Hammock).
The ride had been torturous. I'd fallen off my bike twice when
its wheels went astray in unseen sand traps. There were no
houses, no other souls in motion that Saturday morning except
tiny, translucent crabs. The air was hot and still. To either side
of the road was a phalanx of tall pine trees bursting into green
enthusiasm fifty feet off the ground, where their needles met
the sun. Otherwise I had only the dark forest floor for company, filled with banana-green saplings, palmettos, and unseen,

unsettling rustlings. The hand-painted sign for Racoon Bluff had led me into a grove of ancient live oaks, all strewn with tattered curtains of Spanish moss, which kept a perpetual twilight in the church enclosure.

McFeely says, "There is no echo of Africa in the building," and he's right. It looks just like a nineteenth-century New England church. Africa doesn't linger in buildings, but in people, in Winnie, the free spirit who took on church elders because the mores of turn-of-the-century America didn't suit her. Once again, it is the story record, rather than the written or structural record, that tells the truth. I suddenly slapped a mosquito, drawing more blood as thunder began to growl down by the horizon, which I wearily took as a sign to leave.

I had had a bad night. I dreamt that my shadow had spoken to me, and told me it wasn't mine, it didn't reflect me, that we were mismatched. I tried to peer into it but there was nothing to see but me-shaped shade. Through muddled dream logic, I tried to decide if it were some kind of opportunistic parasite that had wrested my own shadow away and taken its place, or if I had wandered out of my ken into a dark space, and had accidentally picked up someone else's. I never figured it out. After that, I had spent the night staring sleeplessly at the Gardner's off-white, plaster-and-gravel ceiling, which was flecked with bits of mica that shone and glittered like false stars. A raging storm — punctuated by an explosion of light that seemed to happen inside, rather than outside, my eyelids — had unnerved me until sunup.

I returned from Raccoon Bluff under a sky filled with small, round thunderheads, like a snapped string of black pearls. My destination was the island's only store, BJ's Confectionery, where I had bought a can of corned beef hash for my dinner the previous evening. Its counter and aisles seemed abandoned and I turned to go, but then heard a sob from the very back. I wandered down the canned goods aisle until I came upon a few easychairs and a TV at the rear of the shop. Five or six people huddled in front of the set. One woman was crying into a pressed handkerchief.

"What happened," I asked. "What's wrong?"

"It's John-John," said the old lady with whom I had discussed the merits of baloney the previous evening. She spoke as if he were her son. "His plane is missing. It disappeared late last night between New Jersey and Cape Cod. Oh, that poor family."

My flesh crawled with coincidence. I had grown up in New Jersey and spent my summer holidays on Cape Cod. I went to college with John F. Kennedy, Jr.; he had caught my pet ferret when it ran away on the college green. Thanks to television, when his plane crashed into Nantucket Sound, a part of the Atlantic I knew well, my visit to Sapelo Island ended. No one had time for its small stories any longer. Like everyone else in the country, the islanders knew what "John-John" looked like; they could picture him better than their own dead relatives. Just as the TV had brought the Southern battles of the civil rights movement into my living room in the sixties, so it now carried images of New England, of my part of the world, along with weeping members of America's most famous family, into the back room of Sapelo's confectionery. The national story muscled its way onto the island and there was no room left for any others.

I returned to the Gardners' house and showered off the dirt and sand. As I was drying my hair in their improbably decorated bedroom — it looked like a Doris Day movie set, with a semi-circular vinyl settee and French provincial dressers — a young man and his little son Marvin appeared to drive me to the ferry, as the Gardners had prearranged. I said I wasn't quite ready, so they both sat and stared at me as I furiously brushed and blew my hair. In Sapelo terms, I was the afternoon's entertainment.

Fouchena's Tale

JUST BEFORE I LEFT SAPELO ISLAND, one of the residents explained why no one had understood me when I said I was staying in "the Gardners' house."

"Dan Gardner's Sapelo born and bred," he said. "His wife is from Atlanta. That's why it's *his* house. She's not from here."

Later, in Beaufort, South Carolina, I heard something similar. "Everyone in the South wants to know if you *belong,* who your people are," said Natalie Daise, one half of a husband-and-wife story-performing team. "I'm from Syracuse, New York, but my husband Ron grew up here on St. Helena Island. I've lived here for years, but people still call me 'Miss Ron.' It's not just a Gullah thing, it's very Old South. Ron's boyhood community was suspicious of the one next door. It's all very clannish, very tribal. The South is just that way."

I knew what she meant. Cornelia had made it clear that there are two groups of people in the world: Sapelo Islanders, and everyone else. She cast the dichotomy in color terms, which works because Sapelo is almost exclusively African-American, but it is really a land and locality-based division, rather than a racial one: insiders versus outsiders. The man who revealed the Gardner mystery to me also explained some of the current issues facing the island, the hottest of which was whether or not to pave the roads. He was against it. "Heck, right now, you can drive on Sapelo without a license, without plates, probably without a steering wheel. That'll all change with paved roads. But the serious issue is that it'll raise taxes, drive up property values, and pretty soon we won't be able to afford to live here. And if we lose this community, what will we have left that makes us special? We'll be just like everybody else."

His sense of uniqueness is common to many island dwellers, but also reflects a long-held Southern assumption that the South either once had, or still retains, something the rest of the country lacks. Like Orville Hicks, who's aware of his distinction among other men of his generation, the South is acutely mindful of its status as the American Otherworld. A woman interviewed by V. S. Naipaul for his 1989 book, *A Tour of the South,* summed up the attitude: "We are permeated by a feeling," she said, simply, "that the South is special." In *The Mind of the South,* W. J. Cash called it ". . . the general assumption of the South's great difference." When I earlier mentioned the "exceptionalists," I was referring to those who believe in this great difference: that the South is an exceptional place, different from mainstream America. What did Tolstoy say in *Anna Karenina* about happy families? "Happy families are all alike; every unhappy family is unhappy in its own way." The mythos of America is that it is a cheerful place, built on an unbroken chain of successes; the South, however, has a missing link in that chain. The Civil War made it the nation's unhappy family, brooding and fiercely parochial, perhaps, but *interesting,* different and unique.

Adjunct to this Southern sense of specialness, of singularity, is a defensive feeling of entitlement to make decisions about the land that has so shaped one's identity. If you live in an exceptional place, the argument goes that only you and others who live there know what's best for it. My informant on Sapelo went on to say that ultimately the crucial thing, whether the roads are paved or not, is that the people of Sapelo decide the issue for themselves. "We're an old African-American community. We survived all these years, and we don't want to be told what to do by no outsider," he said. At those words — spoken in 1999 by a proud black man — I felt a kind of historical headrush, and shivered. In more than a few interpretations, not being told what to do by no outsider was what Southerners fought for in the Civil War (according to many people I spoke to, slavery had little to do with *their* ancestors' motivations). Asked why he's fighting the Yankees, a character in a short story by Barry Hannah responds tersely, "You want to know what I'm fighting for? . . . For the North to keep off."

The North. It didn't just mean a geographic entity, it meant the Central Government bullying the states (the recent debate in South Carolina about the appropriateness of rebel stars and bars on the state flag is cast by its supporters as a states' rights issue). It meant the Industrial Complex behind the economic miracle of the nineteenth century, crushing the individual. It meant Big Government stripping away the rights of true democrats (democrats with a little "d"). And the ongoing Civil War — literally fought these days by earnest reenactors — is still about these things, except that now you don't have to be a Southerner to fight against the Union. In *Confederates in the Attic,* Tony Horowitz runs into a group of reenactors from New York who insist on taking Confederate parts. "Why?" he asks. "Because," one of them replies, "we don't like one group of people telling another what to do."

In the South, the legacy of this thinking has bred tough independence and place-loyalty, a very real identification with the land — which, through stories and traditions, generates that anchorage in the past that is so attractive to people like David Holt and me — but also a terrible mistrust of outsiders, an almost compulsive fear of Others and any kind of difference. I saw it in Renee Cathou's wary gaze. Vickie admitted to it in an e-mail. More importantly, I've heard it in the story record. Most of the classic Southern stories are about opposition, the pitting of one group against another, which also makes them concerned with winning and losing in a way that the "foreign" tales I encountered, such as "The Girl and the Fish," are not. There is Jack, the local lad, versus the giant (here Jack's "locality" is rooted in his humanity itself, as compared to the superhuman giant); Granny Griffin versus the folks from Bibb County; Brer Rabbit versus Brer Fox; the Mule-Egg Seller, the consummate local boy, versus the Outsiders, the know-nothing city dwellers who, it should be noted, were also Southerners. The Big Story here, of which all these individual tales are manifestations, is the South, the American Otherworld, versus the rest of the country. That place used to be called the North, but now it's really Generic, or Imperial, America (depends if your obsessions run to the social or political). As the Sapelo Islander said, if we become like everybody else, even if everybody is better off, we won't be special anymore.

I waited in the Burger King parking lot on the outskirts of Charleston, South Carolina, as Fouchena Sheppard had instructed. She was late — when I finally called her house she was still in the bathtub — so I got a cup of tea and bought breakfast for a homeless drunk named Leonard. When Fouchena and her elderly mother, Miss Viola, finally arrived, they were resplendent. Both were dressed in wide-brimmed hats and their Sunday best, and they drove a big old '67 Chrysler. We were all going to church together, and then Fouchena was going to tell me some Gullah stories. "We worship the old-fashioned, African-American way," she had warned me on the phone. "It might take some time."

I followed them, increasingly alarmed at the gas spewing out the back of Fouchena's car, on a circuitous route past the Charleston Mosquito Abatement Program and billboards advertising jail bonds and a clothing line called New South Apparel. The latter featured a startling logo: a slap-your-face version of the Confederate flag in African liberation colors, with the tag line, "For the Sons and Daughters of Former Slaves." Finally, we pulled into the parking lot of the Mt. Zion R.M.U.E. Church in North Charleston (the acronym means Reformed Methodist Union Episcopal, a small denomination that broke off from the much larger African Methodist Episcopal Church in 1885).

The church was crowded, and in my casual skirt and sandals I was egregiously underdressed. I was also a little alarmed at the length of the program — twenty pages — but when the visiting minister called for worship, I forgot about it and got caught up in the hush of anticipation like everyone else. It was the last time there would be peace and quiet for another three hours.

One of the first items of business was the suggested value of the day's offering. I was shocked. My memory of Tithes and Offerings time was my dad discreetly slipping two dollars into an envelope when I was a little girl. But this was a prix-fixe service, and it wasn't cheap: $20 a head. The congregation fussed at this, but soon got over it. What became clear as the morning progressed was that church members in turn expected a lot for their money. Going to church was not just about being saved, but being saved *in style*. Song. Dance. Excitement. They wanted their twenty dollars' worth, and they'd stay until they got it. When the collection plate came around, I was looking the other way and Miss Viola accidentally hit me on the head with it. She apologized and said, "If you get a bump, at least it's for Jesus."

We prayed; we were called upon and responded; we sang hymns; we listened to the choir; we clapped and moved our feet to the sound. There were no solos or anthems in this service; everyone knew the words, everyone sang along. The music, as Fouchena had promised, was good, but it wasn't Smokey Robinson and The Miracles. At one point the choir and the organist wandered into different keys and critiques instantly rumbled through the congregation. I was so far beyond my ken — one of God's frozen people, a Presbyterian even, surrounded by folks who actually *enjoyed* church, and didn't mind showing it — that I was in danger of converting the great, noisy, holy, and very air-conditioned gathering into some kind of two-dimensional postcard from The Black South. It was actually their fallibility, thank heavens, that kept the service anchored in reality for me.

Before long, women were up on their feet, swaying to the sound and waving like the Queen of England with one or both hands raised up high over their heads. "I hear you, Jesus!" said a lady behind me. "You tell 'em what Jesus said!" A few were taken by the Spirit. Whenever this happened, a team of appointed women, a kind of holy spirit patrol, jumped up and surrounded the chosen one ring-around-the-rosy style, to make sure she didn't hurt herself or anyone else. The woman in the circle slipped into a frenzied trance, eyes cast heavenward as she trembled, wept, shouted, and danced in a sweaty, ecstatic union with Jesus. God was respected here but not often invoked; Jesus, however, seemed a personal friend.

At one point I looked over and saw Miss Viola, just short of her ninetieth birthday, kneeling backwards on the hard linoleum floor and praying with her hands clasped on the pew. When she finished, she got up stiffly, adjusted the veil on her hat, and smoothed her sea-green chiffon dress, and said, "Thank you, Jesus, that was *great*." She seemed to be having such a good time; I *tried* not to be self-conscious, but the effort backfired in a vicious mental circle. It was a relief when the sermon began, although I — along with the minister, I think — soon lost the thread. I recall something about preparing Thanksgiving dinner, and then a dangling metaphor about reheating it all in the microwave. The content didn't matter: enthusiasm and emotion were the minister's goals, not coherent storytelling. The sermon was simply a means to a state of mind, or for some, a state of grace. Afterwards came a report from the Men's Committee. It was Men's Day at Mount Zion, the day of reckoning when the committee would have to announce how much they had collected on behalf of the church. When the final count was tallied, it seemed that they had come a thousand dollars short of the sum collected by the women. Hoots and howls filled the sanctuary. One woman brought out a dress that the committee chairman had promised to wear if his sex lost the race.

"Hey! There are more women in church than men," one gentleman rationalized loudly.

"That may be true," snapped Miss Viola, "but men make more money than women. Which," she muttered under her breath, "is just plain wrong."

Finally, it was time for people with things to say to speak out. Fouchena stood and offered a prayer for the Kennedy family. John Kennedy's plane had not yet been found, and she urged everyone to pray that he and his wife were still alive somewhere, as she believed in her heart. The congregation clapped and I thought I was home free, but then came the moment I was dreading: Recognition of Visitors.

"This is where you get up, Pamela," urged Fouchena, giving me a little shove. "Go on."

My heart pounding in my ears, I stood up and said that I was a friend of Fouchena's and Miss Viola's, visiting for the day. More polite clapping. My sunburned, white skin stood out like a sore thumb, but it was my shaking voice that banished every other form of embarrassment. I hate public speaking, and this was no exception. Afterwards, in the broiling parking lot, at least twenty people came up and welcomed me and shook my hand, warmly inviting me to join them again. Nearby, a group of teenage girls imitated the women who had been visited by the spirit, twisting and shaking and breaking themselves up into trills of giggles. Fouchena, clearly a figure of authority, gave them a Look, and they stalked off in adolescent haughtiness.

Fouchena lived in the Charleston Projects: block upon block of utilitarian public housing with its own maze of streets, filled with girls jumping rope and young men half-hidden under the hoods of old cars. Her apartment, where she has lived for twenty-seven years, was packed with mementos and books and furniture. Miss Viola changed into a shift dress and sat on a re-cliner in the middle of the living room to watch Special News Reports about JFK, Jr., as Fouchena braided her soft white hair into corn rows. "It's cooler for her," she explained. While she worked, she spoke about her background. Her voice was low and her words perfectly enunciated: each one reached my ears enveloped in its own package of breath. She never ran her words together or slurred them into a Southern accent. When I remarked on her exceptional speaking voice, she said she had taken a Toastmaster Training course.

"I'm one of seven," said Fouchena, "but I'm the only Geechee. I grew up here in South Carolina with my grand-mother, and we spoke Gullah." Her brothers and sisters, she said, had been raised elsewhere by other members of the fam-ily. "I thought everybody spoke Gullah, but I found out in school that white people had decided it wasn't a real language. We were punished for speaking it . . . I didn't allow my daugh-ter to speak it. After I graduated from secretarial school, I couldn't get a job because my accent was too heavy, and I didn't want that for her. That's when I went through Toast-master Training . . . and why I speak like this now."

I asked Fouchena to say something in her first language so I could hear the sound of it. Gullah is the result of a pidgin speech that sprang up on the Georgia and South Carolina coast during the days of the big slave markets, which combined English with several West African tongues. A pidgin is a synthetic language that has no native speakers but that arises when people of many different linguistic backgrounds come together. Eventually, this compromise tongue took over as the primary speech of the coastal community, and was spoken by whites as well as blacks as a first language. I recognized some words that have slipped into mainstream American English: *tote* means carry; *ashantie* means house; a *goober* is a peanut. Cornelia had shown me a written phrase, *UDAT?*, pronounced, "Who dat?" — literally, "Who is that?" — that my Cleveland-born father says all the time. But when Fouchena spoke, I was lost. I had no idea what she was saying (it turned out to be a Gullah proverb, "You don't see eagles fly with other birds, because eagles don't fly in a flock").

Linguists speculate that the word *Gullah* may derive from "Angola," and *Geechee* from "Gidzi," which is the name of a people and language from Liberia. Whatever their ancestry, the two terms mean more or less the same thing. Cornelia prefers Geechee; Ron and Natalie Daise, who used to have a children's show on cable television called Gullah Gullah Island, don't use Geechee anymore. "It's come to mean something like 'hick,'" said Natalie. They like the more anthropological "Gullah."

Once again, my experience living in Wales and learning Welsh came to my aid. Welsh was my conduit for empathizing with speakers of Gullah. Welsh, too, had been marginalized as an inferior, older, useless language. Not long ago, parents who wanted their children to get on in the world refused to teach it to them. I started to explain this to Fouchena, but the television had broken into her attention and held it rapt. JFK, Jr.'s luggage had been found scattered along a Martha's Vineyard beach. She looked at me with tears in her eyes and said, "I pray to Jesus he's still alive. I refuse to give up hope. I can still see him saluting his daddy's coffin when he was a little boy."

The depth of Fouchena's faith so conditioned her relationship to probability that it almost placed us in different perceptual worlds. I wanted to say to her, "Look, it's very sad, but the evidence that the man is dead is overwhelming," though I knew she wouldn't believe me. For Fouchena, prayer was capable of achieving miracles; for all I knew, maybe she was right. She told me that the greatest influence in her life had been her grandmother, who sneaked spirituality into her world when she was a teenager.

"My grandmother's Gullah stories weren't religious, but even within their secular context they taught morals and ethics," said Fouchena. "So she told me stories, and tried to get me to go to church. I was the seventh child — the seventh child is of particular significance in West African tradition — and she believed I was born to be a leader, but no way could she get me into church. I would read to her from the Bible everyday, she especially liked Psalms and Proverbs, and she eventually learned to read to herself when she was sixty-seven, but she knew I wasn't taking it in. So she used my world: she taught me to sing and dance to the scriptures."

Fouchena got up, and there in the crowded, little apartment began to do the Twist. "She let me dance to pop songs," she explained, swinging her hips, "but I couldn't sing along. I had to set the tune to one of the Psalms. So instead of 'Let's Twist again, like we did last summer,'" sang Fouchena, "I'd go, 'All right! To God be the glory . . . ,'" and she twisted to the floor and corkscrewed back up again. "The boys thought I was a tease, but that's how my grandmother reached me."

As Fouchena moved into the Grind, it occurred to me that the proverb she had spoken for me in Gullah was a self-description. She had been ostracized for her language, her dyslexia, her race, her poverty, and even this morning the teenagers at church had made fun of her spiritual zeal (she had been one of the women taken by the spirit). And yet, using white society's tools of language and education, Fouchena had shaped herself into her own proud creation. She showed me the South Carolina African American History Calendar for 1997: she was February's success story.

Later in the afternoon she told me one of her grandmother's family tales about "slavery time." Like Vickie Vedder, Fouchena went far back into her remembrance and inhabited the memory of her grandmother. She began humming, and tilting her head to one side, absently started to stir an invisible pot of beans. When the story was finished and Fouchena returned to the present, something had changed. Perhaps she had revealed too much of herself; whatever the case, there had been a transgression, and she drew back into herself like a frightened tortoise. I instantly knew it was time to go. Shortly afterward she got in touch and asked me not to reproduce the story in my book.

During our interview Fouchena told me she likes to take stock of her audience before she decides what to tell them; no wonder she was afraid of casting a narrative piece of her family's soul out on the wing of a book that might take light anywhere, in any reader's hands. In place of her story I opted to include a condensed version of an old Gullah folktale rendered into English by the writer John Bennett at the turn of the last century. It was told to him by a laborer named Caesar Grant from John's Island, South Carolina, and published in Bennett's

188

1943 collection, *The Doctor to the Dead*. Ron and Natalie Daise, with whom I met only briefly in Beaufort, mentioned the story as *The People Could Fly*; Bennett called it *All God's Chillen Had Wings*. (Natalie also mentioned another of her favorite Gullah stories called *Seven in One Blow*, about a hero who kills seven flies on a peanut-butter and jelly sandwich, and never lets on that he hasn't actually killed seven men. "Big man Jack killed seven at a whack!" I had shouted, startling her and improbably summoning the memory of Orville Hicks telling *Jack and the Varmints* into her exquisite, art-filled home. I guess a mountain man's mud puddle is a Gullah woman's peanut-butter and jelly sandwich.)

THE FLYING AFRICANS

Once all Africans could fly like birds, but owing to their many transgressions, their wings had been taken away. There remained, in the sea islands, some who had been overlooked, and had retained the power of flight.

There was a cruel master on one of the sea islands who drove his people till they died with overwork in the burning summer sun, through the middle hours of the day, although this was against the law.

One day, when all the worn-out Negroes were dead of overwork, he bought a company of native Africans just brought into the country, and put them at once to work in the cottonfield . . . There was among them one young woman who had lately borne a child. She had not fully recovered from bearing, and should not have been sent to the field. She had her child with her, as the other women had, astraddle on her hip, or piggy-back.

The baby cried. She spoke to quiet it, then she went back to chopping knot grass, but being very weak, and sick with the great heat, she stumbled and fell.

The driver struck her with his lash until she rose and staggered on.

She spoke to an old man near her, the oldest man of them all. He replied, "Not yet, daughter; not yet."

Soon she stumbled and fell again. But when the driver came running to lash her she turned to the old man and asked: "Is it time yet, daddy?" He answered: "Yes, daughter; the time has come. Go; and peace be with you!"

With that she leaped straight up into the air and was gone like a bird, flying over the field and wood, her baby astraddle of her hip, sucking at her breast.

Soon another man fell. The driver lashed him. He turned to the old man. The old man cried out to him, and he leaped up, and was gone through air, flying like a bird over the field and wood.

Then the overseer cried to the driver, and the master cried to them both: "Beat the old devil! He is the doer!"

But the old man laughed in their faces, and said something loudly to all the Negroes in the field, the new Negroes and the old Negroes.

And as he spoke to them, they all remembered what they had forgotten, and recalled the power which had once been theirs. Then all the Negroes stood up together; the old man raised his hands; and they all leaped up into the air with a great shout; and in a moment were gone, flying, like a flock of crows, over the field, over the fence, over the top of the wood; and behind them flew the old man.

Where they went I do not know; I was never told. Nor what it was that the old man said . . . that I have forgotten. But as he went over the last fence he made a sign in the master's face, and cried, "Kuli-ba! Kuli-ba!" I don't know what that means.

Minerva's Tale

I'm gonna sit at the welcome table,
I'm gonna sit at the welcome table one of these days,
Hallelujah! I'm gonna sit at the welcome table
I'm gonna sit at the welcome table one of these days
One of these days
One of these days

I DON'T KNOW IF THAT SONG SOUNDS FAMILIAR to you," said Minerva King, "but that's a song that comes out of the Southern black church, and that song was popularized during the civil rights movement, from 1955 to the late sixties. Liz, I don't know about you, you grew up in Kansas, but you have an idea of what things were like during the civil rights period, here in South Carolina, right? I think you're old enough to know a little about that . . ."

"Not really," said Liz, a lovely African-American woman about twenty-five years old. "I don't know much."

"How about you, Pam?"

"I am definitely old enough," I said, "but I grew up in New Jersey, so what little I knew came from the TV."

"Well," said Minerva, tucking her long, flowing, tie-dyed dress around her and kicking off her purple Birkenstocks, "I'm going to tell it as somebody who lived it.

That was one of the popular songs. Another one was,

Oh, freedom, oh freedom, oh freedom over me, over me
And before I'll be a slave I'll be buried in my grave,
And go home to my Lord and be free, and be free . . .

Of course during the civil rights movement we'd change the words to some of those songs. For example,

Paul and Silas bound in jail, had no money for to go their bail
Keep your hands on the plow, Hold on, hold on . . .

That became,

Paul and Silas bound in jail, had no money for to go their bail,
Keep your eyes on the prize, Hold on, hold on . . .

Being the heathen that I am, I wrote this in my notes as "All in silence bound in jail . . . ," and only discovered later, much to my shame, that it was Paul and Silas.

But of course, probably the most popular song during the civil rights movement was one that started right here in Charleston, South Carolina. Back between October 1947 and April of 1948, there was a strike at the American Tobacco Company. Working conditions were horrible; people were earning anywhere from thirty-five cents an hour to forty-seven cents an hour, tops. And, of course, these were primarily women, a lot of women, a lot of black women. And the conditions were very unsafe, very unhealthy. Ventilation was quite, quite poor. People used to get sick all the time. Well, there was already a labor union in place, so the people who worked there got connected with that union, and they went on strike.

Now this was practically unheard of in the South in 1947. It lasted, as I said, for six months. The women picketed everyday, and during a point where the negotiations were not going well at all, and people's spirits were sagging, this one woman from John's Island came up and she started singing.

I want to walk with Him, I want to talk with Him, I want to walk
    with Him, one day
Oh, down in my heart, I do believe, I want to walk with Him
    one day.

And that just sort of lifted the spirits of the people. And they had the motivation and the drive and the energy to continue on their strike. Unfortunately it wasn't an altogether successful movement, but it was a beginning. And it showed people what could be done when people got together and pooled their energy.

Well that woman, Alice Wine, had the occasion to go to a place in Tennessee called Highlander Folk School, where she taught it to Zilfia Horton, the wife of Miles Horton, the school's founder. Now Zilfia was a professional folklorist and folk singer. And she took the song on one of her trips to New York City, and she taught it to Pete Seeger. And together Zilfia Horton and Pete Seeger changed some of the words around, and they added new verses to it, and of course, do you recognize it?

Minerva began to sing, "We Shall Overcome . . ." I looked at Liz who was sitting, bare arms clasped around herself, shivering in the heat. She was staring at Minerva as if she had just descended from Olympus.

And that song became the symbol of the civil rights movement. And it traveled all over the country. Pete Seeger took it and taught it to other people. And they sang it in Albany, Georgia, and they sang it in Selma, Alabama; [the grape pickers] sang it in Oakland, California.

But the song wasn't satisfied by staying just in this country. In the 1960s Mau Mau raiders sang it in East Africa in Kenya. It later went to Czechoslovakia, and to Poland. Lech Walesa and his Solidarity people sang it in Polish. The students in Tiananmen Square sang it ten years ago in China. So it shows the power of a song.

. . . When I was twelve years old in 1956 . . . my father was the state president of the NAACP . . . so we grew up in my family in the civil rights movement. Someone asked me a few years ago, "How did you put up with that?" I said, "Put up? We thought everybody lived like that." We were used to crosses being burned on our front lawn . . . We thought everybody lived like that. We were accustomed to the telephone calls in the middle of the night . . . You know, crosses burned by the Klan . . .

My sister, who lives in Savannah, taught us to always answer the telephone after the first or second ring. Because people used to call at two, three, four o'clock in the morning to wake us up. They threatened to burn our house, bomb our house, kill us . . . So she said, "Listen, we're not going to let these people know they're annoying us," so she taught us to answer that phone after the first, second ring at the most, with the most cheerful, "Hello!" And eventually they got tired and they stopped.

But I can remember as a kid, about ten or twelve years old, going on the city bus, not planning it, but going on the bus. And in those days of course the buses were segregated. White people sat in the front, black people sat in the back. We didn't really plan it, but a girl-friend and I decided we're just going to . . . Well, we sat in that long seat that's opposite that one behind the driver. We just plopped ourselves down. And the driver didn't tell us to move. But he just turned around like this [turns], and I will never forget as long as I live the look on that man's face. Those steel gray eyes. And he said to us, "Live dangerously, die young."

Liz gasped, and I mouthed "Wow." We were sitting in the reception area of a homeless men's shelter, not far from

Fouchena Sheppard's apartment, where both women were volunteers. Immediately after leaving the Projects, I had driven to the shelter to meet Minerva. The staff kept the door locked until seven, when residents could begin to turn in for the night, which meant that when I arrived at five the courtyard was full of men, both black and white, who had nothing to do but wait. Walking past them to ring the bell, I expected harassment, but got only a few raised hats, one bow, and an offer to share a young man's Chinese takeout.

Minerva was a powerhouse: a librarian, storyteller, adjunct professor, substitute teacher, and volunteer. She was also smart, down-to-earth, funky, and as relaxed as Fouchena had been wary. Both women had a wealth of self-confidence, but Minerva's was innate, a perk of class and personality; Fouchena's was learned. When I complimented Minerva on her shoes she said, "When I'm an old woman I shall wear purple and red and spit on the sidewalk whenever I please."

She had planned to tell me "The Flying Africans," but Liz asked about "the civil rights time," and at our urging Minerva changed her mind and told us the story of her life. Men kept ringing and knocking and interrupted the flow: one man had soiled himself, another had been sick, another pleaded to come in early. Yet she never lost the beat, each time returning to her forty-year-old memories as if she had been presenting the evening news. In fact, not that long ago, her story had *been* the evening news — the same medium that had lately been a thorn in my side, or rather my ear. In fact, listening to Minerva made me wonder where the news ended and storytelling began. A Welsh friend once told me that on a tour of the American South she had encountered an old man in Mississippi who left his television on twenty-four hours a day. She had found it hard to converse with him and asked him why he didn't turn it off. "Because I love stories," he'd replied.

The issue, of course, is one of timeliness and veracity. The news is supposed to be "objective"; stories are assumed to be marinated in the particularness of place and personality. Yet pull back far enough, find the bird's-eye view so distant that it links present and past, and they merge: folktales, legends — which folklorist John Burrison defines as "accounts of events believed by the teller and his audience to have actually occurred" — and the news all become episodes in the same, ongoing story.

Another tale from these parts deals with the consequences of black people taking matters into their own hands. Like Minerva's, it is about resistance, but because it is set during the time of slavery and its heroes don't have wings, it ends in tragedy rather than triumph. "Ebo Landing" begins with a shipment of slaves, including members of the Ibo, or Ebo, tribe, arriving at a landing in the Low Country. One version sets the location in St. Simons, Georgia. The slaves from other tribes stand on the docks waiting to be inspected, but the Ebo are proud, and refuse to submit to the slave drivers. They watch the others being sold, and then at a nod from their leader, still in chains and shackles, the Ebo tribespeople walk off the boat and march, chanting, into the sea. "The water took us," they sing, "and the water shall take us away." Tellers add a modern coda: on clear nights, they say, you can sit on Ebo Landing and still hear the sound of the slaves chanting as they drown themselves, over and over again, for eternity.

Like a sudden, quick glimpse of clear sky through clouds, I heard in Minerva's memories echoes of those same chants, and gripped my arms around me, shivering, as Liz had done earlier. She really was telling us the same story she had set out to tell.

I can remember as a little kid going down to the department stores in Charleston, and at that point, restrooms were segregated. Blacks couldn't try on clothing in some stores, couldn't try on hats in some stores. We had separate water fountains . . . They were right next to each other, but there was the white water fountain and there was the colored water fountain. It wasn't black in those days, it was "colored." And I can remember being the mischievous little child that I was, drinking out of the white water fountain and saying to my mother, "Mom, it tastes the same as the colored water . . ."

Charleston, you know, is a peninsula, it's practically surrounded by water. And back in those days you had black beaches and you had white beaches. And you know when I go into schools and tell the students about this, they just sit there with their mouths open. "How could that be?" Well, that just shows the absurdity of the whole system. How in Sam Heck are you going to be able to separate the water? But they would have these poles going out — I don't know how far — into the water, and whites swam on one side and blacks swam on the other. And that's the way it was . . .

I was the plaintiff in the local school desegregation suit . . . I was a senior that year in high school. And they dragged their feet and dragged their feet, and before you knew it I graduated. But my father, in his infinite wisdom, very quickly changed my name to my younger sister's name — my sister's four years younger — and she was able to see it through. So she ended up desegregating the schools in Charleston . . .

When I was fifteen I was in the group that desegregated — or tried to desegregate — the local lunch counters . . . We prepared for several weeks. We did a lot of role-playing, and we chose a day there was no school, so everybody would be available . . . And we dressed up and we were driven downtown, and there were twenty-four of us in the group . . . Word got out that we were coming, but we had a contingency plan. We diverted to another facility. And those folks had not been warned. We walked in a straight line all the way to the back — I don't know about Kansas, Liz, but in the South blacks were allowed to shop in dime stores, but they had lunch counters, and you couldn't eat at the lunch counters. So we got there and we sat down. And of course they were taken for a loop, they didn't know we were coming. And they told us to get up, we don't serve you. And threatened to call the police. We still didn't move. They poured ammonia on the whole counter — you know how strong ammonia can be? — to try to get us to move. We still didn't move. We ended up sitting there, without getting up to use the restrooms and without eating anything . . . for five and a half hours at that lunch counter. And then finally they said somebody phoned in a bomb threat. Which was kind of stupid — Yes, there's a bomb threat, but employees are walking around the store, people are in the store. Yeah, right. We were arrested at that point. We were taken down to the city jail. I think one of us was fingerprinted, then they just said, this is ridiculous. So we were bailed out . . . that was my first time going to jail.

My second time was about three years later — by that time I'd graduated from high school and gone on to undergraduate school in Missouri. Well, I was home for the summer. And by this time — we're talking 1963 — the movement had really escalated. We were having these nightly mass meetings at the churches. And they served two purposes. One, to keep people informed of what was going on. We had the boycott, people needed to know which stores not to go to, and so on. And they also served the purpose of keeping up the momentum, so people wouldn't get too relaxed, and would continue to be pumped up about the movement. Anyhow, at that point, our local newspaper — it's still very, very conservative, but not as conservative as it was back in those days — they kept publishing these very slanted stories about the movement. Well, we decided, we'll get them, and we planned a silent protest. Of course it was all done very spontaneously. We marched from the church down to the Post & Courier building. Well, when we got almost there, they said somebody threw a rock. This was never, ever proven, but it gave the police a reason, and they just started snatching people, just grabbing people out of the crowd. And I just happened to be in the right place at the right time, so I got snatched . . .

They put us on this bus, like a converted school bus . . . I think there's humor to be found in every human situation, and this is no exception. They forgot to lock the back door of the bus. And so when some of the guys realized this, they jumped out the back door. They didn't run home — the whole point was to be there to protest — so they just came right around to the front of the bus, where they got arrested again. I know some guys who were arrested four times that night . . . You know, didn't I see you a couple of arrests back? . . . Well, finally they locked the back door and they took us to the city jail.

That city jail is just the most horrible thing. It's not even open anymore. They called it the Seabreeze Hotel. It was right on the edge of the Cooper River. It was the dinkiest place. There were thirty-one of us. I think there were sixteen girls, and they put us all in one cell. Of course it was summertime, so it was hot, so hot. It was awful. We were there for three nights and four days. Of course, no privacy whatsoever. I think there was one toilet, two beds . . . Anyhow, the NAACP bailed us out, and that was pretty much the end of my Civil Rights activity.

Minerva went on to university, and graduate school, and never lost her fire. When a nonminority person was promoted above her at the Charleston County Library, she filed a grievance and won. Eventually, many years later, she was terminated from her job. "I was fired," she said, "not because I wasn't a good librarian or library manager. Instead, I was fired because I REFUSED to be treated like a second-class citizen."

Tom's Tale

I HAD BEEN IN CHARLESTON, South Carolina for twenty-four hours and had not seen so much as a square foot of the historic district — the pastel townhouses of Rainbow Row, the piazzas, the gardens, the filigreed ironwork balconies, the harbor views, that made it "probably the loveliest city in the continental United States," as my guidebook claimed. After I left the homeless shelter, I retreated to a motel on a commercial strip and spent the evening drinking wine and eating rubbery calamari at the bar at Red Lobster. For a short time I wanted to avoid distinction and bask in uniformity (if one can actually bask, that is, in a world entirely lacking depth).

I returned to my motel room to find a new e-mail from Vickie.

Hi Pam!

I was happy to hear from you . . . kind of like when my daughter writes to me from Korea. The whole e-mail experience is like Christmastime when Santa "leaves you something" — sometimes something that you really want, which, generally, in ordinary life, is acknowledgment from others that you count . . .

As soon as I finish editing the stories about the Dead Man, Sister Collins, and the Bald-headed Bohannon Boys, I will send them to you . . .

As I told you when you were visiting me . . . I am always encouraged when I read the words of the blues songs and can relate to them — there is pain and conflict to Southern life that gets bypassed in discussion. What I mean is: there is a line drawn for no humane reason between blacks and whites as if one suffered more than the other, maybe because the emphasis is always put on slavery. But my own belief puts me in a position to disagree with that. I wish I had better words than I do, and I wish I could articulate my gut feeling when I explain this. There is a common element that connects us (Southerners, black and white) — and I hope it is what disconnects us from innocent Northerners or Westerners. In the South, the blacks and whites are intertwined in wrongdoing — a vicious cycle of hurt. I say that from the perspective of a participant in family violence. When one person (a family or society) commits a violent act on some other person, both people end up hurt. It may take some time for the offender to recognize this, or he may never, but what happens is that the air becomes filled with a tension and a pain, a spiritual hurt . . . In my opinion the South is full of misunderstanding about itself . . .

What is important, I think, is if you're trying to form some opinion about one person in the South, you are usually forced to form an opinion about the whole group first. People say, "What happened to make the South so factious? Are you aware you're pulling in separate directions?" Some people do know; some people don't. I think we (Southerners) have an innocence and ignorance that breeds this kind of separatism. My experience has been that too much focus is placed on blame (black), with obstinacy (white) holding back the help it would take to fully integrate a misplaced culture . . . Nowadays, years after the Civil War, I observe the reverse of what I just said. Blacks are obstinate, and whites blame. Just like family violence, there is a dependence on the other fellow to bend, and until he does, you stalemate. I've seen this in my own family, and it is very analogous to Southern culture as a whole. I see no end to the conflict, no matter how much effort is made by the church, the government, or welfare. Granny would have said, "It'll take the Second Coming to straighten out that mess."

Well, thanks for giving me something to do tonight. I made a pound cake — used a new recipe — MISTAKE. Warmed up spaghetti, drank a glass of "warm" white wine — MISTAKE, not good . . . I ended up acting like Granny Griffin. A flea jumped on my foot — I "grabbed 'im" and toted him to the commode, which is the only sure way not to lose 'im once't ye got 'im 'tween ye thumb and forefanger. What reminded me of Granny was that I TALKED to him all the way to the bathroom! I told 'im: "If you'd a been a smart boy, you would'na got trapped. But no, you couldn't do right no more'n a rattlesnake can be sweet. And THAT'S what got'che in the fix ye in. Now, heah ye go: swim'r drown'd!!!" Can you believe that? . . . We had a wild dog hanging around the back porch, and I feel pretty sure he left me with his dear traveling companions . . .

See you later,

Sincerely, Vickie Vedder

"My theory is that air conditioning revolutionized the South."

At that very moment it was freeze-drying the sweat on my bare arms and legs. Vickie's message of the previous evening was still too hot to handle, I had to let it cool, let it become freighted with faces and names, before I could truly understand what she had said. So for the time being, I had decided to become a tourist. I'd wandered into Charleston's Visitors Center thinking I would take a tour of the city, but was unprepared for the interactive supermarket of options I found. I could take a Ghost tour, a Gullah tour, a Garden tour, a Graveyard tour, an Historic House tour, a walking tour, a bus tour, a group tour, a personal tour. I wound up letting a tourist official decide for me. As it turned out, the tour guide, Tom Dew, and I were the only ones to show up at the appointed place and time. He was all for canceling, until I shamelessly mentioned that I was writing a book. He shamelessly offered to drive me around in his very air-conditioned van and give me his personal take on the city. It was a short, but symbiotic, relationship.

Crowded onto its small peninsula — Tom made a helpful analogy with Lower Manhattan, with the Ashley River standing in for the Hudson, the Cooper for the East River, and Fort Sumpter as the Statue of Liberty — Charleston, as he presented it, was glamorous, insular, and thoroughly seduced by its own superlatives. The oldest *English* city south of Virginia. (The Spanish were already ensconced when Scotch-Irish immigrants arrived in the late seventeenth century. "There was a big turf war," said Tom, smiling. "We won.") One of only three walled cities in North America, the others being St. Augustine in Florida and Quebec City. The richest city in America before the Civil War, with 90–95 percent of white families owning slaves. The biggest slave importation depot in North America. The city that first voted to secede from the union. The only city in the original thirteen colonies that knew, that is, its white citizens knew, how to have a good time.

"We have the oldest theater in the U.S.," boasted Tom, as we dashed through neighborhoods of old trophy houses, their stucco, brick, and clapboard exteriors gleaming again, thanks to recent tourist dollars. Ironically, it was only because Charleston was so devastated by the Civil War that there had been no money to tear old houses down and build ones. These days, the city's chief resource is its architecture of antebellum arrogance.

"Prostitution was legal here until after World War II," he continued. "Up there in New England, while you were waiting around for the afterlife, we in the South had a culture of immediacy. The first act here was the Freedom of Religion Act, which was really the Freedom from Catholicism Act, but it opened the way for incredible diversity. Religious freedom was the greatest marketing tool in the world at the time. See, once upon a time you Northerners were the conservative ones, with a totalitarian grip on religion; we were the liberal free-thinkers, down here in the South. Getting rich was considered a good, healthy thing. Look there," he pointed, "that's the First Scots Presbyterian Church."

As we passed the appropriately somber 1731 building, Tom told me its nickname: the Silent Church. Its bells had been melted down for the war effort, and never replaced. "The saying goes," quoted Tom, "that for as long as the Confederate dead lie silent, so will our church."

As Tom drove, I began to sense a tributary of the Mason-Dixon line running down the middle of the van. Nowhere else, apart from Cyclorama, had I encountered such a long shadow of the Civil War. "I guess," said a friend of mine, who had recently spent time in the Balkans as a refugee advocate, "we had our Kosovo in the nineteenth century." The comparison hit home. Tom's vocabulary was still polarized into "we's" and "you's." "I'm a Southerner," he'd said, "and any Southerner will tell you, deep down, we wish we had won the war, and you had lost." I appreciated his honesty, but it made me uncomfortable. His "we" not only excluded me, but gave me three choices of sentiment by way of response: guilt, sympathy, or a kind of knee-jerk, adversarial wrath. None of them suited my mood. I felt more uncomfortable with this handsome blond man than I did with Fouchena or Minerva. He certainly bore a greater grudge, but then his people had greater reason to miss the old days.

After about an hour, we stopped and picked up Tom's beautiful baby — his wife had to go off to work — fastened him into the back seat, and kept touring. Before long we'd left the SOB quarter (among other things, it stands for South of Broad, referring to the oldest and most exclusive part of the city), and ventured into a dismal neighborhood of uniform drabness. Tom pulled up in front of an old masonry building with barred windows, and unsuccessfully tried to find some shade. I focused the air-conditioning vent on my face as he put the van into neutral. "All right," he said as his son gurgled happily in the back, "I'm going to tell you a ghost story. The city has hundreds of them, but this is the story of Lavinia Fisher. And this, by the way," he said, indicating the ramshackle building, "was once the city jail."

THE STORY OF LAVINIA FISHER

In 1822 a woman and her husband were held here while they stood trial, and were convicted during the trial of being murderers. They ran an inn called the Six Mile Inn, which is on the way into town. There was also a Four Mile Inn, and so on . . .

Their names were John and Lavinia Fisher. You see, a man who was almost their victim escaped and made it into the city, and the police went out and arrested them. They'd suspected them, you understand, because travelers were disappearing. So this huge trial is held. And it's an amazing spectacle . . . so many people were intrigued. There's talk of witchcraft, they think she's a sorceress. She was the first woman ever convicted and sentenced to die in this country.

Well, the day of execution comes and her husband is hung first. There is a gallows set up with two nooses. And there's a huge crowd.

Over two thousand people came to watch her die. And she was also — this is important too — she was said to be an incredibly beautiful woman. The man who was almost their victim, who turned them in, is a guy named John Peoples. He's a skin trader, a country bumpkin. He lived miles from Charleston. He'd been saving up this wagon of skins that he was going to bring to the big city to get a better price. And so he stops at the Six Mile Inn to grab a place to rest, and she immediately tries to seduce him. Now he knows that there's something wrong there, that he isn't deserving of such an advance. He described her as having long, curly brown hair. She had a very full figure, and big brown eyes. He described her as the most beautiful woman he'd ever seen, and said he was not a man that she would be attracted to. So he hides in his room. He makes a pallet and makes it look like he's in his bed. So when they attack he is able to get away.

The trial comes. The husband is hanged. He's dangling. She walks up the gallows. She kisses him on the mouth. She gives her dead husband a full kiss. Before he died he blamed it on his wife, he said she made him do it. Well, it's time for her address. She turns to the crowd, and they said she spoke with a confidence born of insanity. She said, "If any of you here have a message for my devil, you better give it to me now, for I am about to meet him." And she was hung.

This is where she was kept during the trial. And her ghost was known to return to the jail cell where she was held, from 1822 to 1886. Sixty-four years she was trapped here until an earthquake destroyed the jail. They think that symbolically and physically her vault — the jail — was opened and she was released. And that is why she's not returned. But notice where we are. We're in the middle of a housing project. This is low-income housing. But there's no vandalism. There's no graffiti. The grounds of this place are never messed with, because the black population is so terrified of this building. You ask people about this place, and they are scared to death of it. This was a Victorian prison. There was a crank in here. People were tortured. Only white people were kept here. The black jail was actually more lenient.

And that is the story of Lavinia Fisher.

I wrote in my notebook, "With Lavinia, who needs plat-eyes?" I added a few minutes later, "White ghost story in black neighborhood." I wouldn't have been thinking in racial terms if Tom hadn't indicated on the way here that Charleston prac-ticed a kind of de facto segregation. Blacks and whites over-lapped for a few middling streets, but two blocks south of the mixing ground lay an all-white world, and two blocks north lay an all-black one. He said that the city had always supported a brown-skinned elite — I thought of Minerva's family — but that even today the professional classes held few African-American members. There was strife, he said, but there was also "a sweetness here," as he put it. Charleston was a civil city, and no one forgot it. Minerva, surprisingly, had agreed. She'd told me, "Charleston is just as racist, just as ugly, as any other city in the South. But during the protests they never had dogs. We just don't do that here. Even the racists were polite people."

It was past noon in my mind's eye, and Tom and Minerva had begun to cast shadows into Vickie's message, giving it some substance. What I understood from their comments was, We may not get along, but everyone here has something in com-mon, has learned the same lessons, one of which is manners. Place, in a sense, has made us family. Not similar by any means, and more often opposed than united, but like a dysfunctional family we are related in our opposition. And since we know this opposition like the backs of our hands — it has a history, we understand it — we would damn well rather deal with one another than a bunch of busybody Northern outsiders.

In *Red Hills and Cotton,* published in 1942, Ben Robertson

extended the family metaphor to geographical regions of the state. He wrote about the difference between the South Carolina upland where he was from — the area around Walhalla, where I visited Nancy Basket — and the Low Country. "We did not care for magnolias — they were swampy; and as for white columns, we considered them pretentious." He went on to say that "We were Southerners, native-born of the heart of the South, but we preferred the ways of Salem, Massachusetts . . . The North was our mother country," and essentially saddled Charleston and its evil, soft-living ways with the onus for the Civil War. "The Charleston idea, which also became the Mobile-Natchez idea, the idea of all the low countries and deltas, was beaten by the troops of the Federal Union, and Charleston, in losing, took all of us in all the upcountries along with it." Robertson felt that the tragedy of the hills was that its inhabitants didn't hate Charleston enough; and yet, cresting above this tide of bitterness, his conclusion was: "[Charleston] was Southern also and its relationship with us in the hills was always a family affair." The geography that divided the South also, ultimately, yoked it together in a stormy, fatal, familial bond.

I turned the air conditioning vent away because I had chills of my own. This was not an insight that made me feel all warm and cozy. Families, as Robertson knew, can be troubled, destructive units, and in Charleston's the shadows of racial coding fell even into the stories it told itself at bedtime. The most disturbing tale in John Bennett's *The Doctor to the Dead* — "Madam Margo" — concerns a beautiful mulatto woman who sells her soul to the devil so that her daughter may become white. As her daughter pales and prospers, she simultaneously darkens and falls into filth, slovenliness, and poverty. The coda to Tom's story, linking low-income housing and the black population without a word of explanation, confirmed that the two states — destitution and blackness — are still twinned in the Charleston mindset.

But the jail also called to mind another of Bennett's stories. "When the Dead Sang in Their Graves" is about a cemetery gatekeeper and his dog. Appropriately, it takes place in the dog days of summer, the same weather Tom's air conditioning was holding at bay. In the story the evening is hot and still, unnaturally so. Thunder whispers in the distance, and with it a tolling bell, signaling an approaching funeral. But no procession arrives. The dog is uneasy, and the gatekeeper begins to hear a distant song buoyed in the air by many voices. Then the earth cracks open and the dead emerge, singing, in a confusion of bones and moldering garments and splintered coffins. Bennett writes, "Next day came the earthquake. The dog and the dead knew."

It was the same earthquake that freed Lavinia. A Gullah storyteller had taken the results — wrecked graves tossed above ground by the heaving earth — and by altering the chronology of events made sense of a natural disaster, just as Alice's senseless drowning had been assigned to thwarted love. I asked Tom why he thought Charleston was so rich in ghost stories. As I suspected, he had an answer. A multipart answer.

"There are three critical elements leading to Charleston's being a haunted city. The first is age; ghosts are a function of time spent in a place. More dead people, more stories. The second goes back to the Freedom of Religion Act. Every faith has a spiritual realm, and they all got mixed together here. Plus, you had great density of slaves, and this brought African polytheism into the culture. There are survivals today."

By way of example, Tom told me about Miss Rosabell, the nanny who cares for his son. Even in summer, she wraps plastic around her body underneath her clothing; according to her, the evil eye can't penetrate plastic.

"Wow." I wondered if her antiperspirant were up to the job.

He went on to say that he had three chairs in his house that were crooked. "Rosabell won't sit in them. She believes they've been hexed in some way. She assigns the problem a spiritual cause, when I would say it's a flaw in the design. It comes down to a difference in perception." I remembered Fouchena's refusing to believe that John Kennedy, Jr,. was dead. It wasn't a difference in race, it was a difference in faith.

"The third thing," continued Tom, "is tragedy. I like to say that Charleston was cursed by the hand of God and man. We've had more natural and manmade disasters than anywhere else in the country. Eighteen hurricanes; five fires; two earthquakes. You want to know why there's no Spanish moss here? Hurricane Hugo swept it away in 1989. Parts of the city were under seven feet of water. We've fought the Spanish, the French, the Indians. There were more Revolutionary War battles here than in any other colony, only they've been omitted from the Northern history books because of the Civil War. We were bombarded for 587 consecutive days in that war — I think it's a record. Then there's disease. We've had epidemics of cholera, smallpox, typhoid, yellow fever, malaria, whooping cough. Our graveyards are saturated with unfinished business."

Tom capped off his thesis with isolation: after the war the South was left to contemplate its own unfinished destiny with little interruption. "You in the North received wave upon wave of immigrants, so that the culture, the memories, became diluted. Not here. We were left alone to think about what we'd done, and what had been done to us. Our ghosts were restless, and our stories bred and festered."

By this time Tom had cruised back downtown, and we said our mutual thank-yous at Charleston's Circular Church. Owing to some of the disasters he'd mentioned, the structure itself was new, built in 1891; the graves, however, were old by American standards. I stopped in front of one slate tombstone and copied out, "In memory of Mr. Isaac Holmes of Charleston. Merchant. He was a tender Hufband, an affectionate Parent, an indulgent Mafter, and a sincere Christian. d. 1763, aged thirty-four years." What, I wondered, had taken Isaac? Tom was right: what are ghosts but unfinished business? In fact, what is the South itself, the old idea of the South, that modern cities like Atlanta are racing so mightily to outrun, but a kind of national ghost story — an unavoidable chunk of the continental United States haunting America's image of itself?

The culture, the economy, the entire society of Isaac Holmes and his descendants were left incomplete, unfinished, by the Civil War. Few people want that society back again. even supporters of the Confederate flag, like Colonel Rod and his wife Brenda, do not condone slavery or its latter-day shadow, segregation. To them the flag is a tribute to Confederate soldiers, not to the world their victory would have preserved. "We do not like hate groups taking up our flag to spread their hate," said Colonel Rod. "That is not what this flag is about."

Few may want to return to antebellum days, but they don't want the rest of the country's past, or rather, the unfamiliar liberal mores and hard-nosed work ethics that have grown out of it, to complete the Southern story. That is for the South to do. The crucial thing to take from this place is the fact that its story remains unfinished; this is why the South, forever bearing its tragedy of a dead civilization, is America's national ghost story. Like Isaac Holmes and the other residents of the Circular Churchyard, its once-and-future destiny lies open to interpretation. What would have happened if . . .

Like the dead, like Wales, also defeated and incorporated on

sufferance into a mainstream national culture, the South is living a kind of afterlife: a time beyond its own self-envisioning.
That is why, to answer Vickie's question, it is so factious a
place. Everyone tells its once-and-future tale their own way.
Everyone feels they can plant their flag here in the ever-open
furrow of its history. Including me.

Third Journey

RAY HICKS

"Now *it's so,* what I tell you.
Now *believe* it.
I don't tell tales.
I don't tell nobody nothin' that I don't *know* . . ."

Ray's Tale

THE SKY WAS DARK when I set out for Ray Hicks's house. I had seen a church marquee the day before in Verona, Virginia, that read, Faith is the Bird that Sings While it is Still Dark. This time I would find the magic door in the mountains to Ray's house.

Since leaving Charleston I had spent three days at home in New England — doing laundry — before driving eleven hours with my friend Marguerite and the dog Tenby down to visit her parents in Staunton, Virginia. It was to be a holiday. Marguerite's sister Nina, her husband Bernard, and their three children were visiting from Paris for a family reunion in the Shenandoah Valley. I, however, had a date with the Master. I was finally going to meet Ray Hicks.

I had written to Ray's wife Rosa, as David Holt suggested, and had received a reply saying that I was welcome to visit, but not to bring food. They had a garden and that provided for them in summer. If I wanted to donate some much-needed money, however, they wouldn't argue. She also enclosed a map.

Five hours of southwesterly driving along the floor of the Shenandoah Valley brought me, once again, to Boone, North Carolina. At the foot of a very large mountain I found a highway sign, on which five routes clustered in the shape of a hydra-headed cross. Two pointed North, two pointed South, and a third pointed North in the same direction as the Southern routes. This, the impossible direction, was the way to Ray's house.

Again I passed the Mast General store in Valle Crucis; again I climbed switchbacking roads at 15 mph. Consulting Orville's directions and Rosa's map, this time I turned off my former path and onto a single track road cut into the flank of a magnificent hillside. But for the red barns and silos, I could have been in mid Wales. A heat haze took the horizon, but I didn't care. I was folded into a living geometry lesson of immense, angled slopes that were so close to me that I remember individual grassblades, a particular outcrop of gray fieldstone, one improbably exotic, scarlet wildflower. My engine and birdsong were the only noises.

Turning this way and that, creeping deeper and deeper into the mountains' hypotenuse, I noticed that all the mailboxes and the tiny gravel lanes were named for one Hicks or another (women, I'm happy to note, as well as men). I was getting closer. At last I came to a bend in the road protected by a hedgerow of junk: old bicycles, tires, wheelbarrows, flower pots, bits of torn tarpaulin. Leaving the car, I peered down a steep incline, and through a tangle of bushes and trees saw a large, unpainted wooden house at the bottom of the holler. Aluminum pie plates tied to sticks — modern scarecrows — flashed and shone in the sun.

I half-slipped half-ran down the hillside and came to a halt in front of a small, slender, dark-haired woman of about sixty, with a pretty smile and no hint of surprise on her face. "Pam?" she asked.

"Rosa?" I replied. I knew she was expecting me, but given their location, I guess I thought that she, too, should view my arrival as miraculous. She was digging up small round spuds from their potato patch. Suddenly terrified of meeting Ray, afraid I wouldn't understand a word he said, I got down in the dirt and helped her, grinding coffee-colored earth into my meet-the-Master linen dress.

Ray was sitting on his porch in the shade, whittling. Rosa and I heaved the pail of potatoes next to him, and we shook hands. Even sitting down, Ray was tall. His torso, his neck, his arms and shanks, the latter ending in a pair of especially bony knees, were all elongated, as if his body had been drawn by an artist with too much paper to fill. His long-sleeved shirt was buttoned tight at the wrists, and his denim overalls were ancient, and soil-caked. Atop his long body was a small, sharp head, crowned with a thatch of tousled hair. He had a two-day gray stubble and tobacco stains on his chin, and his eyes were wide and the palest blue. The untidy stuff of country life filled the porch.

I quickly produced five twenty-dollar bills — his requested sum — and handed them to Ray.

"Gawsh, a hundred dollars? I didn't think you'd really bring me a hundred dollars!"

A quick memory wrapped itself around my chest, audibly squeezing out the air. In Orville's story, Jack had said exactly the same thing to the King, except in the tale the sum was a thousand dollars. When he spoke, Ray's ancient accent dug deep and hard into the vowels of the word "hundred," harvesting a breathy, punched-in-the-stomach "u" sound from the bottom of his lungs. His consonants were ingrown and his vowels long and distended. His syllables climbed to the penultimate sound, hung there for a long, peaked moment, then fell off abruptly without completing the final one. In fact, the ends of his words seemed more like gulped swallows than actual diction. For "dollars" I heard something like *duhHAAAA-AAAlrs,* with the last three consonants achieved by a simple closing of his mouth. Each word took its own good time to be spoken. I was awed. Ray made Orville sound like a newscaster.

In his speech — I found I could understand *most* of what he said — I could actually *hear* the past. It was a miracle: Ray's tongue and teeth used the same ordinary air I was breathing to produce sounds otherwise unheard for three hundred years. I remembered what his daughter once said — "Daddy has the dialogue that come over with the ships from Shakespeare's country" — and for a moment I actually got a lump in my throat and couldn't speak. In my embarrassment I stepped on their little mutt, Whiskers.

What happened next was that Ray just began to talk. I joined him on the shady porch and the words came flowing by a kind of verbal gravity out of his long, long body.

Well, guess I cay-un tell ye 'bout Grace Hospit'l — whar they go ta barn th' babies. See, it requires twenny duhllars da-yoon, an' another sixty to get'ch'r wife ah-yoot. Well I had n' munny. Eh-yuh. Eighty duhllars seemed like a lot o' munny fer a baby t' be bawrn . . .

That's as far as Ray got. I looked up the hillside that was his front yard and saw two people in city clothes slithering down.

"I hate to bother you folks. But have I found Ray Hicks' house?"

Ray nodded, and the newcomer continued. "See, I heard you were quite a storyteller . . . I do a little television show . . . I wondered if it would be all right if we came out tomorrow to do some filming . . . ?"

I couldn't believe it. This was not part of my good dream of meeting Ray Hicks. Was no sense of the back of beyond sacred? Ray, however, wasn't surprised in the least. Indicating me, he said, "She came t'see me all the way from Rhode Island."

The TV producer and I scowled at each other. "I'm a writer," I said in a prickly voice. "He was telling me a story."

Ray interrupted. "How much would you give me?"

"Well, it's a real small little old television station . . . ain't no big-time, nationwide kind of show . . ."

"She paid me a hundred dollars," said Ray, tossing his thumb in my direction. Get more, get more, I urged silently. "Would you pay me a hundred dollars?" The producer agreed and stalked off, trailed by his assistant. I tried to forget they were ever there. Ray did immediately. He began to roll his second cigarette since our handshake, concentrating so hard that he didn't notice a drop of sweat had gathered on the tip of his nose. It fell straight into his tobacco. Without lifting his head, Ray glanced up to see if I'd seen, met my eyes, and his lips curled, rolling inward like the paper into a long, slow smile. Silently, he twisted off the ends of his cigarette, lit it, and gave it a healthy suck. It was utterly flat when he took it out of his mouth.

So. Twenny da-yoon and sixty if it got ah-yoot OK — if it lived — but ye paid it anyhay-you . . . So I was a-runnin' an ole used car. I had a '39 used 'un . . . Gawsh. An' so I wus a runnin' hit with a tag on hit . . . up t' Beech Mawntain. Ye ever been up on't?

"Oh yes. Looking for you."

Up thar ye're five thousand feet above sea level. An' so, with them that owned it, I was a-pickin' the medicine herbs. An' wild cherry bahrk — it's in th' patent medicines — an' ginsing, an' all that.

"Can you recognize all that stuff?" I asked.

Yay-yah. They put it ah-yoot that a may-un in North Caroliner knows more o' Gawd's plants than any may-un in th' U-nited States or across th' world. Ta recognize th' plants . . . Gawsh. I was a lifetime t'learn hit, from a kid at six years old up t' nay-hew . . . So I was a-runnin' that '39, a-buyin' a tag fer hit. Before that ye could run 'em withah-yoot any tags 'round here. Withah-yoot any driver's license . . . ye could slip by, they had a law, but th' roads were so rough and dug ah-yoot, they couldn't come in t'key-yutch people. An' I started drivin' at eight er nine years old. An' I drove good but couldn't get no drivers license till I wus eighteen. I'd a drove just as good at twelve years old, like Jesus in th' Bible . . .

Nah-you, before she wus t' barn the kid, I'd got to hit th' Beech so's t' pay fer hit. My dad's brother gave m' oldest boy a male pup, one pup. Yup, gave him a pup. They just called him Bouncy. An' then it went on awhile, and they gave him another'n, and just called him Puppy. An' what a dawg. He had t' be alongside a' me lookin' through th' win'shield like he was a-help drivin', Puppy did. Lookin' through th' win'shield . . .

And so I had a new double-bladed sager axe — on credit, I run a credit da-yoon thar in Valle Crusis at th' Ole' Mast Store — an' so I told her I wus goin' out t' hit th' Beech to git that twenty duhllars. An' so I got back thar and found th' pay-pul had hit th' bark till it wus 'bout gah-wun . . . An' so I drove t' th' creek. All that what'er. Springs were a-runnin' everywhar. Cold's ice . . . Some er bottlin' it nah-you . . . S' I went up thar a-walkin', an' th' dawgs were with me. Thar were lawts o' sweet blackburries. Three kinds. An' I broke my way across them blackburry . . . and I got through, and thar was about an acre o' black cherry. They'd a missed it cause it wus grown s' thick. I thought, I'll git mah munny if'n I stay able. (Sometimes it'ud start at ten cints a pay-yoond, an' then it fall t'around sev'hun.) S' I hewed th' rest o' that day and carried it ah-yoot. Carried till mah shoulder was wore ah-yoot. Bleedin' . . . guess it was t' heavy on me. All t' save a little munny what I could, to git that twenny duhllar.

An' I guess it wus twelve o'clock. Th' birds would tell me what time it wus, and th' animals. I never carried no wah-wutch. Th' ani-mals tell you time if you learn hit . . . th' way they holler at that time o' day . . . An' I learned th' time with m' animals. I growed up that way with n' wah-wutch. I ain't carried none in yah-yars. I don't want no wah-wutch. Phooey! Ye git immune to't, seein's ye can't learn that way. I finally got a wah-wutch and carried hit some, and it was a-ruinin' me, so I got rid o' hit . . .

An' so at twelve, I hear'd Bouncy a-barkin ah-yoot by a big rhaw-wuck.

"Rhaw-wuck, rhaw-wuck," I practiced, trying to imitate Ray. To do it right I had to aspirate the whole word out hard, in one breath. It was like playing myself as a musical instrument, maybe one of the woodwinds. Ray saw me quietly mouthing his words and stopped for a moment, narrowing his eyes as he took a drag on his third cigarette. When he exhaled, he harnessed me with his pupils — his focus was so concentrated I didn't dare look away — and continued.

It wus like he was a-bahrkin' at sumbody. But I said, there ain't nobody in here but me. An' I got out t' th' rhaw-wuck an' he's a-lookin' down off hit. An' he's going, Woof, woof, like he's a-bahrkin' kinda at sumbody. An' I looked down. And gawsh, hit's a black bahr. Just under th' raw-wuck. And hit weighed three er four hun'erd pay-yoonds. Gawd!

Ray breathed this last word, "God," slowly and quietly, and with awe. His sentences often dropped off at the end in a kind of hushed reverence, as if he were still caught up in the wonderment of a fifty-year-old tale. It occurred to me that Ray wasn't just telling me this story, he was inside it, living it. And in story-time, the end hadn't happened yet. All the possibilities still existed, for him, for his characters, for his listeners. However Ray told it, the world would be remade according to his words. Ray's phenomenal talent was to convey in each story he told, be it a memorate — what Burrison calls "a firsthand acount of a personal experience colored by traditional belief" — a folktale, or even a joke, this freshness, this sense of happening, of conclusions not yet wrought. It really was a kind of magic. Like dreaming and traveling, Ray's storytelling was special because it was a lived experience as well as a narrative; in its way it was both art *and* reality. That was what made Ray great. That was his uncommon ability.

I considered the man opposite me. Whenever he shifted I could smell sweat from a hundred ancient exertions. I had read an account by Cheryl Oxford, *Ray Hicks: The Storyteller as Shaman,* which basically suggested that Ray, through his stories, functioned as an intermediary between members of the local community and the Otherworld — Jack's storied realm, where the problems of this world were sometimes solved, or at least forgotten. And that this special status made him a healer, or better yet, a resolver, of sorts. That made sense. But then Oxford added, "Hicks believes his stories embody the collective unconscious of a kindred people's yesteryears."

Bunkum. Ray would never have said that. But he does know he is special. He even tells a kind of personal creation myth, essentially acknowledging his talent as so extraordinary that, according to folk logic, it must be assigned a supernatural source. In this tale Ray is a teenager. He, his dad, a friend, and their dogs go into the Beyond — the Hicks family's nickname for the world beyond Beech Mountain — on a hunting trip. Out of the dark, on a rugged hillside, emerges a woman all dressed in black. Ray is surprised to see her — what would a woman be doing out alone in the mountains? — but offers her food and shelter nonetheless. She takes him aside and tells him she's going to put "a 'chantment" on him. She realizes he is shy, and this spell will make it easy for him to "speak to people what time you got left." A terrible thunderstorm breaks out af-

Akbar Imhotep at the Wren's Nest.

Vickie Vedder without her Granny Griffin costume.

Nancy Basket in front of the kudzu barn.

Kudzu vine growing on trees.

Orville Hicks, seated on his "lyin' bench," demonstrates the gut bucket.

Kwame Dawes telling "The Girl and the Fish."

David Holt and his banjo.

Veronica Byrd tells "Taily Po" in
the Moonlit Road sound studio.

Cornelia Bailey on Sapelo Island, Georgia.

Sapelo Island, Georgia *(below)*.

Minerva King in Charleston,
South Carolina.

David Joe Miller and Baybee,
Jonesborough, Tennessee.

Ray Hicks on his porch, surrounded by weather checkers.

Ray Hicks plays the Jew's Harp.

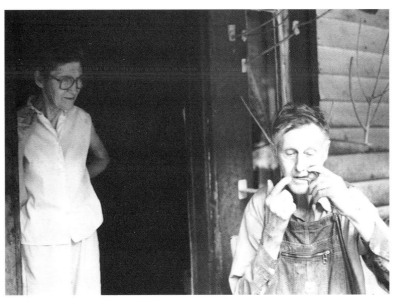

Rosa Hicks in a familiar pose, listening to Ray.

Kathryn Windham in her
back garden.

Mitch Barrett and Carla Gover,
with their daughter, Zoe.

Karen Vuranch as herself, and as Pearl Buck.
PEARL BUCK PHOTOGRAPH COURTESY JURGEN LORENZEN

Oyo Fummilayo backed by a rainbow of hands.

Sign in front of Al Green's Tabernacle in Memphis, Tennessee.

Annie
McDaniel
with the
St. Louis Packet.

Guitar pool at Days Inn,
next to Graceland in Memphis, Tennessee.

Pam and Mammy of Mammy's Cupboard in Natchez, Mississippi.

Marquee-style road sign.

Rose Anne St. Romain and friend.
PHOTOGRAPH COURTESY CYNTHIA S. PORET

ter that, and in the morning the woman is gone. "I ain't never been feared since to talk to nobody," said Ray.

From that day forward he has lived up to the strictures of his fate. To Oxford, Ray acknowledged that when he was young he was set apart from his peers because of his interest in old folks' conversation. In fact even now, when he tells the old stories, he says he still hears them in the voices of his grandmother and grandfather. To other interviewers he has said that he has seen ghosts floating above buried treasure, and has twice watched the "Holy Ghost Dove" wing past him to friends' deathbeds. To me, Ray confessed that his body is so full of electricity that "if'n a louse crawled on my head, it would be electrified to death." He gave me a knowing smile: sure enough, when we'd shaken hands earlier, I'd felt a faint shock.

An' so that bahr's a-lookin' up at us. An' when I got thar, da-yoon on it Bouncy went. Th' others come. And they's all three onto hit . . . S' direc'ly they got s' hot on hit, hit took off at a trot . . . an' they run it up t' what they call in that pretty land th' north pinnacle ridge. An' then th' bahrkin' quit. An' then Bouncy come back a-talkin' tuh me, goin', Eh, eh, eh, eh, an' he had a piece a hide. An' the bahr had hit 'im with a claw . . . A black bahr could slap a dawg's head off if they hit it right. Black bahrs kin with thar strength. An' he'd slapped Bouncy, th' claw'd caught his forehead an' you could see th' skull thar, a little pay-yutch.

Well I put mah bahrk on mah back an' got ah-yoot, an' I said, "Nah-you, I'm a-gonna be killed maybe by a bahr, but I kay-yun't quit, I need that munny. I need that twenny duhllars . . ." Two o' mah payh-pul, yah-yars ago, one killed a bahr with a pine knot an' saved his life . . . Hit it in th' head with a pine knot . . . that's mah related payh-pul, a hun'erd yah-yars ago. Another'n shot one with a hog rifle . . . An' now if they'd a-dun that, I could chop one up with an axe, maybe. I thought, "I'd got t' get that bahrk."

"What happened to Bouncy?" I asked. Ray replied that he had recovered just fine, but my interruption got him off the subject, and for the life of me I couldn't get him back on it. I managed to find out that he'd earned the twenty dollars in the end, and had sprung Rosa from the hospital, but I never discovered what had transpired between him and the bear.

All the time Ray had been talking, I'd been vaguely aware of what looked like pairs of slim antlers growing out of the porch wall behind him. The nearest one stuck out on either side of Ray's head like a pair of antennae. Since I had already interrupted him, I asked what they were.

They's weather checkers, said Ray. Ye'll need t' take one with ye.

I asked what a weather checker was, and Ray's eyes grew huge with disbelief.

Gaaawwwd! They tell ye th' weather. See? Rain's a-comin' nayhew. Gawsh . . .

Ray explained that they were made out of whittled chokecherry wood; you need peach for water diviners, but chokecherry is good enough for weather checkers. "When it's real purty in the weather," as Ray said, they crook in the middle; when a cold snap is coming they point down; when rain is on the way they flatten straight out. I looked skeptical but Rosa said she'd seen them work with her own eyes. You have to know how to read them. Just the other day . . .

Ray coughed loudly, cut in, and took up his narrative. Rosa retreated into the house.

An' da-yoon yander then, 'nother time, I's a-comin' up th' ole' mawntain road . . . an' thar's somethin' black in th' road . . . an' it's a bahr, wantin' t' keel me. They want t' kill ye if ye're a cah'ard . . . But th' biggest part of people is a little cah'ard. See, Gawd created ye t' fear fer yer lahf. An' so I got up thar an' that bahr was a-wantin' t' know if I'd a-run. I wundered what t' do. "If I run it'll keel me." Then I happened t' thank, when I went t' school, nay-hew ye know hit, I thank, when David Crockett smiled a coon t' day-yuth? Ye remember that in yer school? . . . Smiled a coon t' day-yuth. Tried it on a grizzly, an' hit wouldn't smile. So he come on hit an' he cut it up with his knife . . . Way-ull I thought, "I might smile it out, like Crockett." An' I walked up a little closer. Way-ull, I said, "You been eatin' a lot o' mawntain sardines, eh black bahr? How 'bout them cock-a-roaches? They taste good?" An' he begin to turn smiley, jus talkin' to hit. An' di-rec'ly, hit just turned around across th' right buy-yunk — the buy-yunk wus pretty high — an' jumped up th' buy-yunk, an' smiled at me three mohr times as hit went up.

. . . I know a lot about sna-yucks too . . .

"Ray," shouted Rosa over her shoulder as she was hanging laundry, "maybe she wants to hear a Jack tale." Rosa had been silently doing chores ever since I sat down, literally, at the Master's feet.

I feel like talkin' 'bout th' animals t'day. Is that all right with ye?

I told him it was fine with me. Heat-struck flies buzzed slowly around the porch as Ray reached for his tin of tobacco and began to roll yet another cigarette. To hear a Jack tale from Ray Hicks would be redundant, impossible even: I felt as if I had been listening to Jack himself for the past two hours. Like Jack, the trickster hero who didn't have an ounce of self-doubt (which generally served him well, but occasionally made him a fool), Ray was not a man who knew what it was to be self-conscious. The theory I developed as I sat listening was that, thanks to a happy concordance of geography and personality, Ray had never once in his life cared what other people thought of him. Because he lived by his own standards, the opinion of others had never become the capricious yardstick it is for most of us, the means by which we become disappointed in our own behavior, or, when they fall short of our imagined standards, in theirs. Such wondrous self-reliance and lack of disillusionment in kith and kin has left him totally without bitterness. No wonder his world was so full of joy and surprise and enchantment. No wonder that Ray Hicks's own life sounds like a Jack tale, or that for him Beech Mountain was the Otherworld on earth. It simply had never let him down, because like his alter ego, Ray had never let himself down.

One of his signature tales is called *Jack and Ray's Hunting Trip*. In it, the storyteller literally jumps into the story. Ray tells his audience, "Now it's *so*, what I tell you. Now *believe it*. I don't tell tales . . . ," and goes on to say that one day after he finished his chores he said to himself, "I'm gonna go down and see Jack and see if me and him can get into something together." So Ray goes to Jack's log cabin — in an aside to his listeners, he says, "I remember the last log cabins built in these mountains was a-standin' yet when this house was built . . ." — and tells him, "I'm kindly here to go a-huntin' with you, Jack. I heard talk about ye. And I wanted to be with you one time in my life." Jack is willing. "Bedad!" he says to Ray, "we'll do her." And the two go off and Jack has amazing adventures as Ray watches.

Ray is at home in Jack's magical world. And in that world the South is remade: Jack and Ray come upon miraculous streams of sourwood honey — the best, oldest, sweetest honey — running down the limbs of a tree hit by lightning. They catch fifty ducks. While sneaking up on the ducks underwater, the current sweeps thirty-five pounds of trout into

Jack's britches. And so it goes: nature is bountiful, men are clever, and no one goes hungry. What is remarkable about this picture is that it is antithetical to the honor code of the Old South. Two self-assured men have no need to seek public assessment of their worth. Bertram Wyatt-Brown writes that in prewar Southern society, which was regulated by the rule of honor, "the weight of the community lies upon the individual . . . to thwart it is to lose one's honor." Jack — as well as Brer Rabbit, that other self-reliant trickster, whose confidence generally wins the day, but sometimes makes him play the fool, too — exists outside this honor system, in the Otherworld of a South that has never entered the history books, but flourished in storytellers' imaginations.

Wyatt-Brown goes on, "Honor, not conscience, shame, not guilt, were the psychological and social underpinnings of Southern culture." Yet the two greatest heroes of Southern folklore, one white, one black, knew no shame. Honor would not have enticed them to fight in a war in which they had no stake. Like Ray, who probably understands them better than anyone else, Jack and Brer Rabbit did what they needed to do to get by, no more, no less. Their stories are not often honorable, but they are remembered. They are the real heroes of the South — survivors, untouched by tragedy. And so, as their sometime companion, is Ray Hicks, who, no matter where my thoughts took me, was still talking about snakes.

We ain't got n' poisonous sna-yucks nay-hew. We used ta, though. Sna-yucks kah-yoon't see, that's why they bite you. They kah-yoon't see right well, thar scahr'd . . . We got a lot o' little brown sna-yucks, black sna-yucks. They don't bother me. They swaller thar frawgs . . . I used t' keel 'em — they had me teached that way — I don't hardly keel a sna-yuck n' more unless'n if hit be around mah hay-use . . . Un huh.

An' so, . . . Gawd, they come around me . . . They ask, where's Ray at? Others say, Look whar th' crowd is and you'll find 'im. Gawsh.

"How did you come to tell stories so well, Ray?"

Mah gran'father told 'em when I' us little. An' I tried to tell 'em at fivh yay-yurs ole' . . . I liked 'em. Loved th' stawries. An' do yet. Well, at Washington D.C. when I wus one o' th' sixteen winners, in '83, a-ridin' th' bus, they asked, "Mr. Hicks, had you ever preached at some time, th' way ye talk an' th' wurds you speak?" Yay-yuh.

"But you never did?"

No may'yum . . . But like they teached from th' Ole' Testament o' th' Bible, if you one o' Gawd's chosen pay-pul, it make you think t' lead others. One o' Gawd's chosen pay-pul wrote th' ole' Bible . . .

"Do you think you were chosen too, Ray?" I asked. "To tell stories?"

Yay-yuh. Chosen. Chosen vessel.

But I wus a-gonna tell you about th' sna-yucks . . . I learnt 'em when I'us young. If'n ye ponder hit — ye've got t' ponder yer stuff. Now ye kah-yoon't go t' bayd an' sleep s' good and just lit ever'thang go. Ye kayoon think a lot of diff'rent stuff, rememberin', while yer in th' bayd. But most people sleep s'good. Don't punish enough to larn. Give up t' quick.

Nay-hew, this 'us in th' wil' chestnut time — they's a-makin' me drive th' cattle up yander . . . An' thar's this big bunny rabbit. Th' ole' rabbit wouldn't run. So I just picked hit up in mah ahrms an' brought it da-yoon, an' mah muther said, "Whar'd ye git that rabbit?" I said I picked it up up yander in th' field. An' so I put it under a washin' tub, an' my father come in — mah daddy, Nathan Hicks. An' so, muther said, "Nathan, Ray's got an ole' bunny rabbit, said he just picked it up. Brought it t' th' hay-youse an' got it under a tub et thar." An' he said, "Hay-yull, you go show me whar ye got that rabbit." I walked with him up thar. An' he knows. Looked over on t'other side, an' a big black sna-yuck had it charmed. Gonna swallow hit . . . Eh-yuh . . . Ya gotta larn an' keep away from 'em, an' not git swallered like Jonah did . . . like Jonah in th' whales' belly. It puked, vomited 'im up.

Ray stopped for a minute, laughing and scratching his head. A new, already flattened cigarette burned between the fingers of one hand. Then he looked me straight in the eye. Thunderheads had begun to spill over the mountaintop, Gold Rock Point, that towered in front of us, casting the whole holler into sudden shadow.

Way-ull nay-hew, do you believe he was in that belly?

Ray bent close to me, eyes wide with seriousness, but I sensed a hint of amusement at my predicament. He didn't think I really believed, but how would I respond?

"Oh Ray, I don't know. What do you think?"

I used t' did, but I don't no more. He dreamed that. It's Bible stawries. He dreamed he was in thar.

But . . . all th' people thought s' much o' me — Gawsh, t'be with Ray. He's a leader. Yay-yuh. Got t' believe me an' trust me. An' listen hey're, yahrs back, when th' rubber boots come ah-yoot, them ole'-timey rubber boots? Way-ull, thar wus three bruthers. One o' th' bruthers wurked an' he got a pahr o' boots. Way-ull, he went awhile a-wearin' th' boots, an' he died. Way-ull, the second brother wore 'em, an' his leg set up . . . an' he died. Th' thard brother put 'em own, an' went a-wearin 'em . . .

"Now that's just foolish," I said. Ray held up his hands like it hadn't been his decision, and went on talking.

. . . an' he went t' th' doctor's with his ley-ug. T' others didn't go t' th' doctor t' check on 'em. He went t' th' doctor. An' they done told him th' other two died o' wearin' th' boots. An' that doctor, he said, "Go git" — I ferget which foot it'us on, th' right er th' lay-uft — that doctor said, "Go git th' boots, and brang it tuh me." An' he got th' boots and checked hit, an' a snake had struck th' boot an' broke a . . . a fang off in hit, an' hit had scratched and killed th' mey-un.

"Is that true?" My own voice suddenly sounded as if it had been scooped out of the earth. I guessed my latent mynah bird instinct had awoken, and had begun bending my accent to Ray's. I was embarrassed for myself.

Yay-yuh, I'd say hit's true. Scratched, broke off in th' rubber . . . Stone dead, both o' 'em. They told it me when I was young. An' I'd say that's so.

Nay-hew, mah muther and dad moved over t' Bethel in 19 an' 29. I wus sev'hun yahrs old, a little pay-yust. Moved t' Bethel an' stayed three yahrs, then moved back hey're to mah hay-youse. Rented this hay-youse hey're t' people 'bout tore it da-yoon. Way-yull, they made liquor a-livin' in hit. All them rough people an' thar daddy. Stayed in th' penitentiary.

I wus th' faw-urth keed, mah sister wus th' thard keed . . . An' nay-hew thar's Ahrville . . . I started him a-tellin' stawries. Mah children will tell 'em but they won't face pay-pul. Rosey, mah wife, can tell 'em good . . . It's hard, growed up like I did in th' woods, t' face that many pay-pul. And so I wus about t' quit. An' th' prey-chers o' th' church said it's wro-wung t' tay-ell stawries. They gettin' on t' Ahrville nay-hew . . . some of 'em. Say it's wrong t' tell stawries. So I's a-gonna quit. Mah nephew, we's a-goin' . . . we wus goin' t' entertain in Nawrth Caroliner, an' I spoke I wus about t'quit. It's wro-wung with th'Bible t' tell stawries, er pickin' music, they used t' teach. An' Franklin Proffit, mah nephew who picks music, said, "Ray, don't quit, anythang that makes people feel good can't be wro-wung." Gawsh. An' I just kept hit a-goin' . . .

I asked Ray if he remembered David Holt. His eyes shone and he silently held up a finger, indicating "Wait here. Don't leave." He unfolded his legs and rose in the shape of a nearly seven-foot, human S-curve. Age and an old back injury had stooped him into the ergonomically correct position for sitting rather than standing, but despite that he moved quickly. I heard him shouting in the house for Rosa. Seconds later, he returned clutching a wrinkled brown paper bag.

I gonna sing you a saw-wung and play a little on mah harp.

Ray's hand roamed around in the bag until he found what he wanted. In triumph he pulled out a pair of false teeth.

Need mah teeth ta playh . . . Ye ever seen anythang like this?

He held up a delicate bamboo reed.

It's outta Chiner. David, mah friend David Holt, brought me that a few days ago . . . that's a homemade mountain Jew's harp. I kah-yoon't playh hit vera way-ull . . .

He immediately produced some twangy sounds, then grabbed what looked like old pop-top aluminum can lids from the bag. I asked what they were. More astonishment.

Ye mean ye hain't never seen 'em afore? Gawl-ly! . . . Thar mawn-tain Jew's harps.

Ray put one to his mouth and began tweaking it with his forefinger. The big one sounded like an aluminum pig snort-ing a tune; one of the smaller harps reminded me of a song plucked out on a metallic rubber band.

"The people who can play ought to be the happiest people there is, because they can make music," said Rosa, from her position in the doorway.

Ray blew into a harmonica and then sang,

It takes a worried man to sing a worried song . . .

Ray sang for about an hour. Sometimes he had to search around for the right key, but he always found it. "Short life and trouble . . . ," began one song. Hit's an awld song from the mawn-tains, he explained, like a-whar you'd be a-datin' one another.

After singing "John Henry" Ray said, I kah-yoon't playh like some people kin a-playh, but I'm willin' ta trah. An' whin I get done, they say, Gawsh . . . Some tried t' argue that I'd been a-trained. I know: I a-trained in th' woods with mah animals and mah burrrds. They come an' listen at me. Nay-hew, if ye don't take nothin' in th' field t' keel 'em . . . thay'll come listen if you playh muh-sic . . .

It was hard to leave Ray and Rosa. It was hard to get Ray to stop talking: only after reiterating several times that I had a five-hour journey back to Virginia, did he agree to let me go, bearing gifts of a three-pronged weather checker and a bird he had whittled from a pine knot.

A few thousand feet closer to sea level, where roadside shops gathered at the mountains' knees, I bought a bag of boiled peanuts near a church with a marquee that read, The Bible Prevents Truth Decay. To quote Vickie Vedder, "MISTAKE." I hadn't realized that the peanuts were boiled inside their shells, which in my air-conditioned car instantly turned dark brown, cold, and soggy. Since I couldn't drive and shell nuts at the same time anyway, I decided to bring them home as an American delicacy for the French visitors (this did not go down very well, and they sat in the kitchen for a few days before someone mercifully threw them away).

As I barreled north up Interstate 81, all America seemed in motion. I passed trucks bearing fruit, hogs, potatoes, pianos, fuel, new cars, milk, and frozen chicken. I shared the road with fellow travelers from Maryland, Virginia, Texas, Florida, New Jersey, Vermont, and Minnesota (a sampling from my two-hour survey of license plates). Perhaps due to my extreme weariness — four hours of trying to audibly unfold Ray's accent to make it fit into my ears had taken their toll — the cars started to look like speeding metaphors on wheels. The camaraderie between travel and storytelling never seemed so clear. In the old European storytelling tradition (the Great Tradition), tellers were travelers themselves. The tag line at the end of their tales, which Orville Hicks and other American storytellers sometimes preserve, was "And I was there."

"They are emissaries from the magic world of the road (and the story)," writes William Bernard McCarthy in *Jack in Two Worlds,* "come to the prosaic world of settlements." Storytellers either visited on holidays, or created holidays by the mere fact of their presence. McCarthy adds that it was in America, ironically — the consummate mobile society — that storytelling "quit the road and settled down," into what scholars call the Little Tradition. This occurred, he reasons, because in the eighteenth and nineteenth centuries American frontiers were extraordinarily fluid. Since life was in transit, magic and comfort were not found in motion, but in the all-too-often temporary peace of hearth, home, and community. And so Jack put down roots in the Appalachian Mountains, became a farm boy, and joined the Hicks clan.

As a fixture on Beech Mountain for eight decades, traveling only to Jack's Otherworld and back, Ray Hicks is a master of the Little Tradition. In the peripatetic, Great Tradition of my pilgrimage, however, Ray himself provided the meat in the "magic sandwich" which William McCarthy describes below. He was the storyteller truly become the story.

McCarthy writes that the typical *märchen,* or fairytale, such as a Jack tale,

> begins in a quiet, unremarkable place — such as the simple hearth where poor Jack and his widowed mother worry about their next meal — and only gradually opens to the magic world. Taking to the road to make his fortune, the hero finds more magic the further he travels from home. Usually . . . Jack ends his tale by coming home and settling down. The *märchen* is a magic sandwich, in which the miraculous events of the hero's travels are framed by mundane beginnings and endings, and the simplicities of home.

For one summer's day, I was Jack, and Ray Hicks was the giant — albeit a welcoming giant. When I got home, everyone was watching television, and once again, the sky was dark.

Fourth Journey

WILLIAM FAULKNER, *The Sound and the Fury*
"I stood in the belly of my shadow and listened . . ."

Ollie's Tale

A S OUR PLANE TOUCHED DOWN, the pilot announced that the temperature in Jackson, Mississippi was 95 degrees Fahrenheit, but that because of the humidity it felt like 115. Then he suggested that we all have a nice day.

It was a strange beginning to my last, and longest, circuit in the South. There had been a total solar eclipse in Europe that morning. On the news in my motel room I heard that a freak tornado had leveled much of Salt Lake City. A reporter interviewed a man staring at the ruins of his house. "I was reading the paper in the living room," he said, "when I felt the building leaving." In Kansas City the school board voted to ban Evolution from a list of recommended teaching subjects. It did not bode well: the sun blotted out, the Mormons attacked by a wind dervish, Kansas City undoing Darwin.

This trip, to the Deep South, *really* made my friends and neighbors nervous. Secretly, I think, to a lot of Northerners, "Mississippi" summons the same visceral response that "The Dark Continent" did to nineteenth-century Britons. Exotic, dangerous, hot, diseased, and worst of all, populated by ignorant, intolerant whites and ignorant, grudge-bearing blacks. Anthony Walton summed up the feeling in *Mississippi: An American Journey:* "that word — 'Mississippi' — is perhaps the most loaded proper noun in American English. I would always be uneasy there, no matter what I did or how long I stayed. I knew too much, saw too many shadows . . ." One shopkeeper

237

in Providence told me I was crazy to go there alone. I told her that's what the rest of the world says about New York City.

This time I planned to make a great circuit that would take in as many dissimilarities as the South had to offer: coal-mining hills, agricultural plains, seacoast. I would travel from Mississippi eastward to Alabama, north to Tennessee and West Virginia, southwest to Kentucky, and then south again via Memphis, through the Delta back to Jackson. At that point Marguerite was planning to join me — she had traveled around the world with me for my previous book and wanted a foothold in this one — and together we would see the Louisiana Bayou. Rose Anne St. Romaine, a storyteller in Mansura, Louisiana, was our final reward. I had become infatuated with her accent when I'd spoken to her on the phone from Providence. "Be careful!" she'd drawled, pronouncing "careful" *kay-a-ful*. "In August in the South, you really have to keep an eye on your personality."

The road to Laurel, Mississippi began, as most roads in America do, with a commercial strip. Bright, visually lobotomized logos for motels, fast food chains, and gasoline stations towered above miles of tarmac parking lots on poles high enough to be seen from the Interstate. In the garden of our mobile, consumer culture, these were the weeds. The images were so generic that I could have been on a strip in New England had it not been for the occasional, often homemade, Signs of the South: Boiled Peanuts!, Hot & Juicy BBQ, Today's Fresh Crawfish!, Guns & Ammo — Cheap.

The strip was soon conquered by real forest, the beginning of southern Mississippi's great piney woods, some of which had been felled — recently, to judge by the Watch for Fallen Logs signs — to make way for farmland and miniature towns of worn, flat-roofed buildings, clustered at crossroads. The earth was the orange-brown of New Mexican adobe, and kudzu ran riot in the open spaces. A billboard inquired, Got Bugs? Call Murphy!

Shortly before I reached Laurel, I became entangled in road construction. Bare-chested men were digging and hammering and working heavy machinery, but the slender flagman, holding his neon banner, stood still enough to study. It was midday and viciously hot, and the sun seemed to strike him in blows. He even staggered once. In my air-conditioned car, I felt as if I were on a tour bus, sightseeing in Hell.

Laurel at 2 P.M. was a town parched of color. Driving down Main Street made my mouth dry: the brick roadway, the two paved roundabouts, the flat-topped shops all seemed made of chalk and ashes. There were no movements, no people, no sounds. The J.C. Penney store was long abandoned and its windows whitewashed, though otherwise the town looked prosperous enough. It was heat sapping the life from Laurel, not a nearby commercial strip. Heat baked away color and pleated the air into dizzying waves. There were no trees, no hope of relief from the sun.

On a hill just above downtown, however, perched a leafy neighborhood of turn-of-the-century mansions, kelly-green lawns (I tripped over an implanted sprinkler), and magnolia trees. Before air-conditioning, money in the South had meant shade. I found the Lauren Rodgers Art Museum in a very grand neo-Colonial structure, and prepared to meet the afternoon's storyteller: Ollie de Loach. I was in love with her name.

When we had spoken on the phone she had said to meet her in the museum. "Where in the museum?" I'd asked. "You cannot miss me," was her reply. "I'm not like anyone you've ever met before."

I walked into a microcosm of Western civilization. Lauren

had died in 1921 of appendicitis, at twenty-three, and his parents and young widow had given his memory a classically referenced repository of American and European Art. The museum may have boasted one of the largest collections of Native American baskets in the world, but its long, somber corridors and opaque skylights ushered visitors firmly into the Western tradition. The model for Thomas Sully's painting *Ideal Head,* of a round-shouldered young woman with pink cheeks and blonde ringlets, looked like she could have been Lauren's sister.

Here, in this hall of mirrors reflecting centuries of white Taste and Discretion, I found what I first took to be the Burning Bush. When the flaming orange apparition lifted its head, I knew Ollie had been right: how could I have missed her? In her mid-sixties, she wore a floor-length, shocking-orange caftan with a satin flower sewn onto the chest. Her head was bound in a turban, from which gray cornrows spilled out of the top like ash from a volcanic eruption. We retired to a very Victorian, wood-paneled Reading Room so as not to disturb the other visitors.

Ollie began by saying that she had been born in Laurel but had moved at the age of four to a dead-end road out in the country.

"I was raised in isolation. It was the best thing that ever happened to me."

I asked why her parents had left town.

"You don't want to know, but I'll tell you. Back then Jones County was segregated, but it wasn't so bad. We had a reputation for being civilized here; we still do. One day when I was four, I went to Kresge's Department Store with my mom and my little sister. While we were there, a white woman came with a little girl the same age as me. Well, we began to play. The white girl said, 'Let's switch: you drink out of the white water fountain and see how white water tastes, and I'll drink out of the black one to see how black water tastes.' Well, her mother was furious. And when we got home my mother had a fit. She said to my father — she always called him Mr. Ollie — she said, 'Mr. Ollie, I can't take this anymore. You've got to do something.' So my father bought land and built us a house and we moved to the country. All because I wanted to taste white water."

Ollie took a good hard look at me. I fretted that I might seem half-witted from lack of breakfast or lunch. "My great grandmother was a full-blooded African, and a slave . . . One day she went with her mother to gather firewood, which she would have carried back to their hut in a bundle on top of her head. As they were picking up sticks, she was captured." Ollie intensified her stare. "Now, do you know why we are in this country?" I started to speak but she continued. "No, you don't, but I'll tell you. We were captured by other Africans — it was part of an intertribal war — and sold to white men."

"How do you know all this?" I asked, amazed at the extent of the Southern memory. A bronze Nike — the goddess of victory — behind Ollie's head spread her wings on either side of her turban. The effect was less incongruous than prophetic.

"As a child I had contact dermatitis," Ollie explained. "I had to stay inside, so I listened to the adults, my grandmother in particular. Often they didn't know I was listening, but I was."

Ollie's huge eyes gripped me tight. As she spoke, her hands and arms did a kind of dance around her upper body, gracefully investigating one another, her face, the air. All the while her wide-open eyes, emphasized below by deeply etched shadows, never budged from mine. The combination of constant motion and stillness created a wonderfully fresh sense of perpetual discovery; I felt that Ollie was always surprising herself.

". . . so when I went to Ghana, I asked the old people what

they taught their children about the slave trade, about *us*. Now, you should know that I'm the type of person, that when I talk to someone I can *command* them to speak . . . Well, this woman didn't want me talking to her father, but when she left I made him answer me. 'You should be thankful we did what we did,' he finally said. 'You live better than we do. You have more money, better health, better jobs.' I responded, 'But we lost our *stories,* our family history.' He didn't think that was very important."

Ollie smoothed the orange fabric over her knees and settled into a momentary stillness. I could tell what she thought of his opinion. On the phone the previous evening, she'd told me that after she retired she had bought "a big barn of a house," and for twelve years had taken in elderly people whom no one else, including nursing homes, had wanted. She was on an Advisory Council on aging; she worked with children; she brought the young to see the old. "My motto," she said gravely, "is that I want every person who comes in contact with me to be a little bit better for it."

"That takes energy," I responded, feeling perilously sluggish from hunger (I later discovered to my horror that Ollie never sleeps more than four hours a night). The burning bush had been a good simile: Ollie burned so much energy that she siphoned off her listeners' oxygen. I yanked myself back into alertness, noticing her meticulously painted red toenails.

"Here's some wisdom for you to go home and ponder, Pamela. It's just for you: 'The ear tried the words even as the mouth tasted meat.' Job 34:3. Think about it."

It unnerved me that she seemed to know I was hungry; even more so that she thought feeding my ears would be meal enough. Shortly afterward, Ollie began to touch on the topic of storytelling and spirituality: that the stories she told belonged not to her but to the past, which she perceived in an almost personified way, as if her visual imagination were shaped by a knowledge of African ancestor worship. "I know nothing, but *they* know everything," Ollie whispered. "I have to wait for them to tell me."

I sensed that she was speaking from the shadowland between belief and metaphor, and was trying to sift the difference between them when my friend Bryan Holzwanger suddenly blew into the Reading Room on a breeze of anarchy and beer. Two worlds — both in which I had but a toehold — poised to collide.

Physically, Bryan was the antithesis of Ollie. He looked like a rakish cherub reluctantly grown into adulthood: short, stocky, with very thick blond curls and a rosy complexion. Born twenty-six years ago in Mobile, Alabama, Bryan had recently moved to New Orleans. Since this was the closest we would come to each other, I had invited him up to Laurel to meet Ollie and me, and was feverishly wondering if I'd been rash to do so. Bryan had a ferocious intellect and was as attracted to juxtaposition as a vampire to an exposed jugular. It made me uncomfortable that he and Ollie were breathing the same air. I stuttered an introduction and then simply stopped, mouth open, with not a word to say that would make sense to both of them simultaneously. Bryan got the point and, promising "to be a good boy," took his friend Kerry off to see the museum's collection. Ollie returned to her work of making me a better person.

She said that she was the fifth of fifteen children. She had used stories, borrowed from her elders, to keep her younger brothers and sisters quiet when she looked after them. "Not for their sake, for mine," she explained. "So they'd be good and I wouldn't get into trouble." Once, while her mother was out, their pet goat had gotten in the house and charged at its reflection in an armoire mirror. "There was glass everywhere,"

Ollie said, wincing at the memory. No one had noticed the goat because they were so engrossed in her tales.

As she continued to comb images and incidents from her memory, I gradually became aware that, while nuggets of stories liberally peppered her conversation, they rarely grew into full-blown tales. She had too much to convey to me, I think, to settle into the slowness stories demand. She said that she had spent two years caring for an old man named "Mr. Clean," who had once killed an intruder and was so ornery no one else would have him. She told me about "Mrs. Smith," a childless widow feared by parents but adored by children. Mrs. Smith was kind and understanding, and the children had visited her against their parents' wishes. One day they arrived to find that she had had a stroke; yet because they had responded to her kindness rather than their parents' prejudice, they were on hand to save her life.

"Now, you tell me what that story means, Pamela."

"Um, that children aren't weighted down by adult preconceptions?"

"There's no wrong answer. But it means that our children are watching us all the time. They learn by example, not by being told. Now you see why I'm so busy."

I glanced over at Bryan and Kerry, who had been staring at us in silence since they returned from their rather brief tour.

I asked where the story had come from.

"HOW CAN YOU ASK ME THAT?" Ollie shouted. "You should know that, girl! I've just bared my soul to you! What did I tell you I did for twelve years? That I do every day?"

I had only wanted to know if it were based on an incident or if it were a parable of Ollie's beliefs, but it didn't matter. The important thing was that for Ollie, stories were tools with which to shape change, or seeds to be planted in her listeners' conscience. Like verbs, they performed an active function;

they were never the nouns of simple entertainment. For Ollie storytelling was a kind of social work — and when stories didn't work fast enough, she quit telling and nursed and cooked and organized and politicked and championed. "Would you believe me," she asked cryptically toward the end of our conversation, "if I told you I was never a child?"

"Yes, absolutely," I told her. "You had too much to do."

Ollie nodded slowly, smiling.

I was so absorbed in my crawfish and corn chowder that I didn't stop to consider the impression we made: a statuesque black woman of a certain age in orange African garb, two young white men, not long out of college, and a sunburned, sleepy woman in her late thirties with a notebook, all crammed together at a table in a noisy bar. The conversation went something like this. Bryan: "I told Kerry we were going to Mississippi to meet this girl. I said you were pushing forty, but you were cool. You could pass." Me: "Pass for what?" Kerry: "If you look at her forehead in the light, you can see a bunch of gray hairs." Me: "Pass for what?" Ollie: "My name, de Loach, means of the light." Me to Ollie: "I'm not surprised." Me to Bryan: "If I didn't dye my hair, I'd have a skunk stripe like Susan Sontag." Kerry: "Who?" Bryan: "Think 'Bride of Frankenstein.'" Then to me, "Twenty-nine, but only in the right light."

Bryan lit a cigarette and Ollie chastised him. She ordered a Coke and sent it back because it was flat. He took a long sip of his gin and tonic and told her in his lazy, Gulf coast accent, "Ah always say, a fountain Coke is like a rock concert. It may not be that great, but at least it's live." To my amazement they discovered a mutual fondness for Mississippi's slot machines. Ollie said, "I don't gamble, but I like to play the slots. It relaxes me." At this, they smiled at each other over the worn brown table, its surface pocked with pale drink rings like so many scrambled Olympics logos, in a weird, mutual appreciation. I had underestimated them both.

"My grandfather's face looked like this table," said Ollie, smoothing it with her fingers. "He was lined and dark brown too." She told us a story about him and her grandmother: "Ant'ny" — she said this in her grandmother's piercing, nasal voice, with her eyes scrinched up — and "Ole Miss," which she did in her grandfather's baritone. Apparently he never called her anything else.

"Well, a cat got into our smoking shed, where we hung the meat, and it kept eating my grandfather's handiwork. So one day when he knew the cat was inside he stepped into the shed and commanded Ole Miss to close the door. Imagine us: a tall, regal old black woman with all these little black children running around her, leaning against the door to keep it shut. And my grandfather and that cat went to war.

"Finally, we heard him yelling, 'Open up, open up!' and she opened the door and the cat ran out. Ant'ny came next, bleeding all over his bald head. Well, Ole Miss burst out laughing, and we children were shocked. We thought our grandmother wanted our grandfather dead! It wasn't until I heard my mother tell the story to my father later, and he fell about laughing, that I understood it wasn't a real life-and-death battle."

At that Ollie left us to go sit up all night with a sick friend. I looked concerned and she said, "Don't worry, it's only from 11 P.M. to 7 A.M." When the rest of us left the bar a little later Bryan asked me to come over to his car. The sun was setting but it was still very warm. Slow jazz filtered onto the street from another nearby bar. He went to the trunk and produced a big brown shopping bag. "For you," he said with a flourish.

I looked inside and found a bottle of Dalmore twelve-year-old single malt. It was fantastically hot from sitting all day in the beating sun; in fact, there were stains around the top as if it had actually boiled.

"I have a friend," said Bryan, "who's a real Mississippi gentleman. I mean, magnolias and mint juleps just follow him around wherever he goes. So one time I was sitting in a traffic jam with him, and he reached across me to the glove compartment, and pulled out a pint of whisky. He said, 'The traffic in this state just tries mah nerves. If I didn't take a nip or two, I'd probably have an accident.' Since I know the roads down here, I thought you might need some too."

Kathryn's Tale

I WOKE ON FRIDAY THE THIRTEENTH as I always wake, without my glasses or contacts. Instead of drapes, many of the motels I stayed in hung heavy plastic shades across their rooms' large, lone windows. For some reason, wear and tear I guess, these were often filled with infinitesimally small holes, through which the white-hot morning sunlight tried to pour into the room. Against the dark shade, and without my glasses, the tiny bursts of light throbbed and twinkled like so many stars. Every morning, I would wake to a whole galaxy — suns and supernovas and even red giants — in a motel room. If there was magic on this road, I found it in these $49-a-night solar systems. Although I complain about them, I secretly love motels. Like good stories, they offer evidence that ordinary life, even if only its furniture, can temporarily be held at bay. This particular morning, as I lay in bed squinting, I could just make out the constellation Cassiopeia in the Super 8 Motel universe.

Friday the thirteenth was also the day that I would meet Kathryn Windham, a storyteller who lived in the haunted city of Selma, Alabama, with a ghost named Jeffrey. The coincidence wasn't planned, but I reveled in it. Yesterday at the bar, Kerry had been exceptionally quiet (I think he was surreptitiously watching a baseball game on television), but at the mention of Kathryn's name he spun around and faced me.

"You mean you're going to meet the Ghost Lady?" he exclaimed. "Wow! Cool."

In the two and three-quarter hours it took to drive from Laurel, Mississippi to Selma, Alabama, I found more radio stations than things to look at. The scenery principally consisted of pine trees, kudzu, planted trailers surrounded by hubcap collections and dry cornstalks, and old-fashioned gas stations where all they sold was gas. In Demopolis, Alabama, I stopped at a roadside family restaurant for a nightmarish chicken salad plate: a grisly mix of canned pears, bone, and gristle swamped by mayonnaise and, possibly in an attempt at fusion cuisine, topped by a maraschino cherry. After lunch I continued on to Selma in my rented Oldsmobile, which had a habit of honking at will, feeling distinctly unwell.

Walking around Selma in the early afternoon was like wearing a hair shirt made of heat. Its historic district, as shady and grand as that of Laurel, testified to the city's rapid rise after its destruction in the War. Actually, it wasn't quite destroyed. Water Street, which backs up to the unhurried, jade-colored Alabama River, maintains one of the few commercial districts in the South that managed to escape the torch. The two-story buildings, their cornices shaved into flat rows like adjacent, architectural crew cuts, retained a feeling of the old frontier; if they had a motto, it would be that restoration is only for sissies (renovation had a weak toehold on the street). One grand seven-bay-window façade, still wearing its nineteenth-century grillwork, was just that: a façade. I looked through immense oblong windows to see a small meadow and mature trees growing in its roofless interior.

I had to be careful with Selma. As I limped around in the sun (my back was still twisted, and I was all too aware of that chicken salad), my memory kept dragging me back, past the porches and awnings, not to a streetfront forest but to those old, blue-rinsed ghosts, rolling forever on a 1960s television set in my memory. It was in Selma that the civil rights movement had become a nationally visible Voting Rights campaign. In response to the killing of a black demonstrator by a state trooper, Martin Luther King, Jr., and the civil rights leadership had decided to lead a march from Selma, fifty miles east to Montgomery, Alabama's capital. On March 7, 1965 — nicknamed Bloody Sunday — six hundred marchers had just mounted the Edmund Pettus Bridge over the Alabama River in Selma when state troopers attacked, most reports say without warning. The march was televised, so the world saw what I remember. People screaming and running from the police, who were snatching and beating anybody they could reach with billy clubs and cattle prods. These images emerged through a mist of tear gas, which gave the footage the surreal sense of dreamtime: a ghost story and a live report, all at once.

I walked down Water Street to see the bridge. In the sun, it looked homely and humpbacked, like a steel model for an overgrown box turtle. Selma's Chamber of Commerce brochure had this to say about the incident: "Late in 1963 voting rights activity began in the city and this culminated in 1965 with the Selma to Montgomery March led by Dr. Martin Luther King. Months of daily demonstrations led up to this climactic moment that resulted in the U.S. Voting Rights Act . . ." One line later, it added, "In recent years Selma has been the host city for several movie productions. One of these [was] *Blue Sky,* starring Jessica Lange and Tommy Lee Jones . . . The other was *Body Snatchers III.*"

I knew I had found the Ghost Lady's house when I saw the license plate of the car parked out front. It read, simply, "Jeffrey."

Moments later Kathryn Windham warmly invited me into her house: a brick bungalow in a modest fifties development that her friends had warned was becoming a ghetto. ("That means most of my neighbors are black," said Kathryn, who is white, in a "so what?" tone of voice.) I would have said her ordinary house was the last place on earth that could have been haunted, but for Kathryn's *things.* A formal Empire sofa was accented by putty-colored wall trim, the latter painted a shade that spoke more of the owner's love of history (it had "early nineteenth-century" written all over it), than a decorator's need for a neutral tone. Stately antiques were matched with whimsy: a mobile made from a Coke can cut into a propeller plane; a collection of hollowed gourds and bird feeders, hung from the ceiling; an old-fashioned wheelchair pulled up to a writing desk ("It's comfortable," explained Kathryn). I knew immediately it was the human Jeffrey had chosen, not the house.

Kathryn and I sat at her dining room table and drank grapefruit juice. Throughout our long conversation — "You can stay until the [Atlanta] Braves game comes on," she had told me, "then you have to go" — the phone rang incessantly. She answered each call firmly but politely. "Put it in writing, and I'll gladly consider it," she would say, before perfunctorily hanging up. White-haired but agile, her face lined but her eyes huge and alert behind large glasses, I found it hard to believe Kathryn was eighty-one. She did not suffer fools gladly and had no trouble sharing her opinions (she had a hard one, as Granny Griffin would say, on answering machines). If I misinterpreted her, she corrected me. Like Ollie, Kathryn had a twenty-year-old's interest in the world and an old lady's forthrightness. It was a fine combination.

She had been a newspaper reporter for forty years. "I began in Montgomery as a police reporter," she said. "I was received badly. The men told me, 'You should be writing the society page.' I responded that I didn't know enough adjectives. It was lost on them, but I enjoyed saying it." In the fifties and sixties Kathryn covered the civil rights movement and took photographs of all the principal movers and shakers. "It was a traumatic time . . . Selma has a lot to live down, and probably never will," was all she had to say on the subject, though I noticed a copy of J. J. Chestnut's *Black in Selma* lying on the table.

After about half an hour of conversation, I could no longer resist asking about Jeffrey. Kathryn smiled in a tired way, as if signaling, "so it's come to this." I hoped I hadn't disappointed her. Jeffrey, as it turned out, was a shadow in a photograph and a bump in the night. He was simply a benign, occasionally unruly presence. He walked when everyone else was sitting, he locked doors that had been open, he moved furniture, he scared the cat. He even showed up as a vivid and much-tested, but ultimately inexplicable, shadow in the background of a photograph of a young woman. One of Kathryn's children had named him Jeffrey. "As you would name a pet," Kathryn said.

There is no accompanying tale to explain Jeffrey's behavior. He is the most curious of all creatures: an effect without a cause, a ghost without a story — which was perhaps a relief and an outlet in a town already heavily haunted by its past. Sometimes, if we give the wild things, the frightening things, a name, domesticate them, they become manageable. I wondered if it were a coincidence that Jeffrey had turned up at about the same time as the civil rights protests. There had been a lot to be afraid of back then: for whites, a changing world order, and for blacks, retaliation against a campaign for self-respect that could cost them their lives.

In a memoir of her newspaper days, *Odd-Egg Editor,* Kathryn recalled the ugliness of that time, and the conflicting feelings the movement spawned. She remembered men in her church who would line up and try to intimidate the few black churchgoers who dared enter the sanctuary. She wrote that she had protested, calling their actions "unwise and unchristian," but didn't stop attending. She recalled being afraid only once, when "a chorus of angry white women standing near me" had shouted "Kill them! Kill them!" at passing black marchers. She called little attention to her own bravery in signing a desegregation order as a member of the Selma board of education, despite receiving hate calls and having her car shot at. Yet she was also infuriated by Northern whites — "outside agitators" — who came to march in Selma. Didn't they have their own problems? Why didn't they leave the South to work out matters itself? Ultimately, however, Kathryn wrote that her life was essentially undisrupted by the demonstrations. It had taken Jeffrey to shake up her home, to register, in a mild, housebound way, the seismic activity of the era. Perhaps his story, in a very elemental way, a way that preserves the process by which revolutionary change registers in the folkloric record, is, literally, history.

Lacking his own narrative, Jeffrey made Kathryn a seeker of ghost stories throughout the South, which she has collected in six volumes. If ghost tales do contain a core of subversion, a cry of protest from those pushed to extinction, then she also became a quirky champion of the oppressed. "It has become almost a mission with me," she explained. "After the first book, I became aware that we were losing our ghost stories. They were told mainly by old people, and the old people were dying. So I became a collector."

I was no longer surprised when she said that some parents objected when she told ghost stories to children. "They say I deal in the occult," she said, sounding politely dismissive. An officers' wives group once boycotted her appearance when she told stories on a military base. Kathryn thought they were missing the point. "I don't tell ghost stories to frighten people,

I tell them to entertain. To preserve our folklore. Besides, we need to hear something we don't know about. Everything else in our lives is so set and dried and explained away. Ghosts, you see, give us back the unknown."

Whenever she tells scary stories, Kathryn scrupulously provides her audience with an antidote to the heebie-jeebies. It is an old Southern custom, she says, to put your shoes halfway under your bed, one toe facing inward, the other outward. Heel-to-toe shoes are a sure-fire way to ward off being haunted and to get a good night's sleep. I, however, could continue tossing my footwear any-which-way, for Kathryn chose to tell me about a very different kind of ghost, one who only haunts her memory: her grandfather. In her well-bred Southern accent, r's thrown wide open like windows trying to catch a breeze, reminiscing about her family, she swept me out of Selma and into the rural farmscape of southwest Alabama.

THE GRANDFATHER TALES

Now my family just talked. They were storytellers, but they didn't call themselves that. They wouldn't believe that people are paid to tell stories today! We just sat around and engaged in conversation.

"There's a fine line," I interrupted, "between gossip and talking and storytelling."

That's exactly right. And we did all three. And we sang, and just enjoyed each other. That was before television and air conditioning. We would sit on the porch in the evenings — you see it was too hot even for us children to run around — and tell stories. Most of the stories about my grandfather came from my own father. He was an amazing man, born in 1866: the year after the War Between the States ended. My grandfather had been a prisoner of war . . . after the fighting was over, he walked home from the Mississippi coast and married his childhood sweetheart, and had nine children. Well, my father was one of those children. He went to school for a total of three months, and taught himself to read. He always said I could be anything I wanted as long as I could read. He grew up to be the president of a bank . . .

Now I remember my grandfather. He died when I was seven or eight. He was a thin old man when I knew him, with a white beard. I remember him as being OLD. He was an itinerant Baptist preacher. People still come to me with stories about him from all over Southern Alabama. One of the stories my daddy used to tell about him was that one day he had an appointment in Chocktaw county, but there had been heavy rains, and when he came to cross the Tombigbee River — the name means "coffin maker," by the way — he found that he couldn't get across. The ferry had been washed away.

"I'm sorry Brother Tucker," said the ferryman. "You can't cross the river today."

So my grandfather went to an isolated spot and took off his clothes, and very carefully wrapped his Bible in his shirt and trousers, and put them on his horse's saddle. Then he and the horse swam across that river. My daddy never made a moral out of that story, but I got the point . . .

One time an old lady came up to me in southern Alabama and asked, "Were you kin to Reverend Lee Tucker?" I said yes, and she told me that he had stayed in her house when she was a child. She said she liked it when Reverend Tucker came, because her mama made great meals for him. Well, one day he was late. Now this was very unusual, because as you know, my grandfather never missed an appointment. They waited and waited, and he finally showed up. And when he did his shirt was dirty and his tie was all rearranged, and his hair tousled.

Because he was late he had to go straight to church to preach, and the congregation was shocked. He was usually a man with not a single hair out of place. My grandfather took the pulpit and said, "First, I apologize for being late. Second, I have to explain my appearance." Well, it turned out that he had met a man with whom he had had some disagreement years ago. The man had made him get off his horse. "When I did," continued my grandfather, "he slapped me. Now the Bible says to turn the other cheek, so I did, and he slapped me again. After that I couldn't remember any further Biblical instructions, so I gave him a sound thrashing."

There was another occasion as well, when a man came up to me and asked if I were the Reverend Lee Tucker's kin. This man said he had once seen him pray away a cyclone in Nanafail, Alabama.

Kathryn stopped the story for a moment and said, "Isn't that a beautiful name, Nanafail?" I agreed, and told her my favorite name, the Welsh city Aberystwyth. We both repeated the words over and over, like enchantments, and briefly discussed the legendary Welsh prince, Madog, who may or may not have sailed into Mobile Bay in 1170, until Kathryn got up to answer the blasted telephone. She came back bearing two Mini Moo chocolate Bluebell Ice Cream pops, and continued her tale.

Well, this man had been working in the fields one day when a horrible black cloud came up from nowhere. He realized he couldn't make it to his house, so he ran to the barn, which was nearby. Through the barn cracks, he saw my grandfather standing out in his field, holding on to the top of a rail fence. The man watched as his hair was whipped back by the wind. The funnel cloud was headed directly toward him. He could see that my grandfather's face was tilted toward the heavens, and his lips were moving — he was obviously praying, fast and furiously. Well, don't you know that funnel cloud veered away at the last minute, and only damaged some brush? Ever afterward that man told about how he had seen Reverend Lee Tucker punctually pray a cyclone away.

As it was getting to be time for the Braves to begin their warm-up, Kathryn suggested a quick tour of her house. As we passed the garage, she said, offhandedly, "That's where I keep the coffin." I really wanted to say something about my garage being crowded with them and let it go at that, but I couldn't resist: I had to ask. With a smile, she explained that awhile back she had discovered the outrageous cost of dying in this country, and had been particularly shocked at the price of coffins. "So I had a cabinetmaker make me a plain old box for $250. My children know it's there. Right now I keep a twelve-piece set of crystal in it."

Kathryn's backyard again proved why Jeffrey had chosen her to oversee Selma's transition from the nation's bad dream to "Tale Tellin' Capital of Alabama," as it is now called on her behalf (the Chamber of Commerce also tried to get Selma known as the Butterfly Capital of the state, but not enough butterflies came to roost, so the name didn't stick). Her garden was lined with pale aqua-colored insulator caps from old telephone poles, which looked like thick bubbles blown by a passing wind. I admired them and she immediately dug one out for me to keep as a present. It came filled with stubborn orange clay. The very stuff, I thought, of which the Reverend Tucker was made.

Best of all were Kathryn's trees: two live saplings that grew, on their lower limbs, an amazing profusion of blue glass bottles. There were big bottles and small ones, round ones, square ones, tiny ones, old ones. All were made of cobalt-colored glass, and they were hypnotic. Kathryn saw I was enchanted.

"They're blue-bottle trees," she said proudly. "I pull the leaves off the smaller branches, and stick on the bottles. They keep away evil spirits." I told her about the blue trim on the Gullah coast, and she nodded her head. Her trees were a variation on the old African-American theme. As I left Kathryn to her baseball game, and drove off with my insulator and some turkey feathers she had given me, I wondered what spirits she had to fear. Jeffrey was a good ghost, and she had told me that she would not move from her neighborhood until she was afraid. "And I haven't been scared yet," she said. With neither ghosts nor humans to worry about, I surmised that Kathryn had taken the weight of Selma's bad memories onto her branches, and covered them in blue bottles. She could not pray away the cyclone of events which she had lived through in this town — indeed, I doubt she would have wanted to — but she could grow the color of peace from the turbulence of the town's history, and that was a fine achievement.

I found an Econo Lodge on the outskirts of Montgomery, not far from Crazy Bill's Fireworks Superstore (why is it that everyone who sells fireworks is "Crazy" somebody or other?). It is illegal to sell fireworks — sparklers, firecrackers, cherry bombs, that kind of thing — in the North, which meant that whenever my family went South when I was a child, I thrilled to the recklessness of the place. It was the first time I recall thinking that fun might somehow involve illegality. Once installed in my room, I opened Bryan's Scotch, which along with my contact lens solution was near boiling point from sitting in the trunk all day, and called Dick Newman. As we spoke, I absently watched Doris Day mouth "Que Sera Sera" in the Hitchcock film *The Man Who Knew Too Much* that I had muted on television, in which she and Jimmy Stewart did plucky things to save their kidnapped son.

Dick, whom I had also called from Florida for information on Rosewood, was supposed to have been with me on this portion of the trip, but had fallen sick at the last moment. Although he was thirty years my senior, we were close friends, originally drawn together by our appreciation of the fact that Robert Byron, the great travel writer of the 1930s, did a near-perfect drag impression of Queen Victoria. Dick was one of the Northern white boys whom Kathryn Windham had so resented, who came South to join the civil rights movement. He had been a Presbyterian minister, taught theology, run the publishing program at the New York Public Library, married twice (he considered and rejected it countless other times), and had a dog named after the eighteenth-century black poet, Phyllis Wheatley. He now worked at the W. E. B. DuBois Center for African-American Studies at Harvard, and if he could have made a deal with the Devil, like Madam Margot in the Gullah ghost story, he would have chosen the opposite of her request and asked to become black.

"Whatsup?" he asked, from what I assumed was his sickbed.

"Tell me what I don't know about the civil rights movement," I said, watching the ice melt too quickly in my hot whisky. "I was in Selma today and I'm going to Montgomery and Birmingham tomorrow, and I don't want to be ignorant."

"All right," he said, "get out a pencil. Here's Newman's Civil Rights Lecture 101 — the condensed version."

The first thing you need to know is that the movement comes up from below. It's genuinely a people's movement. You get the leadership rushing from place to place throughout the South to direct what's essentially already happened. Now here's the historical situation in which they're operating: by law and custom the South has been segregated for a hundred years. Black people are *never* addressed as "Mr." or "Mrs." The status quo is all about keeping black folks in their place — which is secondary.

Between Reconstruction and the 1950s, there were what? — three to four thousand lynchings? This means that there was always covert resistance, but never anything organized until the 1950s . . . One of the most interesting things about the Movement was that it was a *civil rights* movement. Look, the Thirteenth Amendment ended slavery; the Fourteenth made blacks citizens; the Fifteenth gave them the right to vote. It all happened a hundred years ago! But nothing was enforced! This movement was not radical or new, the purpose was to get the law enforced. The people perceived as defying the law were actually the ones trying to get it obeyed — that was the great irony of the civil rights movement.

Now at the beginning the North was unsupportive. Just some college kids and church types . . .

"Like you," I said. Doris Day was singing like mad now, though I could only tell from her facial muscles. Thank goodness for the mute button. I wondered how Dick could work up so much passion when he was sick. He ignored my interruption and continued.

Then King takes over — King, the Reluctant Reformer. J. Edgar Hoover called him the most dangerous man in the United States. Down there where you are he was called Marxist Lucifer Coon. Now the key thing with King is that because the movement rallies around him, it becomes religiously based. This means that supporters adopt King's strategy of nonviolence, which he essentially takes from Gandhi. The idea was not just passive resistance, but positive action, which virtually invites suffering and confrontation, so the enemy is converted to your cause by your willingness to suffer. It's both a religious concept and a practical device.

Now this sounds perverse, and it is, but the best thing that happens to the Movement is the assassination of J.F.K. Curiously, Kennedy, the Northern liberal, is conservative on race — his intellectual team continually roadblocks their efforts — but Johnson, the Southern hick from Texas, really cares. Johnson, you see, went to teachers college, and started his teaching career in a Mexican school. At heart he has sympathy for the poor. That's why the Civil Rights Act of 1964 gets passed.

So now the movement has momentum. When you have nothing, you have no expectations; but the CRA energizes the leadership.

When you get a little you want more, and you really do become dangerous. On top of that, the mood in the country has changed. People aren't suddenly for Negroes, but they're against unfairness. They're paying attention now.

Okay. The Civil Rights Act in theory desegregates facilities. But the great goal is enabling legislation for the Fifteenth Amendment — voting rights. See, the intractable whites in the South say, "All right, I can live with Negroes in Woolworths. I don't want to, but I can. If we lose political power, though, we're screwed. We'll finally lose the peace we won in 1865."

I wouldn't have understood exactly what Dick meant by his last comment if I had not been to Sapelo Island and learned its history. Political expediency not only took away the forty acres Sherman had promised to the freed slaves on the sea islands, it dragged antebellum attitudes into the twentieth century.

. . . so this is the harder goal. This is the tough one.

"What were the strategies used to keep blacks from voting?" I asked.

You have to realize that there was essentially no Republican Party — the party of Lincoln — in the South. Everyone voted Democratic. So whoever controlled the Democratic Primary virtually controlled the general election. Well, the Democratic Party was defined by law in many Southern states as a private organization — like a club. And this one didn't take blacks. So that was one strategy. Another was illiteracy — illiteracy rates were high — and that was an automatic disqualification. But the most notorious were the examinations. If blacks passed the initial voting exam, they would come to the final question: "How many soap bubbles can you blow from a bar of Ivory Soap?" Guess what? Somehow, your answer was always wrong.

Dick finished with a victory. Congress passed the Voting Rights Act in 1966. We hung up then, leaving the tragedies of the later sixties for another phone call. I turned off Doris and Jimmy, and went to bed.

The following morning, when I turned on the car engine, I experienced a rare moment of cosmic convergence: "Sweet Home Alabama," by Lynyrd Skynyrd, was playing on the radio. I picked out snippets of lyrics: "Singing songs about the Southland . . . In Birmingham they love the Guv'nor / Now we all did what we could do / Watergate does not bother me / Does your conscience bother you? . . ."

When this song was written in the early seventies (not long before the band was decimated in a plane crash), the governor of Alabama was George Wallace, once the best-known racist in America. But the song's lyrics confused me. What did they all do? The last line — "Montgomery's got the answer" — was equivocal. What was the question?

I asked myself that as I wandered through the city in which Rosa Parks, in 1955, had famously refused to move to the back of the bus. The ensuing Montgomery Bus Boycott had been led by a twenty-six-year-old minister, Martin Luther King, Jr., who from 1954 to 1960 was pastor of what is now called the Dexter Avenue King Memorial Baptist Church. I sought it out, and found an unassuming red brick building, a thorn in the side of Alabama's gleaming white complex of state government offices. The church sat halfway up a hill crowned by the glorious state capitol: a big Greek Revival box with Corinthian columns, a clock cupola, and a ninety-seven-foot whitewashed dome (although it was superb architecture, Akbar's warning that context is everything gave it a halo of arrogance). The structure had been completed in 1851, just in time to house the first government of the Confederacy, as a solemn historical marker notes (Montgomery was only the Confederate capital for a few months, before the honor was snatched away by the more aristocratic Richmond, Virginia).

On a Saturday morning, equally devoid of ghosts and the living, Montgomery was empty and unlovely. Nondescript buildings sat without relation to one another, with random spaces in between. It was a city without architectural conversation: no opportunities to pose questions, no proximity to hear answers. I did find a bustling crowd in a farmer's market behind the capital, but vegetables and fruit pies didn't offer much in the way of ballast to anchor the place to the present. Okra, watermelons, peanuts still attached to their stems (out of a familiar context, which for me was in a little foil package on a plane, they looked like tiny, shriveled, pox-ridden yams), more sorry-looking peaches, individual pecan pies, red and green chilies strung together into a wreath: these were all the answers Montgomery had to offer.

I liked Birmingham, once archly known as "Bombingham," better. The radio beamed optimism. As I drove into the city, a caller won a thousand dollars on "Oldies 109." "We're gonna go right out and buy a camper!" the winner declared. From what I overheard of conversations in gas stations and fast-food restaurants, an air of barely contained hysteria at the approach of college football season hung low over the city. When I asked some kids slouching around a street corner how to get to the Civil Rights Museum, they looked depressed at the prospect of my torturous afternoon. "Why don't you go to the Alabama Sports Hall of Fame instead?" one suggested.

Accompanied by a chorus of "Oh no's," I chose the museum. Birmingham had been one of the cities targeted by civil rights leadership with marches and demonstrations. I saw Dick's point about King inviting confrontation and suffering: in Birmingham he had chosen a stronghold of the Ku Klux Klan, and a city ruled by police chief Eugene "Bull" Connor, who vowed that if the nonviolent demonstrations continued, there would be "blood running down the streets of Birmingham." Both men got their wishes. As protesters ignored Connor and continued their marches, white supremacists went on a bombing spree, culminating in the September 1963 bombing of the 16th Street Baptist Church — the movement's headquarters — which killed four young black girls attending a Bible class. (A week after I wrote these words, in May 2000, the Alabama Grand Jury indicted two former Klansmen for the four murders. While no charges were brought at the time of the bombing, the case was reopened in the seventies, which resulted in the conviction of a third bomber who died in jail in 1985. A fourth suspect is also dead. The case was subsequently reopened in 1980, 1988, and 1997, the latter resulting in the current charges.)

The museum was packed with reminders of tragedies and victories: interactive exhibits, explanatory posters, even an old city bus and a couple of water fountains. A Dutch couple and I were the only white visitors. One clip from a newspaper caught my eye. In the spring of 1963, a group of white Birmingham clergymen had published a letter deeming the protests "unwise and untimely." With a jolt I recalled Kathryn Windham's phrase: she must have been making a reference to this letter when she called racist members of her congregation "unwise and unchristian." What courage that must have taken, but what satisfaction she must have felt as a reporter, turning the news on its head.

As I tried to find my way out — the museum was cunningly designed to prohibit a fast exit — I came upon a display of console-style television sets from about the time I was born, 1960, each blue-toned screen flickering with images of brutality. Time and perception telescoped then with a rush, and I flushed with heat despite the air conditioning. It was as if my personal memories were on public display. I had the uncomfortable impression that the country was trying to trap the ugliness of the era within these sets, to prevent it from leaking into the Technicolor daylight of the present. I peered at an image of "Bull" Connor, heavy-set, angry, and balding. His image didn't roll, but it spawned a faint ghost just to the left of it, as if his memory were breeding in some unthinkable, televised afterlife. A cowardly part of me wished that he, like Jeffrey, were also a ghost without a story.

Sharply at 5 P.M., guards hurried me out of the museum, and I joined a foot patrol of well-dressed couples, both black and white, strolling from their parked cars to a concert at the civic center. Birmingham had too much to do — after all, football season was right around the corner — to dwell on ghost stories.

David Joe's Tale

IT WAS A SOFT, SLOW DUSK, almost more tactile than visual, and it seeped through the open car windows straight into my pores. I was driving through northeastern Alabama's lake country en route to Tennessee. At Gasden the pine and the kudzu belts temporarily collided, and for a few miles the roadsides were hung with curtains of topiary, shot through with branches of cool, green sparklers. Insects buzzed in wavering crescendos, and Kathryn Windham spoke quietly on the car's tape player about her two ancient aunts, who had sat on the back porch in summer and tried to pick names and memories out of unidentified family photos. As I listened, her voice wove into the steadily rising countryside, so that I came away with a double-exposed memory, one image of gentle farms and tilled fields entering through the eye, the other, of two old women in long black dresses studying photographs, through the ear.

Without warning, the secondary road petered into a causeway, and led me to the town of Cedar Bluffs on Lake Weiss. The low, clotting sunlight whipped the chop of the lake as if it had been batter for a yellow cake. It was what Willie Morris called, "one of those sudden, magic places of America," spoiled, unfortunately, by a fake log-cabin-style motel lying in wait at the end of the causeway. I was tired but avoided the place as an animal would an obvious snare, and drove on to Tennessee.

I spent the night at Marguerite's brother Nat and his wife Tina's house — they were away but had lent me a key — in

Chattanooga, or Chattaboogie, as they called it. After two hours of fast driving while trying to follow pale, penciled directions in the dark — in a car that kept the mysteries of overhead light operation to itself — I had arrived so shaky that I thought I'd punched in the wrong code on their alarm pad and had tripped the system. But no screeching sirens, no lights, no wails ever came. Giddy with relief that I didn't have to explain myself to the Chattanooga police, I began to explore the forbidden fruits of someone else's home. Neon green Post-it notes covered almost every drawer or door in the kitchen with cryptic messages. "Cat Food Not Yours." "Drink the Wine." It was exhilarating to forage through other people's decisions. Why did they put the silverware here? Why was there a folk art carving on top of the toaster oven? They had mint chocolate-chip ice cream: how much could I eat without them knowing? I studied the topography of scoops in the carton so I could exactly replicate it, albeit at a lower level. It soon became apparent, however, that the house and I had a disagreement about the time. I was living at the nine o'clock hour, and it at the ten. Somewhere, perhaps at the magic lake, I'd lost sixty minutes, and had returned to Eastern Daylight Time. Sometimes this country is just too big.

I spent the next day, the *only* day on my very garrulous pilgrimage, in absolute silence. Tina once told me that she had made friends with a neighbor, a kind woman who gave her recipes and plant cuttings. One day, the woman had excitedly shown her the autograph of her hero — the former KKK politician David Duke. Because Tina, whose best friend in Chattanooga is black, is still fretting about whether or not it's possible to compartmentalize politics, morals, and neighborliness, I stayed inside to hide from the ethical dilemmas across the street.

*

Hazy mountains on the northeastern horizon and dead deer by the roadside; Uncle Bud's Catfish, Chicken and Such; yellow-green fields of tobacco, egg carton hills and valleys; Swiss rolls; barns and silos, trailers and shaded farmhouses; Nanny Goats 4-sale. These were the way marks that led me to Jonesborough, Tennessee: Storytelling Town, USA. As I headed up the spine of Tennessee's eastern border, it occurred to me with a jolt that I was probably only about an hour from Ray Hicks's house, albeit approaching from the opposite direction.

About twenty years ago, Jimmie Neil Smith started a story-telling festival in Jonesborough as a last-ditch prod to eco-nomic development. It succeeded beyond anyone's wildest dreams. Every October the small town is now overrun by tens of thousands of visitors who flock to hear a panel of invited tellers (Ray Hicks is the only one with a lifetime invitation). While other little towns in the area struggle, Jonesborough al-most indecently thrives. Its red-brick homes and businesses are in fine repair; coffee shops, B&Bs, and expensive gift shops dot the main street. As I sauntered around with David Joe Miller, a storyteller who lives in Jonesborough, townspeople called greet-ings and fond teases from their porches. "Watch out for him," one well-dressed man yelled, winking, "he's a *storyteller!*" Two sisters who run the local coffee shop gave us towering Orange Thistles (frozen concoctions of orange juice, sugar, and milk that left my teeth chattering with cold) just because they adore David and his dog Baybee. In Jonesborough I had stumbled on the South — the modest, pioneer-built, highland South — of a tour guide's fantasies (there were even special parking spaces for tour buses). A town not so much found *in* stories, as exist-ing because of them. It was also the oldest town in Tennessee, and once capital of a short-lived state called Franklin, which would have been the first new state to follow the thirteen original colonies after the Revolutionary War, had Congress not rejected it.

Before the Orange Thistles, I had learned to make *real* Southern iced tea in David Joe's apartment. I had complained to him about the obsession with sweet iced tea below the Mason-Dixon Line (there really was little escape from the stuff, so sugary it got into my gills and made me wince). David Joe calmly explained that I simply hadn't had *good* sweet tea.

"First, see, you take your mama's big old teapot — that's the secret ingredient. It needs to have seasoned over years and years. Then add a cup of sugar; then pour in the boiling water. It caramelizes the sugar just a tad. Let it dissolve, then add five tea bags, and let it sit for two hours."

He handed me a glass: I could actually taste the tea, but in my bad-natured, Northern way still imagined I felt it rotting my teeth. David Joe was a gentle bull of a man. Like Kathryn, he was from a family that liked to mythologize itself, though he was the first to actually call himself a storyteller. He was a big man with a thickset neck and a clipped, graying beard. I might have mistaken him for a bouncer, but for a calm gentleness of spirit and earnest brown eyes. He and his dog were soul mates.

Despite his mountain-moving looks, David Joe wore the storyteller's mantle almost apologetically, or maybe his sweetness disguised his ability to take center stage. At least I thought he was shy until he began to speak.

"All right," said David Joe, "this is an old Appalachian folk tale. I really hope you like it, Pam."

THE PEDDLER MAN

There was once a peddler man who lived in a small cabin outside a village. The cabin had a very small front porch, and beyond that, a garden. In the middle of the garden was a cherry tree. Now, every year, the peddler man, he would grow a bountiful garden, and every year he would share his bounty with his neighbors and friends. What he didn't eat he would give away, and what he didn't give away he'd let the animals come and eat.

His friends and neighbors all told him the same thing. "Peddler Man, you give too much away! What you don't need you give away, and what you don't give away you let the animals come and eat. One of these days, Peddler Man, if you don't save up, you're going to come asking for a handout."

I was astounded. Back in Beaufort, South Carolina, Ron Daise had said how important church-going was to story-telling. When the message is good versus evil, the preacher's delivery had better be able to stand up to the subject matter. "Emulation is the key," Ron had said. "My grandmother couldn't read but she sure could *perform*. You even get little ten year olds sounding like Martin Luther King." Here in the highlands, this big, gentle white man drove Ron's point home. David's whole persona changed when he launched into "The Peddler Man." He sat erect; his voice took on a preaching cadence, rising and falling in the hilly patterns his hands traced in the air. He used repetition to create an almost stately delivery. The force of his performance was presumptive: it took over all other mental and physical options and left me with no choice but to listen. He was a changed man.

Well, the peddler man, he was living his life the way he wanted to, and he saw no reason to change it. And he didn't. Why, he'd fill his pouch full of wares, and he'd take 'em into the middle of the village and he'd sell them. He'd lay them all out on a rock and he'd stand there as people would come and look at what he had to offer. There'd be the little girl who'd come up, and she'd see the red ribbons and she'd say, "How much are those red ribbons?"

"Well those red ribbons are two bits."

"Oh, my daddy would never let me spend two bits for something as silly as red ribbons for my hair."

And the peddler man would give those red ribbons to the little girl and say, "Now you go ahead and take 'em. They'd look a lot prettier in your hair than in my pouch." And she'd pick 'em up and run off to show her friends as she was tying them in her hair.

Then a little boy would come up and say, "How much is that jack-knife?"

"Well that jackknife is two bits too."

"Ain't got two bits."

"Aw, you go ahead and take that jackknife. It'll be a whole lot lighter in your pocket than it is in my pouch . . ."

Now, that summer came a drought. And the peddler man's garden didn't prove to be as bountiful as it normally does. So going into the fall of the year the peddler man was running low on food. He'd look into his pantry and he was very low on food. Then the winter hit. And oh, the winter hit that year with a vengeance. The snows flew in from the north, the temperature dropped, and the peddler man found himself one day opening his very last can of food. And he remembered what his neighbors and friends had all told him.

He went to bed that night hungry. And they tell me a hungry man will dream. And in his dream was a vision. And the vision told him to go into town. To look, and he will see all he needs to see. To listen, and he will hear all he needs to hear . . . Well, the peddler man pulled all the strength together that he could muster, and pulled himself up out of that bed. He got his big long overcoat on and he pulled it up high, over his neck. And he opened the front door and the wind came rustling in. He walked that pathway into the village like he'd done so many times before to sell his wares. But never had he been met with such force of wind. The snowflakes felt like needles stinging his cheeks as he walked into town, to do what the vision told him to do.

When he got into the middle of the village he found the spot where he used to sell his wares and he stood there, trying his best to keep himself warm. No one looked him in the eye. His neighbors, his friends, no one would look at him, because they were afraid if they made eye contact then he would ask them for a handout, just as they had told him. So they ignored him. At the end of the day the peddler man was so filled with despair that he couldn't stand it any longer. He was too weak to make it back to his cabin. He decided the only thing he could do was to find an alley and lay down in the corner and give up. He chose an alley off the village square, and started walking toward that alley, but an innkeeper hollered out to the peddler man. He said, "Peddler Man, come over here. I've been watching you most of the day. You've been standing out there in the square in this weather not meant for man nor beast, and you've been waiting on someone. Tell me, who is it you've been looking for?"

Well the peddler man, he couldn't speak, because he hadn't had anything to drink or eat all day. The innkeeper saw this, and gave him food and drink. And when the peddler man could finally speak he asked him again. "Tell me who it is you've been out there looking for, waiting on all day?" The peddler man answered. "Not anyone in particular," he said. "I just been standing out there because I had a dream, and the dream told me to come here and listen, and look."

"Ha! The dream told you to come here in this terrible weather and stand around listening and looking? Peddler Man, you're a bigger fool than I've heard you be. Well, Peddler Man, let me tell you something. I have dreams all the time, and where would I be if I closed up my inn and chased these dreams that I have? I'm gonna teach you a lesson, Peddler Man. Listen to how silly this sounds. I had a dream the other night. And in my dream a vision came. And that vision told me that if I were to follow one of these pathways that led out from the village, I'd eventually come to a modest cabin. And that cabin would have a front porch on it. And beyond the front porch there'd be a garden in the middle of which would be a cherry tree. And that vision told me that if I took a shovel and dug underneath that cherry tree, I'd find a chest filled with gold. Ha, ha!! Do you think I'm going to close up my inn and go off following some crazy dream like that?" And he ran the peddler man out of his inn.

Well the peddler man got up and he thanked the innkeeper for the food and the drink and the advice. And he walked back down the pathway into the woods where his cabin was. When he got there, he went into the toolshed and he got a shovel, and he came back to the cherry tree in the garden and he started digging. And after he dug for awhile he hit something rock solid. And he dug all around it and brought it up on the ground, and he took the end of the shovel and he broke the lock. He opened it up and it was a chest. And that chest was filled with gold. All the gold he would ever need for the rest of his life. And the good that he did with that gold! — I can't even begin to tell you. And that is the peddler's story.

I clapped and David — I had begun to call him David because I felt silly saying "David Joe" — beamed. Baybee, a sweet old mutt with a lot of German Shepherd in her, thumped her tail against the back of her master's giant sofa (sitting on it, my legs didn't reach the floor). After he finished, David told me that one day he had gotten a call from the White House, asking if he were David Joe Miller, the storyteller. He thought it was a joke and almost hung up, but the man convinced him it was the vice president's office calling: would he tell a story to Al and Tipper Gore and a few thousand of their closest friends at a fund-raising picnic for the Democratic Party? David was stunned, but agreed. Like most of the storytellers I've met, he said he had no idea what he would tell until he stood on stage and took stock of his audience. "The Peddler Man" is what came out.

"The audience was from Tennessee, so I gave them something they could relate to," said David. "I also tacked on an obvious ending so they wouldn't have to think too hard."

This was David's coda:

From that story I've learned two things. We must not only follow and listen to and respect our own dreams, but follow and listen and respect the dreams of others. Because you never know when our dreams may be entwined with someone else's. And we can realize our dreams by looking no further than our very own backyard.

After this, there had been thunderous applause. "In its best dreams, that's how the Democratic Party sees itself," said David, laughing.

I pictured Al Gore, standing out in the cold, waiting for the presidency to come to him in a vision. It was a comforting message that David had given him: inward-looking, optimistic, easy, respectful of others. But before his moral edited out the details, the story had also been about suspicion, poverty, and superstition. David essentially offered the Democrats the waking South and the dreaming one — the latter dreaming happy, insular dreams of its own backyard. And like a good politician, he told them which one to remember.

I stayed just up the road from Jonesborough at a Red Roof Inn on the outskirts of the bigger and rougher Johnson City. Just outside the inn's office, his lawn chair nearly blocking the entrance, was an old man with a Lhasa apso on a leash. I bent over to pet the dog and a voice that sounded like a working lawn mower asked, "Where ya from?"

I thought I'd try "Rhode Island" this time.

"Well, well," he said with delight, "what's a Rhode Island Yankee doin' driving a car with Texas plates? Hunh?"

I studied him as I explained that it was a rental car. He had long, sleek white hair swept back under a black fedora, a white beard, and eyes like a basset hound. His outfit — white shorts and a red golf shirt — seemed to belong to someone else. Maybe it did.

"All right, missy, let's see how smart ya are. Where was the first cotton mill in the U-Nited States established?"

"Ha!" I parried. "Pawtucket, Rhode Island."

"Okay, think yer smart, dontcha? It was established by an Englishman named Slater. What was his first name?"

Dang. This was trickier. Then it came to me. "Samuel!" I shouted. "His name was Samuel!"

"Man, girl, you got eyes in you that see! My name's Joe Pace, what's yours?"

At great length, Joe explained that Slater's grandson had migrated to Greenville, North Carolina, and opened the first cotton mill in the South. Joe's daddy had opened the first bale of cotton for its looms in the early 1920s. Joe himself had been born in the mill village, gone to work on the looms at fifteen, married a beauty queen, and become an alcoholic. He had taught English in the Los Angeles County Prison — as an inmate — and then one day eleven years ago, after buying a bottle of vodka for breakfast, decided he was sick of the stuff and poured it away. Joe has been sober ever since. Now he was seventy-five years old and lived at the Red Roof Inn.

I told him that I thought drinking was like bad storytelling, the kind that functions as an reflex defense against listening, or like storytelling only to yourself, or desperation travel: all are ways to retreat from perception. Joe nodded solemnly. William Faulkner, who knew a little bit about drinking, also knew that storytelling could be a means to oblivion as well, and that the South was drunk on escapist tales of its own devising. Following his comment that "We [Southerners] need to talk, to tell, since oratory is our heritage," he added, "we seem to try in the simple furious breathing span of the individual to draw a savage indictment of the contemporary scene or to escape from it into a make-believe region of swords and magnolias and mocking birds which never perhaps existed anywhere." In the rarified atmosphere of Faulkner's unhappy families, and maybe in the big, unhappy family of the South, storytelling is as involuntary as breathing, maybe even as leaving, however it is you choose to go.

Joe hadn't read Faulkner, but he knew the name. "He was an alcoholic too," I said.

"Did he stop drinking?"

"I don't think so."

On my way back from checking in at the motel, I shook hands with Joe and said good-bye, before going off to my room. Then he blew my mind. "Y'know, Yankee," he said, "when men are defeated, they drink. Or they get up and go. A defeated place can't leave itself, so it makes up tales about how it wants to be. Have I understood you right?"

I felt like I'd been slapped. "Man, you've got eyes in you that see," I told Joe, and put Bryan's Scotch back in the trunk for the night.

Karen's Tale

I STILL HAD NOT RECEIVED Vickie Vedder's stories, and I was getting nervous. Every morning and evening I would crawl under dusty beds in motel rooms, plug in my modem, and check for word from her. I was also getting addicted to her messages, through which I learned more and more about Granny, Daddy Runt, and Vickie's views on the South. Dependant as it is on reciprocity and spontaneity — and often bad grammar — e-mail is often more akin to speech than writing, which is so much more solitary and slow. I felt as if Vickie and I were having a summer-long conversation carried out through a medium that synthesized the two of us, the talker and the writer. But she still hadn't told me a story.

Her latest installment kept the promises coming.

Hay!! (That's spelled in what I call Southification)

It's crossed my mind that most stories are based in pain or the threat of it or the detour around it. You know what I mean? Speaking of stories, I promise you, you won't need to worry about the stories not coming. They mean too much to me, and some real-life Southern stuff that's not sooooo old would be good for your book. You know how every-body thinks of the South as the 1800s? . . . What I like about my family stories is that they are old-timey . . . but the people in them have been KEPT ALIVE by everybody TALKING and TELLING about who they were and what they did.

Daddy's family and Mama's family lived through such hard times . . . that their stories are stories of survival. They laughed at blisters from the plow, feeding the mule instead of the babies, planting and picking food, the heat, the sorrow, death, love and affection in unbearable suffering, which all stemmed basically from trying to feed themselves. And that's what they talked about, sitting on the porch . . . And with ten brothers and sisters talking (Daddy was the eldest of ten young 'uns and Mama the oldest of six), with cousins and aunts thrown in, my life was filled to the brim with the past.

. . . I suppose when you live on a farm with no modern amenities there are so many things that can and do go wrong. That is why my family has a little phrase that covers all sorts of trials in life: "Ye gotta have a little backbone." It means you have to rely on a "bit of courage" which, according to Daddy and his family, was bred into you. Unless you happened to have inherited a gene from Uncle Hansel, who was a scaredy cat and a numbskull, but a dandy. They always followed up an account of Uncle Hansel by reminding us that he was handsome and clean. Mama said when she married Daddy, she ended up ironing white cotton shirts for Uncle Hansel everyday. That iron was . . . heated in the fireplace, and wiped clean with beeswax before you could touch a white cotton shirt with it. Mama says, "Lord, gal, it's a wonder we didn't all keel over . . . It wut'n no world back then for no frail sort . . ."

. . . Anyway (that's one of my favorite transition words — the other one is "Let me see, now") . . . it's clear that Daddy Runt, Granny, Daddy, Mama and most of their relatives . . . had plently to say about life, and as they talked about it, they became the characters that I know and talk about. But what

I've tried to do to make all this talking a little less chaotic is to condense it into the voice of one person: Granny Griffin. And everyone talks through her, in a sense . . . She stands for everyone I ever loved on both sides of my family . . . As one old man told me, "There's a bunch'a good people out yonder in that graveyard. I hate'che don' know 'em."

I'll be sending my stuff soon . . .

Sincerely, Vickie Vedder

I was traveling now to the very rim of the Otherworld: West Virginia. Some say it is part of the South, some say not. Either way, it was a long haul from Johnson City, Tennessee, to Fayetteville, West Virginia, where I was headed, and an even longer one from there to mid-western Kentucky, where I would be going next. But I wanted to meet Karen Vuranch and hear about coal mines — besides, she had invited me to spend the night — so North was my direction.

The road to Karen led me back to Appalachia, as the mountains in my windshield attested (West Virginia, in fact, is the only state that falls entirely within the Appalachian uplands). In the early morning mist, which lent the valleys pale green definition, I could see how the mountains cupped one another as they receded northward, looking for all the world like a giant Sydney Opera House.

At the border of Tennessee and Virginia, I stopped in Bristol for gas. It was a functional little place except that it was essentially a bisexual body politic. Half of Bristol lay in Virginia, and other half in Tennessee. Brass markers down the middle of the inappropriately named State Street indicated the dividing line. This quirk made for two local governments, two police forces, and two fire departments, none of which, of course, agreed on anything.

"Ya can't get nothing done here," complained a convenience-store clerk. "One state will build a big four-lane highway that reaches the state border, then just stops."

"Or they'll miss each other by a big fat foot," added a woman who had just walked in to buy cigarettes.

They explained to me that because the sales tax in Virginia is four percent, compared to Tennessee's seven and three-quarters percent, people want to buy things in Virginia, but live in Tennessee, where there is no state income tax.

One thing was clear as I drove northward: no one in New England would be concerned at my visiting Bristol, Virginia, but they would turn up their noses at Bristol, Tennessee. As states go, Virginia has charisma. The 1998 rankings of U.S. cities (based on resident satisfaction) list three for each geographic region, in descending order of size. All the Southern Region winners — Norfolk, Richmond, and Charlottesville — were in Virginia. Anyone who thinks class is not a factor in America should consider this state. The home of Jefferson, Washington, Madison, and Monroe, even though it was capital of the Confederacy, has always conjured graciousness and intellectual achievement, and because of that was given a place in Northern historians' creation myth of America. The rest of the South, or rather, the Further South, wasn't afforded the courtesy. The perception still lingers.

Now West Virginia, as they say, is another story. Until the outbreak of the Civil War, it had been part of Virginia, but had refused to go along with the rest of the state on the issue of secession (because West Virginia had been a slaveholding territory, Lincoln made abolition a condition of statehood; its constitution duly rewritten, it was admitted to the Union in 1862). Around noontime I drove through a tunnel under a mountain in Jefferson National Forest, and came out in this strange little state, Virginia's bastard, that no region really claims, not the

South, not the Mid-Atlantic, not the Midwest. We all carry baggage on our travels, and what I brought to West Virginia was a child's memory of going to see my brother in college, near Wheeling: hollering on hairpin curves, listening to tales of locals shooting at students for fun. I had reveled in the danger of the place. Visiting parents had used words like "backward" and "inbred."

From what I could tell now, as an adult, the only evidence of inbreeding was among the mountains. They humped each other and their knobby little foothills writhed and twisted around their knees. The towns were hardscrabble places, lacking the deeper, flatter South's cultivation in every sense of the word. No apron of farmland added the easy grace of agriculture; only forests pressed against them, and steelworks, and lumbermills. I stopped half an hour from Fayetteville to buy Karen some wine, and remarked to the cashier about a sign I'd seen announcing the town as Birthplace of the Founder of Grandparents' Day. The market's shelves were nearly empty, and the floor covered in trash.

"'Cause there ain't nothing else to do here, ma'am, so folks makes stuff up," she said, truthfully.

I walked into Karen Vuranch's blue farmhouse and fell silent. There was a "Cymru" sticker on her kitchen window. She saw me looking at it, my mouth ajar. "That means Wales in Welsh," she said.

"I know."

"You do?"

Karen and I quickly discovered a mutual infatuation with Wales and storytelling. The West Virginia coal mines had led her to the Welsh valleys, the ancestral home of so many mining families and their stories (the state had reputedly been founded by someone named Morgan Morgan). We looked at each other closely, the way you would look in a mirror. She saw a sweaty woman in shorts and a T-shirt with dark hair sweeping into her face. I saw a barefoot, majestic creature about my age, with wavy red hair and strong, handsome features. She was smiling. We sat on her back patio and drank tea.

Karen was originally from Ohio, from a family that held labor unions sacred. "Never cross a picket line," was her first mantra. She had gone to college in West Virginia, stayed, and wound up running a museum. Stories eventually rose into her life the same way coal comes to us, up from the hilly ground. The earth held the coal and the coal held jobs, and how people worked mesmerized her. Especially women. Like Vickie Vedder, Karen was rare among the Southern storytellers I met in that both she and Vickie filtered the daily experience of their surroundings through women's eyes. Karen spent years collecting oral histories from coal miners who had worked in the 1920s and 1930s, but she tells their stories through the voices of their wives and mothers and daughters: the women who stayed above ground and died of childbirth, pneumonia, or exhaustion, rather than black lung.

Like Vickie, Karen literally lets whole communities speak through one woman, Hallie Marie, a character she created for a performance piece called "Coal Camp Memories." "In West Virginia," she explained, "say around 1910, ninety-seven percent of all miners and their families lived in company-run towns called coal camps, which controlled every aspect of their lives. They were paid in script: think of IOUs that could be redeemed only at a company store. They lived there, they died there, and after the coal ran out, the camps disintegrated. They were so shabbily built that they no longer stand."

"Coal Camp Memories" threads the stories of those places onto the string of Hallie Marie's life. It begins when she is a little girl, progresses through her teen, "courtin'" years and her life as a young mother, and ends with Hallie's widowhood ("I borrowed my grandmother's body for Hallie as an old lady," said Karen, "at least her body as I remember it, stooped with osteoporosis and arthritis"). Karen never leaves the stage, but simply changes her clothes, makeup, and voice in front of her listeners. "It's not a fixed piece," she said, "it evolves with the audience's contributions. Good storytelling is really more about listening than talking. Has anyone else told you that?"

I laughed. David Joe Miller had just said the same thing, as earlier had Kwame Dawes.

"I'll give you two examples. After one show, an old woman came up to me and said that she always put a bit of extra food in her husband's lunch bucket in case he got trapped underground. After that, whenever I did Hallie in her little girl incarnation, she would merrily root around in her father's lunch looking for a treat. As a young wife, however, the innocence was already gone, and she began to slip in a few extras with real trepidation . . . Another time, I was doing the show for a black-lung conference, and these two old guys just talked to me throughout the whole thing. They weren't interested in meeting Karen Vuranch afterwards — they talked to Hallie because they knew her. Come on," she said with gusto, "I want to show you something."

Karen had too much enthusiasm for just one woman. I wasn't surprised to learn later that in addition to Hallie Marie, she also made room in her body's pantheon for Emma Edmonds, a cross-dressing soldier in the Union army; the labor activist Mother Jones; Mary Draper Ingles, an eighteenth-century Indian captive from Virginia; and author Pearl Buck. Right now, however, they all wanted to show me Fayetteville.

It was an attractive but average, dusty little town suffering from the same drought and heat wave that gripped the entire eastern half of the country. But Karen had embraced the place.

She and her husband, Gene, ran a secondhand bookstore there, and had taken over the old cinema, turning it into a community theater.

"Do you sleep?" I asked with genuine curiosity.

"Rarely," she said cheerfully, steering me into the post office to see an authentic American art form: a WPA (Works Progress Administration) mural. During the Depression, Roosevelt's WPA had created jobs for thousands of out-of-work artists, writers, and photographers. This mural had been painted by one of them, Nixford Baldwin, in 1939. In bold earth tones, it showed a muscular black man drilling in the providential earth, a little girl and her dog bidding good-bye to her coal miner father, and in the center, a white workman prospecting for riches. Rarely have I seen such an optimistically expectant image. The promise had been made. The nation would provide. At least it did until Roosevelt died in 1945.

"Now get back in the car," said Karen. "I want you to see the setting for the story that I'm going to tell you tonight." We drove to a place called New River Gorge, and looked down through a green chasm to a snaking river far below. New River is a "National River," which means that like a National Park, it is maintained by the U.S. Park Service. Because the river flowed before the Appalachian Mountains rose from their prehistoric plateau, geologists speculate that despite its name, the New is one of the oldest rivers on the globe, probably going back about sixty-five million years. "Only the Nile is older for sure," said Karen.

Duly noted from above, we drove down to see the river at eye level. Near a roadbend called "Stupid's Corner," where a shabby, shingled house was unseasonably bedecked in Christmas lights and flying plastic reindeer, was a modest bridge hunkered over the water. Karen pointed at it. "That's the Tunney Hunsacker Bridge," she said. "Tunney was a Fayetteville police chief, but his real claim to fame is that he was the first-ever person to box against Muhammad Ali in a professional fight. Ali was Cassius Clay back then . . . You can buy coffee mugs with photos of Tunney on one side, and Ali on the other." Far above us, soaring hundreds of feet higher than the humble Hunsacker, its single arch vaulting into an afternoon heat haze, was the sleek new bridge that spanned the gorge. Residents were so grateful not to have to descend one side of the canyon, cross the old bridge, and climb the other cliff, that they celebrate Bridge Day each year on the third weekend in October.

"Now, what's important to know," said Karen, "is that there used to be twenty coal camps within a fourteen-mile stretch of this river. There were two right here, one on each side. One sold liquor, one didn't . . . The story I'm going to tell you tonight, "Rose and Charlie," is set in one of those camps. It's not a folktale, it's a ghost story that I pieced together out of hundreds of reminiscences I've heard." She explained that the gorge was one of the most isolated places in the eastern United States, until a railroad was built alongside the river. Transportation eventually made coal accessible and profitable and paved way for the camps, as well as some of the bitterest labor disputes in U.S. history.

The smell of roasting lamb filled Karen's farmhouse ("Old-time West Virginians don't like lamb," she had said, "so it was on sale"). Karen and I had resumed our position on the patio while Gene did figure eights around us on a noisy, ride-on lawnmower. Whenever he came too close, Karen would stop talking and take a sip of wine, swallow fast, and pick up her tale as he drove off down the lawn. It gave our conversation a curious, staccato quality. I asked if Karen knew any West Virginia ghost stories. "One comes to mind," she replied quickly, while Gene was out of earshot. "It's not exactly a ghost story, but it's scary. It's called Big Toe, about a guy in a cabin who chops off this creature's toe and eats it and . . ."

"Oh my God, let me guess: then the creature wants it back?"

"So you know the story?"

"I know its relatives."

Karen also talked about the female storytellers who lived in her head, all of whom were associated in one way or another with West Virginia. "When we wake up in the morning, Gene will ask me, 'So who are you today, dear?' Tomorrow, you'll see what he means. I'll be Pearl Buck." Karen beamed at me; I've rarely met anyone with such a warm, ready smile. These storytellers were the happiest bunch of people I have ever encountered.

Karen dresses as each of the women she has researched and tells stories in character about their lives and times. "It's a challenge telling stories as a real person," she shouted. (Gene was circling again.) "For instance, Mother Jones naturally grew out of my work with the coal camps. But she didn't believe in women's rights. For her, feminism wasn't compatible with socialism. When she was asked if she'd ever marry again, she replied 'No, I couldn't, or I'd have to stop working with the labor unions.' I have to find a way to reconcile her belief system with mine, without compromising who she really was. It's tough."

Jones was born in Ireland in the 1830s and emigrated to North America during the Potato Famine. She married a Memphis ironworker and had four children, all of whom, along with her husband, died young in a yellow fever epidemic. After that she moved to Chicago and worked as a seamstress until she fell in with the Knights of Labor, a group that promoted workers' rights and eventually became the United Mine Workers Union. Already elderly — she was an iconic figure in her long black dresses, gray hair, and round wire-framed glasses —

Mother Jones spent the rest of her life traveling the country, leading strikes, and organizing unions. She eventually earned the epithet, "the most dangerous woman in America."

I asked Karen which woman she felt closest to. "Pearl. No question," was her immediate answer. She rummaged through a file and handed me a glossy color photo. It was a studio shot of Karen in a trim blue suit, fox fur, pearls, and a jaunty little hat with a feather. The transformation from the contemporary woman across from me, decidedly unbuttoned in her free-flowing hair and sundress, was breathtaking. Buck had been born in West Virginia but raised from the age of three months in China by her missionary parents. She was the first American woman to win a Nobel Prize for Literature, in 1932.

"Pearl was my kind of woman. She was ten before she saw a child with blond hair and blue eyes . . . The civil rights movement in this country became her passion. Langston Hughes called her 'The Harriet Beecher Stowe of the twentieth century.' She was way ahead of her time. She supported gay rights back in the thirties, and was the one who told Harcourt Brace to publish Betty Friedan's *The Feminine Mystique* . . . She had so much courage. But we don't hear about her anymore because she was equated with Communism . . . mainly because she predicted the Chinese revolution. Henry Luce, the publisher of *Time,* vowed that not a word would be printed about Pearl Buck in his magazine while he was alive."

I watched the Cymru sticker disappear in the steam that was fogging Karen's kitchen window. I had offered to wash the dishes following our outdoor lamb roast, while Karen and Gene visited with some friends who had dropped by to share dessert. By the time I joined them, I was soaked from sweat and splashes, and she was ready to tell stories. It was a relief not to be the only audience member for a change. Karen warmed up with a monologue from "Coal Camp Memories," about women washing clothes and hanging them out to dry. When they heard the train whistle, they would race to snatch them from the line before they became covered in cinders. Not, Karen reminded us, that they need have bothered: everything in the camp was caked with fine gray coal dust. "In a coal camp you can't get away from it. We eat it, we breathe it, we wear it."

Karen then told us a true story about one of her favorite mountain women, Grace Haught of Reeder, West Virginia. "Miss Grace was the organist at the Methodist Church . . . She was one of those women who had a little gray bun at the back of her neck, and white gloves, and pearls. You know the kind — teaches Sunday school? Even though in those days women weren't elders or deacons, Miss Grace ruled that church, and everyone knew it." When it came time to search for a new pastor, Grace invited each of the three final candidates to her house for dinner the night before his sermon. The first two candidates appeared in church the next morning and declared what a delicious dinner Grace had prepared. The third, however — the youngest — was downcast, and told the faithful he probably wouldn't be their pastor. But why? they asked. "Because her dinner was so bad I couldn't eat it," he replied. Later he was shocked to learn he had been the one selected for the job. One day he got up the nerve to ask Grace why he had been chosen. Her response was, "Young man, I made three meals of soup, beans and corn bread. And for all three meals I put too much salt into my biscuits. I figured if you cannot be honest with something as simple as cornbread, you have no business taking care of my soul."

For her finale, Karen told us her coal camp ghost story. It was so quiet, we could hear the tick of her mantle clock.

ROSE AND CHARLIE

The Native Americans called the New River the River of Death because it's treacherous and it travels through an impassable gorge. But when coal was found in the mountains and railroads were built, coal camps sprang up throughout the New River gorge. These were isolated communities with no roads leading to them, only the railroad providing a link to the outside world. A coal miner would live out his days working for the company, and his wife and children would know nothing but coal dust and company stores.

Now life was difficult in these coal camps, there was no denying it. Everybody had the same thing: nothing. No need to lock your doors in a coal camp. There was nothing to steal . . . But the community was strong, and everybody worked hard, even little Rose Davies, whose father was a superintendent in the camp known as Red Ash. She went to school along with the other kids in the coal camp, and her mother took great pains to make sure Rose wasn't dressed any finer than the children whose fathers dug coal for Rose's daddy . . .

Rose grew up playing with the other children in Red Ash. But there was one child who was her special friend. He was a boy named Charlie Malone. He was one of those Malone boys from over on H Row. You know — they all looked exactly the same? Except for Charlie. He stood out in a crowd. His teachers in Red Ash said he was one of the best and brightest pupils they'd ever had. They said to his father, "You should save money and send Charlie to college. He could be a doctor or a lawyer, he's that bright." His father would just laugh and say, "You don't send a boy to college on coal miner's wages."

As Rose and Charlie grew older they began spending more and more time together . . . They would go for walks in the woods, or follow Wolf Creek down to where it ran into New River. Or sit at the edge of the river and look out at Red Ash Island, where all the coal miners were buried after mining accidents. Or then they would climb the top of Beauty Mountain and look out over the world. But the day came, as it inevitably would, when Rose was sent off to a fancy finishing school in Virginia. She found out that summer, after they finished the eighth grade, and she begged Charlie to figure out a way to go to school too, but there was just no money for it. No, said Charlie, he'd have to work for a while in the coal mines, and maybe save money, and hopefully he could go to school eventually.

They promised to keep in touch, and the letters flew between Red Ash and that fancy boarding school. And the next summer when Rose came home, everybody in town said they could see a difference. Rose was growing into a proper young lady, but she was the same Rose Davies. Her eyes still lit up when she saw Charlie Malone. He was workin' regular underground, but he'd see her of an evening, and on Sunday afternoons they'd go out in the woods, and walk along Wolf Creek, and climb up to Beauty Mountain.

Of course, this didn't make her parents very happy. The next summer they planned a European vacation for Miss Rose, and didn't give her a choice. She only came home for one short week that summer . . . Rose and Charlie saw each other just a few times that week, but it was just enough time for them to declare their love for each other, and to make their promises. The letters continued at a fast and furious pace between Red Ash and that boarding school. And long about spring, Rose's parents got a letter from her headmistress saying, I just think you should know that Rose receives letters continually from one Charlie Malone.

"That is enough!" said her father. He'd had enough of this embarrassing and inappropriate romance . . . A few weeks later, when the dayshift was loaded on the man-trap, heading underground, the foreman said that he had forgotten some tools back in the south section, and asked if Charlie would mind going to get them? Charlie said, No, he wouldn't mind at all, and he went back in the south section. Then the miners began to hear a rumble from underground. Charlie's brother tried to go after Charlie, but his father jerked him back in the man-trap and the man-trap was taken out of the mine.

Above ground, the women of Red Ash heard that whistle blowing.

At first it was just relief, the whistle always blew at the end of the coal-mine shift. But this time it kept blowing . . . meaning there had been an accident underground. They all gathered at the tipple as the women of a coal camp do. And they found out there was one death that day. Charlie Malone had died underground.

Ah, there were a lot of folks talkin' that night, over their kitchen tables and on their front porches, but no one was willing to risk their job and ask that foreman just why Charlie Malone was sent after those tools. It was a few weeks later that Rose came home from school. She looked sad and gray . . . No one knew what to say to her or how to comfort her. It didn't matter. She spent a lot of time by herself, just sittin' out by the river, looking out at Red Ash Island, where Charlie's body was buried, or climbing up to Beauty Mountain by herself. And one day Old Jim had brought her home. He was a retired man, spent his days fishing now. He said, "I, I found her on the railroad trestle, ma'am. She was going to jump, but I stopped her."

Rose's mother didn't know what to do with Rose. But suddenly it seemed she wasn't so desperately unhappy anymore. Oh, she still wandered in the woods by herself, but she'd come home and there'd be a light in her eyes and a smile playing around her lips. "There, you see?" said her mother. "I knew she'd come to her senses."

But soon it became apparent that all was not quite as it should be. Rose was heard laughing and talking, as if in deep conversation with someone. And when her mother asked her who she was talking with, she said, "Why, mother, I'm talking with Charlie."

"Rose," said her mother, "you know that Charlie is dead."

"Yes, mother, but he comes to me and we laugh and we have fun like we used to."

Well, things got worse . . . Soon Rose was seen all over town walking like she was holding hands with someone, or had her arm tucked through the crook of someone's arm . . . Even locked in her room her parents could hear her talking to Charlie and flirting with the empty air. Finally Rose's father said, "There is an asylum for people like her . . . I've got the papers here to commit her." Rose's mother wept and begged for her father to reconsider, but his mind was made up. And Mr. Wilson Davies arranged for an attendant to come and escort his daughter to her new home, a young man who would be assisted by a young woman, for propriety's sake.

. . . The day came, and Rose was ready in her best traveling suit: light blue linen with a matching hat and gloves. She sat waiting, holding her purse and raincoat with her suitcase by her side. She looked so excited her mother was relieved, thinking that Rose didn't really know where she was going. About that time a knock came on the door, and there came a young man's voice saying, "I've come to escort Miss Rose Davies."

Her father said, "But you should have a young woman in attendance with you."

"Oh," said the young man, "she's down at the station looking after our luggage. I came along for Rose."

And Rose said, "That's okay, father, I'll go along with him." And after a flurry of hugs and kisses good-bye, Rose was out the door on the young man's arm. Her mother wiped her tears away, and she said, "I wonder why Rose was so willing to go. Did you notice, Wilson, how much that young man looked like Charlie Malone?"

No, no, her father hadn't noticed. He walked over to the window to watch his daughter walk down the street, but she wasn't there . . . About that time, another young man and woman were making their way up the broad steps of the Victorian porch. They knocked on the door and said, "Hello, we're here to escort Miss Rose to Pleasant Hills Asylum."

"No!" said her father, "One of your colleagues was just here."

"We don't have a colleague with us."

"You must have seen them," said her father.

"No, we haven't seen anyone but a few women hanging out their wash."

Her father walked out on the porch. And there on the porch was

Rose's suitcase and raincoat and purse . . . She knew she wouldn't need them where she was going.

An all-out search was launched for Rose Davies and her mysterious escort. But no one ever saw Miss Rose Davies or her escort again. Oh, sometimes you'll be out walking in the woods, and you can hear a man talking and a woman's answering laugh, and come around a bend in the path, and there wouldn't be anyone there. A stranger might hurry on, trying to get to Red Ash all the quicker. But folks in Red Ash knew. It was just Miss Rose and Charlie, finding some happiness at last.

After Karen's guests left, she and Gene — a quiet man in whom I sensed goodness and experienced mumbled, ironic wit — and I bathed ourselves in late-night TV light and watched *Young Frankenstein* until a fantastically late hour. It had been funnier in the seventies. After that, I tried to sleep in Karen's sewing room. The bed was comfortable, but neither my mind nor body could find their way to sleep. It was as if a mild electric current ran through my veins, and whenever the weight of approaching sleep pressed against it, a faint shock sent me back into full consciousness.

I went to the window: the stillness held an expectancy, and a sweetness. Darkness is roomier than daylight, it gives the mind space to be itself. "First the light sinks to shadows . . . / Watch. As the dark comes / Entirely into its own. Watch . . . / The light murdered that the truth become apparent." The night was softer than C. D. Wright's language, but I understood that there was truth in darkness. It offered an invitation I have wanted to accept since childhood. Nighttime was a way to travel light, a refuge from the daytime baggage of sight; a trick of not knowing, or rather of not being told every single, prosaic thing. Of possibilities; of making the world anew. It was, in a way, the precursor of fiction — of stories. I imagined that the perpetual darkness of the coal mines must have been very different, although the introduction to a book I had bought in Gene's shop, *Green Hills of Magic,* by Ruth Ann Musick, about West Virginia stories of European descent, claimed that coal miners were a particularly creative lot, as far as storytelling went, and had filled the dark mines with wonder tales. They had accepted the invitation to use their imaginations instead of their eyes. Musick put it down to the sheer uncertainty of the work; the possibility of dying at any moment.

When she heard I was going on this trip, a Welsh friend, the poet Menna Elfyn, copied some poems for me from *Black Shawl,* which was written by the Appalachian poet Kathryn Stripling Byer. The West Virginian night brought to mind its restless women narrators, the miners' wives, for whom the night was also a beckoning road. Some took it, some didn't.

. . . She learned how to fight her way

> free when she could. When she could
> not, to play dead. To let them make always
> the same boast: *That little gal's not going anywhere.*
> What good to run away into some dark night
>
> where every lamp signified kinsmen?
> And kinswomen who would not look up, not once,
> from the snarls in their warp chains, or carding wool
> bunched in their laps, to say anything?

From "Bone"

> The last thing she did
> before she disappeared was cut

warp threads and leave them
to gather the handful

of blue yarn scraps
next morning. Then she was
over and done with.
Not even a note . . .

. . . She had taken
some two-day old cornbread
and left the back door
open . . .

From "Sisters"

The next morning I went downstairs to join Karen and
Gene for breakfast. Sitting upright in the middle of the
kitchen floor was a little round traveling case, its sides discreetly
covered in plaid fabric — the kind Rose might have left on her
parents' front porch. It looked as if it were waiting there for the
Orient Express. "That's Pearl's," said Karen, still dressed as herself. "She has a storytelling gig today." Pearl and I were both
hitting the road.

The Tale of the Farmer's Smart Daughter

THE SIGN SAID, BLASTING ZONE, but the shortcut on which Karen had sent me en route to Interstate 64 was anything but explosive. The morning mist made sea waves of the nearby hills; the drought had reduced the roadside river to a quiet, contemplative trickle. In the town of Gauley Bridge, population 691, I came upon a shadowed lake. The far mountain shore was still older and higher than the day's sun, and cast the waterface with its own reflection. In the middle of the lake a tiny island was planted with three white wooden crosses of a kind I've seen in other rural areas throughout the South, the handiwork of an itinerant, evangelical wood carver.

The morning quickly shed its soft serenity. Luckless towns clustered in the river valley between manufacturing plants identified by common nouns like "Alloy, Lumber & Supply." There was nothing beautiful in these places but the ignored mountains; the sole attempts at decoration were bands of shiny blue and gold tassels strung across used-car lots. In London, West Virginia, the cemetery took up more space than the high school, where I stopped to watch an early morning football practice. The players, helmeted and fully suited-up, were doing a jumping drill on their riverside field that made them look like pogo sticks with round silver knobs on top. Ominously, an ambulance hovered nearby.

As I left West Virginia behind, I could feel the grip of Appalachia relax; the earth kneeled, then lay down, tamed by Kentucky horse pastures and tobacco farms. Some dim ancestral instinct signaled relief at being out in the open again, where I could keep an eye on the distant horizon. I shifted in the driver's seat and stretched my neck. Colors paled into drought-depleted golds and wrung-out greens. Autumnal cornhusks were still planted in what should have been green August fields.

My goal this day was to drive straight east-to-west, crossing over half Kentucky, and arrive at Hidden Spring Farm, just west of Elizabethtown, at a reasonable afternoon hour. Twice, however, I had to stop at pay phones to call Mary Hamilton, a Kentucky storyteller who had invited me to her parents' farm, and extend my time of arrival (maps sometimes strain my time-and-distance judgment). On the very last stretch, I got stuck behind a school bus that inched along as if stuck in tar. To keep from having fits, I sucked in stoicism from the surrounding landscape. Its thick, flaxen fields rolled tidily into windbreaks of full-figured trees. Now and then a few acres of ultramarine chicory gave my eyes a rest from the strong sunshine. It seemed as if man and land had arrived at a practical equilibrium here — a partnership of such deep symbiosis that I could almost feel placid moderation emanating from the ground (fittingly, Kentucky had been neutral during the Civil War). The drought contributed to the impression of calm: there was no room for fancy in the dry air. On the coast, the rain and steamy heat had bred a constant, low-grade anxiety in me, like a fever (which I had quite enjoyed). The damp, creeping Gothicism and nightmarish stories of the seaboard were utterly alien to Hidden Spring Farm, where nothing was mysterious. Even the spring was discovered by none other than Daniel Boone, who had a hunting camp here in 1780.

*

One morning, a king stood in his doorway surveying his vast landhold-ings and had but one thought. I want more. Now, the land next door to the king's land was owned by a certain farmer. The king sent word for the farmer to come to the king's palace immediately. When the farmer arrived, the king said, "I have decided to increase my landholdings, and your farm is the land that I'm going to increase my holdings by."

The king explained that because he was the king, he could just take the land, but since he was a fair king, he would give the farmer a chance to keep his property. All he had to do was an-swer three questions by the following morning. The king said,

"Here are your three riddles. First, what is it that's the fastest in all the world? Second, what is it that's the richest in all the world? And third, what is it that's the sweetest in all the world? Now go on home and I'll see you in the morning."

Mary lived in Frankfort, the state capital, but had wanted me to "see the place my stories grew," so we agreed to meet on the farm. "Our people," she said soon after I arrived, "have been in Kentucky since before statehood." The six-hundred-acre farm where Mary's dad, Bobby, grew corn, wheat, soyabeans, barley, and tobacco — along with "seventy head of mama cows" — had been in the family since 1919, when his grand-father bought the land he had farmed as a tenant.

"See that clump of trees back there?" asked Mary, pointing to a windbreak several hundred yards away. Her accent was an economical version of Vickie's, peeled of its wispiness in a way related to the lack of humidity in the air. "There's an old house in there. That's where Daddy's grandparents moved when his mother, Mama Elizabeth, was ten." Martha, Mary's mom, ex-plained that when she and Bobby were newly married, Mama

Elizabeth had insisted on building them a big new ranch house on the property with all the modern amenities, where Mary had grown up. It was a spacious house with a sensibly large kitchen and den, cooled by shade trees and overlooking a 360-degree vista of ribboning farmland. "No one wanted anything old back then, so the original house just gradually became a ruin."

How curious, I thought, for Bobby's childhood home to be crumbling within eyeshot, like a shed skin. This lack of reverence for the material past didn't extend to the land — to which they were anchored in every sense, from the historical to the financial — or to the family. "I had ten grandparents when I was born," said Mary with real pride. "My great-great-grandmother died two weeks after I was born, but I had a great-grandmother until 1978."

These long-lived people had instinctively gravitated around their kitchen table, where we sat having coffee. They had welcomed me into their home with an easy, matter-of-fact kindness that left no room for gushing or prying (no one had pried all summer, to my great disappointment). Mary's parents accepted me as yet another of their daughter's foundlings whom they had to feed for dinner, and who was under the awkward impression that they were storytellers. "Look here, I'm no storyteller!" her dad had said as soon as he met me, while Mary winked behind his back. Bobby was a sturdy man with a farmer's narrowed, horizon-line eyes, buoyed up on the crest of a round face. He looked the incarnation of a good neighbor. Her mother was also sturdy, but quieter, as if she were the doer in a family of talkers. Martha and Bobby had known one another since high school. Mary herself — the storyteller — insisted she was the quiet, shy one, the bookish child, who found it easier to perform on a stage than to wedge her way into family conversation. My senior by a couple of years, she was careful about her speech and pragmatic about her appearance:

no makeup; glasses; dark hair pulled back in a ponytail. Her most striking affectation was a tie-dyed T-shirt.

Well, the farmer went home. He could hardly believe what had happened. He sat at his kitchen table, head in his hands, and that's where his oldest daughter found him.

"Why Daddy, you look miserable. What happened? What's wrong?"

And the farmer told her all about the king's plans, and he told her those three riddles. His daughter smiled.

"Oh ho, Daddy! Daddy, don't you worry. Why tomorrow, when you go see the king, you tell him that the fastest thing in all the world, why that's nothing but the light from the sun itself . . . And as for the richest thing in the world? Why, that would have to be the earth itself . . . And as for the sweetest thing . . . ? Well, Daddy, him being a king and all, he's bound to have to make a lot of decisions, and I'll bet some of those decisions just weigh on his mind. Oh, I'll bet the king will have to agree, that the sweetest thing in all the world is nothing but an easy night's sleep, when your mind is troubled."

It was the green beans that started the avalanche in the den. Someone mentioned the hundred quarts of green beans that the Hamilton clan used to can each summer. Everyone laughed.

"What's so funny?" I asked.

"Steve Hoes the Garden," said Mary cryptically. "Family story."

"See, we planted half a row of peanuts and half a row of beans. But Steve thought the peanuts — which we'd never grown before — were weeds, and pulled them all out," said Bobby.

"Then there was the time he lost his hoe. How anyone can lose a hoe, I don't know, but he did. He was afraid to come in and tell Daddy, so he paid my sister a dollar to find it for him. Lost all the money he'd made. See, we were each paid a penny for every thistle we hoed up. Can you imagine? You'd arm six kids with hoes and thistles . . ."

"You used to have tomato fights too."

"That's when we did the Duck Walk."

"Excuse me?"

"See," explained Bobby, "the government controls tobacco production. Today we sell by the pound, so we produce more plants than we need, and only sell the best. We can afford to be sloppier now. But it used to be gauged by acreage: each farm had a history of tobacco production, and based on that, we could only plant so many acres. But we could sell all of that, so every plant mattered. That's where the Duck Walk came in."

"Duck walking was the children's job," said Mary. "We were small enough that we could walk down the rows and peel off the dead bottom leaves so the plants would grow taller."

"How do the tomatoes come in?"

"We'd plant tomatoes around the tobacco — just using up space. All we used to be able to plant was two and four-tenths acres of tobacco."

"And we'd throw the rotten ones at each other."

"Explain pegging to her, Bobby," called Martha.

"Okay, gran'mommy. That's where you'd go through and take out the dead tobacco plants."

"Now stripping, that was something . . . ," began Mary, winking at me again.

"See, you get different grades of tobacco on one plant, so you have to line up teams of people to strip 'em. Different people strip different grades."

"I'll tell you a stripping story. Every stripping room, you see, had a radio."

Martha was already laughing.

"My brother Jeff used to say that Daddy wouldn't let us stop, not even for the National Anthem."

"We'd be listening to UK basketball, that's why the anthem was played."

UK? I was thrown into confusion. The United Kingdom? It was hours later that I figured out this meant University of Kentucky.

". . . stripping between Thanksgiving and Christmas. There was a wood-burning stove at one end of the room, and believe me, the other end was cold."

"But our kids never missed school for farm work," added Martha. "We'd start stripping over the Thanksgiving holiday and finish over the Christmas one."

"We couldn't miss school, you see, because Daddy was president of the board of education for sixteen years."

Bobby shook his head in disbelief at the extent of his service. "The schools changed here in Meade County when bussing went into effect in Louisville," he said. "A lot of people moved out here to Meade. The kind of people who'd say, 'You're not going to tell my child who to go to school with!' It made for a difficult time."

"Tell her what Jeff said he'd do if your dad died and he had to run the farm," called Martha from her "retirement chair" on the far side of the room.

Bobby interjected before Mary. "He said, 'I'd climb up the silo and see what the neighbors are doing, and do that.'"

"Now tell her 'Jeff Rides the Rides.'"

"Well," said Mary, taking a breath, "You know that money we made hoeing the weeds? We'd save up and spend it each summer at the Meade County Fair. It was a family rule that you could go on the rides all by yourself when you were eight years old. Well, Jeff — he's the youngest — he finally turned eight, and Daddy said, 'You can go off by yourself, but when the organ music stops, you come back and meet us at the car.' Well, Jeff went off and he had a great time. And when the organ music stopped, he went back to the car. They asked him if he rode all the rides. Jeff said he rode on all but one, and he didn't ride on that one because he couldn't find out where to buy a ticket. No one knew what he was talking about, so Jeff described the ride. He said it must've been a good one, because there were really long lines for it, and the people waiting looked really anxious, but when they came out they looked really happy. He said that people went one at a time into these tall, shiny white things, and that there was a sign that said 'Port-a-Ca.' He figured that the 'r' was missing. Of course, by that point everyone knew it was an 'n' missing, and that Jeff was trying to ride the portable toilets."

Well, the next morning the farmer went to see the king and he gave the king those answers his daughter had given him . . . "My," said the king, "those are fine answers. Tell you the truth, those are the finest answers I've ever heard."

When the king discovered the farmer had help solving the riddles, however, he declared that his land was not yet saved, and thought up some devilish new conundrums for the farmer's daughter to solve.

"I want you to go home, and I want you to tell that daughter of yours that since she came up with the answers to those riddles, it's now going to be her job to save your land. You tell her that I want her to show up at my palace tomorrow morning, and I want her to be not walking and not riding, neither. And I want her to show up not dressed, but I don't want her runnin' around naked, either. And I want her to bring me a present that won't be a present. Uh huh."

That evening the Hamiltons took me out to dinner at the Doe Run Inn, a converted nineteenth-century stone gristmill that had once pulverized corn and wheat. If they had not been coming to the place all their lives, I might have worried that they had chosen it to fulfill my Northern expectations of the down-home South. We sat at a table covered with a red-and-white checkered cloth, on a screened porch that let in the hum of katydids but kept out the mosquitoes. Central casting sent a Farm Woman with arms like heifer thighs to bring us our fried chicken, biscuits and gravy ("just pour the gravy on everything," advised Martha), green beans, potatoes, and lemon chess pie. And of course, iced tea.

Then we went for a ride. This had been a favorite occupation in my family when I was growing up. Instead of playing cards, or watching television, or visiting with neighbors, my family would "go for a ride." It didn't matter if it were day or night, or if we ever got anywhere in particular. We would just ride, on highways or backroads, usually in silence, each contentedly staring out the window or into his or her own internal scenery. My father heroically drove us north, south, and west; never east, because that led to New York City.

Tonight, however, sitting in the back with Mary like a couple of kids, I was riding in the dark with the Hamiltons, who, unlike my family, had an ulterior motive to their wanderings. They were systematically making their stories concrete for me. We drove to the darkened Meade County Fairgrounds, where we careered around empty fields that in a few weeks would be parked with tens of thousands of cars. Bobby proudly pointed out the horse showring, and the stadium's gladiatorial entrance, from which entrants in the truck and tractor pull would triumphantly emerge. Then he drove us to the darkened banks of the Ohio River, which separated Kentucky from Indiana. At dinner Bobby had told a story about the 1937 flood. His daddy had been pilot on a flat barge for the Kosmos Towing Company. He was on the river when the waters rose, and wound up

saving countless families that he found floating downriver, clinging to the roofs of their bobbing houses. Three days passed before he came home.

"See that light post?" asked Bobby. He pointed to a street-
light on a hilltop high above the riverbank. "That's where he
moored the barge." Afterward he returned to his house so exhausted that he lay down in the front hallway so as not to wake
anyone, and went to sleep. His wife — who by this time suspected he was dead — heard a noise and came downstairs in
her high heels and walked on top of him, breaking several ribs.

"We wanted you to see the lamp post," Mary explained.

"Oh, daughter, you wouldn't believe what that king wants you to
do now." And the farmer told his daughter what had happened. His
daughter smiled. "I have been wanting to meet the king. This sounds
like a perfect opportunity."

The next morning the farmer's daughter appeared at his
palace naked but for an old quilt she had wrapped around herself, hopping on one foot with the other leg thrown over the
back of a nanny goat. In her hand she held a birdcage with a
quail inside. The king was impressed: she was neither naked
nor dressed, walking nor riding. And just as she took the quail
from its cage to hand it to him, she gave it a little push and it
flew away: clearly a present that wasn't a present. The king was
so tickled with her cleverness that he offered to marry her and,
after securing her father's farm for all perpetuity, she agreed.

"One thing I've always known about myself," she thought, "is that
I would be a fine queen."

Just before they were wed, the king added one condition: she
must never butt into his business. She never explicitly agreed,

and one day, sure enough, when he made an unusually poor decision, she butted in. In a rage the king ordered her to leave, to go back to her daddy's house. She meekly assented, but before she left she begged to cook him one last meal and to take one souvenir of having been queen. He agreed, and she fed him so many sweets and so much wine that he fell sound asleep.

When she could tell the king wasn't going to be waking up anytime soon, the farmer's daughter loaded him into the wagon and she hauled him on down to her daddy's house. When they got there she dragged the king inside and dumped him in the bed that had been hers as a child. Then she climbed in bed beside her husband and slept till morning. When the king woke up and saw her in bed beside him, he said, "What are you doing here? I told you you were supposed to go on back to your daddy's house! Now why are you here?" And she said, "Honey, maybe you ought to look around and see just where you are." And the king looked around. "Where am I anyway?" "Don't you remember? You told me that I could take one thing on back to my daddy's house with me, and there isn't a single thing I like more about being queen than being with you . . ."

The king was so moved by her having chosen him as a souvenir, especially when she could have had any of the treasures in his palace, that they made up, went back home, and ever afterward she butted into his business with impunity.

"It's not critical," Mary said, after we'd returned from our ride, sitting on the sofa in her parents' darkened living room, "that I take you into my memory when I tell stories." She explained that when she tells a tale she knows the minutiae of its landscape, the color of a character's hair, her perfume, the cast of the sky, but she is careful not to enforce those details on her listeners. She didn't want to be what Karen Vuranch has called a storytelling Nazi. Although desperately sleepy (I had been musing out of Karen's window the night before, and had driven six hundred miles in the course of the day), I roused myself to consider her methodology. Travel writing, I said between deep yawns, was exactly the opposite. To pull flesh and breath out of narrative memory, it was critical to report the details: that she was curled up on one foot, playing with her hair; that she was giving me the bed she had slept in as a little girl, in a room full of stuffed animals.

When performing for an anonymous audience, I believed Mary did precisely as she said — she offered outlines, and let her hearers color them in. A single listener, however, was captive to her memory. The following morning she drove me a few miles down the road to Big Spring, an abandoned village clustered at a backroads intersection, fast receding into memory. Its shops were empty and crumbling. One in particular, the former general store, was refined even in dilapidation, its façade a puzzle of oblong windows, crowned by a humble wooden pediment that for all its modesty claimed a tracery of diamond shingles. Two screen doors hung at awkward angles at the entrance like crooked front teeth.

This is where one of Mary's favorite stories — "The Ghostly Young Woman in Brown" — was set. (I knew the tale as "A Mother's Love," from The Moonlit Road.) These are the basic elements: a traveling woman and her baby are found dead, and are buried by the local community. Afterwards a young woman approaches a dairy farmer seeking milk, or in Mary's version, she petitions the owner of the general store. She receives the milk and then disappears. Eventually someone follows her to the cemetery and hears a muffled cry. Her coffin is opened and her baby, mistakenly left for dead, is healthily crying inside, holding a fresh cup of milk.

Mary had told me this tale the day before, and as she spoke my mind had followed her words with pictures. I saw the young woman walking beside the sea, approaching a weather-beaten shop on Cape Cod. I knew the cemetery as well: it was sandy and grown over with the wild tea roses that bloom in June.

I didn't mind in the least being kidnapped by the daemon of Mary's mind's eye. But I thought it intriguing that a storyteller in this family of storytellers ("Making everything a long story is the Hamilton in you," someone had said at dinner), ultimately didn't trust words. She used them marvelously — Mary was easily one of the most fluidly engaging tellers I met — but she and her parents betrayed a nagging urge to anchor their words in the physical world. Besides Karen Vuranch, none of the other storytellers had thought to underline their tales in witnessed landscapes; no one else insisted on such concreteness. I put it down to the driving practicality of this landlocked place, wonderfully caught in "The Farmer's Smart Daughter." Unlike Jack, or Brer Rabbit, the farmer's daughter wins the day through cleverness steeped in practicality, not through cunning. I had expected her to challenge the king through a metaphysical game of words, to play cat and mouse. But instead she had taken his riddles at face value and solved them with the material things of ordinary life: a nanny goat, a blanket, a quail. Nothing fancy, just serviceable items in a land squabble. The boy who would climb a silo to see what the neighbors were doing, "then do that," and so run the farm in the event of his father's death, was clearly a relative of the farmer's smart daughter.

It was also evident, however, that this belief in the seen world, as opposed to the ever-encroaching invisible world of the seaboard, had not been bred from an immunity to coastal-style disasters. In addition to the 1937 flood, Bobby had spoken the previous evening of a tornado that touched down unexpectedly in 1974. Thirty-one had died in a town of only three thousand. He recalled the winds uprooting tombstones; he had been among the rescue crews that carried bodies to a gymnasium-turned-morgue. But events like these did not seem to inspire ghost stories. They were anomalies within man's beneficent partnership with the earth. The story record rather stressed heroism, humor, and family. The one ghost story that Mary told was not only a tale borrowed from Georgia, it pivoted on domestic sentiment and love from beyond the grave: very, very different stuff from "The Gray Man" and "Lavinia Fisher."

The one truly scary moment I had at Mary's, I am ashamed to say, was self-inflicted. The previous evening I had fallen asleep immediately, but woke in the middle of the night, opened my eyes, and looked up at the ceiling. Directly above the bed floated a giant green skull, winking at me. I bit the blanket rather than scream — a decision I now applaud — and forced myself to understand what I was seeing. Finally, after about ten horrible seconds, I figured it out. The answering machine was signaling that a call had come in while we were at dinner by flashing its green indicator light. This shone up through the interior hardware of Mary's bedside lamp, and the chartreuse shadow cast on the ceiling just happened to resemble a death's head. Honest.

Just as I was leaving Hidden Spring Farm — I had arranged to meet a Japanese storyteller named Oyo in Danville, Kentucky, three hours drive back east — Mary stopped me. There were two more things I had to see. One was simple: the barn where Bobby's tobacco leaves had been hung up to dry. She walked me into an open shell of a building so unexpectedly beautiful it made me gasp. The tobacco leaves, hanging from the ceiling and on pegs along the side walls, conjured up an impossible concept: an ephemeral cavern. The leaves were each about two to three feet long. Their edges curled like lace, but otherwise they hung straight down in shades of yellow and brown like a clutch of paper-thin, fragile stalactites. The barn had a reedy smell, something between freshly mowed grass and an unlit cigarette. "I've never smoked," said Mary. "You should see the gum that comes off on your hands from just touching the leaves."

The other thing she wanted to show me was a little more complicated. Mary wanted me to see Flaherty High, where she and her siblings and parents had gone to school. She wanted me to see St. Martin of Tours church, a place of comfortable holiness, with stained light pouring through the windows and a faint odor of grape juice, where she had been confirmed. She wanted me to see the cemetery where her ancestors lay. "That's my uncle," pointed Mary, "and over there, see? Those are my grandparents, and there are my great-grandparents."

I could practically see roots curling out from the soles of Mary's feet into the Kentucky soil. But the real reason she wanted to show me St. Martin of Tours was to give substance to another tale, an unfinished story she calls "The Baptist Boyfriend." Mary once had a suitor who lived just over the hill on a nearby farm ("When I first called and said it was Mary Hamilton, his mother asked, 'Of which Hamiltons? The Hamiltons from over the hill?' That meant us: the *Catholic* Hamiltons.") She had invited the boyfriend to Christmas Eve service at her church. She remembered, she said, having been so proud of the purple vestments, the decorated statue of Christ, the music, the splendor of the holiday pageant. He had gone stiff with horror. "You worship monuments," he told her later. That anyone could use the word "monument" to refer to Christ on the crucifix flagged his speech, she thought, as some kind of foreign language.

"He thought we were heathens. You know, you think you

have a shared geographical experience — I mean, he lived in the very next valley. But we didn't share the same spiritual reality at all. I guess the point of this story is that we can't imagine we know someone else's experience, just because we're neighbors."

Flannery O'Connor wrote a short story that makes a similar point. In "Everything That Rises Must Converge," two women meet on a bus shortly after desegregation, one white, one black, both wearing the same Godawful ugly purple-and-green hat. The white woman — elderly, living in a half-imaginary memory of a paternalistic South — offers the black woman's young son a shiny penny, and his mother takes umbrage and strikes out with her handbag. Moral: even though they wear the same hat, the women perceive the world in vastly different terms. And yet, desegregation was an umbrella over both of their heads. They rode the same bus, just as Mary and her Baptist boyfriend did, day in, day out, on their way to Flaherty High School.

Oyo's Tale

I ARRIVED EARLY AT THE YMCA on Danville's main street, and took a moment to survey the town. It looked a sturdy, prosperous, profoundly unexciting place, full of solid citizens in solid houses, the latter built when construction crews used plaster instead of wallboard. I was wallowing in the happy discordance of finding a Japanese storyteller there, when a voice from inside the Y shouted, "Hey, you Pam? Come on in here, girl!"

My jaw dropped like a nutcracker's. "Are you Oyo?" I asked.

"Sure am. Come here and have a seat."

Framed by a rainbow of children's hands imprinted on the wall behind her was a large African-American woman in a brown and purple caftan incongruously paired with thick, white running shoes, her hair bound up in an open turban with cornrows running out the back. Her magnificent smile drew every feature of her face into a gesture of such warmth and welcome that I instantly forgave her for not being Asian.

"I thought you'd be Japanese," I said in a small voice. "You know, your name, *Oi-o* . . ."

Oyo laughed so hard her cornrows came to life, dancing every which way behind her head.

"It's 'O-yo.' Now tell me: do I look Japanese?"

I had to admit she did not. Oyo was Kentucky's gift to me that afternoon. Smart, and so down-to-earth she was practically subterranean, I realized after half an hour in her company that I had taken my shoes off, put down my notebook, and shown her the gray roots beneath my suspiciously dark hair (I honestly can't recall why I did this). She told me a Yoruba creation myth from Africa — "I'm wearing this outfit for your benefit, girlfriend. I usually wear jeans" — but in spite of checking my tape player several times to make sure it was recording, when I tried to play it back I found the tape completely empty. In a way I was relieved. Oyo's best story was Oyo: a creation unequaled by any narrative.

Oyo had been born in Kentucky and raised in Ohio by Cousin Anne. "A part-time voodoo woman and bootlegger . . . The IRS did a sting on her. When Cousin Anne went to prison, I came back home." Instead of returning to her mother and six brothers and sisters, however, she went to live with two old women. "Why I was the chosen one, I never understood," she said, but although she wasn't raised by her mother, the two became close later in life.

"My mother always talked in code. Things like, 'A woman can run further with her dress up than her pants down.' I never knew where she got this stuff . . . Another favorite was, 'You've been married once — you're a Mrs. — so now every ship will sail under the same flag.' That was a reference to my tribing with other men I didn't marry, and having their children."

A few years ago Oyo performed a slave wedding for Kentucky's public broadcasting television station. Slave weddings had not been legally binding, but were important events on the plantation, traditionally overseen by "the Missus."

"Everyone would attend, white and black, so we got a crowd of about eighty to a hundred people together. And they would have brought tons of food, so we did that too, just like in the old days. Old fashioned food like Hoppin' John [black-eyed peas and rice] and Corn Pone [cornbread mixed with onions and corn kernels]. But was it hot? It was hot. Too hot for couth. I always say, any time we try to do anything ethnic, God heaps the heat on us. Can you imagine working in the fields in heat like that? I'd have chopped off my feet and hands before I'd have picked cotton . . ."

Oyo had played the role of the Griot, or storyteller, who initiates the wedding ceremony. First, there was drumming, and then a calling of names, when she had asked everyone in the community to call upon the spirits of their ancestors. "You know," said Oyo, "to keep things holy. Did I mention that it was hot?"

As Oyo spoke and smiled — it was almost one gesture — her eyes turned up at the outside corners, forming the lovely arc of a second smile on the upper half of her face. It filled the dingy, cavernous room with warmth, outshining the overhead fluorescent lights. Because the YMCA management had decided to close the facility, it was nearly empty: just a pool table and some bookshelves and chairs standing around awkwardly in the center of the room, as if awaiting their next incarnation in life.

The chief feature of the slave wedding, said Oyo, was Jumping the Broom. Diane Williams, a storyteller I had met briefly outside Jackson, Mississippi, had also talked about this custom — the act that indicated a slave couple was actually married. Diane had researched its origins, and found that in Africa jumping over a broom was considered bad luck. "So it's indigenous to the States," she had said, "with regional variations. In Virginia, for instance, they jumped three times; in Kentucky, only men jumped." In Oyo's ceremony, the broom had been laid on the ground, and the couple jumped backwards over it. "The idea was whoever landed first would rule the house."

"Who landed first?" I asked eagerly. "The bride or groom?"

"They tied. Did I make it clear to you it was Godawful hot that day?"

Oyo picked up something that had been lying on the desk in front of her and absently started flipping it. Her crimson nail polish glinted under the lightning-white lights. It looked like a shoehorn with hair.

"What's that?" I asked.

"A cow-tail switch from Uganda. It's a symbol of authority. I got it from a cookie lady in Louisville."

Oyo had lived in Louisville for many happy years, "a real cultural hub," as she described it, where she and a group of friends used to get together to cook and then "lay around on the floor like a bunch of sated lionesses." But she had moved to Danville for work. "If the world should ever end," she said, "this is the place to be. Danville will give you another decade of good living."

I asked her if she got along with folks here. She gave me a look that took me straight back to Granny Griffin. A real, you-don't-know-what-door-you're-opening-girl look.

"Well, I kind of rocked the boat immediately," said Oyo, who proceeded to tell me the following tale. When she had first come to Danville and was looking for a place to live, someone had put her in touch with the local black Baptist church. Because its current minister owned his own home, the manse was unoccupied. So they offered it to her for a minimal rent. Oyo hadn't been there long when she discovered varmints in the fireplace, and so called the deacons, who were in charge of maintaining the property. The deacons brought in a fumigator named Buddy — "a little old white guy," as Oyo described him. While the deacons were seeing to other matters, Buddy put his hand on Oyo's back and started rubbing it up and down. "Do you ever fool around?" he whispered.

Oyo threw what she called a dignified fit, and asked the

deacons to escort Buddy out. Then she brought up the matter before one of the church committees. The response was, "Oh, let's just keep this quiet. I'm sure he's never done anything like this before . . ." Oyo threw a bigger fit — "Like that's true," she said in disgust — and lodged a complaint with the local NAACP.

Shortly afterward, two of the deacons arrived at her front door. "Now don't get mad," they said to Oyo, "but do you ever, you know, do woo woo?"

"Do I do what?" asked Oyo.

"You know, woo woo," they said mysteriously, bringing their hands close to their faces and wiggling their fingers while they made *Twilight Zone* noises. "Did you woo woo Buddy?"

Oyo was mystified. Finally one of them whispered, "Voodoo. You know, spells. Buddy the Fumigator was never sick a day in his life, and yesterday he just up and died. We were wondering if, maybe . . ."

Oyo had laughed so hard she slid down the wall in the entrance hall. "You think I killed Buddy?" she managed to blurt out between seizures. "I'm Catholic, for God's sake!" Finally, seeing that they weren't laughing, she picked herself up and said calmly, "I would not put a spell on a bug man. Now, see Bank One right down the street? If I were going to put a spell on anything it would be that bank, and you'd see dollar bills floatin' down here right this minute to my house."

Oyo later told the story to her son, who replied that because she burned so much incense, what else were they to think? "I had billows of frankincense and myrrh blowing down the street," she laughed. "I'd tried to light one little corner and the whole thing went up in a big Poof! Honestly, I was just trying to keep the mosquitoes away . . ."

Despite repeated attempts on Oyo's part to pay her rent, the deacons stayed well away from her, and she wound up spending months at the manse for free.

After the Buddy story, I glanced out the plate glass windows of the dying YMCA. The sky looked like half-lit charcoal. "I shook my rain-stick this morning," said Oyo. "It's gonna come chucking down any minute now." I offered her a ride home and she grabbed me and hugged me hard. We pledged to stay in touch. Then she accepted the ride on account of the fact that she was blind.

I staggered out of her arms. "You're what?"

"Legally blind. I can't see poop," Oyo said cheerfully.

I had spent almost three hours with a blind woman and had never once realized that she couldn't see.

Mitch and Carla's Tale

IT WAS NOT A LONG DRIVE from Danville to Berea, Kentucky — I was heading back into the tail end of the Appalachian highlands — but the Old Testament weather added miles of anxiety. The storm began the very second Oyo closed the door of her sturdily weather-stripped home. After that, twisting on a back road between planted fields, I became a moving target. Platinum lightning bolts jammed into the earth before, behind, and beside me. Rain and hail fell so fiercely I had to turn off a radio alert about severe thunderstorms because I could no longer hear it. Young trees were bent double, and in the sky, hovering uneasily near the horizon, a ridge of clouds the color of smoky quartz rose overhead with the intimidating mass of a mountain range.

I thought biblical thoughts. Words like wrath, retribution, and justice rattled around in my head while my hands sweated on the steering wheel. The earth badly needed rain, but it was too hard and dry, and this storm too fierce, for much water to be absorbed into the ground. I sang some of an Elvis Costello song to myself: "All this Useless Beauty."

I emerged into Berea via a rain-sleeked commercial strip, which carefully siphoned off the area's consumer vulgarity so that the town center could maintain its prestige. Berea is an upscale little spot renowned for its arts and crafts. I wasn't surprised to find storytellers there, especially a young couple who on the phone sounded hip yet mellow — the requisite combination for smart, Southern, bohemian-yuppies. My guess was that they'd moved to Berea from Louisville, or Atlanta.

Carla had advised me to meet her husband Mitch at the Wan Pen Asian Restaurant behind McDonald's, so that we could bring Thai food home for dinner. Aha! I thought, how New South of them (by "New South" what I really meant was, "how much like home"). I had just begun scanning the menu when Mitch appeared, with two visiting teenagers in tow. About my age, he was eye-catchingly handsome, with wide, pale blue eyes and brown hair gathered in a long braid. In a voice that was not bred in Louisville or Atlanta, or even Berea, he told me they had thought it a good idea for him to meet me on the strip, as I'd never have found their holler on my own.

Mitch Barrett's voice wasn't just "Southern." To make an English analogy, it was Cockney compared to Kathryn Windham's Oxbridge. Later he said, a little bitterly, that his Appalachian accent "gets you stereotyped all over the States as some kind of backward hick." Unlike Vickie Vedder's voice or Mary Hamilton's, both of which held agriculture in their syllables, Mitch's had something feral in it. It was twangy and sharp, nasal, a voice of the Appalachia Mountains, but without Orville Hicks's folksy vocabulary or leisurely rhythm. Not a voice I'd normally associate with Pad Thai.

They were right in thinking I would never have found their house. I followed Mitch about fifteen minutes out of town, climbing and turning on nameless roads deeper and deeper into forested hills as we reentered the southernmost corner of Appalachia from the fertile tableland of central Kentucky. Finally, I glimpsed a sign identifying a rutted dirt track as Barrett Lane, and Mitch's car came to a stop. "This here's our holler," he said, waving his arm vaguely across a hillside already lost in dusk. "My whole family's from here. This is where I grew up."

All right, so I was wrong, I thought, they're not city people. And Oyo wasn't Japanese: it was just one of those days. Ahead, however, lay a house patterned on an aesthetic that was anything but native to an Appalachian holler. "I built it myself in the seventies," Mitch said proudly, as if my squint demanded an explanation. It looked like it belonged in Northern California: natural woods, rough-hewn logs for posts and beams, a giant circular window in front lit with white Christmas lights. All around the grounds were tokens of slightly outdated hipness: a cow skull painted bright blue, fitted with wrought-iron antlers; a stone Buddha; a mosaic of marbles set in concrete; and on the porch, the floorboards of which had recently been painted lavender, a tall cactus and bright purple chairs. The front door had a sign that read "We see beauty and goodness in all things."

Inside was just one great room in a state of terminal disarray, overseen by an open loft. Looking up, I could spy the corner of a crumpled duvet, suggesting an unmade bed just beyond eyeshot. Carla had greeted us at the door holding a beautiful toddler named Zoe. Carla was at least a decade younger than Mitch, barefoot and fresh-faced, with shiny, dark blond hair. I asked to use the bathroom and she indicated an open door in the corner of the room. "There's a curtain — you can put it down if you like . . ." she called over her shoulder. Which meant, of course, that I couldn't and still be cool. As I furiously prayed that no one else would need to relieve him or herself, I heard Vickie Vedder chastising me in my head. "If you're trying to form some opinion about one person in the South, you usually have to form an opinion about the whole group first." That was exactly what I was trying to do with Mitch and Carla, but the groups to which they seemed to belong — leftover hippies, Appalachian hill folk, people just like me — gleaned from misleading clues like accent and style, kept shifting every few moments.

We ate our Thai food in near silence, then the teenagers, a friend's son from the posh city of Annapolis, Maryland, and his buddy, sent to Mitch for a week to experience "backwoods living," announced they were taking a walk.

"That's all they do," said Carla. "Where do they go? How many walks can you take?"

"As long as the police don't bring 'em back, they're all right," said Mitch.

After dinner the rest of us sprawled beneath the big circular window and tried to find some common ground. Like just about everyone else, they knew David Holt and Ray Hicks.

"I have an old friend," said Mitch, "plays the banjo. He said David went to see him once. 'That boy lay on the floor and watched ma fingers. Strangest thang I ever seen,'" said Mitch, adopting an old man's voice. "A lot of folks 'round here can't imagine what they do is worthwhile."

"This is still considered Appalachia," said Carla, as if in explanation. "People in town don't think of themselves as Appalachian, but out here they do. Like Mitch's family."

"I come from a family of storytellers," said Mitch. "We's British Isles, you know, Scotch-Irish-Welsh, all mixed up. Storytellers goin' way back. The old folks'ud tell us stories when we were workin' the tobacco. It was always s'hot, we had to take breaks, then the stories'ud start up . . . I heard some of the best ones in the strippin' room, with ma grandfather, ma uncle, ma aunt, ma granny. We'd strip for two weeks straight. Got out of school. It was acceptable to take off from school at strippin' time."

The Hamiltons suddenly seemed very bourgeois to me, listening to basketball games on the radio and never missing their studies. Despite the Thai food, Mitch was shadowed by a much older world.

"The stories were usually about my grandfather," said Mitch. "Fox-huntin' stories — no, not that kind of fox huntin'," he said, laughing at me — "stories they used to tell while they was sittin' around the fire, waitin' fer the dogs to snuffle out some old fox."

"We still hear stories on your granddaddy," said Carla, cupping in her hands a dying, sea-green moth that Zoe had found on the window ledge.

"Th'other day a blind old banjo player asked me who my people were. Said, 'I reckon I know yer grandpaw.' That happens all the time. Ma dad died recently, and at his funeral this old guy — a fox-huntin' buddy — come up and said, 'Bunk,' that was my grandfather's name, 'had no patience fer animals. He had a mule that balked. So he whacked him on the rump. Nothin'. Switched him. Still didn't move. So he built a fire under that mule's belly and he moved four feet.' Now that's what I call a Standard Lie."

"No, that's true," said Carla.

"He taught me a lot of things, like how to make a rabbit trap. Everyday we ate somethin' he caught in the woods. I remember goin' out there with him and ma sister at five A.M. We'd be so sleepy, we'd be leanin' against each other, an' smellin' his tobacco . . . And he could sing, too. Once I shut off ma car engine when I saw ma grandfather's truck, and I heard him all alone out there, singin' in th' woods. 'These weddin' bells were never meant for me . . .'"

Mitch roamed through his good memory. "Ma granny was great. She raised all these weird crops like peppers. She didn't need the money that bad; she just wanted us grand-kids to learn how to do it. Same with keepin' and killin' hogs."

"I was real close with my grandma too," added Carla. "She's

the one who told me my stories. She lived with us, and took my education seriously. She taught me how to cook, and quilt, and garden. It was incredible what they had to know back then to live a subsistence lifestyle. She also taught me how to call down a load of bees when they were swarmin'. You beat on a dish pan and holler, then ease in real slow and get the queen."

By now Zoe's hands were covered in a soft, green phospho-rescence from the moth. She wiped them on Carla's silk-screened T-shirt.

"But I had a real hard time getting my values figured out," she continued. "My grandma was born in 1898, but I came of age in the 1980s. She taught me the values she'd inherited from her mama, from the mid-nineteenth century. Like shaving your legs was something only racy women did. And I couldn't go to a dance — that was wrong."

"Appalachia is hard on youngsters," said Mitch. "When we go into the schools to tell stories, we can spot 'em: we call 'em 'grandma and grandpa people.' The ones raised around old folks. They're like little old men and women, but they're just kids. It's like they're marooned in an older generation, and don't know how to relate to their own."

This is the downside, I thought, to the protection Vickie Vedder found in living among the elderly.

"You throw it away at first," mused Carla. "You can't wait to get out of the holler. Then you come back to it — everything you grew up with — and hold on to it real tight. Then you have to let it go. We're trying to keep the good stuff for Zoe and just let the rest go."

As she spoke, I saw my whole summer's pilgrimage begin-ning to coalesce around their words. I looked into Mitch and Carla's giant round porthole, now black with night, and saw myself rushing up Interstates and slaloming along backroads from Florida to West Virginia to Mississippi, wondering always why Southerners were right about what Cash called "the South's great difference." And wondering, too, why I was so deeply attracted to this elusive place, and sometimes scared by it. Storytellers had been hinting at an answer all along. Vickie Vedder and Veronica Byrd, Ray, Oyo, Kathryn Windham, Cornelia Bailey, and Ron Daise: they all credited their story-telling careers to growing up in the proximity of old people. "The important thing to know about Granny," Vickie had said, "was that she was *old*."

The same reasons that the South is predisposed to story-telling — its rural isolation, poverty, and until recently, relative lack of immigration; its consequent tight-knit networks of fam-ily, church, and community — also meant that families stayed put. Grandparents were not in nursing homes or condomini-ums in Florida; they were in the kitchen, cooking. And the stories they told when it was too hot to work anymore, in a bit of shade on the front porch, were funnels for passing on older ways of thinking. "My life was steeped in the past," said Vickie. Through this funnel of tales came spilling all of the past, the good and the bad. Granny Griffin's dislike of outsiders; in-visible terrors like plat-eyes; deals with an ever-present Devil; the belief that prayer can turn back tornadoes; Jack and Brer Rabbit's tough, every-man-for-himself philosophy; the courage of homesteaders like the rattlesnake couple, Ross and Anna. The ancient morals and prejudices and opinions of these charac-ters — their worldviews — were, incongruously, the birthright of the baby-booming storytellers with whom I had spent the summer, and of their listeners as well. They were all recipients of a tradition that was like an open tap through which yester-years flowed unfiltered. It occurred to me that for outsiders to get to know the South, a geographical map of the United States was insufficient; a temporal map, like a topographical one but made of light and shadow instead of flat and raised surfaces, was necessary as well to really locate the place.

Vickie said that everyone thinks of the South as stuck in the 1800s. There is a very good reason for that. In my experience growing up in the urban North, the past, the long-distant home of the dead, was the Otherworld that I knew only from pictures and history books. It didn't touch me; there was no mechanism like storytelling to bring it into my world. In the South, however, to this day children carry the past to school with them for Mitch and Carla to see. They are marked by it. Yet these children also live in the same daylit world that I inhabit (and which I seek, ironically, to dig beneath) — the world of commercial strips and smooth-legged women who have a constitutional right to an abortion — and the two clash like opposing weather systems. The resulting thunder is the sound of today's South. It was rumbling toward me from Mitch and Carla.

"There's a difference," Mitch began, "between what people in the South tell each other — you know, real stories, like the one I'm gonna tell you, 'Wicked John' — and what gets told about us in the rest of the country. Like Appalachian Kentucky: people just think of this cycle of violence and fightin' and inbreedin' . . . I mean, I have some of those stereotypical stories too. My grandfather used to tell tales on Great Uncle George, who was the last person hung in Indiana. The FBI trapped him in an ambush — the same FBI agent who caught Bonnie and Clyde . . . And for a while there my family was involved in a feud. My grandfather carried a .45 . . . There'us one time, in the mid-sixties, I guess, they was shootin' at each other up on Blue Lick Mountain. Ma mother broke it up by drivin' up there and calling fer ma father by his full name. 'Ray Barrett! You come out here right now!' That did it."

"I thought you weren't gonna tell her that stuff," reminded Carla. "You're just reinforcing it."

"Sometimes I find myself holdin' onto the bad stuff, you know, just to hold on to somethin'."

"My family comes from coal," said Carla, definitively. Mitch picked up a toy fishing rod and started casting across the floor, with Zoe between his knees. "Why don't you tell her a story?" he suggested.

Carla blushed, and said that Mitch was the real storyteller, and fussed with lighting some incense, but eventually ran out of distractions and I turned on the tape recorder.

HOW MY GRANDMA WAS MARKED

This is a story about how my grandmother was marked. I guess you need to know that in the mountains there's something we believe in called marking babies. If something happens to the mother while she's carrying the child — usually something of a strong, emotional nature — then the child's got a certain kind of birthmark.

Well, it was 1898, and my great-grandparents, Martha and Felix, were riding into town on a wagon to do some business, and my great-grandmother was expecting my grandma, and you know, she was cravin' stuff. Well, they passed a blackberry bush, and they were just hanging there, ripe, and she wanted some so bad. She just had to have some. And Felix wouldn't pull over the wagon. She begged him, and he just drove on to town. I guess he was in a hurry. So, three months later, when my grandmother was born, she had a big blackberry-shaped birthmark on her back.

Now that's not the strange part. You know, I can hear all these skeptics out there sayin' "coincidence," but here's the other part of the story. When I was a kid, I really liked to pick blackberries. It was one of my favorite things. We'd make jellies, and cobblers, and just eat 'em. The only trouble was, I'd go pick 'em up on the strip mine, which was a long, hot, dusty hike. And I hated to hike up there and then not have 'em be ripe . . . Now, the thing about my grand-mother's birthmark was that most of the year it was red, like a black-berry is when it's not ripe. Then when the blackberries would come ripe in July it would turn dark. Turn dark purple like a blackberry, you know, like a ripe blackberry. So that I wouldn't have to hike up, I'd just lift up her shirt and it would be purple, and I'd know it was time to go up and pick. And then when blackberry season was over it would fade throughout the winter. And it really did, you know, I saw it.

"And it hadn't turned color from the sun, right?" I asked. "It was hidden?"

"Yeah, it was hidden under her dress. And it happened her whole life. But I don't reckon I marked Zoe anyway." Carla smiled. "At least not yet."

Just as she had finished her story, the teenage moochers re-turned, and threw themselves on the sofa. Carla scooped up Zoe for a bath and Mitch took her place, eyeing his two charges with an amused scowl.

"Y'all wanna hear a story?"

They shrugged.

"Okay then. Now listen up. I learnt this story from my pa. My daddy's — no, my mama's daddy. Foller me? Good."

WICKED JOHN

A long time ago, a way back long time ago, back before you was born . . . You know how every story starts "Once Upon a Time"? Well this story's so old it was before anybody ever said, "Once upon a time."

The boys folded their arms across their chests, and fixed Mitch with the same look he'd just given them.

Naw, I'm just making all that up.

There was this feller named John. Now John was a blacksmith . . .

Well, this particular blacksmith was the orneriest, nastiest old man. Well, he was wicked. People called him Wicked John, the black- smith. He was just wicked. He was one of those people — I don't know, maybe he had gout or something, his feet hurt him all the time — because he was always in a bad mood. People'd say, "Howdy John," and he'd just bite yer head off. That's just the way he was. You might know somebody like that.

Anyway, people took real good care of their tools, because they didn't want to have to go see Wicked John. Well, Wicked John was workin' in his blacksmith shop one day, and this old feller — he must've been a stranger — now he's old. I'm talking about old, old. Did you ever see anybody get so old that they git crooked? Yer back all humped up? This old man, he's bent over and a-walkin' on the cane, and he had a long beard hanging down like this . . .

Mitch pulled his long braid across his face, under his chin.

And he come walking up to Wicked John's fence. And he said — Mitch lapsed into a rickety voice — "Excuse me, kind sir, can you spare a drink of water for an old man?" Wicked John said, "Furriner, who are you? This ain't no rest area! Git on down the road."

The old man says — Mitch borrowed his braid again — "Please kind sir, I jist need a drink of water. I ain't had nothing to drink for seventy-eleven days."

Wicked John — well, something came over him. He looked around to make sure nobody saw him being nice, and he said, "All right, old man, come through the gate, go down the well, git you a drink of water, then you hit the road."

"Thank you kind sir." And he walked over to the well. And Wicked John hauled him up the bucket, you know, pulled it up out of the well, set it up on the edge there. Now in the well there was a gourd dipper. Ya ever seen a gourd dipper? Know what a dipper is?

The boys shook their heads no.

Well, this is one of them garden-gourd dippers. Know what I'm sayin'? Big long handle. Just cut the top off, and scrape the guts out, throw the guts on the ground, grow more gourds . . . Kind of like a gourd factory. But that's a different story. Anyway, there was one of them gourd dippers hangin', so he just took that gourd dipper, and he dipped it in that bucket and he put the dipper up to his lips. Slurp. Oh, it be good, you know, right out of the earth. This is way back before Wal-Mart and stuff. Anyway, he gave him one more drink. He put it up to his old lips and said, Slurp. When he was done, John grabbed it and said, "That's enough! Ask for more drink, and you drink ma whole well dry. And that's the truth. You people, ya give ya an inch and ya take a mile. Now you git on outta here."

And the old man said, "Thank you kind sir. Thank you." And he started to walk off, but then he smelt something. Sniff, sniff. He said, "Excuse me kind sir. Ah couldn't help but notice that smell a-comin' from yer house. It smells like lunch a-cookin'. Ah ain't had nothing to eat for, ah, eleventy-seven days." Wicked John says, "Ah don't care if you never eat again, old man. I didn't take you to raise. Now git on the road." He said, "Please, I hate to die in yer yard." Wicked John says, "No, no, don't want ya dyin' in the yard . . . All right, come up to the house, and we'll fix ya a plate of food. You eat the food, and then you git on out of here."

So Wicked John helped the old man up to the house . . . Wicked John pulled him up a chair, and the old man set down. Wicked John went over to the stove. And he had a big skillet full of cabbage. He fried it. Mountain people fry everything. Makes it better. Whelp, he fried the cabbage. And then he poured a big glass of sweet milk — that's what it's called, cow milk, it weren't buttermilk, it were sweet milk — so, he poured him a big glass of sweet milk, and set that down. Then he went over and opened the oven up and pulled out another black skillet — one of those big iron skillets — and he thumped it on the table and the corn bread fell out. Big old pone of corn bread. Now, Wicked John may have been wicked, but he could cook, and this corn bread was good . . . The skillet — see, he knew the secret — you never wash the skillet. That way it'll always make a real nice crust on the cornbread. So that's what he done. He cut him off a big piece of cornbread, and he split that piece in two, and it opened up, and the steam comin' up out of it. And he took some fresh cow butter and he smeared it on that bread. And he set that down there, and he pushed that plate up there, and he said, "Now eat, old man." And the old man said, "Thank you kind sir." And he started eatin'.

Man, it was good. It was so good, he had to tap his foot while he was eatin'.

Mitch began tapping his foot.

Ever eat anything that good? (They're all noddin' their heads, readers.) Well, he's eating . . . and Wicked John just lookin' at him. He finally finished. And he brushed the crumbs from his old beard, and he pushed his chair back from the table. And he stood up. And I mean he stood up. All the cricks come out of his body and he stood up real tall and straight. And his beard was kind of glowin' silver-like, now. I ain't lyin, I'm telling you a story. He was St. Pete. Right there in Wicked John's house. Wicked John couldn't believe it. St. Pete looked at him — that's how he talked now — Mitch had dropped his voice low and deep — "Wicked John, I been sent here to test you. And you passed the test. So I'm gonna grant you three wishes, John." And John said, "Three wishes!!! Just like on *Jeopardy*. Let's see, the first thing I want is . . ."

"Now wait a minute, John, before you use up any of your wishes, John, I want you to think about your soul." John said, "Ma what?" He said, "Your soooouuuullll." John said, "Ma soul?" He thought about it and said, "You know ma good hammer, layin' over there? Everytime I want to use that hammer, somebody runs from down the road to borrow it to build them a treehouse or somethin'. And then they leave it out in the yard, the rains comes, rots the handle out, and I have to make another'n. My first wish is that the next person who teches ma hammer, it just stick to their hand, and hammer 'em, and hammer 'em, and hammer 'em, and hammer 'em, till I say let 'em go."

And St. Pete said, "All right John. Now John, you got two more wishes now, think about your soul." And John says, "My soooouuuullll! Ma second wish — you know ma good rockin' chair? Everytime I want to sit in that rockin chair, some stranger's in it. Come in here in ma shop. Have to run 'em out of ma own chair before I can sit down and take me a little rest. Ma second wish is that the next person teches that chair, it just suck em down in there and rock 'em, and rock 'em, and rock 'em, till I say let em go."

St. Pete said, "You're a strange man, John, but it'll be. Now John, you got one more wish, but John please think of . . ."

He said, "I know, I know, ma soouuulll." He said, "No, John, eternnniitttyy." John said, "Eternniittyy! You know, out there by my porch. I ordered this bush from the Sears & Roebuck catalogue, and it's called a Fire Bush. Big purple flowers on it. But them fox hunters come through here, and they take all them flowers for their girl friends. Don't leave me nothin' on that bush but them big old sharp thorns. Ma third wish is the next person that teches that firebush, that it just suck 'em down in them thorns and stick 'em, and stick 'em, and stick 'em, till I say let 'em go."

St. Pete said, "Okay, John, it'll be. Now you've used up your wishes, John. Thank you for the cornbread." And he turned around, and Bam! he'd disappeared. I ain't lyin', I'm tellin' you a story. Well, Wicked John? He settled right back into being . . . wicked. People see him and they'd shake their heads and say, "Wicked, wicked, wicked." Well, about two months went by, and Wicked John was sittin' around in his shop one day, and he hears, tap, tap, tap, tap. And he says, "Uh, come in." And the door come open. Creeeaaaakkk. In stepped a little devil about two-foot tall. Had little red horns on his head, yeller eyes, green teeth, swishing tail, forked foot, and a pitchfork in his hand. And he said, "Wicked John, my daddy sent me up here to get you and bring you back down there to talk to him."

Wicked John said, "Is that so?" And the little devil said, "Yeah, old man, that's so." Wicked John said, "Well, little devil, I'd love to go down there and talk to your daddy, but I got work to do as you can plainly see. I can't just go off and leave my shop." Said, "I tell you what, little devil, you help me get ma work done, and then we'll go see your daddy." And the little devil said, "Whater I got to do?" Wicked John said, "Pick up that hammer over there." That little devil walked over and he picked up that hammer. Wicked John set an old wagon wheel up there and he said, "Hit it right there." That little devil rared back, and he started to hammering. Hammering, hammering, hammering, hammering. All of a sudden, it just stuck to his little red hand. Hammer! Hammer! Hammer! Hammer! He looked at Wicked John. Hammer! Hammer! He looked at that hammer. 'Bout that time it took off with him. Hammer! Hammer! Hammer! Hammer! Went across the room, up the wall, Hammer, Hammer, Hammer, across the ceiling, Hammer, Hammer, Hammer, Hammer, his little red legs a-floppin' in the wind. He said, "Wicked John! Wicked John! Make this hammer turn me loose." Wicked John said, "No way, little devil. Not till you promise never to come around here again." That little devil, his legs are a-floppin', you know, and he's goin across the ceiling, that little devil said, "I'll promise you anything, Wicked John, just get me off this hammer." When he got off the ceiling Wicked John said, "Turn him loose." Clap! Shwwwwt! Lickety-split, down the road he went.

Well, Wicked John snickered about that for about fifteen minutes. Then he settled back into being . . .

We all chimed in unison, "Wicked, wicked, wicked." By now the boys' eyes weren't leaving Mitch's face.

Well, about two weeks later Wicked John was working in his blacksmith's shop, and he hears, Knock, knock, knock. "Uh, come in." And the door come open.

"Crrreeeeeaaaakkk." We all made the noise.

In steps that little bitty devil's brother. He's about thirteen years old. Worst kind of devil. The boys smiled. There he was. Red horns on his head, yeller eyes, green teeth, swishing tail, forked foot, and a pitch fork in his hand. And he said — oh yeah, he had on them big baggy britches too, look like they's gonna fall off? — he said, "Yo, Wicked John. What up?" Wicked John said, "What up wi' you, little devil?" Mitch started laughing. He said, "My daddy sent me up here to git you, and bring you back down to talk to him. And he don't like what you done to my little brother, neither." Wicked John said, "Issat so?" And the little devil said, "Yeah, old man, that's so."

Wicked John said, "Well, I'd love to go with you to see your daddy and your little brother. But I got work to do around here. I can't just go off and leave ma shop. If you'll help me . . ." He said, "Uh, un, old man. I ain't touching no hammer." Wicked John said, "You don't have to help me work. Just have a seat in that rockin' chair. I'll be with you in a minute." So that little devil, he sauntered over there to that rockin' chair, and he hiked up his britches so he could sit down, and he set hisself in that chair, and he started rockin'.

Now this is one of them old ones . . . Probably put together green, made everything swell together good and tight, and it kind of squeaks when you rock in it. Gives you that wompity-womp thing goin' on on the floor, 'cause rockers are kind of crooked, you know. He got to rockin' in it, and he got good on it. You know, he liked it, he's a-getting into it, and all of a sudden, it sucked his little red butt down in that chair, and it started rockin' him. Whamity-bam, whamity-bam. The back of his little head was hittin' that chair, whamity-bam, whamity-bam. He said, "Wicked John, Wicked John, get me out of this rockin' chair!" Wicked John started laughing. He said, "No way little devil, not till you promise never to come round here again." He said, "I promise anything! Just git me outta this rockin' chair!" Wicked John let him go for a few minutes, then he said, "Turn him loose." Clap! Phewt. Lickity-split, down the road he went.

Well, time passed, and Wicked John, he snickered about that too. But pretty soon, he settled into being . . .

In unison, "Wicked, wicked, wicked."

Well, one day, he was workin' in his blacksmith shop, and he hears, Boom! The door flew off the hinges. In stepped the big D himself. Great big horns on his head, big yeller eyes, green teeth, garlic breath, swishing tail, forked foot, and a pitchfork. And he said, "Wicked John. I don't like what you done to ma boys, so I comed up here to git you myself." Wicked John said, "Issat so?" And the old devil said, "Yeah, old man, that's so." Well, I don't know if y'all ever watch big-time wrestling, but Wicked John did. Ya never watch big time wrestling?

The teenagers and I both shook our heads no.

Well, Wicked John, he reached and he got a hold of that devil, and he got him in one of them, ah, head locks. Yeah, got him in a head lock. And he give him one of them, ah, nuggies. He nuggied him good. The old devil reached down and he got a hold of Wicked John's leg, and he throwed him up in the air, and they're rollin' across the room . . . They rolled out onta the porch, and Wicked John — he mighta had cable TV or somethin', he knew how to do one of them karate moves — Weha! Ha! He jumped around, and he grabbed ahold of that old devil, and throwed him right down in the middle of that . . . Fire Bush.

Well it got real quiet. And Wicked John looked down there in them thorns, and he said, "Oh, Devil, are you in there?" And he heard a little bitty voice way down in there in them thorns — Mitch dropped down to a croak — sayin', "Wicked John, whatever you do, don't shake the bush." Of course Wicked John shook it. "Aaagggghhhh!" Old Devil said, "Please, please, please, don't shake the bush! Oh oh oh oh oh oh oh!" He said, "Please, Wicked John, don't shake the bush, let me outta here, please, let me outta here." Wicked John said, "I ain't lettin' you outta there until you promise ta never to come 'round here again. And I don't want to see none of your kinfolk neither." He said, "I promise anything! I'll let everybody know. I'll e-mail all my relatives and I'll tell 'em not to ever come round here again!" He said, "All right, turn 'em loose." Clap! Whush. Lickity-split, down the road he went.

While Mitch spoke, Zoe ran around us half-clad in a towel, flashing everyone. She finally dropped it altogether and toddled off to the kitchen.

Well, Wicked John laughed at that for about an hour, then he settled right back into being . . .

In unison, "Wicked, wicked, wicked."

Well, one day, Wicked John was workin' in his blacksmith shop, and he died. That's right. Got old, kicked the bucket, passed on over yonder, as they say. Well, he got up there to heaven, to the Pearly Gates, and he knocked on the door. Knock, knock, knock. And the gate come open.

The boys and I made a squeaking noise.

Naw, it didn't squeak, it just made, Swush! (We swushed.) Out stepped St. Pete. And he said, "Well, John, what are you doin' here?"

John said, "Well, Pete, I died. Thought I'd have me a look around, maybe move in." He said, "Well, that's nice, John, but you see, you can't even so much as step your foot inside the gate until we look at the book." John said, "The book?" He said, "That's right. The book that lists all the good things you done in your life, and all the bad things you done in your life. You wait here John."

Pete went back there and he got this big book, and he brought it out and he opened it up. He said, "Wicked John, that'ud be in the Ws, won't it?" So he flipped it over there. "Wicked Jane, wick . . . Wicked John! Says here, John, you gave an old man a drink of water." John said, "Yeah, I gave him a whole dipper-full. It'us real good, too." Pete said, "Yeah, it was good water, John. Also says here you gave an old man a plate of food." John said, "Yeah, I gave him a whole big plate of cooked cabbage. I put pepper on it, and salt, and a big piece of corn bread, and a big tall glass of milk." He said, "See Pete? I'm a good guy, let me in." Pete said, "John, it was good cornbread. But . . . We've got to turn the page now and look at all the bad things ya done." So he did, he turned the page. Full pages on the other side, completely full. Written down in between the margins. Know them little yeller sticky things ya have by the phone, for writin' notes on? Them things was stuck all over it, because they'd run outta room to write all the bad stuff that Wicked John had done.

St. Pete said, "I'm sorry, John, but you can't come in here." John said, "Wull, what am I supposed ta do? I done died."

"Ya gotta go down there." John said, "Down there?" He said, "Yeah, down there." He said, "Wull, I reckon I will." And he started off down there.

Meantime, down there, behind the fiery gates, them little devils, they was ah, ah — Mitch stopped for a moment, just this side of laughter, considering the boys — throwin' frisbees. Fire frisbees. They's a throwin' it back and forth — that's what little devils do — they throwin' that fire frisbee back and forth. One of them looked up and he saw Wicked John comin' down the road. He dropped his fris-bee and said, "Daddy, daddy, daddy! Here, come quick, it's John!" And he come runnin' up and he said, "Get in behind me, boys, I'll protect you." And he closed the gate and put a big padlock on it and a chain, and put all his furniture up against it. Put up a Do Not Dis-turb sign too. And Wicked John walked right up to the gate and rang the doorbell. Ergggguhhhhh — I just made that part up — he just knocked on the door, Knock, knock, knock. And old Devil said, "What do you want, John?" And he said, "Well, old Devil, I died, thought I'd have a look around, maybe move in down here." Old Devil said, "Un uh, John, you're in the wrong place, you got to go up there." He said, "I been up there, they sent me down here." Old Devil shook his head. He said, "Naw, thought about it, John, and you're too wicked to be in Hell."

John said, "Well what am I supposed to do?" The old Devil said, "You just wait here." And he went back and he opened up his old fiery furnace, and he reached way in the back of that furnace and he got this hot burning coal outta there. And he took it and he stuck it out the gate, and said, "Here, Wicked John, you take this burning hot coal, and you go off, and you find your own Hell. Start your own Hell."

So, to this very day, in the Appalachian Mountains, Smokey Moun-tains, up in Eastern Kentucky — right out here the other night — I seen something. Some people call it foxfire. Glows in the dark up in the woods at night. Them scientist fellers say — Mitch assumed a dignified voice — "It's a mushroom that glows in the dark." The old timers, they'll all say — now in a creaky voice — "Why, it's fox fire." And the really old-timers, they'll say, "That's Wicked John."

We clapped till our hands hurt, and the boys beamed in a very unteenage manner. I had seen "Wicked John" mentioned in a list of old Irish tales transplanted to the South, but I'd never heard it before. After he finished, Mitch admitted he'd had trouble with the ending — "It's a bit of a downer, besides, I don't like that whole Hell thing" — and had added the part about fox fire.

"What's that?" asked one of the boys.

"It's a light, like a phosphorescent light, that rotting wood sometimes gives off," explained Mitch. "Looks spooky, but it ain't."

Afterwards, while Carla and Zoe made cookies in Zoe's kiddie oven, we cajoled Mitch into telling us one more tale. This one was called "Whickity-Whack," a Jack tale he'd learned from Ray Hicks, about Jack trapping Death in a sack (the very tale Ray told to the president of the United States when he received his award from the National Endowment for the Arts). Mitch said he hadn't quite finished working on this one, which I thought a curious comment, until he began speaking. Then I understood: the tale was a bridge across time that Mitch had built word by careful word. But for a few rough spots, it was nearly complete. In Mitch's world, a hybrid of New South and Old Appalachia, Jack watches Martha Stewart and Death carries a weed whacker instead of a scythe; the princess is anorexic. Through Mitch Barrett, Ray Hicks met daytime television, and the boys loved it. It seemed that of all the Hicks clan, Jack was the one who had gone upscale and moved into a condo.

We ended the evening very late, with me yawning desperately and Mitch and Carla each playing guitar and singing (they have recorded an album together, and have a new CD in the works). Then, because the boys were in residence, Mitch announced I was staying with his mother, just around the corner.

"But I don't know her!" I cried.

"She don't know you neither, but she invited you. C'mon."

The Barrett family continued to foil my expectations. In the few minutes it took to cross the dark hillside, I populated the little ranch house ahead of me with a tiny, gray-haired old lady; instead, Peggy opened the door, still extraordinarily young-looking at fifty-eight, in pajamas, with a long dark braid down her back to match her son's. Her home was the antithesis of Mitch and Carla's: neat, proper, rich with knickknacks. We chatted for a little bit, and I learned that she had married at fifteen and had Mitch at seventeen, and then Peggy announced she had to leave for the greeting card factory where she worked at five A.M. but that she'd be real quiet.

"You just get up whenever you like. I'd leave breakfast, but Carla already offered to do that. Just go back to their house — they'll be gone too, they're telling stories at a school a few hours from here — but the front door is always open."

"But, but you don't know me," I stammered, nearly adding that for all she knew I was planning to rob or maim or murder her in the night, then thought better of it.

"Oh, any friend of Mitch's . . . ," she said generously, showing me where to find my towels.

The following morning I woke in silence. The only noise in the holler came from a motion detector in the shape of a frog on Peggy's front walk. Whenever anything crossed its path, which I did several times, it croaked a loud, electronic warning.

I knew Mitch and Carla's house was less than a minute away, but I didn't know the direction, and wound up wandering for fifteen minutes before I found it, feeling as solitary as Wicked John. The name raised a visible shiver on my arms. I had been so caught up in Mitch's telling last night that the sudden, existential awfulness of the ending had curdled in my ears. "Here's an ember: go start your own Hell." In the South, where evil has always had a close, familial quality, caught up in a cycle of intimates inflicting violence on one another (the very geography of the South, bordered by the Appalachian range, the Atlantic, the Gulf of Mexico, and the Mississippi River, reinforces a claustrophobic, regional intimacy), to be cast out of the family, however grim, is the ultimate expulsion. To travel always and have no home, not even in Hell. To be alone, without conversation or kin — it is a Southern storyteller's nightmare.

The Bell Witch's Tale

I WAS DRIVING THE FINAL STROKE of the backwards "Z" that my recent travels had traced on the map: west from West Virginia to central Kentucky; east from there back to the Appalachian outskirts of Berea; and now, west again, across the long rectangle of Tennessee toward Memphis. In the north-central part of the state, somewhere on Interstate 40, my car radio entered a strange dimension. One channel, playing oldies out of Knoxville, said it was ten A.M.; another, playing classic rock out of Nashville, said it was nine. This riff in chronology unsettled me. If we can mess with anything invisible to us, like time, and make it bend to our comfort, surely the invisible world can make us uncomfortable as well. You see, I was on my way to Memphis, but I planned to stop at a haunting along the way.

In 1818 — coincidentally, the year Mary Shelley wrote *Frankenstein* — some very interesting things began to happen to a family in Adams, Tennessee, which today is a little farming community about twenty miles north of Nashville, near the Kentucky border. In morning sunlight the countryside looked ordinary enough: tidy seas of chicory bobbing in a light breeze, red barns battened up tight, with smoke curling out from under their eaves (actually this seemed a little sinister, and for a time I considered calling a fire department, until I figured tobacco was drying inside). Adams was just a collection of houses casually calling themselves a town. It was only by chance that I found the sign I was seeking on a secondary farm road:

> Historic Bell Witch Cave
> Daily Tours 10–6 May thru Oct.
> Private tours available
> Alcohol strictly prohibited

Another sign added, Closed when Flooded.

In the early nineteenth century there was even less of a human presence in this part of Tennessee than today. The Bell family, prosperous homesteaders and pillars of the small community, had for a time been disturbed by unidentified scratchings and knockings outside their home. Then in 1818 the noises moved inside. Four sons who shared a bedroom were bothered by the sound of a rat gnawing their bedposts; when they searched, however, no animal was ever found. Next the covers began slipping off their beds, as if being pulled from the foot, accompanied by the sound of someone smacking their lips and gulping for air. The same things happened to their sister Elizabeth in the next room, who was also bothered by noises of dragging chains and stones thudding on the floor. It was when the shivering Bells tried to pull their bedclothes back up that the real trouble began. Invisible hands twisted around their hair and yanked hard, or pricked their skin with pins, or pinched them. Elizabeth was "frequently crimsoned as by a hard blow from an open hand," her brother Richard wrote later.

Their father, John Bell, forbade his family to speak of these incidents until Elizabeth, especially, became so tortured that he asked a neighbor in as a witness. When the nightly tumult started, the neighbor cried out, "In the name of the Lord, who or what are you?" There was no reply except an immediate, temporary silence, which they took to mean that the disturbance understood their words. After that the Bells' secret was out, and more neighbors came to pelt the air with questions, and were audibly slapped in response. Progressively, the spirit began making whistling sounds, then unintelligible whisperings; finally it spoke, answering the question, "Who are you and what do you want?" by saying "I am a Spirit; I was once very happy but have been disturbed."

Thereafter the Bells, quite against their will, and their in-house Spirit became celebrities. For two years people came from all over the States and England to witness the phenomenon (the Bells' English relatives had passed the word), including President Andrew Jackson. Locally the voice became known as the Bells' Witch. It took an active interest in the lives of the community, gossiping about locals' private doings, meddling in Elizabeth's love life — it refused to let her marry against its wishes — and going on for hours singing hymns and quoting whole chapters of the Bible verbatim, at top speed. It chastised anyone who misquoted Scripture. It played tricks. Once it declared itself to be the spirit of a person buried nearby, whose grave had been disturbed; another time it said it was a neighbor woman's witch; once it announced it was the spirit of an early immigrant who had buried treasure on the Bells' land. It instructed several people to dig for this treasure in a certain spot — they did so exhaustively, and found nothing — then it recounted the adventure to newcomers for a month, making uproarious fun of the gullible treasure hunters it had duped. Curiously, it was also intensely prejudiced against the Bells' black slaves, and harrassed them with beatings and slaps.

Finally, the Spirit announced its intention of hurrying John Bell, or "Old Jack," as it called him, into his grave. At the same time it showed real love for Bell's wife, Lucy, caring for her when she was sick and bringing her presents. It also brought a gift to the Bells' daughter-in-law, Martha — black silk stockings, "to be buried in," it told her — when she moved to Mississippi. But John Bell was its target. The Spirit cursed him viciously, and one night in 1821, finally poisoned him. Bell was discovered unconscious with a vial of dark liquid nearby (when the family tested some on a cat, it immediately went into convulsions and died). The disembodied voice announced gleefully, "It's useless for you to try to revive Old Jack — I have got him this time; he will never get up from that bed again." As usual, it was right. Bell died and the Spirit sang a drinking song — "O, row me up some Brandy!" — at his funeral. Afterward, it said it was leaving the household but promised to return seven years later. Sure enough, in 1828 the Spirit came back, and this time had a tête-à-tête with John Bell, Jr., to whom it fairly accurately described the upcoming Civil War, and World War I.

"Some say it never left," said Chris Kirby, a pretty blonde woman who along with her husband now owned the former Bell farm. She wore a T-shirt printed with an icon of a witch — a figure in a tall hat, riding a broomstick — superimposed over a big yellow bell. Her familiar was a friendly black Lab named Panther. The Kirbys had built an open-air pavilion in the middle of one of their fields, with a corrugated iron roof overtop to create some shade. The pavilion functioned as a kind of outdoor office; although the Bell's house had been razed long ago, for five dollars the Kirbys took visitors on tours of the "Bell Witch Cave," a cavern on the property. The cave had its own body of folklore, including a story I had heard on The Moonlit Road about a little boy who had gotten stuck in it, and had suddenly been jerked out by unseen hands.

"We're the Number One haunted spot in America," Chris announced proudly.

Before touring the cave, Chris told me a ream of spooky

stories under the pavilion, while Panther licked his private parts and the roof creaked in the heat. "There's somethin' here, I don't know if it's the Bell Witch or what," Chris began. "When people takes pictures in the cave, weird things come up on the film." She opened a photo album and began pointing out strange lights and glowing spheres on otherwise ordinary photographs. "We had a guy come through with one of them night cameras, like they used in the Gulf War? Here's what come out."

She showed me a second-by-second sequence taken by a thermal-imaging camera inside the cave, that depicted some kind of aperture opening and closing in quick succession in one of the crawl spaces; one image clearly showed a face contorted in a scream, seemingly being torn apart by the aperture. My skepticism had a tussle with my eyes, and there were no winners. "Now look at these," she said. "They were taken by ordinary folks who've visited us. They send me copies of the real good ones."

Chris first pointed out a snapshot she herself had taken of her daughter and a friend. She had accidentally moved the camera and created a double exposure. The curious thing was that in the primary image of her daughter the girl's hair was off her face, while in the shadow, or ghost image, it fell across her forehead. I looked at Chris and raised my eyebrows. She smiled and rubbed her forearms, which were covered in goose bumps. "Real creepy, ain't it?" she commented, handing me another snapshot, this time labeled March 1977. It was an ordinary color shot of a family on vacation, taken next to a crumbling wall.

"Tell me what's weird about that," she challenged.

I peered at the people, who all looked normal enough, if unfortunate victims of seventies fashions. Then I glanced at the wall: almost formed by the cracks and peeling paint and lichen, but not quite — it was too vivid to be a suggestion — was the colorless outline of a woman in a long skirt, holding a baby, with a child by her side.

"That's been tested by labs an' everything, and it ain't a doctored photo."

At that moment a fierce, hot wind came whirling out of the calm afternoon and shook the pavilion, scattering photos and papers every which way. Chris and I looked at each other and laughed, but we both fumbled unnecessarily with the photos, shaken though too skeptical to admit. At that point we were also joined by a portly mother and much-pierced daughter from Nashville, the latter sporting beet-red hair and blue fingernails. They came with us, along with Panther, on our excursion to the cave. The additional flesh was somehow reassuring.

The Bell Witch Cave was on a cool, ferny hillside above the Red River. Chris explained that we had to be on the lookout for canoeists who sometimes tried to sneak up the bank. The Kirbys had been forced to install an electronic alarm system around their entire property, because so many people — *teenagers,* she said pointedly, nodding at the daughter — tried to sneak in at night to have themselves a good scare.

The cave mouth was outfitted with a sturdy iron gate; inside, its entrails were wonderfully cool, so cool that steam rose faintly from Panther's back. It was not a particularly beautiful cave. Stunted stalagmites and stalactites, no bigger than wax drippings, fixed themselves to a cluster of immense flowstone formations that writhed and twisted alongside the central passageway. The floor was uneven, and water dripped from the ceiling. Panther lapped noisily from a puddle. The colors replicated every shade of copper penny, from brand-new (orange-rose) to ancient (deep brown). Chris told us that three-thousand-year-old Native American graves had been discovered above the cave, and pointed out a small stone sarcophagus to one side of the pathway. It was about three hundred years old and had contained the skeleton of a young girl, until someone had stolen it. That reminded her.

"*Never* take anything from the cave," she cautioned. "I took an arrowhead once, and three days later I got a serious back injury. Then my daughter took a rock, and the next day one of our barns collapsed. We lost $25,000 worth of tobacco. You bet we put all that stuff back."

I looked in horror at my sneaker, which was covered in ocher mud. Did sediment count? As it turned out, fear was the only thing that haunted me from the Bell Witch Cave — that and a curious impression. What the Bells called their "Family Trouble" made for a first-rate ghost story, but in many ways it was a very *human* haunting. The Spirit had preyed on personal relationships and employed, to my mind, fairly low-level methods of nuisance-making. It even stooped to poisoning. Although it claimed to be from "heaven, hell, and earth," its manifestations and concerns fell within the sphere of mortal activity, so much so, in fact, that unlike other ghosts it was obsessed with the present and future, rather than the past. This human orientation puts the Bell Witch in a different category from the ghosts I had encountered earlier on my journey — those incarnations of the terrible, impersonal predations of the coast: the storms, the disease, the Devil lurking in overwork, heat, and stagnant swamps. Whatever shape they assumed, from human to plat-eye, coastal ghosts were ultimately part and parcel of the elements, which is what gave their stories such sensory-soaked fatalism. The heat, the thunder, the damp: the weather there was always ripe for recalling old hauntings, always threatening to create new ones.

But we don't expect such terrors in the hardy soil of Adams, Tennessee. So where did the Bell Witch come from? She — the Witch was gendered female from the very beginning — had an all-too-human fanaticism about her, from her imperious judgments about what was best for members of the family, especially the lone daughter, to her rabid dislike of blacks, her overwrought citations from Scripture, her autocratic sense of right and wrong, her violent outbursts. In an eerie way the Spirit prefigured a very "Southern" brand of intolerance that scarred the twentieth century. Consider the repeated attacks on the teaching of evolution (the Scopes Trial of 1925, in which a biology teacher was found guilty of breaking a state law prohibiting the teaching of Darwin's theories, was held in Tennessee). Consider the white-supremacist ravings of the Ku Klux Klan, and the three thousand lynchings of African-Americans of which Dick had spoken; the decision of the Southern Baptist Church, the largest Christian denomination in America, to cease ordaining women ministers in the year 2000. All of these descended from the attitudes of the Bell Witch. I could not help thinking that those black-and-white TV ghosts that rolled in my memory, the same ghosts I found trapped in old television sets in the Birmingham Civil Rights Museum, were forty year-old incarnations of the Bells' Witch, returned as she had promised (the Spirit had made allusions to coming back to earth a century later), to haunt America.

Had the presence that tortured the Bells been a kind of mirror reflecting the family troubles of the South, or a warning that went unheeded? When, in 1994, Byron de la Beckwith was found guilty of murdering NAACP field secretary Medger Evers in 1963, Evers's widow employed language that summoned the Spirit in order to dismiss her. "I recall this feeling of release that was very spiritual . . . it was as though all of the demons in my body exited through every pore of my being . . . For the first time in all those years, I became free, my children became free and I felt that Mississippi became freer, as did all of America."

"Freer," emphasized Ms. Evers-Williams. Exorcism, unfortunately, is not an event but a process.

Annie's Tale

THE PREVIOUS OCCUPANT of the guestroom in Mike LaRosa's Memphis bungalow was a Peruvian artist named Nicario. To show his gratitude, Nicario had painted the fieldstones of Mike's fireplace oxblood-red; he then divided the wall above the mantle into an arched triptych with painted columns, and placed an image of St. Michael spearing a smarmy red devil in the middle.

"See?" said Mike excitedly. "It represents the imposition of Christianity on indigenous Inca culture. Can you tell?"

My gift, a tea towel, suddenly seemed somewhat inadequate, so I retired to the guestroom to check my e-mail. There was a message from Karen Vuranch. "How much money would it take to describe me something like this?" she asked: "Her svelte figure is the envy of runway models, and her slow, modulated speech was easy to understand." I wrote her back telling her how to make a direct deposit into my bank account.

There was also another message from Vickie — still no sign of her stories — that mentioned an African-American friend of Granny Griffin's named Ol' Rennie. "Where Granny was a tough ol' bird from a white woman perspective," wrote Vickie, "Rennie was her equal according to her race. She'd seen some hard times, Pam — different from Granny's. As I told you . . . the South was a hard place to survive during the Depression and up until now for that matter, but particularly [for] women . . . And black people had an added measure of severity because of their color. My heart winces and stammers at the thought . . ." She added that it would take her hours to find the words to bring Ol' Rennie to life in a sentence. She'd have to "describe and describe to get the dusty picture accurate."

I wrote back and begged her to do exactly that. At least it made a nice change from hounding her about sending Granny's stories. Then, disastrously, I relaxed and spent a serene, twilit hour doing nothing but rocking on Mike's porch swing. Afterwards, having lost the traveler's slightly paranoid edge that I had been honing for weeks (which manifested itself in obsessively gathering directions to storytellers' houses and fretting about running out of gas), I called a teller named Wanda Johnson to arrange a meeting. She lived in Pritchard. I related the good news that I was nearby, in Memphis. Well, that's good, she said uncertainly, and gave me directions that involved many sightings of water. I said how nice it would be to see the Mississippi, and later recounted the route to Mike.

He screwed up his face in a pained smile as if dismissing my intellect wholesale. "Where are you going?"

"Pritchard."

"Pritchard, where?"

"Pritchard, Mississippi. See?" I got out the map and showed him a town near Memphis, on the Mississippi River.

"Why then, Pamela dear, do her directions lead you to Pritchard, Alabama? *See?*" He flipped the page and showed me a town on the Gulf of Mexico.

After I phoned my regrets, Mike tried to cheer me up by taking me to see a different Wanda. It was "Wanda Appreciation Night" at the nearby P&H Café, a dive I had been introduced to on a previous visit to Mike's, that was part frat-boy den, part family hamburger joint, and part tourist attraction for slumming college professors, like Mike. The last time we were there, we had sat next to a table of witches.

Wanda was the proprietress. The many caricatures of her lining the walls might as well have been photographs: exaggeration was her body's natural asset. On that first visit Wanda had told me she'd worked in bars all her life, but didn't drink. "That's the trick to makin' money, honey," she'd said. She looked about fifty. A Neolithic Venus figure dressed up as Stevie Nicks, with long, curly hair and tight, yet oddly wispy, clothing. Tonight was a P&H anniversary — P&H means "Poor and Hungry, darlin'," as Wanda told me, not Pneumonia and Hepatitis, as Mike suggested — which featured mud wrestling (it was actually chocolate pudding) between women in patent leather hip boots and hot pants, and the Wanda Booth, which breathlessly advertised Kiss Actual Woman!

By the time Mike and I arrived, the crowd was swaying as one with a tidelike drunkenness, cresting over the sidewalk into the gutter. Some kid offered to stamp our hands in exchange for the entrance fee. We looked at each other, grimaced, and went home to bed.

"Two Wandas down and counting," called Mike as I fell asleep.

"There's Graceland, if you care." Mike pointed to Elvis's white-columned brick mansion as we hurtled past, driving in the central, fifth lane, the abominable "chicken lane," of a divided highway. All the commercial strips I had seen throughout the summer reached their collective zenith around Graceland, which is what, I imagined, attracted the high-fat, low-priced flotsam of the culture in the first place.

"Stop! Stop!" I yelled. "There's the Days Inn."

"But we'll be late for church."

"Just for a second," I pleaded. Mike pulled in the parking lot and the smell of chlorine led us to the pool. My guidebook was right: it *was* built in the shape of a guitar, in homage to the King. A bright blue, shimmering guitar, decorated around the edges by a series of buttocks marks left by swimmers in wet bathing suits. We snapped photos then hurried on to Al Green's Full Gospel Tabernacle, two blocks down.

There is a vast body of apocrypha as to why the famous R&B singer Al Green became an ordained minister. All stories seem to agree on one point: he was in the bathtub when his wife — either mentally ill or enraged at discovering him with another woman — poured either boiling water or hot grits on top of him. The important point is that afterward he founded a church, which we in turn found thanks to the electric marquee sign out front, advertising an upcoming revival. Mike pointed out that someone had put one of the s's backwards and used a dollar sign for an ampersand. "Very Memphis," he said dryly.

The church was modern, air-conditioned, and outfitted with a state-of-the-art sound system. We were asked to sign the visitor's book. The addresses betrayed that Reverend Green had hit it big in the European guidebook market: Italy, France, England, Germany. Mike and I took our places in a pew next to a French couple (*"Mais où est Al Green?"* the man kept asking with increasing concern), in what were clearly the voyeur seats. The congregation on that Sunday in August was actually a pretty good microcosm of Memphis. A handful of white people — in this case all clones of Mike and me, youngish, liberal, and casually dressed, though Mike was the only one with a goatee and a Boston accent — trying to pretend we knew how to sing and dance as well as the overwhelming black majority. (Throughout the summer I had repeatedly received the impression that whites sense that blacks have a better time than they do, and want in on the secret.) Taking another cue from the city outside, blacks and whites sat in separate neighborhoods of the sanctuary.

The service was similar to that at Fouchena's church in

terms of kinetic enthusiasm, but the program was more free-form. In fact, the sermon and readings and responses were just a slight scaffolding built to house the music, which was so good it took over the beat of my heart. The choir had only ten members, but each one sang as if he or she were a headliner in Vegas. Whenever they began a new number, women in hats shaped like nineteenth-century bustles rose, held their arms aloft, and rotated their palms like the queen waving to her people. Reverend Green himself was an hour and a half late — stuck in the Atlanta airport, he explained with lingering irri-tation — but the service only really began with his arrival. I cannot remember what he said; I was too distracted by the medium to consider the message. Al Green's speaking voice was the audible equivalent of mercury: a smooth, shiny, malleable, metallic sound that slipped sensually into the curves of the ear. It seemed not to issue from his mouth, or his chest or nose, but from his gills, those sensitive hollows right below the ears where the sweetest sensations register in a kind of exquisite, quiver-ing pain.

That evening I lay down in bed with Al Green's voice still stroking my inner ear, anticipating a fine night's sleep. Just as I was drifting off I became aware of my feet. They itched. I scratched a bit, then turned over and waited for unconscious-ness. My feet itched more. By two A.M. I was frantically pulling ice from Mike's freezer to rub over the fourteen little red welts on my ankles, insteps, between my toes. When Mike woke at six, I borrowed a bottle of Caladryl that he had bought in Colombia — "Where bugs are *big*," he said — and covered my pox marks in pink liquid. It helped for about three minutes.

"You've got chigger bites," he pronounced.

"Your porch!" I cried. "It must've been sitting on your porch . . ."

"They lay little chigger eggs in there, that's why it itches. See . . ."

"Stop!" I shouted. "That's disgusting. I don't want to know. What are chiggers, anyway?"

A former student of Mike's was visiting and had overheard my raised voice. "Nasty little bitin' bugs. You want to put nail polish on those, if they are chigger bites," he advised. "That way the eggs can't breathe, and they die." Mike and I looked at him with full-blown New England skepticism. "Really," he said. Then he wished me luck, because I was heading to what he called "the redneck part of town."

Annie McDaniel had been recommended to me by another Memphis storyteller as "the real thing," whatever that meant. She lived in Frayser, a white neighborhood of modest, one-story homes not far from the city beltway. I spotted her way mark immediately, a camper parked in the driveway with a Day-Glo For Sale sign in the back window. A compact woman answered my knock. Although elderly, she was pretty, in an elfin way normally associated with the young and perky. Her home was stashed full of crafts and knickknacks and her husband's sturdy handmade furniture; it was clearly a house in which people *did* things with their hands. In fact, a kind of stamina emanated from Annie. I thought of her as the proverbial early bird, a plump, busybody on restless stick legs, the latter covered in tight pink stretch pants.

She brought me a Coke and we sat down next to a triple-decker model steamboat displayed on the coffee table. An odd assortment of objects, including a button on a string, a model tent, and a metal leg trap lay beside it. "My father built that packet boat fifty-five years ago," she said. "It was modeled after a real ship that ran between Memphis and St. Louis — the *Robert E. Lee.*"

Annie began to unpack her memory for me. Unlike anyone else I had met, except Minerva King, Annie's story was, quite simply, her life. Her father, a strapping man who was part Cherokee, had lost an arm in a hunting accident in 1909; after that he couldn't find work, and so became a fisherman, hunter and tracker on the banks of the Mississippi. His family, which eventually included ten children, moved onto the river year-round to be close to him.

"I was born in 19 and 14, in Vicksburg, Mississippi," Annie announced, "and left the river in 1932."

"My God, that makes you . . ." — it took a second to do the math, — "eighty-five!" I blurted out, astonished. I was surreptitiously pressing the Coke can against my burning feet.

Annie gave me an indulgent look. "I do pretty well for an old lady," she said, and continued to deal out memories as from an orderly deck of cards. Like Orville Hicks, Annie had spent her childhood in a world no longer known to the young. Her stories, like his, had subsequently acquired the patina of much-handled icons. "We didn't know this way of life would disappear," she said, still a little surprised.

The family had lived on bargelike houseboats, unless someone took a liking to their then-current home, and her father sold it. In that case, they had camped out in tents along the riverbanks and on islands and sandbars. "We ate whatever Daddy caught. Coon, mink, muskrat, possum, rabbit, wild duck, turkey, fish, you name it. When you're hungry, you'll eat anythin' that don't bite you first. Have you ever had raccoon meat?" she asked, showing me how a steel leg trap worked by prodding it with a pencil, which it viciously snapped in two.

Not to my knowledge, I told her.

"It's real tasty, but you got to get the kernels out from just underneath the front legs. It's this bit of real dark meat —

glands, maybe, I don't know. If you don't, it tastes just like wet dog smells."

Annie's parents had put an enormous amount of ingenuity into using raw materials of the river to replicate housebound life. Her mother had taught the children their ABCs by drawing in the sand with driftwood; she had made them dolls out of cornhusks, and had invented the button toy that lay on the coffee table. The object was to spin the string and make the button move from one end to the other. Annie and her husband Jesse were both masters of this art, but I failed miserably. Jesse took both my hands in his, and tried to override my hand-eye coordination with his own, but even this was unsuccessful. I finally had to wriggle free to scratch my bites.

"Oh you poor dear, are those chigger bites?" asked Annie. "You want to put some nail polish on those, it kills the larvae." Not waiting for a response, she popped up and ran to the bedroom, returning with a bottle of clear polish. "Cover 'em right up," she advised, which I did as she talked, successfully gluing several toes together in the process.

Annie's mother had used willow trees along the riverbanks to make brooms and toothbrushes; she had sewn the girls' dresses from flour sacks, and had baked holiday pies over campfires built on sandbars. She determined it was safe to drink Mississippi water if it sat for a day and the sediment filtered out, but not Wolf River water; she taught herself about medicinal herbs and barks, and made her children wear something called asafoetida — a stinky member of the carrot family — around their necks. "It supposedly kept germs away, but since it smelt like onion gone bad, it kept *everythin'* away."

While her mother was doing all that, to prevent Annie from wandering too deep into the river and drowning, she would draw charcoal rings around her legs. If Annie came home and

357

the rings had washed away, she'd get a whack from a willow tree switch. "Once I went in too far and drew new rings on my own legs so Mama wouldn't know. She did. I never found out how, but she knew."

For a time the family lived on Mud Island, which hunkers in the Mississippi just off the Memphis shoreline. Mike pointed it out a few days ago: an urban cul-de-sac now silted to the eastern bank, bulging into the coffee-with-milk colored river. Today it houses a Legolike maze of expensive, waterview condominiums. Seventy years ago it had been a little wilderness with sandy edges. While the family camped there, a preacher came every other week and held services under a brush arbor that her father had rigged up. Other times, when they were living on houseboats or camping on sandbars, they had attended services at the black churches that huddled along the riverbanks. I doubted they had felt like holy tourists, as Mike and I did, perhaps because they were there to hear God rather than music.

"There weren't many blacks on the river," recalled Annie. "They were all working in the big plantations up on the banks. We traded with them for eggs, butter, and milk, and shared their religion."

SHUG

Now I remember in 19 and 19 — the winter of 19 and 18 and 19 and 19 — it was a terrible winter. Papa could not keep the snow and ice off of the top of our tent. We lived on Mud Island then, and the tent fell in. So we moved off of Mud Island to the southeast corner of Front and Auction Streets, into a huge house. We didn't know who owned the house or anything, but we moved into it. I guess Papa found out, because we stayed there that winter.

Now the 'flu epidemic — the influenza epidemic — was raging. My sister Grace and I both were in bed with the 'flu, and my grandma died in that house in January with the 'flu. It was terrible, terrible. I think it came from Germany during World War I . . .

And there was a black family that lived behind this house in a alley [pronounced halley]. And they had a little girl my same age, and her name was Shug . . . And Shug and I run around together. I thought Shug was so pretty. She had skin that looked like black satin, and her lips was nice and thick, and I just thought she was so pretty, and I just wished I had lips and all like Shug.

Well, everybody had cook stoves, and they burned wood or coal. And back in behind that cook stove there is a place that is about this wide — Annie indicated a foot or so — so you could open that cook box and get all of that soot outta there. Because if your pipe filled full of soot too much, it could catch a fire.

Now I had platinum blond curly hair. Both Shug and I — her mother was gone this day — and so Shug and I got in that soot box. And we blacked me with that soot. Every inch of me that stuck out of my clothes, we blacked it. Even my hair. And I was so proud of me, because I was like Shug, you know? And Shug and I went to my house to show Mama. Well, Mama wasn't happy. Mama said, "When I get through with you, you're going to be red like an Indian!" And I was. So I couldn't be black . . . She like to never have got all that soot out of my hair!

So since I couldn't be black like Shug, Grace and I took Shug and we's gonna make her white. We greased her all over with, ah, grease, and then we took flour, and we just patted that flour all over Shug. All in her hair . . . Well, we covered her with that like we did me in the soot. And her mother wasn't happy either.

While Annie went to get us more Cokes, I looked around her house. A homemade Christmas ornament — two plastic Champagne glasses glued together and filled with confetti — lay on a side table waiting to be trimmed with ribbon. Annie's own nostalgic oil paintings hung on the walls. The paintings had the awkward, urgent charm of paradox: fleeting shadows cast by a remembered life, transferred to canvas in the primary colors of the present. Looking at them, I realized that Annie had become a curator of the vanished nomadism of her youth. Ironically, it was her mountain of things, her paintings and crafts, her models and souvenirs, that now recalled a childhood of fluid minimalism. Unlike her stories — she had learned the art of telling on the river — the contradiction pushed the past further away.

MY FIRST EXPERIENCE WITH A FLUSH COMMODE

Now I'm going to tell you my first experience with a flush commode. My sister Grace was two years older than I, and Grace and I were always into something. Grace was not afraid of nothing, absolutely nothing. We lived in the woods, and she'd have to get up and go to the bathroom at night, black as night — it's midnight — and she'd get up and go on out there and come back. But me, I've always been afraid of my shadow. I'm not adventurous at all.

So, my grandpa's sister, Aunt Nan, moved to Memphis from Illinois, and she rented or bought a big two-story house down on Adams, or Washington . . . well, down where they've got all the police now. So we went to see Aunt Nan.

Now I'm about three and a half, four years old — I's always mama's little Pillsbury Dough girl. And Nan had shrubbery. Now, like I told ya, we didn't have a bathroom, we had to go in the woods. And Nan had shrubbery running all around the back of her house and down one side. So she called Grace and I to her, and she said, "Look, now if you have to go, you don't go in my shrubbery out there. There's a little room at the head of the stairs that you go in." Well, Grace and I had never been to a room. We didn't know what kind of room that was. So up the stairs we went, and found a little room. And back in the back corner, attached to the ceiling, there's a square box. And there's a long chain hung down from it. And at the bottom of that chain there's a commode. It looked more like a pot. But it was a commode. It's about this tall — Annie waved her hand around her knees — perfect for an adult, but impossible for a little dumplin' like me to get on.

And that commode was plumb full of water. Well, I leaned over that commode and run my hand down in that water, and I ruffled that water in that commode, and I said, "Grace, is that river water?" Grace said, "I don't know . . ." Well, we ruffled that water, and Grace said, "I wonder what would happen if I pulled that chain?" I said, "I don't know, Grace, but pull it." So Grace reached up and she pulled that chain, and that water in that pot went, ugh ugh ugh ugh, shwoosh. And every bit of it went out of that pot.

There's no water on the floor, none in that pot. We thought we'd broke it. We didn't know what had happened to it. A few minutes later, it started coming back up. Well we felt that water, and we didn't know if it was the same water or not. Grace said, "Wonder what would happen if you sit on that?" I said, "I don't know." Grace said, "Well sit on it."

Well I couldn't even get up there. So she helped me up on it, she turned me around, she set me down on that thing. I went all the way down in there. My seat stopped it up, and my legs from ma knees out were hanging out over the top, and I'm hanging my arms over the seat, a holdin' on, my head stickin' up, and water was plumb up to my neck. And I'm screamin' and hollerin' for Grace to get me outta there. Well Grace wasn't about to get me outta there, she's havin' a ball. So praise the Lord, mama heard me hollerin', and she's on the way upstairs to see about me. And I'm hollerin', "Grace! Get me outta here! Get me outta here!" Grace hung on to me and she said, "I wonder what would happen to you if I pulled that chain?" I said, "Oh Grace, I don't know, but please don't pull it, please don't pull it!"

She said, "Well I am." And she did. She reached up and she pulled that chain. Well here come all a that water. My bottom had that thang stopped up, and I'm already in water up to my neck, and the water can't go nowhere, and it started runnin' over me, and I'm hangin' on, going "Gulp, gulp, gulp, gulp." About that time Mama came in and got me outta there. And if she hadn't'a — well, I was born and raised on the river, but I would have drowned in my first commode. And I didn't get back on it till I was old enough to get off by myself.

Angela's Tale

THE RAIN FELL WITH SUCH FURY that Northern Mississippi had about as much visual coherence as a story told by one of Faulkner's addled narrators. The world was reduced to blurry, green confusion. Bits and pieces of information, a planted field, an abandoned shack, a carpeting of kudzu, filtered between the windshield wipers through gaps in the downpour. Oxford, Faulkner's hometown, was entirely obscured. I could tell its center of gravity was that very Southern landmark, the courthouse plunked squarely in the middle of town, but that was all I could tell. At best, as I drove, the landscape took on the uncertain familiarity of a dream, of which I culled only adjectives — rural, poor, half-tame — rather than nouns.

In the midst of the storm I had to stop for gas. The fattest woman I have ever seen put down a bag of potato chips long enough to ring up the sale. Her flesh looked like a recent lava flow, but pale and partly clothed. "See ya got sum chigger bites," she drawled as I bent down to scratch my dripping ankles. "Don't scratch 'em. Bad fer ya."

That morning Mike had taken me to a diner named Mike's for a farewell sausage biscuit, as I was on my way back to the Jackson airport to pick up Marguerite. After the waitress and I chatted, he commented on the rapidity of my speech. "You got in at least three words to her one," he said. "I'd like to say you were thrice as bright but that would be just a supposition . . ."

Now again, in front of the fat woman, I felt overwound, and forced myself to slowly explain that indeed, I — breath — had — breath — chigger bites. To tell the truth, I had begun to wonder if I hadn't made a ghastly error, and put nail polish on mosquito bites by mistake. It wasn't helping in the least.

The rain let up by the time I reached Coffeeville, a town Mike had added to my itinerary in honor of his caffeine addiction. A clutch of fairly substantial older houses suggested that people had once been comfortable there; a mushroom-crop of campaign posters — advertising five or six candidates, including two women — testified that enough people remained to mount a contest, although, like so much of the rural South, the good times seemed to have passed. Main Street was almost as wide as it was long. Its frontier-style, flat-topped shops shared the street with manufacturing yards. The drugstore (named The Drug Store) was just a few doors down from a whole block filled with brand-new fiberglass shower stalls, glistening from the recent rain. Their uprightness and immobility embodied Patience, as if they were members of an elderly tour group waiting for their bus. Another block was taken up by children's swing sets; still another with overwrought front doors. The pizza joint and video store were across the street from an encampment of shiny, reproduction antiques.

I bought the local paper for fifteen cents and learned that on August 19, fifty years ago, Coffeeville had received electric power. An election advertisement assured me that a candidate for chancery clerk was a deacon of the First Baptist Church and had been married to his wife for thirty-three years; a young blond woman with a background in PR wanted to be District County Judge. Despite their smiles, Coffeeville wasn't a very friendly place. No one was outside in the now-steaming afternoon; inside, the newspaper office, the drugstore, eyebrows shot up over blank stares, asking "What do you want?" rather than "Where ya from?"

Now that the rain had stopped, the countryside held more interest. Most signs of humanity looked like casually tossed dice — tiny boxlike buildings advertising Hair 911 Beauty Salon or Washeteria — in the damp green lap of the earth. Limousin and Hereford cattle grazed with proprietary contentment, as if they were the ones who casually bought and sold the tired commuters hanging around bus stops in clumps, seeking shade. The air smelled of pines and photosynthesis and cigarette smoke.

That night, back on the outskirts of Jackson, I discovered Vickie's latest message.

Hi Pam!

I just read your e-mail. I'm a bit behind myself because of my daughter's wedding.

About Ol' Rennie — of all the things that would be difficult to describe, it would be a black woman from Gordon, Georgia. Granny is difficult enough, and I lived next door to her. Without that intimacy, I would never be able to put her into words . . . On top of that . . . Granny lived until about 1992, but her experiences from 1900 and her mother's and grandmother's experiences from the 1800s were a large part of her persona — so that automatically puts her living her life out with perspectives from a time that most people document nowadays as that in which white people committed atrocities against a whole race . . . I say all that to say this: I'm not sure how to approach Rennie without a whole lot of investigative work with a whole lot of black people who have a recollection of the times. I spoke with a black man from Gordon the other day about Granny's life and times, and he spoke about his

family. We had a good time in private talking about how segregation caused all of us to adapt. It's a painful subject, and with
our new consciousness, it seems like a bad nightmare happened
to everybody. The good that came out of that conversation was
that, somehow, black and white relationships sprang up like the
one between Ol' Rennie and Granny — a relationship that accepted the limits, but at times broke through the limits.

Where the problem with culture comes up is that Rennie
was "the maid." And when you combine that with the fact that
Granny was a peasant who could hardly afford paid help, you're
deeply into explaining how those two things go together. Both
women were dirt poor. If I could work on this some so that
both women are seen for who they really were, it would be a
great story. But writing about blacks is tricky business because
how they see themselves is often not how they're seen, and I
think the period from 1900 to the 1990s is a time of consider-
able transition that The South is still confused about. As I told
you when you were in my living room, truth is a painful subject for anyone, but when you have a situation where you have
people looking at "the truth" from every angle, you end up with
a lot of individualized truth that none of the truth-seekers is
willing to agree on. And that pain leads each one to nurse his
hurt, which then makes the truth a sword . . .

So Ol' Rennie's personal story would end up having two
sides to it and they would both have to be explained with exquisite care in order to bring her to life — and as we'd say in
the South — "not hurt anybody's feelings."

Write me back if you don't understand any of that.

Sincerely, Vickie Vedder

I sat in the motel room with my hands poised above the
keyboards. "Write me back if you don't understand any of
that." I tugged at my hair: did I or didn't I? What if Granny —

whose friendship had broken the color barrier — had told Rennie's story? Would it still have two sides? I understood Vickie's reluctance, but I initially balked at the idea of Rennie casting two different shadows, like the nonidentical twin double exposure of Chris Kirby's daughter in front of the Bell Witch Cave. Did the Southern past have to resolve into a single neat image before it could be pasted into the country's photo-album? Was that the only way Rennie could come back to life? Would the exceptionalists, both black and white, have to accept the mainstream for the South to fall in line with the American Success Story?

Perhaps; but it would be more interesting if American mythology made room for all the blurry images and contradictory stories of the South. I learned in Wales that there will always be the Big Story of the center and then, flung into the margins, centrifugal narratives spun hard against the wall of history. Some of those stories belong to individuals like Rennie; some belong to continental regions like the South. The real issue does not lie in the validity of these marginal tales — they certainly exist — but rather in who tells them, which circles back to Vickie's conundrum. As usual, she put her finger on the crux of the problem. And she was right: we do need to listen to the cumbersome double exposure of Southern history, which is not so much a resolution into one story as a tale-in-tandem. As Martin Luther King, Jr., wrote in *Letter from a Birmingham Jail,* "Too long has our beloved Southland been bogged down in a tragic effort to live in a monologue rather than a dialogue." We need Vickie's Rennie and an African-American–remembered Rennie as well, if anyone remains to tell her tale. Ever since slavery cast the races into an unequal relationship, all Southerners have, indeed, cast two shadows.

I closed the laptop. Vickie had addressed my questions before I'd asked them.

*

"It tastes like mold." Marguerite was speaking with her mouth full of grilled catfish sandwich. We both examined our rolls for telltale greenery and decided it was the dark bits of the fish that tasted like old river bottom. Marguerite had risen in Rhode Island at three A.M. in order to fly into the Jackson airport by ten. She is from the South — Virginia, by way of Brazil, where she spent her childhood — but Mississippi and Louisiana seemed as far-flung to her as they did to me, which is why she wanted to come along on this portion of my journey.

Our goal was Mansura, Louisiana, where Rose Anne St. Romain lived, vocal emphasis on the *Saint,* but our route was wayward. At first we followed the Natchez Trace parkway, an ancient Native American hunting path used by the Spanish and mapped by the French, now a green tunnel from which kitschy paraphernalia has been ruthlessly banned (driving it was a little like watching educational TV: after a while you miss the trash). An exit at mile 39.2 — the Trace runs from Natchez, Mississippi to Nashville, Tennessee, and is painstakingly mile-marked — led us to Port Royal, another little town deemed "too beautiful to burn" by the Union Army. The Presbyterian Church steeple there was topped by a twelve-foot golden hand, the index finger of which extended straight up, pointing to heaven. I figured it was intended to mean, "Follow me, it's this way," but the finger looked a little cheeky, as if the Presbyterians were warning God not to get too rowdy over there with the Baptists, and to mind his manners. I wondered if it had ever been hit by lightning (we learned later that, rather than lightning, the original wooden hand had been attacked by woodpeckers, and had been replaced by a metal one).

In Natchez we found the Mississippi, wide as a yawn, sluggish and still coffee-colored. Signs advertised Knock You Naked Margaritas and Boudin Tamales, which we took to be a culinary rapprochement between Natchez's former incarnation as a Spanish outpost (it belonged to New Spain from 1779 to 1798) and Creole Louisiana across the river. On a strip outside the city's exclusive neighborhood of antebellum homes, I made Marguerite take a picture of me in front of Mammy's Cupboard. A postcard informed us that "This unusual structure was built of brick in 1940 by Mr. Henry Gaude . . . Typical Mississippi fried and barbecued chicken and beef dishes are served." I was amazed no one had burned it down. The building itself was shaped like a rounded pyramid, but actually formed the skirt of a giant black mammy. On top of the pyramid, like an anthropomorphic finial, rose her busty torso and bandana-wound head, awkwardly sculpted in concrete. But the biggest affront was the windows piercing the brick base, which seemed like an invitation to passersby to look up her skirt. In the postcard, which was probably at least fifteen years old, her skin was painted shiny dark brown; now it was more of a politically correct mulatto shade, much like the Mississippi. Mammy was closed, otherwise we might have had a piece of pie.

It was in southern Louisiana, skirting New Orleans and heading west on backroads toward Baton Rouge, that I felt my journey start to rewind. The air thickened, and I saw that the glaringly white sky was veined with rainclouds — the kind of weather that breeds suspicion in a person. Arthritic live oaks marked out fields and cast misshapen shadows over the damp ground (the fields were planted with a roughish, thick-bladed weed that to our mortification we dubbed "swamp grass" before realizing it was sugarcane). Spanish moss crept between tree branches like dirty spiderwebs. Evacuation Route signs began to appear on Highway 18, along with hand-painted shingles advertising Psychic Readings. It was ungodly hot. The humidity was like a fourth dimension.

"You needn't have pined about missing the South Carolina and Georgia coast," I told Marguerite, who had indeed been pining. "It's here." The low-grade fever of the lowlands was back, and I welcomed it. I'd had enough of the high, dry ground, where humans had more to fear from one another and made their own ghosts. Like any good Romantic, I preferred to be menaced by something suprahuman, like The Weather.

As we drove along Route 18, a kind of green blindness afflicted us both in the right eye. To the left, on the Gulf side of the road — we couldn't see the Gulf of Mexico, but we could smell it — were oil refineries, Chevron and Union Carbide, and fields of sugarcane, and a few plantation great houses raised off the ground like women with hiked skirts (a good excuse for grandiose staircases) in anticipation of floods. I'd seen their architectural kin in the Caribbean, colonial India, and northeast Brazil. There were several modern, semisuburban housing developments also called "plantations" after family estates long since sold off for cash. To the right, however, was just one solitary earthwork: a great, grassy levee that ran the length of the highway and protected the other side from the Mississippi River.

By the time we reached Interstate 10, we were riding above a mer-world of black water and gray stumps. The road was elevated on a causeway over miles of swampland — what in Louisiana is known as the bayou. This struck parallels in my memory and, again, in chimed the South Carolina Low Country. Here, however, the swamp terrors — death borne by sickness, flooding, heat, and disease — were embodied in the Loupgarou, a creature eerily evocative of his eastern cousins, the plat-eyes. The Loupgarou is a half-man half-wolf fiend that haunts the dark, Delta waters. *The Treasury of Southern Folklore* declared that "Loups-garous (loogaroos) are not so plentiful as they used to be, but . . . every once in a while a man or woman is missed." Some fear only werewolves, but others say the Loupgarou is trickier, that the danger lies in his malleability, his penchant for assuming animal shapes to cover his evil-doing ways.

I learned about the Loupgarou from Angela Davis, a storyteller I had met briefly on the outskirts of New Orleans. She had suggested a rendezvous at a coffeehouse at dusk. I was proud of myself for having found the right exit off the highway without having to double back several times, but I emerged from the adrenaline rush of the road into the shock of complete cessation and silence. I had exited into an immense cemetery, one of the Cities of the Dead for which New Orleans is famous. Acres of white marble vaults, sooted and soiled from automobile exhaust, camped like a forgotten army guarding a ghost town. Night shadows fell across them — the dark moving over the dim — cast by the nervous interplay of streetlights and tree branches.

At first I was relieved to find Angela in a clean, well-lit place smelling of hazelnut coffee, but her words dragged me right back outside to the tombs. We had been speaking of storytelling — she didn't have time to tell me a tale, she said — of how stories "create a space in people that's kind of like a prayer." Of how stories lure the imagination with possibilities, and in so doing create the future. "Who knows what we are creating today with our tales?" asked Angela. "Someday we'll fly. Someday a child will hear a story, and will up and do it." Then, when I confessed to getting lost among the sarcophagi, she leaned closer and said in a soft whisper, "I went picking herbs in that cemetery one day."

"In broad daylight, I hope."

"Oh yes," she said, "but a storm came." And she proceeded to tell me how the day had begun to turn "dark and greenish," and that a plum-faced man had suddenly appeared behind her.

He was dressed in black and held a key to one of the tombs; when the rain hit, he invited her inside for shelter. After a short silence the man said, "I remember when Audrey came and killed so many of my people."

It did not help me to realize I had been sucked into a ghost story — that happens all the time in New Orleans — it was Audrey that gave me goose bumps, not the invented ghost who had mentioned her. Audrey was a hurricane.

"There is a culture of death in this city," said Angela. "The veil between the living and the dead is very thin here."

We think we are clever in inventing stories, in scaring ourselves with phantoms and imaginary creatures, but how many of our tales are premade for us by geography and climate? The stories we tell about ourselves are really often about our environment, in a way I only came to understand by inching my way slowly across the South, listening to the shadows speak. The Atlantic seaboard and the Gulf coast were bound together in the story record as surely as if a land bridge vaulted high over the interior of Georgia, Alabama, and Mississippi and connected their words. Alice and the Gray Man needed only to learn French to be at home in the Delta. I wanted to tell them that; I wanted everyone to know how much they had in common.

Angell Brothers' Swamp Tours: the sign pointed toward a dirt road that led atop another levee, which in this case kept the Atchafalaya Basin from preying on the town of Henderson, Louisiana. Not that there was much to prey upon, just a few modest bungalows with signs announcing home businesses: Hair & Nail Care; Vietnamese Food (advertised in English and Vietnamese); Exotic Skins & Taxidermy Services. We mounted the levee and blinked in glare and wonder. Before us, unsuspected for miles, was what looked like an inland sea circling a half-drowned forest. It was the antithesis of the brooding swamp we had seen yesterday. In the morning sun the basin waters winked and glimmered under a pale blue sky, and the greens looked young and full of promise.

I left Marguerite in the air-conditioned car and dashed through scalding daylight into a shack by the water's edge. Inside in the cool gloom were a bunch of guys sitting around a bar drinking their morning Budweisers; one of them shouted into a back room, *"Quelqu'un pour te voir."* An Angell appeared and sold me two tickets for the upcoming swamp tour. To me he spoke a rapid-fire English that jammed on the phonetic brakes after all words ending in "d." It made him sound like a backwoods Canadian, but the setting — sun, swamp, heat, all wrapped in the smell of beer — stripped his accent of any northern earnestness and gave its abrupt rhythm a Cajun virility. (The Canadian connection is no flight of fancy. French-speaking "Cajuns" migrated from Canada to Louisiana after France lost Nova Scotia and parts of New Brunswick — called "Acadia" — to the British in the mid-eighteenth century.)

For nearly two hours we careened around the basin in a flat-bottomed "Cajun Cadillac," the Angells' awning-covered swampboat, with three other English-speaking tourists and four French speakers from Quebec, France, and Belgium. Our guide poured out information in English: the swamp covers one million acres of fresh water; Spanish moss is a member of the pineapple family; wild boar season runs from October to January; eighty thousand 'gators were "harvested" last year, and their meat sold to the Japanese; five species of catfish live in the basin, but crawfish are the most important industry. Then he repeated himself in French. One of the French tourists, a woman literally armored in turquoise jewelry, leaned over and whispered, "I cannot understand a word of his French, so I listen to the English. It is better, yes?"

We cruised past abandoned natural gas wells and floating fishing and hunting camps moored to cypress trees; the latter had the look of mobile homes tacked on to rafts. Emerging from the flat, shallow water were occasional stands of cypresses, their trunks characteristically flared at the base like bark-covered bell-bottoms. In these trees was invested all the authority of the swamp. Their verticality lent them the dignity of elders; even our bilingual guide showed them an instinctive deference. At one point, just before we turned back to shore, the boat passed directly under Interstate 10, and our Angell brother stopped for a moment so we could all gaze down the endless corridor of pilings that held the highway aloft. It looked like the nave of a very long cathedral, flooded with water. Each set of concrete pillars formed a square shadow on the basin's surface; by a trick of perspective the squares grew smaller and smaller, overlapping each other and receding into the distance until all we could see was a pinhole of light at the very end that refracted into four diffused rays shining down the long dark tunnel.

When I stood to take a photo, my own shadow fell atop the nearest square of shaded, luminous green water, and in that instant I heard rather than saw. In my head a memory spoke: "I stood in the belly of my shadow, and listened . . ." Cars and trucks raced overhead with such speed that the concrete shook, but despite my usual fear of underpasses I was caught up listening. William Faulkner wrote those words in *The Sound and the Fury* — the tale of a Southern family trapped in a cycle of pain and familiarity and love and confusion. All that summer I had listened to a chain of shadows out of the deep past that, if diagrammed, would look much like the one before me; only the shadows I chased had been cast with words rather than shade. And from the depth of my own Northern, urban silhouette, I had stopped to listen. Now here, at rest under the highway, was the image of my journey mapped for me on the restless face of the water.

The boat rocking with a slight wind in the intense morning heat, I watched the shadow squares recede to that pinpoint of light and thought that so many of the Southern stories I had heard were really origin myths — explanations and reasons for the way things are today. That was not how they started out, especially the old folktales, but perhaps those tales have lingered into the present precisely because they do help buttress our world. From simple myths like "The Hogaphone" — David Holt's mountain ancestor of the telephone — to "The Peddler Man," which preceded the Democratic Party's neighborly, activist self-image (is it an accident that the last two Democratic presidents have come from the South?). From Minerva King's reminiscences of the civil rights years to Karen Vuranch's star-crossed ghosts, Rose and Charlie, whose tale anticipated the death of Appalachian coal mining. And, in a storied class by himself, Wicked John, in whose solitary ember glows the lonely, ornery, proud independence of the American South. In that ember also burns Jack and Brer Rabbit's self-sufficiency and the South's ancient, antifederalist passion for states' rights. Come to think of it, Wicked John is the father of the Southern states — or rather of everyone in the South who believes the Civil War was fought "for the North to keep off."

Rose Anne's Tale

ose Anne St. Romain lived very near the Sweet
Potato Capital of the World. We were late getting to
her house — we had stopped at Prejean's Restaurant
for a shared order of "Tout que'que chose," which translated
into a platter of crawfish tails, fried shrimp, mushrooms, frogs
legs, boudin balls, fried cheese, and alligator, and took some
time to eat — and I was in a snit.

"Relax," said Marguerite, "she's not going to forget her stories because we're half an hour late."

What I had not told Marguerite, who gets deathly seasick
and therefore has a healthy suspicion of watercraft, is that Rose
Anne wanted to take us out into the bayou on her dad's barge.
Marguerite would not be pleased by two boating adventures
back-to-back, but I really wanted to see more of the swamp
and I was anxious to hear Rose Anne's stories. And it was getting late to do both.

We sped past plum and peach orchards and tomato and
melon fields. Just as Marguerite was copying down a notice on
a church marquee that read, Don't let the hearse be the one to
bring you to Church, I glanced in my rearview mirror and my
palms went cold. The flashing red lights of a police car were
signaling for me to pull over. I groaned. Marguerite's age-old
declaration that I deserved a speeding ticket had finally come
to pass. We were on a secondary road and, unlike me, the speed
limits kept changing from 60 to 45 mph I pulled over to the

side of the road and a beefy, very young cop in a tight tan uniform shouted for me to get out of the car. "Do whatever he says," Marguerite warned. "Don't argue."

"Did you know, ma'am, that you were goin' 62 in a 45 mile-'n-hour zone?"

"Yes sir, I know. I didn't slow down soon enough. I'm sorry, sir."

"Y'know, you Texans, you think you can just drive on through Louisiana like ya owned th'place. But let me tell you, this ain't Texas where you can go any old damn speed ya like . . ."

I saw my salvation and I jumped at it. "Excuse me, sir, but this is just a rental car. I'm actually from Rhode Island."

"Rhode Island?" His face fell. His friend, sitting in the passenger seat of the police cruiser, pointed at the donut in his hand to indicate, I think, that they were going fast.

The cop clung to the hope that I had stolen the Oldsmobile until he ran a check on my license and I came out clean. "Well, hell, you really are from New England," he said miserably. "Well then, y'all just drive slower, OK? I'll let ya off with a warning today."

I continued with the exaggerated care of the truly exasperated to the Chicken Palace in Mansura — "population two thousand, with cows," Rose Anne said later — where I asked for directions to Large Road. In two minutes we were in front of a tiny, salmon-pink cottage sheltered by a stand of trees, but otherwise adrift in the flat, fertile vastness of central Louisiana. The cottage looked like it belonged in a fairy tale. It had a miniature white picket fence and window boxes filled with flowers. It was almost more an idea than a dwelling, like a child's drawing of a House, underlined with a straight green line that meant Ground. Then Rose Anne appeared and made her house look even smaller. She wasn't big, but she had enormous presence. She wore a long white dress, perfectly straight and unaccented but for a big alligator claw hanging around her neck. Her hair was pulled back in a bow. The simplicity accentuated her operatic good looks: high cheekbones, wide mouth, vivid dark eyes. Her beauty was like Vickie Vedder's, in that it came from strength and intensity rather than any facile prettiness.

She thought it was funny we had stopped at the Chicken Palace. "It's not really Large Road — 'round here it's just called The *Large,* pronounced the French way. It means a wide open agricultural area. I had a friend stop there once, asking the same thing. They grilled her about who she was looking for. She said, 'Rose Anne St. Romain.' They didn't know who that was, so she described me. 'Oh,' they said, finally. 'You mean Edmond's unmarried daughter.' That's my identity in these parts, even though I was born and raised in this town. I grew up behind the livestock auction."

Rose Anne may have grown up in Mansura, but she left town for college and graduate school, marriage and divorce, before returning five years ago to live large in a little town. She invited us inside and gave us food and wine, talking all the while about whatever entered her head. Like storytelling: "It's a good bridge between conversation and theater." Or, "I think of telling stories as writing with sound in the air." About "improving" folktales: "There's no need to reset most of them. That's just narcissistic." About red wine: "It goes with anything." About starting a new hobby: "One day I decided to learn to tell lizards apart." She said she felt hounded into becoming a storyteller. "I felt I was being called to do something enormous and important."

Rose Anne said that she became aware of the value of the spoken word when she was young. "We were only allowed one hour of TV a day, and my eight brothers and sisters and my mother — Daddy probably wouldn't have been home yet — had supper together every night. And we were expected to *talk,* but only pleasant conversation. And," she held up a finger, "no singing at the table." Her mother had told stories during those long meals about growing up in a family of dirt farmers, and picking cotton at the age of five. She had been raised in a bilingual household, but Rose Anne's father had spent his first eight years speaking only French. "He was finally taught to speak English by German nuns," said Rose Anne, in a rural Louisiana accent sculpted into art by training and practice. Her voice was so smooth it lacked the hard right angles of a typical American "r." "That accounts for the way he sounds today. You'll meet him."

She explained that Avoyelles Parish, where she lived (Louisiana is the only state that divides itself into parishes instead of counties), was settled by Creoles, descendants of original French immigrants, rather than French-speaking Acadians, called Cajuns, come down from Canada. Many people in the parish still spoke French. (Rose Anne didn't put too fine a point on it, but she was not the only person I met to note the difference between Cajuns and Creoles, and then specify her own ancestry.) Rose Anne said her family had been in the state since the 1760s.

When she got up to fetch us more snacks, Marguerite leaned over and whispered, "Ask her why she's wearing a claw around her neck."

"You ask her."

"No, you."

"This?" said Rose Anne when she came back, in answer to my question. "I bought it at a convenience store in Breaux Bridge, Louisiana. It was dirt cheap and the guy had a ton of them. I have this theory that you can tell a lot about a local culture from what they sell in the convenience store. You know, some sell ammo, some have suntan lotion. I always check 'em out when I travel."

It grew quiet for a moment and we all noticed that the sun, which only a short time before had filled Rose Anne's house with an almost fireside glow, had now fallen lower than her windows. The living room corners were already shaded in with night. "Yo, Ladies!" said Rose Anne, suddenly jumping up. She had the rampant enthusiasm of a teenager grafted on to the sophistication of a forty-two-year-old woman. "I have a story all set to tell you, but I want to do it in the right setting, on my daddy's boat in the middle of the bayou. We'd better get going if we're gonna get out there tonight."

"Boat?" asked Marguerite in polite alarm. "What boat? There's *another* boat?"

I told her about the party barge as we followed Rose Anne's dust — the inevitable aftermath of tires on gravel — to her family's "camp" on the bayou, where we had been invited to spend the night. After about fifteen minutes we came to a halt in a place as closed and secret as the grounds of her house had been wide and open. Trees grew close together and almost obscured the darkling cobalt sky and young moon. The air was busy with the noise of unseen things: frogs and crickets and locusts. I was secretly terrified of getting more chigger bites, but didn't want to break the mood.

The door of a long, low house banged open and out strode Edmond, Rose Anne's handsome father, still strong and vigorous in his early seventies. I couldn't quite hear German nuns in his voice, but there was plenty of humor. "When I was a boy," he began, "I spoke only French. And I went to school with other French-speaking students, but the teachers wanted us to speak in English. Well, we didn't know English, but that didn't stop them. One day they said, 'Today, you learn your numbers.' So they said, 'Say Zero.' We said 'Zero.' Then they said, 'Say

One.' We said 'One.' Then they said, 'Say Two,' and we all went home."

"Get it?" asked Rose Anne, laughing. "*C'est tout* in French means 'that's all.'"

"If we're going out on the river, we better do it now," said Edmond, gesturing toward an absence between two banks of trees. "It's getting late." Rose Anne hurried us toward the lagoon, the main channel of the bayou, about thirty feet from the house, and into a kind of aquatic garage. Floating in the bottom was a large, flat boat set on a pair of pontoons, with a barbecue grill rigged up in the stern. We all piled in — Marguerite being a good sport, although sending me surreptitious looks of suspicion — then glided silently out onto the canal past a stand of twelve bearded cypress trees that Rose Anne's mother had named the Twelve Apostles.

The banks were dark but for occasional flickering camp lights. In the uncertain twilight, not yet night, but no longer day, the river took on the viscosity and translucence of soft honey, and seemed to absorb into itself the dark indigo of the sky. Heading east, we left a trail of pale orange sunset on the faint ripples of our wake. It was silent but for the low throb of insects. All experience felt as if it had been run through a sieve and strained of anything rough or coarse: we were smooth, and liquid, and dark.

"The glow of the sun is gone now," said Edmond to himself, up at the wheel.

In a whisper Rose Anne told us that five years ago she had come down with an inexplicable low-grade fever that had so sapped her energy that after storytelling performances she would often collapse into bed for hours. She had been diagnosed with chronic fatigue syndrome, and had only recently regained her health. We stared at her in disbelief: it was impossible to conceive of an enervated Rose Anne St. Romain.

It was at that time, she said, that she had called her dad and asked him to find her a little piece of property back home in Mansura. "Sure, baby," he'd responded, and together they had slowly fixed up her cottage. She had proved so adept at carpentry, despite her illness, that one day Edmond had said, "You know, Rosie, you're so good at this you should've been a man." "I said, 'Daddy,'" recalled Rose Anne, with a toss of her chin at her father, "'I'm not a man. But you've got to admit, I'm a hell of a woman.'" It was the same year that Rose Anne's mother had been diagnosed with Alzheimer's disease.

"Now I'm going to say something that may sound corny to you," she said, as we outcruised the western sky and it grew dark. "The thing you cannot overlook in this culture — my French culture — is Catholicism. A really profound belief in God. It's where my storytelling comes from."

We must have looked heretical because Rose Anne laughed. "No, I don't mean it's a gift from God or anything. I'm not *that* good. What I'm talking about is the French Catholic habit of *telling* — of prayer. You tell people everything about yourself so they can pray for you. We freely tell our personal stories so we can get on each other's prayer lists. That's one reason why storytelling comes naturally to me." She gave the example of her sister, who had told everyone in the family she was having medical tests, something most people tend to keep quiet about, so they would pray for her. "See," said Rose Anne, "the more people you got callin' on God, the more chance you have of getting his attention. So you tell everyone *everything*." She had once been deeply shocked by a friend's mother, who had had cataract surgery without telling her son. "We don't operate that way. We have to talk, to tell, because we believe there's a powerful source of good out there, listening. And when you believe in that source of goodness, then it gives you license to have a broad and bawdy sense of humor — to live a little. Telling your stories to others, and to God, having that deep, abiding verbal connection, it gives you a strong footing that lets you joke around a lot."

As she spoke, Edmond soundlessly glided the boat around its own wake and we turned back for home. I spun the reels of memory. "We need to talk, to tell, because oratory is our heritage," Faulkner had said of the South; and long ago, at the beginning of my first trip, Vickie had shown me that thinking really *was* a form of speaking. Was the South's obsession with narrative, with public performance and *telling,* a kind of communal praying? Did the sum total of all the stories I heard throughout the summer amount to a Southern prayer for respect; a prayer for the rest of America to stop, to listen, to take the South seriously? Like Rose Anne said, the more people who hear your stories the better your chances of catching the ear of the Powers That Be.

"And we never stop talking," continued Rose Anne. "Through prayer we can access the souls of dead people too, and just keep talking to them as if they were still here. We tell them stories. And sometimes," she paused for effect, "they tell us stories too."

We sat quietly for a few moments, listening to the night we could no longer see. Then Rose Anne spoke again. "I can't communicate with my mama, though. She's still alive, in a nursing home, but she no longer recognizes me or Daddy, or even herself. I can't access her soul through her body. And I can't pray to her in death. So where is my beautiful mama's soul right now?"

Another silence fell and I knew we would not hear Rose Anne's story on the bayou. Her pain was so acute that I found myself stretching it, pulling it taut over the whole South, so that it became diffused and less intense, and lodged in my head instead of my heart. A soul caught between death and life —

between an exceptional past and an assimilated future: that was an apt description of the South itself. My summer travels, too, what had they been but a kind of peripatetic prayer, in that, like a conversation with God, I hoped that they would answer some of my questions. What else is a pilgrimage, really, but prayer's visible footsteps? Like Ray Hicks's magical storytelling, like dreams and travel, prayer, for the faithful, also belongs to both art and reality, in that it is narrative we believe capable of action, of intervening in our lives.

Unlike Rose Anne's mother, whose soul hovered beyond the tug of imploration, there were moments, I think, when I did access — or rather fleetingly glimpse — the soul of the South. At that very moment, even, my body tingled with a kind of gut comprehension. How different the South was after all. But I cannot speak for the rest of the country, so I must return to where I began: to myself. The South was different from me.

All along, I had been so wrapped up in what Southern stories said that I didn't stop to consider the telling. Ollie de Loach really had given me an important clue: "The ear tried the words even as the mouth tasted meat." I had been chewing on the meat of these stories for so long I had ignored what was behind the impulse to tell them. Why were these people telling tales? Because each one of them believed along with Rose Anne that there is a powerful source of good out there. This is not to say that they are all Catholic, but they all did *believe*. They believed in the old shamanistic notion that storytelling can change the world. That stories are essentially secular prayers that instruct and educate and warn and thereby prepare for the future, all the while preserving the ghosts of the past. And perhaps it is this belief that is more important than isolation or poverty or ancestral heritage in explaining why the American South is and has always been a hotbed of storytelling.

The South is a famously (and infamously) religious place —

almost every storyteller with whom I spoke was an active churchgoer — and prayer is one of the reflexes behind this worldview. Yet something older lurks there too, that goes back to a time before history when stories explained the natural world and made it accessible to the human mind. As for me, I too believe that the world holds plenty of good — I had seen it in action all summer — but I did not believe in a powerful source of good out there, *listening* to us. I could not share Fouchena Sheppard's profound reliance on prayer to prevent John Kennedy, Jr., from being dead. The facts told me he had died in that plane crash, and I believed *them*.

I had gone to the South seeking a place-bond that American Southerners seemed to exclusively enjoy. But I went there as a Romantic, looking for a relationship between soil and history and stories. I did not approach it as a missionary, in the way of the storytellers I met who felt a responsibility to tell the ancient tales of the South because they resonated and played an active role in the present day. My pilgrimage was private, not public (one might also call it selfish, not altruistic), and the South, within its own, familial confines, is a very public place. I came to love the best of it in a visceral sense: the scenery, the weather, the elemental South. The stories that bore their history did lend me temporary anchorage, but I did not find a home there. My sense of belief fell short.

Earlier I had asked a question in Russell's Pharmacy, back in Forsyth, Georgia: what did it mean that I was brought up in the suburban North, with television and family photographs, and Vickie in the rural South, where her childhood had been shot through with family narratives that trailed back into the distant past? What did it mean that her inheritance was one of communication stretching across generations, and mine one of images and wordless love? The answer, I think, has little to do with old North–South dichotomies; it simply means that as adults we must find our sense of wonder through very different venues. Vickie's older, landbound magic, which I still envy, is wrought through the secular prayer of public storytelling, and mine (which I know she envies), through a very contemporary *landlessness,* through restlessness, through the private act of traveling in search of new landscapes in which to quarry for metaphor and history. Ironically, while my pilgrimage in search of a mooring in place and past brought me to the South, it was the journey itself that held my magic: my entry into the Otherworld of twinned art and reality was through travel — the art of lived storymaking. This is hardly a novel realization, but it was a shock to find that it applied to life — *my life* — as well as literature. The voice I had been looking for turned out to be the voice that has told the tale of this trip. This has been my story.

The St. Romains's camp was Edmond's lair. Just as Rose Anne's car was filled with rocks and old shoes and birds' nests that she had scavenged on her storytelling travels, so her father's house on the bayou was a museum of found rarities. An old jukebox that played big band hits; a massive butcher block in the middle of the kitchen linoleum, crosshatched with ancient guttings; Rose Anne's mother's photos of the bayou; a lifesize, concrete alligator; a wooden cigar Indian; a pair of ancient gas pumps. Marguerite and I were teetering on the edge of exhaustion, but Rose Anne made us sit down side by side on an old vinyl sofa, and cleared a performance space.

"Would it be rude to go to bed?" whispered Marguerite.

"Yes. Besides, you'd regret it for ever and ever," I responded. Rose Anne was preparing to tell us her story. On the wall was a poster-size photo of her parents on their wedding day surrounded by pictures of the eight St. Romain children as youngsters. "Mom made the collage a long time ago," explained Rose Anne.

"Now I know this would've been better on the boat, but you've just got to use your imaginations. This is an old Creole story. It's Creole in the sense that it is a combination of a number of different cultures. It has French, English, Native American, and African elements all woven together. It was inspired by a book I read a number of years ago, and it's evolved over the years as I've told it, all over Louisiana and all over the United States. It's actually a trickster tale. Features a little song I heard by one of my favorite groups — an all-female band called the Dixie Cups — at the New Orleans Jazz Festival, called *Iko, Iko.*"

Rose Anne tucked in her head and drew backwards a bit, then, like a runner springing out of a crouch, suddenly stood up tall and straight and stuck out her chin. Her head was directly under a ceiling fan that spun pinwheel shadows around the pink walls.

THE SONG IN THE MIST

Whooooo, hoo, hooo, hooo, hooo, sang Rose Anne in a high, lilting wail.

Way down deep, in South Louisiana, run all sorts of little bayous, lined in cypress trees, drippin' with moss. And along these bayous, and in these bayous, live all kinds of creatures. But there is one bayou where lives a strange and mysterious creature. This creature hasn't been seen for years and years. But folks would hear this creature, and would hear it early in the morning, when the mist was rising up over the bayou, and late in the evening, when that mist came drifting down. Through that mist would come a song. A strange, sad, sighing song.

Whoooo, hooo, hooo.

And nobody knew who sang it, or why. Until one day . . .

There were these three buddies happened to go camping right down that particular bayou. Now they didn't know they were on the bayou where the creature lived — at first. They pitched their tent, got there kinda late at night, spent the night out there. Next morning, two of them were still sound asleep, when one woke up. He was feelin' kinda hungry. He decided he would go and try to catch some catfish for their breakfast. Now, he'd grown up in that area, so he was mighty familiar with the ways of the bayou. He jumped in his little pirogue — that's a little flat-bottomed boat that Cajun people use — and he started paddling down that little bayou. And that morning mist was so thick that he could hardly see where he was goin'. But all of a sudden, through that mist, came that song.

Whooo, hooo, hooo

It wrapped itself around him and he felt like he was hypnotized. He couldn't help himself. He followed that song deeper and further down that bayou than he'd ever been before. Saw things he'd never seen before. Stand of cypress trees he'd never noticed. An old beaver dam. A mother nutria and her three little babies jumped in the water, splash, splash, splash.

Whoo hooo hooo.

Round and round swirled that mist and that song, pullin' him deeper and deeper in to the swamp, until finally, he saw where that song was coming from. Right up on the side of the bayou was a little house about that tall (Rose Anne indicated her waist). It was made of mud and moss and sticks all packed together, and he could practically see that song seepin' out of those cracks in that mud. He paddled fast as he could toward that little house, jumped out of his pirogue and pulled it up on the banks. He ran up to that little house, banged on the door, and he said, (breathlessly) "Who's in there? Come on out, I know you're in there, I followed your song here. I can't wait to meet you!"

Silence from the house. He knocked again. "Come on, you might as well come out. I gotcha cornered. Folks have been hearin' your song for years. My mama told me about it and her mama told her about it. I never heard it myself, but I found you now. Come on out now, I wanna meet you!"

Silence from the house. Waaay on back in his memory, something jogged, and he remembered something his grandmother had taught him, called Manners. He got down on one knee, he tapped kinda gently, and said, "Excuse me, ma'am, I, I didn't mean to startle you, I'm just excited is all. I followed your song to your little house . . . Oh, man, that's the most beautiful singing I ever heard in my life. I would be so honored if you would come out of your house and sing a song for me out here in God's cathedral, under the cypress trees. Wontcha please, ma'am? My name is Tom, and I'm fishing with my buddy and his cousin over down the bayou there . . ."

At that, the little door slowly creaked open. And out came the head of a great, big, old . . . turtle. A gigantic, ancient, grandmother snappin' turtle, with eyes as brown and deep as the muddy bayou bottom. She looked up at Tom and said — at this point Rose Anne took her slow time, shrinking into her shoulders and stretching out her neck, rotating her head from side-to-side as if her eyes, like a turtle's, were locked into one-directional peripheral vision — "Did you really like my singing?"

"Like it? Ma'am, your singing is legendary. I'd never dream it was a turtle singing a song like that. I didn't know turtles could sing. Heck, I didn't know turtles could talk either. Oh, ma'am, I'd really like to hear how you sound if you'd come out of your little house — I bet it would be really beautiful. Please, come on out and sing for me out here." The turtle shook her head and said slowly, "I don't think so. I just sing to pass the time. I used to sing . . . in New Orleans when I was a girl. But the crowd got so wild, I came back to the swamp. Now I just sing to please myself."

"Oh ma'am! Don't do this to me! Don't leave me without another song! If you come on out and sing another song, well, I can make a story out of it. I'll tell my children, and they'll tell their children, and oh, ma'am, your story and your song will live on way after you're gone. Woncha please, ma'am, it'd mean a lot to me."

The turtle was a born entertainer, and no entertainer can refuse an audience. She said, "Well, if you insist." She pushed that little door slowly open. She ambled out of that little house, slowly, slowly. When she was all the way outta that little house, Tom staggered back in amazement. It was the biggest turtle he'd ever seen in his life. She must be a couple of hundred years old, he was thinking. Her shell rose up from the ground in a green and brown mound. And then she did somethin' he'd never seen a turtle do. She pushed with her front legs, like that, and she stood up on her hind legs, just like a person.

"I like to stand when I sing, you see, I get more breath into my lungs. Let's see now, what song shall I sing for this concert, my first in so many years?"

While Turtle was going over her repertoire, Tom's eyes were movin' from her front shell to her back shell. You don't often see the underside of a turtle. Well, that front shell was beautiful, all ivory and patterned with brown, and his eyes traveled from that front shell to that back shell, and back again, and somehow, somewhere — maybe it was just the old South Louisiana boy in him — his brain got stuck in the middle. And he stopped thinkin' about singin', and started thinkin' about how many pounds of turtle meat there was between those two shells. "Man, I'll bet there's about seventy-five pounds between those two shells. You know, if I could trap this old turtle, and go get some of my friends, they'll bring everything we need to make turtle soup. I can pay back all the people I owe suppers to and get it all done in one night.

"Yes ma'am, what song you gonna sing for me, Miss Turtle?"

"Well," said the turtle, "I think I'd like to sing an old New Orleans favorite for you, Mr. Tom, if you don't mind?"

"No ma'am. You go ahead, you sing whatever song you like." He thinks, "I think I'm gonna need about ten pounds of onions, and about fifteen pounds of bell pepper — now where'm I gonna get that? Oh yeah, Miss Des Moines, her garden came in early this year. She always plants in February, you know. Oh, where am I gonna get that much sherry? My cousin, yeah, his still's about ready. I think I can get it from him.

"Go ahead, sing whatever you like, Miss Turtle."

The turtle said, "Well, all right, here goes." Tom continued to make up his recipe and his menu. Turtle took a deep breath. She imagined she was down right along the levee in New Orleans on a smoky Saturday night, and she sang.

Rose Anne broke into an earthen voice swaddled in the blues. I glanced sideways at Marguerite, whose mouth was slightly open, eyes wide in wonder. She saw me looking at her and whispered, "You were right. I'd never have forgiven myself if I'd gone to bed. She's amazing."

Summertime, and the livin' is easy
Fish are jumpin' — I know they jumpin', baby, there goes a
   choupique

(I later found out that a choupique is a bottom-feeder known as a "trash fish"; Rose Anne said it has a muddy taste and doesn't freeze well.)

And the cotton is high — actually it's not that high, we could
   use some rain
Yo mother's rich — yeah, she won the lottery!
And your daddy's good lookin' — you're not so bad yourself,
   Mr. Tom
So hush, little baby,
Don't you cry

While she was leanin' back hittin' that last note, Tom saw his chance. He lifted up his great big foot, clad in a heavy leather boot, and he kicked her right in the stomach. Turtle rocked over on her back, her eyes wide with surprise. Tom clamped her to the ground and said, "You gonna be my supper, turtle. I don't care if you can sing like Louis Armstrong, you comin' back to the camp with me and I'm makin' turtle soup with you."

He picked up that big old turtle and he put her in his pirogue. He lay her on her back. And when a turtle's laying on her back, she just as helpless as — you know those little bitty black june bugs come around your screen in the summertime and they lay there "ehehehe-hehehehe," can't go nowhere? Turtle was just like that. All she could do was watch and see where Tom was taking her. She was horrified. Hundreds of years down here in the swamp, and now she was going to be made into soup.

Well, when Tom got back to campsite, his two buddies were just wakin' up. His friend, Jake, was a South Louisiana Cajun boy. Jake's cousin Willie was in for a week in the summertime, and Willie didn't know too much about the bayou. It used to scare him, so they were always trying to teach him the ways of the bayou. Now Willie and Jake were just getting up, and they were what we would call, couillot — it means stupid. They were yawnin' and scratchin'.

"Whatcha got there, Tom?" Jake said. Tom got outta that pirogue carrying that turtle like it was a trophy. And in a way it was, you know. He put that turtle on the ground on her belly. He said, "Lookid what I got there, Jake, lookid what I got. I got us a turtle. I'm gonna get all our friends. They're gonna bring everything we need, and we gonna have turtle soup for supper tonight. Now, you and Willie, y'all watch that turtle, don't let her get away, all right?" And before Jake could say anything, Tom jumped in his pirogue and paddled away.

Now Turtle was scared. And you know what a turtle does when she's scared? Pulls inside her shell. All Willie and Jake could see was that big old shell. Between them bein' so couillot, and it bein' so early in the mornin', they were mighty puzzled. Jake said, "Willie, you think that's really a turtle or what? How can it be a turtle, man, it don't have no head." Willie said, "I don't know. I don't know. I don't know if that a turtle or not. Looks kinda big to be a turtle." Rose Anne dug a huge breath out of her lungs. "Looks kinda just like a big old rock to me never seen a rock that big though never seen a turtle that big seen plently of turtles without their heads on 'cause where I'm from the first thing we do when we get a turtle is cut its head off what bothers me is don't have no arms don't have no legs don't have no tail don't see how it can be no turtle it don't have no arms . . ."

"Would you be quiet, Willie? Why you talk so much? Be quiet. I know what's wrong with it. It's scared. It went in its shell. Look, help me build a little cage so she don't get away, 'cause if it gets away, Tom's gonna be mad, mad, mad, yeah! Come on!" So they looked around and found some sticks. Whittled down one end, knocked 'em in the ground all around turtle. Took some ropes and string, wound them around, made a little cage for turtle. All the while, turtle can hear everythin' goin' on. She knows she's really trapped, but all the while, she's in her shell, and she's thinkin', thinkin', thinkin', and finally, she got a plan. She stuck out her head a little bit, her fingertips, toes, the tip of her tail, and she said, "Good mornin', gentlemen."

Jake jumped about that high. "Agggghhhwillie!!! Willie, look, man, look that hand, look that hand, look that feet. Wait a minute! It was talkin'! It's a turtle and it was talkin', man! It's a talkin' turtle! I never seen no talkin' turtle. Willie, you ever seen a talkin' turtle?" Willie said, "No, no, no, can't say that I have. I never seen no talkin' turtle I never seen no turtle that big I never seen no rock that big I never seen nothin' that big 'cept one time I saw somethin' that big my Aunt Edna had a family reunion she was bendin' over getting somethin' outta the ice chest . . ."

"Shut up, Willie! We gonna talk about Aunt Edna's backside when we got a talkin' turtle? Now be quiet. Uh, er, good mornin ma'am.

Uh, comment ça va? Uh, uh, ma'am, I don't know what to say to an old turtle, I'm kind of nervous, you know?" Turtle said, "Listen, Jake, you don't have to be nervous. I can do all the talkin'. You fellas seem a bit surprised that I can speak. Well, I got another surprise for you. I can not only speak, (giggle, giggle) I can sing. Would you boys like to hear me sing?" Jake said, "I'd like to hear you sing. I never heard no singin' turtle, that's for sure." Willie, said, "No, no, no, can't say that I have. I never seen no singin' turtle I never seen no talkin' turtle I never seen no turtle that big I never seen no rock that big, I never seen nothing that big, 'cept, oh yeah, one time at night I was outside late and saw somethin' big and gold in the sky like that might have been a UFO 'cept it didn't say UFO on the side so I'm not sure if it was a UFO or not . . ."

"Oh would you hush? Uh, yes ma'am, we would like to hear you sing."

So Turtle pushed with her front feet and she stood up on her back feet. She started snappin' her fingers, tappin' one foot, she sang,

> My grandpa and your grandpa
> Sittin' by the fire
> You and me in a chinaball tree
> Climbing higher and higher,
> Talkin' 'bout . . . ,

And she stopped singing. Jake said, "You can sing. Dat was good. You can sing. But uh, why you stopped? I was just getting the rhythm. And I know dere some more verses to dat song."

Turtle said, "Why, you know, I, I don't like to brag on myself, but I can not only sing and speak, but I can also, (giggle) dance. Would you boys like to see me dance?" Jake said, "Oh, you can dance too? I'd like to see you dance. I never saw no dancin' turtle, dat's for sure. Willie, you . . . never mind, Willie. Yes, ma'am, we'd love to see you dance." So Turtle backed all the way up against that little cage. She started snappin', and tappin', and she sang,

> My grandma and your grandma
> Sittin' by the fire
> You and me in a chinaball tree
> Climbin' higher and higher,
> Talkin' 'bout
> Hey na, hey na, hey na, hey na
> Iko, Iko an day
> Jacques et moi fino, a na nay
> Jacques et moi fi na nay

She stopped again. Jake said, "Ho, I can't believe my eyes! Ha! Dat was plumb astonishing. But how come you stopped? I know dere's a lot more verses to dat song, it's like the stations of the cross, it's got thirteen or fourteen verses like dat. Keep goin', keep goin'."

Turtle said, "Well, I can't really dance for you. I don't have enough room. I just feel so confined in this little cage. I'm accustomed to a much larger stage. But if I had more room, then I could show you how I can really shake my shell."

Jake said, "Ho, I'd like to see dat, dat's for sure. I can give you some room, ma'am. Hold on. Come on, Willie, let's move dat cage." Quick as a wink, Willie and Jake pulled up those sticks and ropes and strings, and threw 'em aside. And now, there was nothin' keepin' turtle from the nearby bayou 'cept a little muddy stretch of ground. She looked to see how far away the bayou was. About two verses. "Thank you," she said. "I feel so much better." She stretched herself out, and backed up a little — Rose Anne started snapping and tapping,

> My maman and your maman,
> Cookin' up some dinner

Blackberry dumplins, chicken stew,
Oh! each one is a winner,
Talkin' bout,
Hey na, hey na, hey na, hey na
Iko, Iko an day
Jacques et moi fino, a na nay
Jacques et moi fi na nay

She moved back about halfway to the bayou and she stopped again. Jake was about to have a fit. He said — Rose Anne taps awkwardly, as if she were Jake — "Don't stop, do it again, I think I'm catchin' on, I think I just about got dat rhydm." Turtle said, "Well, Mr. Jake, I could see you were about to catch on, that's why I stopped. Now this time, you and Mr. Willie, well, you all dance along with me. And you just let the music moooove you. You might even want to close your eyes, if you know what I mean. Okay? Okay, we got it." (More snapping and tapping.)

My daddy and your daddy
Workin' in the cotton,
Rains all night
Ruined the crop,
So cotton it was rotten
Talkin' bout,
Hey na, hey na, hey na, hey na
Iko, Iko an day
Jacques et moi fino, an na nay
Jacques et moi fi na nay

Turtle jumped into the bayou, swam away. Willie and Jake didn't even notice at first, they were kicking up a storm. "Jacques et fino, who, who, who, Jacques et moi fino, who who . . . Who took the turtle? Willie! Willie! Who took the turtle?"

"I don't know, I don't know. What we gonna do?" Well they thought and thought and started walkin' around, tryin' to think of what to do. And lo and behold, Willie stumbled across a rock about the same size as the turtle's shell. Now I realize there's no rocks that size along the bayou — we don't even have rocks in Louisiana — but in the story, you can put in whatever you like. So they picked up that big rock, and they took that big rock, and they put it right where Tom had left that turtle. And they got some mud, and some berry juice, and they smeared it on that rock, and they hoped their friends wouldn't notice. They knew their friends were in their early forties, really needed bifocals, but instead they were heavy into denial, they didn't have 'em. Got that little cage back, and they waited for their friends to come.

Pretty soon Tom came back, ahead of just about a parade of pirogues following behind, and people bringing everything they needed to make turtle soup. Someone had a great big old hundred gallon washtub to boil that turtle in. Mrs. Lemoine was there with her early vegetables. Somebody brought potato salad. Somebody else brought corn casserole. Somebody had oyster dressin', someone had cornbread dressin', somebody had rice dressin'. Not a thing on a sugar-buster's diet, ladies and gentlemen.

Tom directed the cookin'. "All right, Willie and Jake, take that big old wash tub and fill it up with water." And so they did. "OK, Mrs. Lemoine, go ahead and start choppin' your onions. And the bell peppers too. Chop 'em real fine. I don't like to feel 'em too much, they get caught in my teeth, you know?" And so she did. "All right everybody, set out that food. All right, Willie and Jake? Now get that big old turtle right there and throw 'er in the water. We gonna boil her all afternoon, that's the only way to do it, man."

And so they picked up that big old rock and they thrup! dropped it in the water. Well, all afternoon, that seasoning was boilin' and churnin', and man, it smelled really good, you know? So they sat around all day tellin' jokes, havin' spittin' contests and such, drinkin' beer, havin' a good old time. Late in the afternoon, after a couple of hours, Tom called everybody and he said, "Awright! Time to eat, everybody, come around. Willie and Jake, fish that turtle on up outta that pot."

Well, they fished that big old rock out and they brought it over to 'im, put it out in front of him. Had some sawhorses with boards across 'em, makeshift table. "Awright! Awright, everybody, I caught this turtle this mornin', man, and it's gonna be fresh. Spent the night in the bayou." They love to say that around here. "Give me that butcher knife, Willie. Willie handed him his butcher knife. Here we go, everybody, fresh, hot turtle meat." He brought that knife down. Whang! Bounced right off. "Man, don't worry, everybody, it's an old turtle, big shell, you know what I mean? Anybody got an axe?" Of course somebody had an axe — these are south Louisiana woodsmen. "Thank you sir, thank you. Awright, awright, everybody, here we go. Fresh hot turtle meat." He brought that axe down. Whang!!! It bounced off. "Man. It's really tough. Uh, anybody got a, uh, sledgehammer?" And somebody had a sledgehammer. "Thank ya, yeah, yeah, 'preciate that. Okay, here we go everybody, fresh, hot turtle meat!" He brought that sledgehammer down. Whamp! That rock exploded into hundreds of pieces. Pieces flyin' this way and that way, hittin' people in the backside, they jumpin' outta the way. Tom looks down at that mess. He said, "Man, we overcooked her. She's hard as a rock. I thought we needed to boil her a long time, make her tender. I'm sorry, y'all, I never made turtle soup with a turtle that big, but, uh, well, we still have the broth, the potato salad, and everythin' else, come on, let's eat."

And so they did. They ate. They didn't care. They just needed an excuse to get together and eat anyway, that's the way it is. They ate up, and ate up, and after awhile they all sittin' around, rubbin' their round bellies, digesting that food, burpin' every once in awhile. And sun starts goin' down, and that evenin' mist starts floatin' down over that bayou, and all of a sudden, through that mist, came that song.

Whooo hooo, hooo hooo . . .

Tom jumped up. He said, "Y'all heard that? Ya heard that? That's the same song I heard that old turtle singing this morning. It can only mean one thing. Willie, Jake, come heah. Ya heard that song? You know what it means? I'll tell you what it means. Hum? She has a sister back there. And tomorrow morning we getting up early and we gonna go catch her. We gonna have turtle soup again, everybody! I'm gonna get you all some turtle meat yet!"

Well, they say Tom, Jake, and Willie got up early next morning, and they paddled through that bayou, and the mist was real thick, but they never heard that song. Tom paddled on down to where he thought that little house was, but he couldn't find it. He must've gone off, down the main channel or something. Far as I know, nobody's ever seen that turtle again, 'cept for one person . . . After all, where do you think I learned this from? I learned it from the turtle, who sings the song in the mist.

Granny Griffin's Tale

S TORIES END; TO BE TIDY ABOUT IT, this one wrapped up a day after we left Rose Anne's camp, when Marguerite and I boarded the plane in Jackson, Mississippi, and flew home to Rhode Island. Sometimes, however, stories have codas, which exist beyond the bounds of their geographical and chronological narrative, but were generated by it. This is one such coda.

Back home in New England, the days shortened; the leaves fell, we turned back the clocks. A new millennium began, and we folded the old one up and put it on history's bookshelf. In the imaginations of students in millennia to come, I wondered, as the past continues to recede and the weight of years presses us, shalelike, into centuries that preceded ours, will we merge with the Romantic poets, with Columbus and the Inquisition, the invention of the fork? Just as Alexander the Great and the Trojan War are chronological neighbors in my sense of passing time, will our era live someday in the mind's eye next door to that of William the Conqueror? I wondered these things as I pulled on heavier woolen sweaters and began to write this book. It even got cold in the South.

Then one day, completely unlooked-for, I was transported back to the heat of the previous summer. Vicki Vedder had finally sent me "Granny Griffin's Tale." But it wasn't what I had expected. Vickie was planning her daughter's wedding and didn't have time to transcribe a single live performance, so in a breathtaking fit of confidence in the U.S. Postal Service, she mailed me an eight-inch stack of original manuscripts that seemed to amount to her entire oral inheritance, in type and ink. Most stories appeared to be in Granny's voice, but others gave me a peek at her father, her mother, Daddy Runt, even her daughter. There were hundreds of scrawled-over pages, and each one of them was a protest against the fixedness of writing. I could almost hear countless, long-dead Griffins and Hamms murmuring beneath the black and white pages, trying to argue their way out of the prison bars of typeface that held them to one rendition of an event for all time. Vickie would type a story in Granny's voice, then tell it in a different manuscript in her mother's. Then she'd give in to a visible yearning for conciliation, and atop each would insert in pen bits of the other's version. Historically, we talk about a moment when the suppleness of orality gave way to the rigidity of the written record, but we no longer expect to find traces of the battle in the present day. Vickie's stories literally showed me what it looked like.

Which was fascinating, but hellish when it came to sifting out a coherent tale which would approximate one that Vickie might actually tell in a performance. I struggled and read and reread and kept coming back to one story — a tale told by Vickie in the persona of Granny Griffin, though some of the details were her mother's additions — that existed in more versions than any other. It was called:

THE DEAD MAN
'Bout the dead. The Dead is dif'unt'n us, and bein' dif'unt is what's the trouble with most things. A dead man ain't no nawmal feller, but tryin' to convince 'im is a waste'a time, and fer now on a hunderd

years Granny's the onliest one that know'd the inside on The Dead —
which is why she's goin' to the trouble'a tryin' to learn ye sump'n
'bout it.

Granny gathers "the Inside" like some folks picks peas — what'che
loves is what'che picks, and if'n it's peas, then Granny says: "get at it.
Find'je some dirt and git them peas in the ground 'fore the first frost
hits." And the dirt is 'xactly where The Dead's headed, too, 'ceptin'
the dead man's garden is The Graveyard. Now then. First of all 'bout
dyin' — the Dyin' Man, he ain't never been dead before, so in so many
words, he's ig'nernt. He's jes slap eat-up with ignerence same'as some
not-dead folks Granny knows uv, and goin' frum smart to stupid is
prob'bly a mite hard to git used to . . .

. . . Right off the bat, if'n the Dead Man's right with the Law-erd,
that search-light from heaven hits the poor fool right 'tween 'is eyes
like a young'un's done slung a ball'r a rock jes as hard as one'a the
rascals can sling one; and when the speed — which ye cain't see
but'che ken feel — lands jes in the right place where God aimed it,
ye go blind. Perm-nut. So Granny'd say that heaven's a mite dif'unt'n
sittin' heah on the front porch swing with a 'skeeter bitin' the tar out'n
ye kneecaps. It's prob'bly a fact, or leastwise, Granny's uv the under-
standin', that eyes ain't even naissisary in heaven. She cain' prove it,
but that don't make it less true. Some thangs calls fer trust, and
Granny's uv the opinion ye could hang ye coat on the one 'bout not
needin' eyeballs in Paradize . . .

Now, as to that si-che-a-shun with The Dead, Granny's seen
more'n her share'a suf'frin', and some'a that there suf'frin come at the
hands'a dead folks carryin' on in they caskets worse'n the live ones
sittin' there in the front room at the Wake. First off, they's Ol' Man
Henry Birdsong. Folks al'ays ast's Granny: "Why'as Ol' Man Birdsong
berried face down, Granny? Wuz he a Dead Man, Granny?" And por'
ol' Granny, she ought'n to know since she'd been 'round s'long she'd
set up wid plenty'a dead folks . . .

Just as I was in the midst of reconstituting Henry Birdsong, the Dead Man, I got an e-mail from the living storyteller herself, who, by sitting up at nights with her computer, inhabiting her equally dead grandmother's memories and impersonating her voice, was keeping all three of them alive.

Hi Pam:

I've been meaning to write you, but there's been a nightmare of activity. About "The Dead Man" story. The story behind the story is that Granny Griffin really believed in ghosts (haints to her), and with that being kept close in mind, you can imagine that "sitting up with the dead" was a favor to the neighbors that would put Granny on the spot in a hurry . . . This was called "the viewing" and the term is still used in my family. The widow needed support from her lady friends, and two things happened in quick order: everybody made 'tater salad, deviled eggs, fried chicken, and biscuits and brought that to the kitchen of the dead man's house; secondly, everyone helped "sit up" with the dead until such time as it took for everybody to get a good look at him, talk about his good deeds, the troubles his chillin' (offspring) had brung on him, and what a good wife he had all them years considering how stubborn, mean, cruel, sorry and no'count he had been all his life. Each person visiting would start this conversation over and over and over.

Once't way back, Granny Griffin took little ol' Sarah Laverne, Granny's eldest and the only good young'un she had — the rest'a uv'em was a pack'a rascals — ova to Twiggs County to comfort the dead and the grievin'. Henry Birdsong'd done up and keeled ova from old age and the wida, Myrtice Ryal, needed a little sleep frum all her squallin'. They wun't nothin' really wrong wid Henry, but he died anyhow. Some folks does that. Now, long 'bout midnight, Granny thanks it wuz — Granny weren't a'wartchin' no clock, but it'uz good[n'] dark and them shadders wuz a'fallin' in frum the winders that kep the cold out. Long 'bout midnight, Granny, she gits up to pat the dead man's hand. Granny know'd . . . ye gotta sit up wid the dead to make sure they stay put. Dead folks gits to stretchin' and twitchin', and if they ain't careful — which most ov'em ain't — heah they go rite ou'n they berryin' box and out'n the middle uv'tha floor. And gittin' a Dead Man back in his caskit ain't no easy thang.

So, Granny, jes as she leans ova the Dead Man, the Dead Man decides to go and stretch hisself. Now heah Granny is wid her face in the Dead Man's face. His hands shoots straight up in the air like a Hallelujah from the Sunday mornin' choir; and if that wut'n enough to aput the fear'a God in ye, heah he goes and sits straight up. Granny has see'd a heap'a thangs in her time and heird a heap, but thish h'yer wuz the worstest. Jes as Granny went'a thankin' this wuz the worstest, what'da you thank the Dead Man done? The Dead Man, he looks Granny squa'har in the eyes, and says: "Ha'bout gittin' a feller a cup'a coffee?" Now, little Sarah Laverne, she'as a standin' rite there, and what does that gal do but take off th[r]oo the house a'hollerin', "The Dead wants a cup'a coffee 'fore we berry'im tomorrow!"

Things went from bad to worse for Granny. Henry followed her into the kitchen and, in the midst of drinking his coffee, fell headfirst into the saucer and drowned, inconveniently dying a second time a good distance from his coffin. Granny had to wrestle him back into the parlor and heave him into it, in the process managing to get him in upside down. Afterwards she took out "a sturdy length of quiltin' yarn" and tacked Henry to the lining, so he wouldn't get back up again. Then she roused the household and held a midnight funeral.

As I read "The Dead Man," it occurred to me that one of the pitched differences between hearing a story and reading it is the matter of time. In an oral performance, listeners are aware whether they're enjoying a tale, but they don't have time to analyze it; the best one can often do is simply follow the narrative thread. Reading, however, with its private opportunities for pondering and dwelling, breeds a different type of audience, one at leisure to formulate questions. In the case of "The Dead Man," as I read through the story I crossed a line I never even broached in any of the other tales I had heard over the summer. I wondered how much of it were true.

Truth is an issue I hadn't really addressed before — in most cases the veracity of a tale pales beside its necessity. Yet telling the truth versus telling make-believe is a complex subject. Listeners on the Georgia and South Carolina sea islands prize storytellers who excel at what in the Gullah language is called, "de lie." Appreciation is granted not to feats of memory, but feats of invention. And yet "the truth" does play a role in the contract between audience and storyteller. Scrupulously traditional tellers in Appalachia, for instance, conclude even the oldest, most often-told, most outrageous tales with lines like, "And that's just the way it happened. I know; I was there." No one believes this claim, but the words throw a mantle of creative authority around the teller. Without them, listeners might wonder if he or she hadn't borrowed someone else's style, someone else's surprise ending. The old tag lines are, in fact, a mark of originality, like a signature on a painting (but from the days when neither storytellers nor listeners knew how to sign their names). The wink and nod and pretense of truth in this case betrays more about the nature of community — and whether a story may be taken out of one and still mean the same thing — than it does any moral issue involving the tug between fact and fiction.

At the end of "The Dead Man," Granny says, Sometimes a gal's gotta use a little gristle, and this was one of 'em, leastwise 'til a decent amount 'a time pase't, when Granny would divulge tidbits of the truth fer entertainment's sake later on. Folk'ses 'round Twiggs County loved to talk about The Dead, and this would turn out to be the best of the best, on down the road a piece. Granny know'd that. And she set right here on it and treated it jes like a good hen treats a good egg. In Granny's hardscrabble world, entertainment was valued more than verisimilitude, and her phrase "tidbits of the truth" acknowledged her community's preference and her storyteller's authority within it. I betrayed that pact by e-mailing Vickie to ask "What Happened?"

As soon as I sent the message I regretted it. Granny's "truth" should have been good enough for me, even outside its oral context. Besides, I have exempted myself from having to answer this question in regard to some of my own stories, mainly because it uproots my enjoyment of them, but also, paradoxically, because in one case it actually interferes with that great intangible, The Truth.

When I was very young, I used to go to sleep at nights with my hands clenched on the bedsheets. I did this for fear that as I was falling asleep, contentedly listening to the murmur of television voices from the living room below, I would float up to the ceiling. I couldn't help it. No matter how firmly I gripped the mattress, my body would lighten and irresistibly rise, until my nose touched the plaster. I *remember* having to turn my head to the side so I could breathe. This would happen night after night, always accompanied by the fear, not that my rising to the ceiling was something powerfully out of the ordinary, and therefore terrifying, but that I'd get in trouble if my parents found me up there. What is curious to me today is that the memory of floating is usually sparked by cleaning the house: dust isn't odorless, it has a faint, forlorn aroma, and when I clean I'm reminded of the smell of the dusty ceiling (no offense to my mother's housekeeping).

After I had been up there awhile, I'd sense a faint breeze,

which would gradually grow strong enough to suck me around the four corners of the room. I'd spin faster and faster, totally out of control. Then, just as I felt about to disintegrate, I would wake up in the morning back in my bed. I mention this for two reasons: like my talking slides, this must have been a dream, but I prefer to recall the memory from the file in which it accidentally got stuck — the file of lived experience. The truth has no place in this story. Secondly, the feeling of being about to disintegrate, of lost control, prefigured an actual event. Like Granny's, this was my closest encounter with The Dead, though instead of meeting them I almost joined them.

In the late eighties, I was in a train wreck. My passenger train collided with a slow-moving freighter outside Baltimore, Maryland. The engine exploded; the front cars flew into the air like pick-up sticks and landed on one another, with mine balanced atop the heap. There were the usual consequences: people died, hundreds were injured, television programs were interrupted with the news, ambulances and photographers rushed to the site, residents of the woodsy, working-class community in which we crashed lined up to give blood. This, so the reports tell us, is What Happened.

"My God, what happened?" I once wrote. "It rings out like a tax collector's cry, calling everyone to rally around and pay up in observations. The tithes are gathered together toward the greater good of justice, understanding, and reports on the evening news . . ." But here's the rub: amassing people's stories and material evidence into an overview of the accident is to betray the experience of the wreck. The completed picture, for better or worse, is a construction, and a train wreck is precisely the opposite: a de-construction.

The "truth" of the experience lies in chaos and fragmentation and *not* knowing What Happened. There was no narrative logic guiding those involved in the crash. I likened the violent braking before the impact to music turned up so loud you lose the words and can only absorb the throbbing, screaming bass with your body: no communication, just blind, visceral discomfort, in this case, shuddering metal, flying bodies, and train seats ripped loose from their moorings. After the crash my usually roving eye telescoped ever inward, at first blinkered by pain and fear, then quite literally by the bandages that two kind women, one black, one white, wrapped around my head. I lost my sensory input, my point of view, even, when asked by a paramedic, part of my name (I answered "Pam" because it seemed too difficult to attempt the entire "Pamela"). After I was treated at the triage site, the whole affair lost its quality of rampant chaos and took on an equally uninformative, bureaucratic boredom. Take a numbered ticket and wait for the ambulances.

This is the truth of a train wreck: the erasure of What Happened. I never saw the "crumpled mass" of the locomotive, as *Baltimore Magazine* called it. I never thought to look in that direction. The Dead must have been all around me, but I didn't notice them. This utter lack of curiosity and context, the twin pillars of good storytelling, is What Happened to me. Filling in the gaps makes the crash comprehensible and also dramatizes it — it makes it a *story*. And sometimes stories do not tell the truth.

More often, however, they don't have to. While The Wreck of the Colonial, as most written accounts dubbed the crash, may never be reconstructed as an honest narrative, I do believe it would make a terrific ghost story. Those metaphorical deconstructions we call ghosts cleave closer to my blinkered, worm's-eye point of view than the so-called "disaster literature" about the wreck. As I imagined in Alice's graveyard back in South Carolina, hauntings are anticipations trapped in dead-ends, much as I was temporarily trapped in my shrunken perspective. Granny would understand that the story, if there is to be one, belongs to the sixteen people who died in the wreck. She would tell their tales and help them haunt the memories of the careless men who caused it. She would tell young Griffins and Hamms how on certain snowy afternoons in January you can still hear the screech of metal fruitlessly gripping metal; how you still choke on invisible smoke; how ghostly passengers search the thin woods for their suitcases, their books, their tickets. How they repeat their families' telephone numbers over and over, hoping someone will call with the impossible news that they survived. How they frantically seek their coats, shivering so violently you can hear their broken bones clattering together, because for them the temperature will always be at the freezing point, just as it was on January 4, 1987. And Granny would be telling the simple truth: that the dissolution of the most basic of all narrative sequences — the rhythmic course of a train running over its tracks — derailed forever their expectations of reaching the ultimate destination of growing older. That is the haunting thought.

Granny's granddaughter, however, is a different kind of storyteller, one with experience of both worlds. She grew up with ghost stories but has grown accustomed to the nightly news. Vickie can tell me the tale of "The Dead Man" but she can also, without betraying Granny's trust, confess in an e-mail What Happened the night Henry Birdsong sat up in his coffin. Being her contemporary, and a reader as well as a listener, I abandoned my regrets and called it up on my screen:

> The gist of Granny's story is simple: the man was dead, or was supposed be, but lo and behold, when everybody cleared out of the room and went to sleep, Mama looked over at him just as he rose up stiff as a board, but in the sitting position. Granny, of course, had "to do something." What she did was summon

up all the courage she had and walk over to the casket — being Granny, the first thing she did was speak something sarcastic to the dead man, trying to sound as ordinary as possible (just in case he weren't dade!). She wouldn't want to hurt nobody's feelings, that's what she said . . .

Over the years as she told this story to us, she added details that made the tension mount and the suspense of the ending more and more far-fetched . . . But my Mama told this story maybe even more than Granny Griffin, because the real event actually scared the daylights out of her. She was just a girl, maybe ten or eleven, and where this all come about was in Twiggs County, out in the middle of nowhere, near the clay holes where chalk was mined. It was a scrappy, mosquito-infested, dry sort of place with pine thickets and measly-looking wild plum trees growing everywhere. The roads were narrow pig-paths that ran up through the swamps, so, generally speaking, it was a spooky place . . .

I really feel like Mama saw this moment in her mind — from the time she heard she was about to set foot in the house with a truly-dead person to the point where the dead man sat straight up, I think she began drawing pictures in her mind about "what is death" and how "do they act" — meaning the dead. "What do they do?" "What do you do with them?" "What if something happens?" I think all this went through her mind, and so Mama's version is less factual than Granny Griffin's, and that is what gives it character — there's a childish quality to it even today when Mama talks about it.

One thing to tell you, though. The dead man — in reality — was a hunchback. When you hear my mama say "he was a hunchback," you get this eerie feeling of severe physical retardation. She comes from an era and a country place where "odd" was not okay — every flaw in the physical makeup of every person living over there in Twiggs County was noted by all — if you were beautiful, they went on and on about it; and if you had imperfections, Lord help you, because they went on and on about that, too.

So when Mama says "he was a hunchback," she means he was stooped in the back and shoulders. And that's kind of how Old Man Birdsong looks in my mind today — he was bent forward and a tad on the heavy side — a big, lumbering giant of a man. You have to get that vision because the next part leans heavy on that. See, Old Man Birdsong was TIED to the bottom of the casket with a measure of twine 'cause'a being bent forward. When they put him down in the pine box, he wouldn't stay down! He leaned up by the nature of his spinal problem, and they couldn't nail the top shut with his body being in that condition. That is WHY Ol' Man Birdsong sat straight up that night — THE TWINE BROKE because of his weight and the pulling of riga-mawtis settin' in, to boot! . . .

I'm sure movement of any kind would terrify Granny and Mama, so they made the most of this story, and they always saw themselves as something between victim and hero for being there. They'd say: "Thank God por ol' Myrtie wut'n put throo more'n she could bear. It was us that took that lick fer'er." And then on other occasions they'd say: "Wouldn't ye know it'ud be us who'as there when that sorry soul busted loose and hopped out'n that box? Life do dole out some carryin's-on fer womenfolk. What's next, do you reckon?"

I'll write you later. Love, Vickie Vedder

I replied immediately, telling Vickie about the train wreck and how I thought Granny would have loved to tell the story of its "haints."

"It occurs to me," I continued, "that the train must have crashed just as it neared or crossed that old invisible boundary

ll haunts us all: the Mason–Dixon Line. I looked it up. It
urveyed in the 1760s by two English astronomers, of all
le, to settle a boundary dispute between Pennsylvania and
yland. Of course, it's famous for separating free states from
e-holding states: the line that divides North and South.
d that's precisely where my speeding, northbound train de-
iled. We were going too fast, and because of it, became a
ghost story. Which side do you think the ghosts haunt? Or
have we outgrown that question? Perhaps The Dead, unlike
the rest of us, found an eternal home straddling the line."

Story/Storyteller Index